D0027556

CATASTROPHE

Clinton's Role in
America's Worst Disaster

Edited by Christopher Ruddy
and Carl Limbacher Jr.

A NewsMax.com Book

NewsMax.com

Publisher: Christopher Ruddy
NewsMax.com Inside Cover Editor: Carl Limbacher Jr.
Cover Design by: David Willson
Copy Editor: Rita Samols

Printed in the U.S.A.

ISBN 0-9716807-5-2

© Copyright October 2002 by NewsMax Media, Inc., Publisher NewsMax.com
Inc. P.O. Box 20989, West Palm Beach, FL 33416. All rights reserved. No part
of this book may be reproduced by any means or for any reason without the consent of the publisher. For additional copies call 800-485-4350.

Table of Contents

CHAPTER 3

The CIA Failed

CHAPTER 4

The FBI Failed

CHAPTER 5

The Media Spin

PART 2
New Dangers

CHAPTER 6
Weapons of Mass Destruction

CHAPTER 7
Bioweapons

CHAPTER 8
New Threats

CHAPTER 9
Freedoms

CHAPTER 10
New Dangers New Responses

PART 3
The Axis of Evil

CHAPTER 11
The Leaders: Russia and China

CHAPTER 12

Iraq

Introduction

As we write this introduction, a full year has passed since the most devastating attack on U.S. territory in our country's history.

Yet both Congress and the press have refused to undertake a thorough investigation into the national security failures that left America vulnerable.

Yes, Bush administration officials have been skewered in congressional hearings, as well as on the front pages of almost every newspaper in the land. The president himself has been lanced by headlines like "Bush Knew," suggesting that he could have prevented the 9/11 attacks because of a vague warning of "hijackings," but didn't.

His FBI director, Robert Mueller — on the job just four business days before terrorists struck — has been raked over the coals for not "connecting the dots."

FBI whistle-blower Coleen Rowley was celebrated by the establishment press after she charged that Mueller had engaged in a deliberate post-9/11 cover-up.

Bush Attorney General John Ashcroft has been accused by no less a media personage than CBS News anchorman Dan Rather of taking advantage of intelligence warnings to remove himself from commercial flight travel, while leaving the flying public to the mercies of the 9/11 hijackers.

Meanwhile, with the exception of the Internet and talk radio, news of the role played by the Clinton administration in decimating U.S. capacity to prevent a 9/11-type strike has been almost completely ignored.

One can imagine the response if events similar to 9/11 had taken place shortly after Ronald Reagan left office. Without doubt the media would have unceasingly linked the conservative Reagan to such events, claiming negligence and malfeasance on his part.

The media today seem more interested in protecting the Clintons' reputation.

Since 9/11, Bill Clinton has rarely been asked to explain his handling of national security matters. His wife, Hillary, has not been queried about why her husband did not do more to protect America.

Fearing the media's wrath for pursuing yet another "Clinton investigation," congressional probers on both sides of the aisle remain uninterested in grilling ex–FBI Director Louis Freeh about how his agency, which had dubbed terrorism the number one threat to national security in 1998, managed to miss the handwriting on the wall.

Former Attorney General Janet Reno, who makes herself available to reporters several times a week as she campaigns for the Florida governor's seat, has yet to be asked to explain how her Justice Department dropped the ball, not only at the FBI, which she oversaw, but also at the INS, another agency under her command.

Doris Meissner, who headed up the Immigration and Naturalization Service under Clinton, hasn't been called upon to answer for the virtual open-borders policy that allowed the September 11 hijackers to slip in and out of the U.S. at will.

On the other hand, Clinton CIA Director George Tenet, who inexplicably retains his post in the Bush administration, did testify before Congress in February — fully five months after the catastrophe of 9/11.

But rather than accept any responsibility for the intelligence failure leading up to 9/11, he denied that his agency had failed at all.

"Intelligence will never give you 100 percent predictive capability on terrorist events," he explained shamelessly to the Senate Intelligence Committee.

Those who worked under Tenet, however, disagree — pointing to the restrictive spy recruitment policies ordered by the Clinton White House that went unchallenged by Tenet.

Less than 24 hours after the 9/11 attack, NewsMax executive editor Christopher Ruddy reported on an e-mail exchange he had that night with a former CIA field agent. It was the first report anywhere on what was likely the single most important factor in the agency's inability to predict the attacks.

"Roger," Ruddy's CIA source, had resigned from the agency in disgust because, he said, his bosses had lost interest in obtaining human intelligence, a task the veteran agent knew was key to fighting the war on terrorism.

The CIA in the mid-1990s had implemented a "human rights scrub" policy, he revealed.

"Clinton's anti-intelligence plants implemented a universal 'human rights scrub' of all assets, virtually shutting down operations for six months to a year," Roger told NewsMax.

"This was after something happened in Central America (there was an American woman involved who was the common law wife of a commie who went missing there) that got a lot of bad press for the agency.

"After that, each asset had to be certified as being 'clean for human rights violations.'

"What this did was to put off limits, in effect, terrorists, criminals, and anyone else who would have info on these kinds of people."

Roger told Ruddy that the CIA, even under new leadership, had never recovered from the Clinton administration's "human rights scrub" policy.

Roger's information turned out to be 100 percent on the mark.

In a report issued by the House Intelligence Committee in July, limitations put on the CIA's spy recruitment program were cited as a key reason for the agency's inability to anticipate the 9/11 attacks.

Since the ex–CIA agent gave his account to NewsMax, dozens of others with inside information have stepped forward, some with accounts just as startling.

But none have been given the Coleen Rowley star whistle-blower treatment by the press, and their reports were relegated to the op-ed pages — when they were covered at all.

One of the most persistent has been Mansoor Ijaz, a Pakistani-American investment banker and one-time major Clinton contributor who acted as the White House's unofficial liaison between the U.S. and the government of Sudan during the late 1990s.

Ijaz's story is well known to NewsMax.com readers.

But it's a measure of how thoroughly his remarkable account has been swept under the rug by the prestige press that it has never garnered any headlines.

The one-time Clinton operative says officials in Sudan, where Osama bin Laden had settled after being booted out of Saudi Arabia, offered the U.S. three separate opportunities to take the notorious terrorist out of circulation — and were rebuffed by the Clinton White House each time.

"By May of 1996 the Sudanese had decided to get rid of bin Laden because he was becoming a problem there as well," Ijaz explained in May to Fox News Channel's Sean Hannity, one of dozens of interviews he has granted that mainstream reporters have ignored.

"They called the Clinton administration one last time and said, 'If you don't want him to go to Saudi Arabia, we're prepared to hand him over to you guys directly.' And the Clinton administration's response to that was 'We don't have enough legal evidence against him.' "

Ijaz explained that he had turned over reams of files to the Senate Intelligence Committee on his bin Laden negotiations with Sudan, but had not been called to testify under oath.

But committee chairman Bob Graham, D-Fla., wasn't particularly interested in Ijaz's story and even trashed the London *Times* for covering it last January.

"One thing we've learned is to be a little skeptical of these London-based news accounts," Graham told Fox News. "So I'm not prepared to give them an initial presumption of credibility."

Attacks on Ijaz grew sharper as it became obvious he wasn't going away, with Democratic National Committee spokeswoman Jennifer Palmieri telling one interviewer that he was "a crackpot" who was "lying."

Asked to respond to Ijaz's account, senior Clinton National Security Council aide Nancy Soderberg told Fox News Channel, "He's living in a fantasyland. There was no such Sudanese offer."

The media seem to be taking their cue from the doubting Democrats.

In May, both *New York Times* reporter Judith Miller and NBC news-woman Andrea Mitchell told radio host Don Imus they declined to cover the bin Laden extradition story because they didn't find it credible.

The mainstream press silence continued even after Ijaz's story was cor-roborated by former Clinton administration Ambassador to Sudan Tim Carney, who confirmed to Fox News that "there was an offer to send [bin Laden] to us." He explained that the Sudanese deal was rejected because "we did not have an indictment [against bin Laden] at the time."

How desperate is America's Democrat-media complex to cover up Bill Clinton's responsibility for 9/11? Desperate enough to ignore even a bombshell audiotape of the ex-president himself admitting he had the chance to extradite bin Laden to the U.S., but decided instead to let him off the hook.

In August 2002 NewsMax.com released the shocking audio, which we obtained exclusively while covering Clinton's address to a New York busi-ness group in February.

Through a link to the startling clip on NewsMax.com's website, readers from around the world have been able to access the tape.

The clip proves beyond a shadow of a doubt that Ijaz's account of Clinton turning down a deal for bin Laden's extradition was accurate all along.

In the explosive audio, the ex-president responds to a question about whether he would have handled bin Laden differently knowing now what he didn't know then.

Clinton explains that he was criticized at the time for being "too obsessed" with bin Laden and al Qaeda, then maintains he just barely missed the terror kingpin when he launched the August 20, 1998, cruise missile attack on his terror training camp in Khost, Afghanistan.

The mission failed, said the former commander in chief, because the attack plans were "ratted out."

In the next breath the ex-president defends his simultaneous cruise mis-sile attack on a Sudanese medicine factory, claiming subsequent testimony from the trial of the 1993 World Trade Center bombers proves that attack was justified.

Then Clinton makes the devastating admission he has never repeated before or since — that Sudan was ready to hand bin Laden over to the U.S., but he said no even though "we knew he wanted to commit crimes against America."

Here is a verbatim transcript of a portion of the ex-president's astonish-ing remarks:

"Mr. bin Laden used to live in Sudan. He was expelled from Saudi Arabia in 1991, then he went to Sudan.

"And we'd been hearing that the Sudanese wanted America to start meeting with them again — they released him.

"At the time, 1996, he had committed no crime against America so I did not bring him here because we had no basis on which to hold him, though we knew he wanted to commit crimes against America.

"So I pleaded with the Saudis to take him, 'cause they could have. But they thought it was a hot potato and they didn't and that's how he wound up in Afghanistan." [*End of Transcript*]

Despite smoking-gun audio that's every bit as clear as the Nixon Watergate tapes, the establishment press had shown little interest in covering the story by the time this book went to press.

ABC and CBS News completely ignored the story. NBC initially planned a segment on some of the taped revelations — then backed out at the last minute, citing other "breaking news." The network never rescheduled.

CNN considered the story for its *Crossfire* debate show, but never followed through.

Only Fox News Channel gave the story prominent coverage, with entire segments devoted to NewsMax's taped revelations on both its popular *Fox & Friends* morning show and *Hannity & Colmes*.

(Is there any wonder why Fox seems to be the only news operation currently gaining audience share?)

Ironically, the Japanese media seem more interested in the Clinton–bin Laden tape than their American cousins, with the Japan Broadcasting Corporation planning to include the audio in a late-summer 9/11 documentary.

The cover-up is no mystery to Ijaz. "I'm absolutely convinced that the Democrats are desperately trying to find a way to deflect the attention from the complicity of the Clinton administration in letting this terrorism problem get so far out of hand," he told one radio interviewer.

Ijaz isn't the only 9/11 witness the Democrat-media complex wishes would go away.

Dick Morris, the former political consultant widely credited with turning Bill Clinton into the first Democrat to win re-election since FDR, has written column after column for *The New York Post* describing how his former boss was asleep at the wheel when it came to terrorism.

The former White House political guru revealed, for instance, that when the World Trade Center was bombed by al Qaeda–connected terrorists in February 1993, his ex-boss never even bothered to visit the site.

"When the bombing happened, he just issued a statement saying we'll fight them and all that. And then he gave it his Saturday radio address," Morris said. "It was never a big priority."

The ex-president gave the same back-of-the-hand treatment to terrorist warnings against U.S. targets in the Middle East, says Morris, who recounted a complaint by Clinton's number one foreign policy troubleshooter, the U.S.'s then–U.N. ambassador.

"In 1996, I got a phone call from Dick Holbrooke," the one-time White House insider revealed earlier this year.

"He said, 'We're getting hard intelligence that terrorists are planning another hit on our guys in Riyadh. I've been trying to get a hold of the president for two weeks about this and we're getting increasing reports about [the threat]."

Incredibly, Clinton's own U.N. ambassador felt he had no choice but to importune Morris to intercede, begging, "Can you call him?"

Despite these accounts and others like them, Bill and Hillary Clinton have not only not accepted any responsibility for what happened on 9/11, they've actually attempted to shift blame to the Bush administration.

"At least in my time, more of these things were prevented than occurred," the ex-president claimed bizarrely to Fox News in June.

"I spent an enormous amount of time on this when I was president," he insisted. "We must have talked about bin Laden several days of every week for the last few years I was president. We did a lot of work on it."

In November 2001, Mrs. Clinton claimed the Bush economic program had left the U.S. vulnerable to terrorism, telling CNN, "If we hadn't passed the big tax cut last spring, that I believe undermined our fiscal responsibility and our ability to deal with this new threat of terrorism, we wouldn't be in the fix we're in today."

Astonishingly, neither of the Clintons' comments made mainstream news headlines.

Many political observers, conservatives included, argue that because Washington's number one power couple no longer control the White House, their off-stage antics are largely irrelevant. But it's easy to forget the sway the Clintons still have over that indispensable element of any democracy — a free press.

Nor should we dismiss the notion that, with such cozy support from the big media, the Clintons will be back in the White House in 2004 or 2008, when Hillary runs.

The real story of 9/11 is not about the tragic events of that day. It is about the hijacking of the institutions that are meant to protect us, institutions like the press, law enforcement agencies such as the FBI and INS, the Executive Branch and the people's Congress.

These organizations have been hijacked by the left wing with its politically correct agenda. With the help of the biased press, the idea of accountability — so essential to a democratic republic — has almost vanished from the public square.

Any appropriate examination of the causes of 9/11 by the press or Congress has been greeted by the left establishment with mantras like "Don't point fingers" or "Let's not play the blame game."

But accountability is not about one side gloating over the malfeasance and negligence of those in power. It is about sound governance. It is about the future. If a business offers no accountability for the actions of its employees or its books, that business will go bankrupt.

Though governments and societies can't go bankrupt, the effect is the same. A society can become weak and hollow, without purpose and vulnerable to attack from the barbarians at the gate. In these times, those barbarians may be Islamic fanatics carrying suitcase nuclear devices into American cities.

The stakes today are extremely high. We believe the future of America as a great nation hangs in the balance.

We are not Johnnies-come-lately to this view. In January 2001 we co-edited and Newsmax.com published *Bitter Legacy: NewsMax.com Reveals the Untold Story of the Clinton-Gore Years.*

This book was a compendium of our news reports – many of which received no major media play — during the final, impeachment years of Bill Clinton.

Bitter Legacy was not a sensational book about the Lewinsky sex scandal. Instead, we warned America about how the Clintons had unraveled America as a civic nation at every level — economically, morally, politically, militarily, legally.

We predicted, accurately, in January of 2001 that America's economy would go into a tailspin. We noted that for eight years the Clinton administration willfully rigged economic numbers to keep the U.S. economy buzzing and interest rates artificially low.

We also warned, ominously, that America after Bill Clinton would enter a period of great danger — including terrorist attack. Here is an excerpt from the Introduction to *Bitter Legacy:*

"Even worse, because Bill Clinton castrated America's military, the country is vulnerable to great threats from terrorist nations; an unstable, nuclear-armed Russia; and an emerging China."

While President Bush has done a remarkable job, along with Defense Secretary Donald Rumsfeld, in shoring up America's defenses, it will take many years to re-establish our national security infrastructure, so artfully deconstructed during the Clinton years.

Thus, America remains in grave danger.

Terrorist groups like al Qaeda are no doubt supported by states like Iraq, Iran, Cuba and North Korea. These rogue states hate the U.S. and wish us destroyed.

Behind the rogue states are China and Russia, with elements in each country that harbor significant animus toward America. These nations have long been friends with almost all the rogue nations, if not actually strong military allies. During the Clinton years, many of these nations began aligning in a new axis against America.

Sadly, America will continue to pay the price for Bill Clinton.

Winston Churchill to his dying day called World War II the "unnecessary war."

In the 1930s there had been a refusal to confront the facts of the evil of fascism and to hold officials in the democracies accountable for their passivity. The result was predictable for those with clear vision, like Churchill: A worldwide conflagration was loosed upon the earth.

America can still rise to the challenges ahead.

But we must do so with an accurate compass and an understanding of what happened in recent years to bring us to the point of catastrophe. Only then can we make necessary reforms. Only then can we insure that this great experiment in democracy that Abraham Lincoln spoke of will survive as the last great hope of mankind.

Christopher Ruddy
Carl Limbacher Jr.

PART 1

How It
Happened

❖

Chapter 1

September 11
Day of Infamy

Astronauts See Smoke From New York

Inside Cover
Tuesday, September 11, 2001

Astronauts living in the International Space Center, orbiting the earth more than 200 miles out, report they are seeing plumes of smoke emanating from Manhattan from the collapsed World Trade Center buildings.

Warning: More Attacks, Use of Weapons of Mass Destruction Possible

NewsMax.com
Tuesday, September 11, 2001

NewsMax's national security expert, Colonel Stanislav Lunev, is traveling abroad.

The highest-ranking military officer ever to defect from Russia, Colonel Lunev has served as a consultant to the CIA, the FBI and the Defense Intelligence Agency.

He called NewsMax and gave the following analysis:

1. Last year, Colonel Lunev wrote that the U.S. had been the main target of terrorist groups and the nations that support them. The actions today against the U.S. should not be surprising.
2. The successful attack today by this well-organized terrorist group is the result of almost 10 years of the deterioration of America's national security apparatus — including the emasculation of American intelligence-gathering capabilities.
3. American officials and experts have been saying the threat of an attack like this or worse has been a real one. Little or nothing was done, though many knew the threat was real.
4. What countries are involved is difficult to say. It is Colonel Lunev's belief that more than one country was involved in this operation — and perhaps several.
5. Do not forget that Russia remains the number one sponsor of training for terrorist nations. You will find the countries behind this will have very close ties to Russia's military and intelligence agencies.

6. Simple logic cannot be applied to the behavior of these terrorist groups and states. I believe that the terrorist acts conducted could be the first wave of more significant acts that could take place — even in the next few days. Perhaps for the next three days there will be quiet, and then another strike, perhaps more massive than those already delivered.

7. These people are not stupid. They'll use all weapons available to them. Do not underestimate the brutality of these people. The next time, even in the next several days, do not exclude the possibility they will use chemical, nuclear and biological weapons against America.

Caution

Phil Brennan
Tuesday, September 11, 2001

The horrific events that shocked the world today simply defy one's ability to accept and digest the magnitude of the tragedy. The normal mind cannot deal with the images that form upon contemplation of what was endured by passengers in the jets as they raced toward the targets designated by the madmen who had hijacked their aircraft, or the final thoughts of those who faced certain death within the inferno in the towers and or were driven to leap into eternity to avoid the flames.

Sitting before a TV screen, transfixed by the sight of the majestic twin towers of the World Trade Center as they were first devastated by kamikaze attacks and then collapsing in a monstrous cloud of dust and smoke, I found myself wondering if what I was seeing was real and not a nightmare from which I might hopefully awaken.

It was real, and it was perhaps the worst thing I've seen in all the 75 years I've lived in this vale of tears. To begin with, it was personal — I am a native of that city I once loved, and a member of a family whose history was intimately entwined with the history of New York from its earliest days.

Moreover, those two towers stood on the site of the Singer Building, which was built by my children's great-great grandfather, Frederick G. Bourne, who was then president of the Singer Sewing Machine Co. and whose top floors were known as the Bourne Tower.

As my initial shock wore off, my first confused impressions were replaced by a couple of certainties. First, that the most important reaction to the tragedy must be caution. Within minutes, rumors were already spreading — rumors that were quickly disproved. There was a rush on food markets in New York City as residents feared that food staples might be scarce — a report quickly disputed by the mayor. If ever there was a time when all of our abilities must be focused on getting the aftermath right, this is it. We are about to find out what we're made of.

Fingers were instantly pointed, for example, at Osama bin Laden as the culprit behind the attack. While he may well have been, there is enough evidence already available to suggest that he may not have had the resources to mount such a sophisticated military-style operation.

He has been for some time the designated villain allegedly behind a series of terrorist attacks, but by immediately pinning the blame for this latest outrage on him, we becloud the issue and waste investigative resources that should be aimed at other possible terrorist groups.

Most important is the need for this country to be one in our determination to gather behind President Bush in the waging of what is now acknowledged to be an all-out war — different from any we've ever fought, but a war nevertheless.

And in such a war, it is of the most vital importance that such partisan attacks as those waged by a sniveling corps of Democrats and their toadies in the media on the legitimacy of George W. Bush's presidency be stopped and stopped now. I have one thing to say to them: Get over it. You tried to steal the election, and you failed. He won. He's president. And you do no service to your country to question his right to occupy the nation's highest office in such times as these.

Yet, even as I write this, NBC's Andrea Mitchell is on TV questioning President Bush's ability to lead the nation. What a wonderful thing to tell the American people and the world in the midst of one of the worst crises in our history. These people have no shame.

Moreover, you people who have got it into your muddled heads that anyone not a member of the Democratic Party is automatically a presidential usurper should get down on your knees and thank God that we have in the White House in this time of crisis a tough, hard-nosed Texan and not his indecisive, weak-kneed opponent in the 2000 election campaign.

Caution. Take it easy. We face tough times in the immediate future — current problems with the economy may well be worsened, the flow of oil could be disrupted — but we've lived through worse and we've come out on top.

This has been compared to Pearl Harbor. I remember those times, and I remember how my fellow Americans reacted. Most of our Pacific fleet was lying at the bottom of Pearl Harbor; we were woefully unprepared to fight a two-front war; the Japanese, practically unopposed, were swarming all over the Pacific — and we hadn't a doubt in our minds that given a little time and a lot of effort we would win. So we simply rolled up our sleeves and went to work and we prevailed in the greatest conflict in world history.

There was a slogan and a song popular at the time: "We did it before and we can do it again." Let's see if we can this time as well.

Ora Pro Nobis.

Phil Brennan is a veteran journalist who writes for NewsMax.com. He is editor and publisher of Wednesday on the Web (http://www.pvbr.com) and was Washington columnist for National Review magazine in the 1960s. He also served as a staff aide for the House Republican Policy Committee and helped handle the Washington public relations operation for the Alaska Statehood Committee, which won statehood for Alaska.

'A Great People' Fights 'Despicable Acts of Terror'

President George W. Bush
Tuesday, September 11, 2001

Editor's note: This is the White House transcript of President Bush's remarks to the nation tonight.

Good evening. Today, our fellow citizens, our way of life, our very freedom came under attack in a series of deliberate and deadly terrorist acts. The victims were in airplanes, or in their offices; secretaries, businessmen and women, military and federal workers; moms and dads, friends and neighbors. Thousands of lives were suddenly ended by evil, despicable acts of terror.

The pictures of airplanes flying into buildings, fires burning, huge structures collapsing, have filled us with disbelief, terrible sadness, and a quiet, unyielding anger. These acts of mass murder were intended to frighten our nation into chaos and retreat. But they have failed; our country is strong.

A great people has been moved to defend a great nation. Terrorist attacks can shake the foundations of our biggest buildings, but they cannot touch the foundation of America. These acts shattered steel, but they cannot dent the steel of American resolve.

America was targeted for attack because we're the brightest beacon for freedom and opportunity in the world. And no one will keep that light from shining.

Today, our nation saw evil, the very worst of human nature. And we responded with the best of America — with the daring of our rescue workers, with the caring for strangers and neighbors who came to give blood and help in any way they could.

Immediately following the first attack, I implemented our government's emergency response plans. Our military is powerful, and it's prepared. Our emergency teams are working in New York City and Washington, D.C., to help with local rescue efforts.

Our first priority is to get help to those who have been injured, and to take every precaution to protect our citizens at home and around the world from further attacks.

The functions of our government continue without interruption. Federal agencies in Washington which had to be evacuated today are reopening for essential personnel tonight, and will be open for business tomorrow. Our financial institutions remain strong, and the American economy will be open for business, as well.

The search is under way for those who are behind these evil acts. I've directed the full resources of our intelligence and law enforcement communities to find those responsible and to bring them to justice. We will make no distinction between the terrorists who committed these acts and those who harbor them.

I appreciate so very much the members of Congress who have joined me in strongly condemning these attacks. And on behalf of the American people, I thank the many world leaders who have called to offer their condolences and assistance.

America and our friends and allies join with all those who want peace and security in the world, and we stand together to win the war against terrorism. Tonight, I ask for your prayers for all those who grieve, for the children whose worlds have been shattered, for all whose sense of safety and security has been threatened. And I pray they will be comforted by a power greater than any of us, spoken through the ages in Psalm 23: "Even though I walk through the valley of the shadow of death, I fear no evil, for You are with me."

This is a day when all Americans from every walk of life unite in our resolve for justice and peace. America has stood down enemies before, and we will do so this time. None of us will ever forget this day. Yet, we go forward to defend freedom and all that is good and just in our world.

Thank you. Good night, and God bless America.

Aftermath: The Questions Begin

NewsMax.com Wires
Wednesday, September 12, 2001
Half a dozen current and former U.S. officials interviewed by United Press International in the aftermath of Tuesday's series of attacks against the United States all agreed that the country is at war. In the aftermath, U.S. intelligence officials, both former and active, are asking a lot of hard questions.

- How did terrorists manage to outwit airport security systems, not once, but four times?
- Were explosives on the planes or did the jet fuel act as bomb enough?
- What was behind the attack?

And so on down a long list. The target was perfect, according to a U.S. intelligence official.

"The two most conspicuous buildings smack dab in the heartthrob of American imperialism," he called them.

But what was behind it all? Some think they know. "American policy in the Middle East," a former senior CIA official said.

"We underestimate the depth of hatred for America in the Arab world," he added. "To that world, America is the great Satan and Israel is its illegitimate offspring."

Former chief of CIA counterterrorism Vince Cannistraro agreed.

"I have stated publicly, again and again, that unless America took a more active and a more impartial role in the Middle East conflict than we have done so far, Americans would become targets."

Larry Johnston, a former State Department expert in counterterrorism, condemned bias in reporting by the American media. He said he was "tired of seeing the Middle East tragedy presented in U.S. newspapers as the plight of a poor, victimized Israel at the mercy of a horde of bloodthirsty Palestinians."

Referring to the talks between Israeli Foreign Minister Shimon Peres and Palestinian leader Yasser Arafat, the former senior CIA official said, "In the past the closer we got to some sort of deal, the more likely there would be some sort of outrage to bust it up. But if you had something going, something good one side was extending to the other, then you knew you could get past it."

That is not the case today, he said. Instead, he said, "there's just violence breeding violence, different publics hating each other."

James Woolsey, CIA director in the Clinton administration, echoed widespread suggestions that Saudi exile terrorist suspect Osama bin Laden was involved. But he added that a state sponsor could possibly be involved as well.

"There is a reasonable chance this was planned by a state and the terrorist group [was a] subcontractor," he told United Press International Tuesday. "We have to look to see not only who was involved, but who was behind the curtain," he added, concluding "there was a possibility this was Iran [but] this is less likely than if it was Iraq, and it may have been neither."

Others dismissed talk of Iranian involvement. One CIA official with many years' experience in the Middle East, said Iran would only be involved "at many removes."

Iran was too vulnerable, he suggested — it has a capital city with no real air defense, and most of its leadership is housed in public buildings within easy reach of U.S. Navy cruise missiles.

"Iran is far from being the focus yet," he said. And bin Laden?

"There are a lot of his fingerprints on the operation, but we misconceive bin Laden," said a former senior State Department official who spoke — like most interviewed for this article — on condition of anonymity. "We picture [him] as the man sitting at some mighty Wurlitzer organ of terrorism, prodding all the keys."

In fact, "the key to this is compartmentalization," he said. "For technical assistance the terrorists go there; for fake documents, they go here."

All of the sources interviewed by UPI agreed that security at Logan Airport in Boston was terrible.

"What do you expect when you pay people $5 or $6 an hour?" said one. Pressing questions center on what, if any, terrorist communications the National Security Agency intercepted before the attack occurred and how much they picked up while it was in progress.

One former CIA official said that the NSA's technical collection had been plagued with problems of "speed of processing and distribution," and that the agency had been "in the doldrums for several years."

One former senior State Department official suggested that hindsight was likely to reveal many shortcomings.

"Today's events will be like Pearl Harbor in this sense," he said. "In the aftermath, I think we are liable to find that all the clues to what happened, we already had."

COPYRIGHT 2001 BY UNITED PRESS INTERNATIONAL. ALL RIGHTS RESERVED.

President's Statements This Morning

Wednesday, September 12, 2001

"These are more than acts of terror, they are acts of war … this is an enemy that has no regard for human life … they won't be able to run for cover forever … they won't be able to hide forever."

"This enemy thinks its harbors are safe, but they won't be safe forever."

"We will conquer this enemy … we will rally the world … we will be patient, focused and steadfast … we will take time, and we will win."

"Government is open for business, but it is not business as usual."

"We will not allow this enemy to win by changing our way of life or restricting our freedom."

"We will spend whatever it takes to respond … and to protect citizens."

"This is a monumental struggle of good and evil."

Terrorists Targeted Bush

NewsMax.com
Wednesday, September 12, 2001

Tuesday's terror attacks targeted President Bush, federal officials said today.

Attorney General John Aschcroft said that on each of the crashed planes there were three to six people armed with knives and box cutters or making bomb threats.

He also said:

• The White House and Air Force One were targets.
• The FBI has numerous and credible leads and has outposts at each of the crime scenes.
• The recovery of the black boxes is under way.
• All response capabilities have been organized.

FBI Director Robert Mueller told reporters that there were 4,000 agents assisting investigations, including lab personnel at all sites, and an additional 3,000 support specialists.

Their objectives are:

1. Identify hijackers.
2. Gather evidence on those assisting the terrorists in the U.S. and overseas and "remove them."

Manifests have been used as evidence, many of the hijackers have been identified, and associates are being pursued. However, there have been NO arrests, only immigration holds, Mueller said.

Brave Passengers Fought Terrorists

NewsMax.com Wires
Thursday, September 13, 2001

PITTSBURGH — Just minutes before his plane crashed, Jeremy Glick phoned his wife and told her that he and other passengers had come up with a plan to resist the hijackers.

"They were going to stop whoever it was from doing what whatever it was they'd planned," Glick's brother-in-law, Douglas B. Hurwitt, told *The Washington Post*. "He knew that stopping them was going to end all of their lives. But that was my brother-in-law. He was a take-charge guy."

According to the *Post:*

Anticipating his own death, Glick, who celebrated his 31st birthday on September 3, told his wife, Lyzbeth, that he hoped she would have a good life and would take care of their 3-month-old baby girl, Hurwitt said.

Glick told his wife that the plane had been taken over by three Middle Eastern men wearing red headbands. The terrorists, wielding knives and brandishing a red box they claimed contained a bomb, ordered the passengers, pilots and flight attendants toward the rear of the plane, then took over the cockpit.

Fellow passenger Thomas Burnett phoned his wife, telling her the plane had been hijacked but that he and other passengers were determined to "do something about it," the *Pittsburgh Post-Gazette* reported Wednesday.

"I love you, honey," were Burnett's last words to his wife, Deena, before United Flight 93 crashed about 60 miles southeast of Pittsburgh with 45 people aboard.

Authorities don't know exactly what caused the plane to crash at 10 a.m. EDT Tuesday, but it appears that Burnett, 38, of San Ramon, Calif., and other passengers were determined to tackle the hijackers.

During the call Burnett said that one of the passengers had been stabbed, the family's priest, the Rev. Frank Colacicco, told the *San Francisco Chronicle*.

"He said, 'I know we're all going to die — there's three of us who are going to do something about it,'" Colacicco said.

The Federal Aviation Administration reported that as the San Francisco-bound flight neared Cleveland, the pilot requested a flight change and turned the Boeing 757.

The plane was one of four hijacked by suicidal terrorists who destroyed the World Trade Center and badly damaged the Pentagon, but apparently did not intend to hit a grassy field 80 miles southeast of Pittsburgh.

Burnett was the father of three and chief operating officer for Thoratec Corp., a Pleasanton, Calif., medical devices company. The *Chronicle* reported that he told his wife a passenger had already been killed after the doomed flight took off from Newark, N.J.

"This is a great professional and personal loss for all of us at Thoratec," said D. Keith Grossman, the company's president and chief executive. "We are all shocked and saddened by yesterday's senseless and ruthless acts that took from us our friend and colleague."

The FBI interviewed Deena Burnett, 37, about her husband's call.

Meanwhile, the *Pittsburgh Tribune-Review* reported Wednesday that the pilot may have been fighting with the hijackers.

U.S. Representative John Murtha, D-Pa., said finding the black box was key to solving the mystery.

"We think the pilot may have intentionally brought the plane down to avoid attacking another building in Washington, D.C.," Murtha told the *Tribune-Review*.

COPYRIGHT 2001 BY UNITED PRESS INTERNATIONAL. ALL RIGHTS RESERVED.

Bush Vows Victory in Terrorism War

NewsMax.com Wires
Thursday, September 13, 2001

WASHINGTON — President Bush, his face grim and his manner somber, Thursday vowed to lead an international coalition to victory in the first "war of the 21st century," which has already cost the lives of several thousand people, grounded every private aircraft in the country, halted the financial system and obliterated part of the U.S. military command center.

"This country will not relent until we have saved ourselves and others from the terrible tragedy that came upon America," said Bush, whose eyes glistened with tears at one point as he spoke of the Americans who died in the massive terrorist attack of Tuesday.

"The nation must understand this is now the focus of my administration," Bush said, and though it will continue with domestic issues, "now that war has been declared on us, we will lead the world to victory — to victory."

The president made his remarks during a televised telephone call to Mayor Rudy Giuliani and Governor George Pataki of New York and in an exchange with reporters in the Oval Office.

Speaking extemporaneously and punctuating his statements with hard, direct looks at reporters, the president said in answer to a question: "I don't think about myself right now. I think about the families, the children. I am a loving guy, and I am also someone, however, who has got a job to do — and I intend to do it. And this is a terrible moment. But this country will not relent until we have saved ourselves and others from the terrible tragedy that came upon America."

Bush in New York Friday

Earlier the president declared Friday as a national day of mourning for the untold thousands who lost their lives in the attack. On Friday morning he will travel to New York at the invitation of Mayor Giuliani to see directly for the first time the devastation of the World Trade Center.

"I look forward to joining with both of you in thanking the police and fire, the construction trade workers, the restaurant owners, the volunteers — all of whom have really made a huge display for the world to see of the compassion of America, and the bravery of America, and the strength of America. Every world leader I've talked to in recent days has been impressed by what they have seen about our nation, and the fabric of our nation. And I want to thank everybody when I come," Bush said.

Bush said he has been on the telephone with world leaders over the past 24 hours.

"I've been on the phone this morning, just like I was yesterday, and will be this afternoon on the phone with leaders from around the world who express their solidarity with this nation's intention to rout out and whip terrorism," Bush said. "They understand, fully understand, that an act of war was declared on the United States of America. They understand, as well, that that act could have easily have happened to them."

Bush said the leaders had sadness in their voices, but also "understanding that we have just seen the war of the 21st century."

Pakistan's Response

The president said he appreciated the response of Pakistan.

"I would refer you to the statements that the Pakistani leader gave about his — I don't have the exact words in front of me — but his willingness to work with the United States. And I appreciate that statement, and now we'll just find out what that means, won't we?

"We will give the Pakistani government a chance to cooperate and to participate, as we hunt down those people who committed this unbelievable, despicable act on America."

Pakistan, Afghanistan's neighbor, has enormous intelligence contacts in Afghanistan. During the Afghanistan-Soviet war, its intelligence services assisted the United States in feeding arms to Afghan rebels. But Pakistan has not assisted the United States in the past in attempts to locate and punish Osama bin Laden, in part because it is a radical Muslim nation. Secretary of State Colin Powell called the relationship of the United States with Pakistan up and down.

White House spokesman Ari Fleischer said Bush had been in touch by phone on Thursday with Jordan's King Abdullah, Japanese Prime Minister Junichiro Koizumi, Italian Prime Minister Silvio Berlusconi, NATO Secretary-General Lord Robertson and Crown Prince Abdullah of Saudi Arabia.

On Wednesday, Bush spoke with British Prime Minister Tony Blair, Canadian Prime Minister Jean Chretien, French President Jacques Chirac, German Chancellor Gerhard Schroeder, Russian President Vladimir Putin (twice) and Chinese President Jiang Zemin.

The leaders he spoke to "heard my call loud and clear, to those who feel like they can provide safe harbor for the terrorists, that we will hold them responsible as well, and they join me in understanding not only the concept of the enemy, that the enemy is a different type of enemy," Bush said. "They join me also in solidarity about holding those who fund them, who harbor them, who encourage them, responsible for their activities."

Bush would not say whether the administration had evidence of the alleged involvement of bin Laden as media attention increasingly focused on the billionaire Saudi dissident believed to be behind two other terrorist attacks on the United States in recent years. And he warned reporters that his administration will not talk about intelligence operations. This warning was echoed by the secretary of defense and the attorney general.

Bush Urges Respect Toward Muslims

But he urged Americans to avoid lashing out at Muslims in the United States.

"We must be mindful that as we — as we seek to win the war, that we treat Arab-Americans and Muslims with the respect they deserve," Bush said.

Shortly after the Oval Office appearance, Bush and the first lady visited a hospital where victims of the Pentagon attack were being treated.

COPYRIGHT 2001 BY UNITED PRESS INTERNATIONAL. ALL RIGHTS RESERVED.

Democrats Attack Bush in Moment of National Crisis

Inside Cover
Friday, September 14, 2001

In the midst of the national crisis brought on by Tuesday's terrorist attacks in New York and Washington, Massachusetts House Democrats Marty Meehan and Richard Neal slammed President Bush as bumbling and ineffective — with Meehan even suggesting that the White House was lying about Bush being on the terrorists' target list.

"I don't buy the notion Air Force One was a target," the Bay State liberal said. "That's just PR. That's just spin."

On Wednesday, White House spokesman Ari Fleischer told reporters that the Secret Service had received a specific and credible threat that Bush was a potential target, with a caller warning that after the World Trade Center attacks, "Air Force One is next."

Senior White House adviser Karl Rove told *The New York Times* the threat came with code language that indicated insider knowledge of White House procedures and Bush's whereabouts.

Apart from charging that the Bush team had fabricated the threat to deflect criticism over Bush's delayed return to Washington after the disaster, Representative Meehan suggested that former President Clinton would have handled the situation better.

"[Bush] is a new president and he doesn't have the experience that Bill Clinton had," said Meehan. He then added snidely, "Under the circumstances, he's done pretty well."

His Democratic colleague Representative Richard Neal also slammed Bush for what he said was a disappointing performance.

"In politics you have to use imagery to send a message to people," said Neal. "Leadership delineates the difference between a town manager and a president. A president should know how to use imagery, symbolism to lead."

Neal said Bush didn't measure up to Clinton's handling of 1995's Oklahoma City bombing.

"If President Clinton had a better moment than he did in that hangar in Oklahoma City, I never saw it," said Neal. "He lifted the spirits of an entire nation that day. That's what a president does. He provides comfort. And he finds a way to inspire people, to lift them up as well."

Meehan's and Neal's comments were first reported in Friday's *Boston Herald*.

Barbara Olson Eulogized by Clarence Thomas

Inside Cover
Saturday, September 15, 2001

Noted author, TV commentator and one-time Clinton scandal investigator Barbara Olson was eulogized by Supreme Court Justice Clarence Thomas at an Arlington, Va., memorial service Saturday.

Olson, wife of Bush Solicitor General Ted Olson, died Tuesday while aboard an airplane hijacked by kamikaze terrorists who crashed it into the Pentagon.

"This is indeed a sad occasion," Thomas told a gathering of 1,500 at St. Thomas More Cathedral. "One to be repeated thousands of times by our fellow citizens across the country."

The ceremony, which included prayers for the Olson family as well as childhood anecdotes recalled by Olson's brother, David Bracher, moved many on hand to tears.

In his own remembrances of Olson, Circuit Judge J. Michael Luttig described her as "above all, a patriot," a characteristic he said "far transcended her feisty partisanship."

"She was passionate and devoted to our country," Utah Senator Orrin Hatch told The Associated Press. "She always had a smile on her face."

"The service was moving. I thought it just captured the moment and spirit of the United States," another Olson family friend told the AP.

Olson became a familiar face to cable news TV audiences in 1998 and 1999, arguing on venues like *Hannity & Colmes, Larry King Live* and *Rivera Live* that then-President Bill Clinton should be impeached and removed from office.

In 1996, as lead investigative counsel for the House Government Reform and Oversight Committee, Olson prepared formal interrogatories for Hillary Clinton that later became the basis for independent counsel

Robert Ray's finding that Mrs. Clinton provided false and misleading answers about her role in the Travelgate scandal.

In 1999, Olson authored the book *Hell to Pay*, based on her experience investigating Mrs. Clinton.

Just before her death, Olson completed another book, on the Clinton pardon scandal, entitled *The Final Days*.

Bush: 'When I take action, I'm not going to fire a $2 million missile at a $10 empty tent and hit a camel in the butt. It's going to be decisive.'

Inside Cover
Sunday, September 16, 2001
Washington and the liberal media may be getting the message: George Bush is for real and he's no Mr. Nice Guy when it comes to war.

Even *Newsweek*'s Howard Fineman, a liberal Bush-basher, has had to do a double take this week.

Writing in his column of an Oval Office meeting with four U.S. senators — including Hillary Clinton — Fineman described Bush as "relaxed and in control."

Fineman, drawing a comparison with Winston Churchill's defiance during World War II, quoted the president as telling the senators: "When I take action," he said, "I'm not going to fire a $2 million missile at a $10 empty tent and hit a camel in the butt. It's going to be decisive."

Hillary must have shuddered when she heard that, a clear hit on her husband's eight years of appeasement of terrorists and their backers.

Fineman says Bush is "exceeding expectations, learning on the run before our eyes. ... His feet were on the ground, his bearings set: a late bloomer blossoming in the nick of time. ... Cheered on by voters' hopes, he'd become, in the words of a priest at the National Cathedral, 'our George': the designated dragon slayer, a boyish knight in a helmet of graying hair."

Farrakhan Warns of Armageddon if U.S. Retaliates

Marc Morano, CNSNews.com
Monday, September 17, 2001
Minister Louis Farrakhan has warned President Bush that declaring war on terrorism could "trigger the war that would end all wars, the war of Armageddon."

Farrakhan is the leader of the Black Muslim separatist movement Nation of Islam and the architect of the 1995 Million Man March in Washington, D.C.

In a speech Sunday at a Chicago mosque, Farrakhan implied that U.S. foreign policy is to blame for last week's terrorist attacks on Washington and New York. He called on American officials to summon "the courage to look at the foreign policy" and asked if the policies have "produced this danger and hatred toward America."

He described the events of last week as a "dark hour in American and world history." He defended the Palestinians celebrating in the streets after the terrorist attacks because they have "sustained injustice since 1948," which refers to the year Israel became a state.

"They dance in the streets not because they have no feeling for American life, they dance because they wanted America to feel what they feel."

According to Farrakhan, the terrorists that struck America are the product of "despair and hopelessness."

"This is what causes children to strap themselves with bombs. They care nothing for their lives. They want others to feel the pain of what they live with every day."

He then accused the American government and media of unfairness toward Muslims. He noted that convicted Oklahoma City bomber Timothy McVeigh professed to be a Christian, yet the U.S. did not fear all Christians.

"Even though his crime was the most horrific committed up until that time, no one said Christian Timothy McVeigh [actually an atheist], they just said Timothy McVeigh," he noted. He called McVeigh's actions "un-Christian-like" and he declared the attacks last week on the U.S. to be "un-Muslim-like."

He said Muslims throughout the world have no quarrel with the citizens of America, only its foreign policy. He believes these are policies "that the American people know nothing about."

"A better foreign policy of America would defeat terrorism forever in the world," he declared.

COPYRIGHT 2001 CNSNEWS.COM. ALL RIGHTS RESERVED

Bush Tells World: 'Justice Will Be Done'

Scott Hogenson, CNSNews.com
Thursday, September 20, 2001

President Bush was welcomed by Congress Thursday night with standing ovations as he told the nation that "we are a country awakened to danger and called to defend freedom," and promised that "justice will be done" in response to the September 11 attack on the United States.

In an address before a joint session of the House and Senate, Bush said the American people are "joined in a great cause," and he called the terrorist attack "an act of war."

Bush placed blame for the attacks on the World Trade Center and the Pentagon on a group of "loosely affiliated terrorist organizations" in as many as 60 nations, which he said were behind the bombings of the American embassies in Tanzania and Kenya, as well as last October's attack on the U.S. Navy warship the USS *Cole*.

The president issued a list of demands on the ruling Taliban faction in Afghanistan: Deliver all terrorist leaders hiding in Afghanistan; release all foreign nationals; protect foreign reporters and aid workers; close all terrorist training camps; and hand over all terrorist supporters.

Bush received cheers and applause from Congress when he said the demands are "not open to negotiations or discussion."

The president also issued something of a global ultimatum when he said, "Every nation in every region now has a decision to make. Either you're with us, or you are with the terrorists."

In a display of new policy, Bush named Pennsylvania Governor Tom Ridge to head the newly created White House Office of Homeland Security, which will be focused on combating terrorism.

"Many will be involved in this effort," said Bush. "All deserve our thanks, and all have our prayers."

Members of the American military heard Bush repeat his message to them from this past weekend. "Be ready," said Bush. "I've called the armed forces to alert and there's a reason. The hour is coming when America will act, and you will make us proud."

"The civilized world is rallying to America's side," said Bush, who also asked the American people to be patient as the U.S. confronts the current and future threats of terrorism.

"I ask for your patience with the delays and inconveniences that may accompany tighter security, and for your patience in what will be a long struggle. I ask your continued participation and confidence in the American economy. Terrorists attacked a symbol of American prosperity. They did not touch its source," said Bush.

Bush also vowed that "we will rebuild New York City" as a symbol of American resolve.

The president said it was up to the current generation to "lift a dark threat of violence from our people and our future. We will rally the world to this cause by our efforts, by our courage. We will not tire, we will not falter, and we will not fail."

Speaking of his own resolve, Bush said, "I will not forget the wound to our country and those who inflicted it. I will not yield. I will not rest. I will not relent in waging this struggle for freedom and security for the American people."

Response to Bush's speech was almost uniformly positive. Following the speech, Senate Majority Leader Tom Daschle, D-S.D., said "the president has called us again to greatness, and tonight we answer that call."

Joining Daschle was Senate Republican Leader Trent Lott, R-Miss., who noted that after a presidential address, the opposition party traditionally is entitled to a response. "Tonight there is no opposition party. We stand here united," said Lott.

House Speaker Dennis Hastert, R-Ill., said he was "confident that the president has the support of the civilized world to pursue these terrorists and to preserve the free world."

House Republican Conference Chairman Representative J.C. Watts, R-Okla., expressed similar confidence in the American people. "We regard freedom as precious and absolute in this country. It cannot be bought, bartered or borrowed. It must be vigorously defended," Watts said.

COPYRIGHT 2001 BY CNS.NEWSCOM. ALL RIGHTS RESERVED.

Flags Pulled From Berkeley Fire Trucks

NewsMax.com Wires
Thursday, September 20, 2001

BERKELEY, Calif. — Citing past experiences with unruly protesters, Berkeley Fire Department officials ordered the removal of American flags from fire engines in advance of an anticipated series of anti-war rallies at the University of California.

Large red, white and blue American flags were mounted on the city's trucks and engines in the wake of the terrorist attacks on the World Trade Center and Pentagon, but concerns that the banners would draw trouble-makers during the planned march prompted city hall to order their removal.

"Based on past experience, these flags may be inflammatory to people and provoke them to take the flag or whatever else," Berkeley Assistant Fire Chief David Orth told the *San Francisco Chronicle*. "I don't want a fire-fighter defending a flag in lieu of fighting a fire or rescuing somebody."

The Berkeley campus was one of most tumultuous during the Vietnam War, and more recent protests have frequently degenerated into vandalism and agitated clashes with police.

"I think it was wise for the Fire Department to take them down," said Ronald Cruz, an organizer of the march. "Some people are upset how the mass grief of the nation has been manipulated into support of war."

A peaceful march Thursday drew several hundred protesters, and additional rallies were anticipated in the coming weeks and days.

The *Chronicle* said that while the decision on the removal of the flags sorely pained Mayor Shirley Dean and considerably irked many of the city's 124 firefighters, most saw it as par for the course for Berkeley's politics.

"It's no big deal," an anonymous firefighter told the newspaper. "Knowing the history of Berkeley and the city itself, we don't want to be targets, otherwise we won't be able to help anyone."

COPYRIGHT 2001 BY UPI ALL RIGHTS RESERVED

Poll: Majority Want Broad War Against Terrorist Nations

Inside Cover
Friday, September 21, 2001

A *Washington Post*/ABC News poll, taken immediately after President Bush's speech to the nation last night, found that an overwhelming 91 percent of Americans support the president.

As many as 80 percent of Americans said they watched the president's historic address to the nation.

And almost two-thirds of the nation — 63 percent — agreed with the president that the war should not be limited to a small number of terrorists, but widened to "a broader war against terrorist groups and the nations that support them."

Americans are not expecting speedy results either. Some "57 percent said it would extend for several years."

'We've Found God Again'

E. Ralph Hostetter
Saturday, September 22, 2001
These words come from a CBS TV channel, introducing a Hollywood-related program, of all things: "And we've found God again."

The statement was part of a prologue listing values such as flying the American flag, coming together as a nation and a revival of patriotism — values that were rediscovered following the worst terrorist attack on American soil in history, leaving thousands dead at the World Trade Center, the Pentagon in Arlington, Va., and United Flight 93 in a field in Pennsylvania.

Prayers seemed to be on the lips of most Americans this week. President Bush prayed and called for a day of prayer; the Cabinet prayed; the Congress prayed; the Supreme Court prayed; and the churches across America held special prayer services. The prayers for the thousands lost in the carnage came from the lips of Americans all across the land.

But our schoolchildren, probably the most frightened and psychologically damaged of all our population, were denied the solace and comfort of seeking help in prayers to their God. Their prayers were denied by a 1963 Supreme Court decision prohibiting prayer on public school property.

And yet the president prayed in the (public) White House; the Supreme Court prayed in the (public) Supreme Court building; the Congress prayed and sang "God Bless America" in the (public) Capitol building. Denial of prayer in public schools resulted from a decision by the high court, under Chief Justice Earl Warren, "interpreting" the "establishment clause" of the First Amendment to the U.S. Constitution.

The "establishment clause" represents only half of the first clause of the First Amendment.

The term "establishment clause" was coined to give the impression that the entire clause was all about prohibiting Congress from establishing a state religion. Not so!

The complete wording of the clause in the U.S. Constitution is

"Congress shall make no law respecting an establishment of a religion, or prohibiting the free exercise thereof." The liberal Warren Court addressed only the first part of the so-called "establishment clause."

The case, *Murray v. the United States*, involved certain state laws requiring the recitation of the Lord's Prayer and reading of verses from the Bible.

The U.S. Congress had never made any law that could remotely resemble the establishing of a religion.

By apparently ignoring the second part of the "establishment clause' — "or prohibiting the free exercise thereof" — the Warren Court, for all intents and purposes, "threw the baby out with the bath water" by denying all prayer in public schools, including voluntary prayers of student bodies.

The term "prohibiting" is a far cry from the "free exercise thereof." The Warren Court, in its zeal to make law, closed the door on all prayer.

Today the Supreme Court decision of 1963 has grafted onto itself the prohibitions of Christmas nativity scenes in public squares as well as the banning of the Ten Commandments, the basic law of civilization, in town halls and courthouses across America. "Kick God out of America" seemed to be the movement in this country until 8:45 a.m. on September 11, 2001.

A means must be found to have the U.S. Supreme Court revisit the entire first clause of the First Amendment to the U.S. Constitution to give meaning to "or prohibiting the free exercise thereof."

"And we've found God again." This simple phrase may well pave the way to permit Americans to freely exercise their God-given — and constitutional — right to pray whenever, or wherever, they wish.

Poll: Arab-Americans Support Racial Profiling

Inside Cover
Wednesday, October 3, 2001

By a margin of more than 2 to 1, Arab-Americans say they support racial profiling by law enforcement in the wake of last month's terrorist attacks on New York and Washington, D.C., a survey taken by the *Detroit Free Press* shows.

Sixty-one percent of Arab-Americans said they backed stricter scrutiny of those of Mideast descent, while 28 percent disagreed. Eleven percent were undecided.

The *Free Press* questioned 527 Americans of Arab background late last week. Half identified themselves as Muslim, while 43 percent said they were Christian. The two most common countries of origin were Iraq (36 percent) and Lebanon (27 percent).

Arab-American support for racial profiling comes even though 40 percent of those surveyed told the *Free Press* they had experienced anti-Arab bias since the September 11 attacks.

Metro Detroit has the nation's most visible community of Arab immigrants and descendants, estimated at 200,000 to 350,000, the *Free Press* said.

The poll had a margin of error of plus or minus 4.4 percentage points.

Cheney Announces 'Bush Doctrine'

Inside Cover
Thursday, October 18, 2001

In his first major public address since the September 11 terrorist attacks on the U.S., Vice President Dick Cheney announced the Bush Doctrine for dealing with worldwide terrorism.

"The president has made clear in this struggle there is no neutral ground," Cheney told the annual Alfred E. Smith political dinner in New York.

"Those who harbor terrorists share guilt for the acts they commit. Under the Bush Doctrine a regime that harbors or supports terrorists will be regarded as hostile to the United States."

Cheney said that the al Qaeda terrorists had inflicted great damage on the U.S. and forced America to adopt security changes that would last indefinitely.

"Many of these changes we've made are permanent — at least in the lifetime of most of us. Vigilance against the new threat is not just a temporary precaution. It is a responsibility we all share."

Cheney made his remarks after touring Ground Zero, site of the Twin Towers destruction in lower Manhattan. He described the devastation, which he witnessed firsthand Thursday for the first time, as "staggering."

White House Staff Told 'Run for Your Lives' on 9/11

Inside Cover
Friday, March 1, 2002

As a hijacked airliner headed for the White House on September 11 last year, panicky Secret Service agents ran through the halls ordering Bush administration staffers to "run for your lives."

Rebecca Cooper, an ABC TV-News reporter who was at the White House the morning of the World Trade Center attacks, described the scene for WABC Radio's John Gambling on Friday.

"The Secret Service came in scared. You could tell that they were scared, and that's quite unnerving to see the Secret Service scared. And they told us to 'run for your lives,' that there was a plane headed for the White House."

Cooper said she later interviewed a woman on the staff of first lady Laura Bush who "literally ran out of her shoes and ran several blocks barefoot to get to the safety of her apartment, because Secret Service was so scared that we were all going to die if we stayed at the White House."

The ABC reporter told Gambling she doesn't fault the Secret Service at all, noting that "there was a plane, it was headed to the White House — as we know now." The plane, American Airlines Flight 77, ultimately ended up hitting the Pentagon instead.

Cooper said that fears the White House could have been destroyed contributed to President Bush's decision to reactivate a doomsday "shadow government" plan first implemented by President Eisenhower to help the U.S. survive a nuclear attack.

The shadow government plan "underscores what President Bush has been saying all along — the federal government thinks that the United States will be attacked again," she added.

We Could Have Prevented 9/11, Congressional Intelligence Chairman Says

Phil Brennan, NewsMax.com
Wednesday, June 12, 2002

There is no reason why the U.S should not have known about the September 11 attacks in advance and taken steps to prevent the disaster, says Representative Porter Goss, co-chairman of the congressional committee investigating 9/11.

"Should we have known? Yes, we should have. Could we have known? Yes, I believe we could have because of the hard targets" CIA operatives were tracking, Goss told *Washington Post* reporters Dana Priest and Juliet Eilperin.

With reams of intelligence data from the CIA at their disposal, Goss and the joint committee he co-chairs are learning how much vital information concerning terrorist intentions was available to the U.S.

While admitting that U.S. intelligence agencies failed to unravel the mass of data available to them and reach the conclusion that a 9/11-type attack was in the offing, Goss, a 10-year veteran of the CIA, told the *Post* that neither he nor Congress nor successive administrations nor, for that matter, the American people were willing to take the steps required to prevent what happened last September.

"You read the file and you say, 'Why didn't we listen?'" Goss said.

According to the *Post*, Richard A. Clarke, who was Bill Clinton's anti-terrorism coordinator and is President Bush's cyberspace security adviser, was the committee's first outside witness Tuesday. During the Clinton administration, the *Post* recalled, Clarke had repeatedly warned about al Qaeda's plans to attack U.S. targets.

Members of the committee said Clarke provided them with "a timeline of events and information about al Qaeda and other terrorist groups," intermixing it with what the government did with the information.

He went into detail about "planes as weapons," said Representative Timothy J. Roemer, D-Ind.

During several hours of testimony Clarke spoke openly about "some deficiencies in some specific areas," said Representative Sherwood L. Boehlert, R-N.Y.

And Representative Ray LaHood, R-Ill., reported that Clarke's work with several presidents gave him a broad picture of the government's approach to intelligence-gathering. "He's got the perspective going way back," he said.

According to the Post, the committee's path through the investigation has been charted mainly by Goss, with the support of co-chairman Senator Bob Graham, D-Fla. Goss, the *Post* reported, "is leading the committee through a 16-year history of terrorism and the U.S. response to it."

As of now, Goss said, there have been no bombshells or smoking guns discovered in the tons of documents provided the committee by intelligence agencies.

And Goss doesn't expect there will be any that indicate that anybody in the U.S. government knew the details of the 9/11 attacks before they happened.

The most damning evidence yet revealed, Senator Graham noted, was Minnesota FBI agent Coleen Rowley's statements that the FBI fumbled clues that might have stopped Zacarias Moussaoui, the man U.S. intelligence believes intended to be the "20th hijacker." But there is no indication that had the information about Moussaoui been acted on, it would have prevented 9/11. Goss told the *Post* not to expect any smoking guns to emerge from the probe. "You can't tell me there were people out there who knew" about the September 11 attacks, he said.

That conclusion is in line with what Goss told PBS in an earlier interview last year.

"Well, we certainly had plenty of alerts that there was something going to happen," he recalled. "What we didn't have was the where, and the when, and the how."

Former CIA Chief:
World War IV Began on September 11

Dave Eberhart, NewsMax.com
Thursday, July 25, 2002

Former CIA Director R. James Woolsey told a Washington audience Wednesday, "We are in a world war, we are in World War IV." He said World War IV began on September 11, 2001.

Woolsey, former director of central intelligence (1993–1995) under President Clinton, warned a packed audience at a Washington, D.C., symposium that this current world war will be unlike any other in history. The symposium discussed intelligence requirements in the new century and was hosted by the Institute on World Politics.

Woolsey said that America won the Cold War, which he described as

World War III, and he expects America to meet the challenges of the new war.

The former CIA chief did not mince words as he challenged the administration to continue to pound out the message that America is not simply on a mission of self-defense but on a sacred campaign to safeguard the ideals of democracy.

"For the fourth time ... we are on the march, and we are on the side of those they most fear — their own people!" Woolsey exclaimed, pointing his finger at Iraq as the primary opponent of America in the new war.

Woolsey suggested it would be futile to wait for a "[former Soviet President Mikhail] Gorbachev figure to evolve" in Iraq. He said Iraq is ruled by a murderous family that will not give up power.

"Iraq can only be dealt with effectively by military action," Woolsey said. "I like to draw analogies. Iraq is like Hitler's Germany in the mid-1930s. There's no sense waiting, as the situation will only get worse."

Woolsey voiced his strong opinion that it makes sense to wage war against Saddam Hussein even without the "smoking gun" of a clear and provable nexus to 9/11.

"His general support of terrorism is enough," Woolsey concluded, pointing to the dictator's cease-fire violations, the testimony of defectors describing hijack training within Iraq, the meetings of the former Iraqi ambassador to Turkey with al Qaeda members, and the Czech intelligence service's repeated public reports of meetings with bomber Mohamed Atta in Prague.

"Put all this together with the foiled attempt to assassinate the senior George Bush in Kuwait," Woolsey advised.

And Woolsey made it apparent that he was not impressed with Iraq as a potential battlefield opponent, noting that Saddam's standing army is much depleted from the days of the Gulf War.

He also cited the edge of the "smart bomb," suggesting that only 5 percent of the ordnance dropped on Saddam's forces in the Gulf War were smart weapons.

"Sixty-five percent of the bombs used in Afghanistan have been smart weapons. There will be at least that level in any campaign in Iraq," Woolsey said. "The U.S. is totally capable of success."

Woolsey said the U.S. military needs to deploy only 100,000 to 200,000 troops to successfully invade Iraq.

He noted that the U.S. will likely gain access to one or more countries in the region that could be used as jumping-off points for an invasion. He specifically noted the U.S. will likely get the green light from Turkey, Kuwait, Bahrain and Qatar to allow U.S. troops.

As to dealing with al Qaeda, Woolsey suggested the conflict will be protracted.

"We will have to deal with them in their lairs. It will be a long and bloody conflict lasting years, perhaps decades," he said.

"We've got to get busy," Woolsey advised, noting that only an aggressive policy will keep things from going from "bad to catastrophic." He described al Qaeda as a canny and dangerous enemy.

"For two years the FAA [Federal Aviation Administration] was being warned about flimsy cockpit doors." According to Woolsey, al Qaeda sat back and added up the elements: flimsy cockpit doors, box cutters allowed on board, and a general policy to be passive in hijack situations.

That lesson, said Woolsey, should be extended to potential enemy attacks on the U.S. infrastructure, such as the country's electrical grids. "We need to be asking, 'What are the functional equivalents of a flimsy cockpit door?' "

Woolsey emphasized that the victory in the new world war will be won by echoing themes that led us to success in World War II.

"We won before because we were fighting for freedom," he said.

David Eberhart is the former news editor for The Stars and Stripes *and* Stripes.com. *A retired military officer and the published author of five novels, he recently contributed to* The New York Times *best-seller* Chicken Soup for the Veteran's Soul.

Chapter 2

Bill Clinton's Role

CIA Officials Reveal What Went Wrong — Clinton to Blame

Christopher Ruddy
Wednesday, September 12, 2001

The worst, single most tragic day in the history of America has just passed.

There were likely more American casualties yesterday than at the Battle of Antietam on Wednesday, September 17, 1862.

Already the media spin on yesterday's events is relentless.

The talking heads are pushing several themes, including:

- Now is not the time to point fingers at responsible parties in America, i.e., political figures like Clinton or our own security agencies.
- The events of Tuesday are the "worst-case scenario" — the worst is over.
- Osama bin Laden is the culprit.

On these points of spin, the first one is baloney. Of course we need to find why our security failed. This is basic.

And unless the big media are consulting a psychic better than the one I use, no one knows what the future days, weeks and months may yield.

This is not the worst-case scenario. A worst-case scenario is a 25-megaton nuclear bomb detonated in New York or a full-scale attack against the U.S.! These should not be ruled out.

These dangers can be avoided, we pray, but only if we stop listening to the media idiots who feed us a diet of blow-dried nonsense. Is Katie Couric going to say how bad she feels for the terrorists who were driven to these cowardly acts?

Big media and the hack politicians are the ones who led us to this nightmarish day.

Smart to Examine Who Failed Us

We are Americans, so let's get our feet back on the ground and use common sense.

The media say we shouldn't point fingers. (Funny, isn't it, how the media have spent 30 years pointing fingers at Richard Nixon for his alleged crimes, but when one of their liberal favorites is due for some blame, they feed us mantras like "Let's move on!" and "No time to point fingers!")

Common sense dictates that we need to critically examine the people who are to blame for this incident, both the perpetrators (and if you believe Osama bin Laden was the major mastermind behind this, I have a bridge in Brooklyn I want to sell you) and the people we pay to protect us — that is, our national security agencies.

Without question, these agencies failed miserably in preventing this sophisticated, wide-scale and coordinated attack against America.

Intelligence Agencies Failed Miserably

On Tuesday I received an e-mail from a recently retired high-ranking CIA official. I will identify him as "Harry." Here's what Harry said:

"… Reacting effectively and justly to this [attack] makes us hugely dependent on intell [intelligence] capabilities that failed us miserably. This is an enormous liability, which we shall not be able to fix before we have to react. Payback time for the last eight years!"

He continued: "There were clearly enormous failures here. This operation was ingenious in its simplicity, which would have limited the size (number of people, actions) of the operation and hence detectability. But it could not have been that small for at least a dozen men to hijack four carefully chosen aircraft (routes, fuel load) with carefully coordinated timing. And to get through security with knives big enough to subdue four relatively large crews. If the intell and security systems claim that this challenge is simply too hard for them, they have to be replaced, root and branch. Because this challenge is the challenge. It is now pretty self-evident that claims of reform and adjustment [at the intelligence agencies] to new realities that we've heard over the past eight years or so are hollow."

Of course, it's obvious why the media doesn't want any finger pointing.

Guess who ran the U.S. government and was responsible for our national security for the past eight years?

You got it: Bill Clinton, Hillary's husband.

Clinton Responsible for Unpreparedness

The Clintons were supported vociferously by the media through the worst imaginable scandals.

During that time I was one of the lead reporters opposing the Clintons. I was mocked and vilified by my colleagues for doing so.

I said throughout that period that Bill Clinton's personal corruption was wholesale and mirrored how he was corrupting America's national security.

I wrote articles and said repeatedly that, sadly, America might end up paying a heavy price for Bill Clinton and the major media's complicity.

Brutally, we witnessed our weakness yesterday.

I don't believe the worst has passed. We remain vulnerable and weak.

During eight years, Clinton decimated America's military. Our forces were cut almost in half under his stewardship.

Research and development on all new weapons systems were brought almost to a halt as other nations continued to build. Clinton destroyed nearly our entire arsenal of tactical nuclear weapons. Monsters like Saddam flourished as Clinton bombed aspirin factories, tent cities in Afghanistan and worthless radar stations in the Iraqi desert.

These are open facts, easily verifiable.

Clinton, Ever Clever

But Clinton, ever clever, was more insidious. Little, systematic changes were undertaken to destroy America's intelligence agencies.

Let me explain. A regular NewsMax reader, "Roger," was a CIA spy in the Middle East. I met him almost two years ago. Roger wanted to tell me why a gung-ho American quit the CIA in disgust.

Roger said the CIA was not interested in recruiting spies.

Clinton and company knew they could not just tell the CIA to stop recruiting spies. That would look stupid and embarrassing.

So they just changed the rules of how spies are recruited, raising the bar on requirements to such a high degree that the most valuable spies could never meet CIA standards and couldn't work for us.

Previously, I wrote how Clinton effectively stopped the recruitment of Chinese nationals by demanding that only high-ranking embassy officials could be recruited — knowing this is almost impossible. Roger told me that. Roger reminded me of this again today.

He noted that Clinton policies reached their zenith under CIA Director John Deutch and his top assistant, Nora Slatkin. The pair ran Clinton's CIA in the mid-1990s and implemented a "human rights scrub" policy.

Here's how Roger described it in an e-mail Tuesday evening: "Deutch and Nora, Clinton's anti-intelligence plants, implemented a universal 'human rights scrub' of all assets, virtually shutting down operations for 6 months to a year. This was after something happened in Central America (there was an American woman involved who was the common law wife of a commie who went missing there) that got a lot of bad press for the agency.

"After that, each asset had to be certified as being 'clean for human rights violations.'

"What this did was to put off limits, in effect, terrorists, criminals, and anyone else who would have info on these kinds of people."

Roger says the CIA, even under new leadership, has never recovered from the "human rights scrub" policy.

Perhaps that was the intention.

But we the American people, Congress and honest media need to examine all of these issues, now and quickly. If we don't, we risk even graver dangers than those we just lived through.

CIA Official Confirms Ruddy Terror Exclusive

Inside Cover
Wednesday, September 12, 2001

A former CIA official said late Wednesday that U.S. spy recruitment had been decimated by strict Clinton administration rules that tied the agency's hands in its war against terrorism, a development first reported by NewsMax.com's executive editor, Christopher Ruddy.

"We don't have enough people on the ground in the right places," former Iraqi bureau station chief Whitney Bruner told Fox News Channel's Bill O'Reilly.

"Partly it's because there's a culture that I think has developed in Washington concerning human operations over the last several years," Bruner said, a policy that limited the kinds of people the agency could deal with.

"When you're dealing with a terrorist target, you are dealing with what might charitably be called slimeballs — very, very unpleasant-type people who probably have criminal records," the former station chief explained.

But the people in a position to know about terrorists' plans were off-limits under Clinton-era CIA regulations.

"We're not allowed to deal with them … if the person you are trying to recruit against a terrorist target has questions of human rights or other kinds of crime," Bruner revealed.

Nearly a day before the former CIA official spoke out, a CIA source identified only as "Roger" told NewsMax.com's Christopher Ruddy that the CIA's "human rights scrub" policy, developed during the Clinton years, made the recruitment of intelligence assets nearly impossible.

Admiral Moorer: Clinton Policies Led to Disaster

NewsMax.com
Wednesday, September 12, 2001

The catastrophe that struck America was the result of a decade of military cuts and the undermining of U.S. intelligence agencies, Admiral Thomas H. Moorer has told NewsMax.com.

Admiral Moorer served as chairman of the Joint Chiefs of Staff, the nation's highest-ranking military official, and brought the Vietnam War to a conclusion. He has served in three major wars.

Yesterday's events brought back memories of Pearl Harbor, he said. Admiral Moorer, then a naval aviator, was present at Pearl Harbor on December 7, 1941.

Admiral Moorer made the following analysis for NewsMax. His quotes are in bold.

1. The Clinton administration had a view of intelligence agencies similar to the Carter administration's. They didn't like using spies. This is why we had no warning.

"You absolutely need spies. You need them to melt into a society and tell you what is going on. You can't rely on satellites and technology alone."

2. The actions taken yesterday were the result of perceived weakness of U.S. armed forces.

"President Clinton brought the military down and down. He made the military like it was before Pearl Harbor."

3. The U.S. must significantly increase its use of human intelligence — that is, spies on the ground in foreign countries.

4. America must remain vigilant.

"This is like what Yamamoto said after Pearl Harbor, 'A sleeping tiger has been aroused.' We can't just strike back and go back to sleep. Next time the attack could be even more serious."

5. Soon terrorist groups will have access to nuclear weapons.

"This is inevitable. Countries like Russia and China are providing countries like Pakistan, Iraq and Iran with this technology — the same technology Clinton gave to the Chinese."

6. Missile defense is needed now.

"The media is dead wrong when it says this proves we don't need missile defense. Soon, the same countries that supported these terrorists that just attacked us will have missiles capable of hitting the U.S. We need to defend against their use."

7. No additional attacks will occur in the immediate future.

"I believe they reached the limits of their capabilities with these attacks. But they will try again later. They want nuclear weapons."

Report: Clinton Nixed Hit on Bin Laden

Inside Cover
Thursday, September 13, 2001

As recently as last December, former President Bill Clinton was presented with reliable intelligence pinpointing the whereabouts of suspected Word Trade Center terrorist Osama bin Laden — along with the U.S. military's plan to take him out.

But Clinton declined to green-light the operation.

The information on bin Laden's location came from "eyes-on intelligence," The Associated Press reported Thursday, meaning he was spotted by a tipster on the ground or via satellite surveillance.

The intelligence coup is said to have spurred "a high-level debate" among senior White House officials over whether this was Clinton's last chance to eliminate bin Laden before he left office.

Former Clinton administration national security adviser Sandy Berger admitted to the AP, "There were a couple of points, including in December, where there was intelligence indicative of bin Laden's whereabouts."

But in the wake of reports that bin Laden masterminded Tuesday's attacks on New York's World Trade Center and the Pentagon, Berger sounded somewhat defensive, complaining, "I can categorically tell you that at no point was it ripe enough to act."

He also attempted to shift blame to the military for the decision not to act, saying, "There was never a recommendation from the Pentagon."

Among the factors weighed in the decision to spare the deadly terrorist in December were concerns about collateral damage, i.e., the deaths of innocent civilians in Afghanistan.

In 1998, Clinton ordered a cruise missile strike on a suspected bin Laden training camp in Khost, Afghanistan, resulting in the deaths of 20 suspected terrorists.

The total number of Americans killed in Tuesday's World Trade Center attack will run into the thousands.

Clinton Rushes to Beat Bush to Disaster Site

Inside Cover
Thursday, September 13, 2001

In a craven attempt to upstage his successor, George W. Bush, ex-President Bill Clinton rushed to the site of the World Trade Center disaster Thursday, where he attempted to reprise his role as "comforter in chief."

Earlier in the day, Bush had told New York Mayor Rudy Giuliani and Governor George Pataki that he would travel to Manhattan Friday to survey the wreckage and send the city a message of support.

But just hours after Bush announced his New York trip, Clinton materialized at the scene of the collapsed Twin Towers, coaxing several women who were distraught over missing relatives into awkward hugs.

One sobbing woman accosted by the ex-president was clearly more interested in having the photo of her loved one broadcast on TV than participating in any photo-op with the has-been politician.

It's unclear how Clinton, who had been traveling in Australia, managed to re-enter the country — since the nationwide ban on air travel had been lifted only hours before he arrived in lower Manhattan.

At one point during Clinton's attempt to upstage Bush, Fox News Channel's Brian Kilmeade grilled him on whether he missed a chance to prevent the worst terrorist attack in world history during his own presidency.

KILMEADE: Mr. President, there's a report today that you had the best shot at [Osama bin Laden] in December, in the waning weeks of your presidency, and at the last minute you said, "No, too much of a risk." How true is that?

CLINTON: No, it's not true. The best shot we had at Osama bin Laden was when I bombed his training camp in 1998 and we missed him by just a matter of hours. Maybe even less than an hour.

KILMEADE: Do you feel somewhat responsible?

CLINTON: Well, let me say this. We tripled the intelligence budget for counterintelligence — for counterterrorism. Because I believed, as I said, that these kind of threats would be the most likely ones.

How Clinton Shielded Afghanistan

John L. Perry, NewsMax.com
Tuesday, September 18, 2001

Why wasn't Afghanistan on the list of terrorist-sponsoring "rogue states"? The answer in three words: William Jefferson Clinton.

During his presidency, Clinton consistently kept Taliban-controlled Afghanistan off his State Department's annually updated list of regimes that harbor and abet terrorist organizations, such as that run by Osama bin Laden, the world's most-wanted terrorist, whose safe haven has for years been the badlands of Afghanistan.

The number one suspect behind the September 11 attacks on the World Trade Center twin towers and the Pentagon was long known to be hiding out in Afghanistan with relative freedom. Indeed, during his tenure as president, Clinton had some of bin Laden's training camps bombed, but not very seriously.

What Does It Take?

Even that didn't qualify Afghanistan as the sanctuary of a major terrorist operation in the eyes of the Clinton-Gore administration.

The most-recent annual State Department report, issued in the final year of the Clinton-Gore administration, failed to list Afghanistan, despite the known coddling of bin Laden by the Taliban militant Islamic movement, which is the actual ruling power in the Afghan government.

According to Cable News Network last year, "In regards to Afghanistan, the State Department says it is a threat because it continues to shelter [bin Laden]."

Notwithstanding, Afghanistan wasn't put on the "rogue state" list, along with communist Cuba, Iran, Iraq, Libya, communist North Korea, Sudan or Syria.

'Not Sponsoring Terror'

The Clinton-Gore State Department "does not believe [either Afghanistan or neighboring Pakistan] is actually sponsoring terrorist acts," CNN reported.

"In general, sources tell CNN, the State Department believes that state-sponsored terrorism, as a whole, is less of a concern."

At that same time, ABC News said that the Clinton-Gore administration "does not recognize Afghanistan's Taliban rulers as its legitimate government, and so cannot formally sanction them."

The State Department list of state sponsors of terrorism has remained static for the past three years with just the current seven countries identified.

Sounds About Right

The department defines terrorism as "pre-meditated, politically motivated violence perpetrated against noncombatant targets by sub-national groups or clandestine agents, usually intended to influence an audience."

The official State Department attitude has obviously changed under the Bush-Cheney administration. After the September 11 assaults, Secretary of State Colin Powell warned the Afghan government that if the Taliban does not hand over bin Laden, dire consequences will follow for Afghanistan.

Powell's attitude toward another world-renowned marionette of terrorists, Iraq dictator Saddam Hussein, also is more severe than that of his predecessor, Madeleine K. Albright.

'Not a Drop in His Veins'

At a news conference two days after the terrorist attacks, Powell was asked: "Of all of the seven countries on the State Department's state sponsors list, only one of them, I believe, has not condemned [the attacks], has not said anything. Does it raise any red flags with you that Saddam Hussein and Iraq have been silent about this?"

To which Powell replied: "I am not surprised. He is one of the leading terrorists on the face of the Earth, and I would not expect the slightest drop of the milk of human kindness to be flowing in his veins."

The State Department might wish to consider tacking up a sign over its front door down in Foggy Bottom: "Under New Management."

John L. Perry, a prize-winning newspaper editor and writer who served on White House staffs of two presidents, is senior editor for NewsMax.com.

Clinton Blames CIA for Implementing His Own Spy Restrictions

Inside Cover
Wednesday, September 19, 2001

In an interview with NBC anchorman Tom Brokaw on Tuesday, ex-President Clinton tried to dodge blame for restrictions on spy recruitment implemented during his administration, suggesting that the rule change was the CIA's decision alone.

"The CIA had put in place a directive saying that if unsavory characters — that is, people that have abused human rights themselves, for example — were going to be used as sources and paid, that there had to be approval above the field level," Clinton told Brokaw.

During the 10-minute interview, the ex-president never acknowledged any responsibility for the spy recruitment directive, which officials now say may have helped terrorists conceal their plans to attack New York and Washington.

After distancing himself from the decision, Clinton defended the new limitations.

"The director of the CIA says there's not a single instance in which the CIA has declined to use a source in a terrorist case," he told NBC, then added, "but apparently some field operatives feel they may be somewhat constrained. That ought to be reviewed and if so we ought to change the rules."

Still, the ex-president maintained the new limitations did nothing to hurt U.S. intelligence-gathering efforts.

"So far as I know, every potential human intelligence source was explored," he told Brokaw.

Just hours after last Tuesday's terrorist attacks, a former CIA official who was once stationed in the Middle East told NewsMax.com's executive editor, Christopher Ruddy, that the Clinton administration order decimated the CIA's ability to gather human intelligence.

"[Clinton CIA Director John] Deutch and [top aide] Nora [Slatkin], Clinton's anti-intelligence plants, implemented a universal 'human rights scrub' of all assets, virtually shutting down operations for 6 months to a year," the CIA source said.

"After that, each asset had to be certified as being 'clean for human rights violations.'

"What this did was to put off limits, in effect, terrorists, criminals, and anyone else who would have info on these kinds of people."

Bill Clinton, the Appeaser, Still Off-Limits

Christopher Ruddy
Wednesday, September 19, 2001

Why does Bill Clinton still remain "off-limits"?

Last night Bill Clinton was at the top of Tom Brokaw's nightly news, feted as if he were still a sitting president.

I was hoping Brokaw might ask some hard questions of the former president, who was the steward of America's national security during the past eight years.

Other than a softball question about why had not done more to get bin Laden, nothing of substance came from Brokaw.

Since the attack of September 11, major media personalities, figures including Dan Rather, Tom Brokaw, Peter Jennings, Mark Shields, Katie Couric, Howard Fineman, Alan Greenspan's wife Andrea Mitchell and many others have sought to attack our sitting president in a crisis situation for, among other things, his communication skills, his decision not to immediately return to Washington, and his lack of involvement in the "peace process."

Still, despite all of the hours of coverage I have watched on the major networks, I have not heard one media personality or talking head even question the handling of America's national security by Bill Clinton.

There is good reason to discuss Clinton's role in all of this. Only by knowing what went wrong can we fix the problems and prepare for the future.

NewsMax first broke the story about Clinton's activities at the CIA. Now that story about the CIA's failure to recruit spies in these terrorist networks has been talked about by many.

Still, Clinton's role in creating the policy that led to such disaster is never mentioned by the major media.

Even conservative talking heads don't mention Clinton. Why?

Because many of these pundits have read the tea leaves and know they just might not be invited back by TV producers if they criticize the sacred cow Bill Clinton and, by association, his wife.

It's OK for major media to attack Bush, but no one in the media seems willing to question Clinton's performance before and after the tragedy.

Clinton has been behaving as he always has: with no class.

How could he go to Ground Zero in Lower Manhattan before the sitting president?

It was a clear attempt to upstage President Bush, and everyone knew it. (I might note, and this never made the news either, that many of the rescue workers, police and firemen, gave Clinton, and later his wife, the cold shoulder and didn't shake their hands. Bush, however, was enthusiastically received.)

It has been protocol in times of crisis for former presidents to give quiet counsel to the current president, but never to grandstand. Clinton even used the occasion of the National Prayer Service to grandstand, as he politicked on the steps of the cathedral for almost a quarter of an hour.

Clinton obviously has little use for appropriate protocol.

If he wants to put himself in the limelight so much, why, then, should he also be shielded by the major media from scrutiny and criticism?

Why can't the media ask him why there was never any retaliation after the 1993 World Trade Center bombing? If that bombing had fully succeeded, it would have caused even more deaths than the present catastrophe.

Why did the administration continue to coddle terrorist nations like Syria after numerous bombings on U.S. facilities during the past eight years?

Why was the Clinton administration so quiet during Iran's buildup of its nuclear weapons program? Why did we continue to aid Russia while it gave technological expertise to the Iranians to build these weapons?

Most importantly, why, after eight years of the Clinton administration, is Saddam's military almost completely rebuilt?

Remember, former President Bush left Saddam flattened when Clinton assumed the presidency. But today, Saddam has an estimated 5,000 tanks and the same number of troops as he did before the invasion of Kuwait.

Even worse, in 1998 Clinton withdrew U.S. demands that Saddam allow U.N. inspectors to monitor his weapons programs. Richard Butler, the former head of the U.N. program, has no doubt that Saddam's program to build nuclear, chemical and biological weapons has been expedited because of Clinton policies.

At the same time the U.S. pulled its demand for monitors, the Clinton administration was giving the green light at the U.N. for Iraq to begin selling oil on the world market.

Billions have now poured into Iraq, giving that country the type of financial resources it would need to wage war, including one of global terror against the United States.

For some reason the liberal media, so quick to assign blame to President Bush, do not want look to the recent past and to Clinton's appeasement of the nations that sponsor terrorism.

As we begin this war, we should look at how Winston Churchill and the British people handled the calamity that befell them in 1940.

Upon assuming the mantle of prime minister, Churchill had appeaser Neville Chamberlain humiliated and assigned to the backbenches.

To his dying day, Winston Churchill called World War II "the unnecessary war."

He didn't do it for political reasons, such as scoring points in opinion polls.

He never stopped explaining the cause of that horrific war and assigning blame and responsibility to those leaders responsible. Churchill said the war was caused by appeasement. He named the guilty parties.

He did this for good reason. Unless we understood why the war happened, we would be doomed to repeat it.

Hillary Panned for Sour Demeanor During Bush Speech

Inside Cover
Friday, September 21, 2001

Hockey fans at Philadelphia's Rangers-Flyers game Thursday night were so enthralled with President Bush's speech that they actually forced the cancellation of the game's third period to continue watching on the arena's Jumbotron.

But seated in the House chamber, New York Senator Hillary Clinton was rolling her eyes, looking bored and remaining seated as her colleagues gave Bush one standing ovation after another.

Friday morning her disengaged demeanor was being roundly panned by talk radio hosts everywhere.

"You know why she reacted that way," WABC's Curtis Sliwa told his partner, Ron Kuby. "She just saw her hopes to run for president next time around go up in smoke."   •

Down the radio dial in New York, nationally syndicated talker Don Imus was even harder on the former first lady.

"She was disgraceful," Imus told his partner, Charles McCord. "She looked irritable, rolling her eyes and talking."

Imus didn't care much for Senator Clinton's post-speech comments either.

"I mean she was going out of her way to point out how she'd spent the entire week down at Ground Zero, which is not true, by the way. But I think we know what that's all about."

Imus then turned his ire toward Mrs. Clinton's husband.

"I just thank God that he's not still the president, that's all, because we didn't have to endure the self-aggrandizing display of lip-biting and head-wagging and 'I love you' to some bimbo in the balcony."

Judicial Watch: Clinton IRS Turned Blind Eye to Terrorists

Inside Cover
Sunday, September 23, 2001

While Bill Clinton's IRS pursued his personal enemies with great enthusiasm — auditing Billy Dale, Gennifer Flowers, Paula Jones, Juanita Broaddrick and dozens more — America's enemies, it seems, got a free pass from the same agency.

That's the claim from the legal watchdog group Judicial Watch, which has filed a complaint with IRS Commissioner and Clinton holdover Charles Rossotti, charging that Osama bin Laden's al Qaeda network, Hamas and other terrorist groups continue to use tax-exempt U.S.-based charities to bankroll terror, unencumbered by even the hint of an audit.

At least 16 U.S.-based nonprofit entities have been linked financially to bin Laden, the legal watchdog group says.

The decision not to investigate these groups is especially difficult to understand given that the information in the Judicial Watch complaint is hardly a state secret. To the contrary, the complaint is based largely on reports published over the last three years in venues like *The New York Times.*

One such questionable nonprofit, the Islamic African Relief Agency (IARA), has been directly linked to earlier attacks on U.S. interests by bin Laden.

"IARA reportedly transferred money to Mercy International, another nonprofit Muslim organization that purchased vehicles used by Osama bin Laden to bomb the U.S. embassies in both Kenya and Tanzania on August 8, 1998," the complaint notes.

Not only did Rossotti & Co. not investigate, that same year the Clinton State Department showered the IARA with $4.2 million in grants.

Other nonprofits said by Judicial Watch to have ties to Hamas include:

The United Association for Studies and Research
Islamic Association for Palestine
North American Islamic Trust
The Islamic Relief Association
Muslim American Society

The Cultural Society
the Muslim Arab Youth Association
The Alaqsa Educational Fund
Council on American Islamic Relations
Islamic Society of North America
Islamic Circle of North America
American Middle Eastern League for Palestine
Quaranic Literacy Institute

Though Judicial Watch doesn't say so, further investigation may lead even closer to the Clintons' doorstep. For instance, Rossotti's decision to look the other way happens to coincide with a series of generous donations by Muslim nonprofits to Hillary Clinton's Senate campaign.

In Boston — the same city where two hijacked planes departed before slamming into the World Trade Center nearly two weeks ago — Mrs. Clinton held a June 13, 2000, fund-raiser hosted by the American Muslim Alliance.

According to a report on the group's website, "The reception was attended by nearly 100 American Muslim leaders and activists."

As NewsMax.com reported at the time, candidate Clinton "clearly understood that her hosts were concerned that the U.S. war on terrorism might be too harsh."

In her speech, "Mrs. Clinton vowed to pursue fairness and justice in the issue of secret evidence and the Anti-Terrorism Act," the AMA website noted.

At the Boston event, the former first lady accepted a $1,000 contribution from Abdurahman Alamoudi, an official with the American Muslim Council, who once vowed to eliminate Israel and had previously boasted, "We are the ones who went to the [Clinton] White House and defended what is called Hamas."

When Mrs. Clinton's campaign reported Alamoudi's American Muslim Council donation to the FEC, the AMC was camouflaged as the "American Museum Council."

Alamoudi had pledged his $1,000 at a fund-raiser held a month earlier at the Washington, D.C., mansion of Yasser Arafat crony Hani Masri — a gathering Mrs. Clinton's campaign went to great lengths to conceal.

"The event, which sources said raised more than $50,000, was closed to the press, which wouldn't have known about the event anyway, since it wasn't listed on Mrs. Clinton's public schedule," the Jewish newspaper *Forward* reported at the time.

Sooner or later someone's bound to start asking: Was Mrs. Clinton's active fund-raising within the radical Islamic community behind the Clinton IRS's decision to take a pass on tax-exempt groups with ties to terrorists?

Report: Gore Airline Safety Commission Bought Off

Inside Cover
Sunday, September 23, 2001

A presidential commission on airline safety formed in the wake of the July 1996 TWA 800 disaster diluted its recommendations to tighten security procedures after the major airlines donated hundreds of thousands of dollars to the Democratic Party, *The Boston Globe* reports.

Less than two months after TWA 800 exploded in a fireball over the ocean off Center Moriches, New York, the Gore Commission issued an ambitious set of proposals, including baggage matching and enhanced training for airport screeners.

But the airlines complained that the new procedures would be too time-consuming, exacerbating delays and missed connections.

Days after the new recommendations were announced, major air carriers made a series of contributions to the Democratic Party:

TWA: $40,000
American Airlines: $265,000
Delta: $120,000
United: $115,000
Northwest: $87,000

In all, the airlines gave the Democratic Party $585,000 in the closing weeks of the Clinton-Gore administration's bid for a second term, the paper said, adding, "over the preceding 10-week period, the airlines gave the Democrats less than half that sum."

Former FAA inspector general Mary Schiavo pointed to a quid pro quo, saying that the political contributions helped the airlines avoid expensive new requirements.

A former FAA chief, Billie H. Vincent, and two Gore Commission members, Victoria Cummock and Kathleen Flynn, told the paper they agree with Schiavo.

What Was Al Gore's Role?

Neal Boortz
Monday, September 24, 2001

Did Al Gore let the airlines off the hook so he and Bill Clinton could have a little more campaign cash?

Here's the story, according to NewsMax.com and *The Boston Globe*.

After TWA Flight 800 crashed in 1996, Al Gore was named chairman of the White House Commission on Aviation Safety. It came to be known as the Gore Commission.

So, on September 9 of that year, the Gore Commission produced a preliminary report — one that proposed several measures to improve security at airports. The proposals included matching every piece of baggage to a passenger and better training for airport screeners.

But the airlines complained. They said the new procedures would cost too much money. They said that more rigorous screening and baggage matching would take too much time, causing more delays and missed connections.

Ten days after the preliminary report came out, Gore sent a letter to Carol Hallett, an airline lobbyist. He promised her that the commission's findings would not result in any loss of revenue.

Within the next two weeks, the Democratic National Committee received a series of contributions from the following airlines:

TWA: $40,000;
American: $265,000
Delta: $120,000
United: $115,000
Northwest: $87,000

That's a total of $627,000 for the 1996 Clinton-Gore presidential campaign. *The Boston Globe* notes that "over the preceding 10-week period, the airlines gave the Democrats less than half that sum."

Then, after the election, Gore issued a draft of his final report. All of the security measures from the preliminary report were gone, according to one insider. Two members of the Gore Commission balked. So did CIA Director John Deutch. Gore pulled the draft final report.

The final report came out a month later. It included the tough security requirements of the preliminary report — but gave no deadline for meeting them. Basically, without a timetable, the report wasn't worth the paper it was printed on.

It doesn't end there. Gore capped his commission's report with a lie. In a meeting with other commission members in 1997, Gore said he would allow room for dissent by those who disagreed with the report. But minutes later, he announced to Bill Clinton and the public that the report was the work of a unanimous commission!

The true Clinton-Gore legacy is starting to emerge, my friends, and it ain't pretty. It's a legacy that includes gutting intelligence budgets and letting the airlines off the hook in exchange for political contributions. Would [those who died in the 9/11 terrorist attacks] be alive today if the CIA had had the necessary resources and the airlines hadn't been so damned lax on security? We'll never know.

Clinton Haunted by Failure to Get Bin Laden

Inside Cover
Tuesday, September 25, 2001

Acting like a man who knows he has much to answer for, ex-President Bill Clinton is seeking out anyone and everyone who will listen, to explain that the World Trade Center disaster that killed thousands of Americans wasn't his fault.

After telling Fox News Channel's Brian Kilmeade, NBC's Tom Brokaw and countless private audiences over the last two weeks that he did everything he could to nail prime suspect Osama bin Laden, Clinton has taken to accosting total strangers on the street to offer his excuses.

One such New Yorker is Saul Finkelstein, who says he was corralled by the suddenly guilt-ridden ex-prez Saturday while out for a bike ride with his sons.

For a full 15 minutes the ex-commander in chief unburdened himself to Finkelstein, who reported the episode to *The Washington Post*'s Lloyd Grove.

"In 1998, the U.S. Navy launched a series of cruise missile attacks," Clinton insisted to the stranger. "We missed him by an hour."

He seemed to want the passerby to understand that if President Bush succeeds where he failed, it won't be because Bush tried any harder.

"The president can't say this," Clinton reportedly explained, "but it will not be that difficult to get bin Laden [today] because unlike in 1998... the U.S. will have the cooperation of surrounding countries."

By comparison, he said, his task was more difficult because he had to "fight this guy from 1,000 miles away."

The bottom line, Finkelstein said, was that Clinton wanted him to understand that "what happened on September 11 could in no way be traced to some failure on his administration's part."

Dick Morris Tells NewsMax:
Lewinsky Affair Impeded Hunt for Bin Laden

Inside Cover
Thursday, September 27, 2001

Ex-President Clinton's affair with Monica Lewinsky interfered with his ability to hunt down Twin Towers terrorist Osama bin Laden, one-time White House political guru Dick Morris tells NewsMax.com exclusively.

"My sense is that the affair made him passive and risk-averse," Morris said Thursday.

"As a result, I think he was less inclined to interfere with the military or to order long-term involvement," explained the man who engineered Clinton's second-term election victory.

The statements of the key Clinton aide come in the wake of the ex-president's recent claims that eliminating bin Laden was one of his administration's top priorities.

"I authorized the arrest and, if necessary, the killing of Osama bin Laden," Clinton told reporters late last week. "And we actually made contact with a group in Afghanistan to do it. And they were unsuccessful."

Just two days after the Twin Towers attacks, the former president specifically denied that the risks of military commitment hampered his efforts to take bin Laden out.

"No, it's not true. The best shot we had at Osama bin Laden was when I bombed his training camp in 1998 and we missed him by just a matter of hours. Maybe even less than an hour," Clinton told Fox News Channel.

But, like many skeptics of that effort, Morris believes that the cruise missile attacks on bin Laden's camp had more to do with the burgeoning Lewinsky sex scandal than nailing the deadly terrorist.

"I also remain suspicious at the juxtaposition of the strikes and his need to show that he was an active, involved president during the scandal," he told NewsMax.com.

Last week *The Boston Globe* reported that Clinton was distracted by legal issues prompted by his affair with Lewinsky while he was trying to focus on taking the terrorist out.

"He met with national security and military advisers to plan the attacks between sessions with lawyers to prepare for his grand jury testimony," the paper said.

Worse still, "he authorized the attack on the same August weekend in 1998 that he confessed his affair with Lewinsky to his wife," the *Globe* noted, describing the predicament as "an added strain."

Hillary Compares Her Critics to Osama Bin Laden

Inside Cover
Wednesday, October 3, 2001
Former first lady, now New York Senator Hillary Rodham Clinton says she knows what it's like to be the victim of the kind of maniacal hatred that cost thousands of her constituents their lives in the September 11 attacks on Manhattan's Twin Towers.

"Oh, I am well aware that it is out there," Mrs. Clinton said of the "murderous anger" that drove Osama bin Laden to conspire to turn two commercial jetliners into kamikaze dive-bombers and plow them into the World Trade Center.

In an outrageously bizarre attempt to co-opt the Twin Towers tragedy for her own political ends, Mrs. Clinton explained to *The New Yorker* magazine:

"One of the most difficult experiences that I personally had in the White House was during the health-care debate, being the object of extraordinary rage.

"I remember being in Seattle. I was there to make a speech about health care. This was probably August of '94. Radio talk-show hosts had urged their listeners to come out and yell and scream and carry on and prevent people from hearing me speak."

Senator Clinton told *The New Yorker* the experience gave her "firsthand looks" at what it's like to confront terrorism head-on.

"There were threats that were coming in, and certain people didn't want me to speak, and they started taking weapons off people, and arresting people. I've had firsthand looks at this unreasoning anger and hatred that is focused on an individual you don't know, a cause that you despise — whatever motivates people."

Coming next from Senator Clinton: How Osama bin Laden modeled his al Qaeda terrorist network after the Vast Right-Wing Conspiracy.

Gingrich, Morris Slam Clinton for Bin Laden Failure

Inside Cover
Wednesday, October 3, 2001

Former House Speaker Newt Gingrich slammed ex-President Clinton late Wednesday for failing to arrest Twin Towers terrorist Osama bin Laden when he had the chance in 1996 — five years before the terrorist killed thousands of Americans in coordinated attacks on New York and Washington, D.C.

"You had this whole weird experience with the Clinton administration that [Osama bin Laden] was behind the bombing of two American embassies," Gingrich told Fox News Channel's *Hannity & Colmes*.

"They all believed [bin Laden] was behind the World Trade Center [attack in 1993]."

But, the former Republican leader explained, "they were so tied into the rule of law, in the narrowest American sense, that they had an opportunity for Sudan to give them bin Laden and they couldn't take him."

Gingrich continued:

"Now, I would just suggest to you that there is no national security explanation for why we allowed bin Laden to get away with the Sudanese offers.

"If the story that came out today is true, that the Sudanese literally offered to give us bin Laden and the Clinton administration could not figure out a legal rationale — this is an administration that argued over what the meaning of the word 'is' is.

"Now, if they couldn't figure out a way, an argument about bin Laden, to keep him, there was something profoundly wrong with the psychology of the [Clinton] administration."

Former Clinton White House political guru Dick Morris concurred with Gingrich, telling Fox News Channel's Rita Cosby that Clinton was too distracted by the Monica Lewinsky sex scandal to concentrate on getting bin Laden.

"[Clinton was] distracted, disheartened and depressed and not terribly focused," Morris told Cosby late Wednesday.

"And also I believe [Clinton was] risk-averse," Morris said, in an observation he first shared with NewsMax.com last Friday.

"I think that one of the reasons we sent in cruise missiles as opposed to commandos [in 1998] was that he was averse to risk," he told Cosby. "He didn't want to suffer casualties. He was worried about criticism for that."

Morris said he was skeptical about the Clinton administration's excuses for failing to apprehend bin Laden in 1996.

"It's very hard for me to believe that the United States could not muster a case against bin Laden," Morris told Cosby.

"I have to believe that if Bill Clinton were not a distracted president during this period that there would have been a much greater focus on the terrorism issue."

Trulock: Security Lapses Are Clinton's Fault

Wes Vernon
Wednesday, October 10, 2001
WASHINGTON — The former highest-ranking intelligence officer in the Energy Department says you can blame the Clinton administration's pervasive inattention to security throughout government leading to last month's terrorist attacks.

Further, says Notra Trulock in an exclusive interview with NewsMax.com, some Clinton appointees had a blame-America-first attitude. This in turn bolstered the belief in some government quarters that perhaps the world would be better off if the U.S. shared its nuclear secrets with China and other nations that hated us.

"It was a failure across the board," says the man who blew the whistle on the Chinagate scandal, not just in intelligence (that much is all too obvious), but also "in law enforcement. It was a failure in imagination" and ultimately a failure of policy.

"I put it at the feet of the Clinton administration for the complacency they displayed on any threat to American security — not just terrorism, but anything that put in jeopardy their specious arms control and foreign policy objectives was really minimized and downplayed and dismissed as 'a worst-case scenario, a phrase of ridicule that Trulock heard over and over again as he tried to warn the Clinton appointees in the Energy Department of the loose or almost non-existent security procedures.

Since September 11, the Bush administration has been taking remedial measures, though it took the new White House some time to begin to undo the damage.

The vulnerability to our nuclear secrets was "so difficult to close." And this did not apply only to Trulock's area of jurisdiction.

"My counterpart in the physical part of the Department of Energy encountered the same kinds of resistance and a will to disbelieve that there could be any serious threat...to the nation's laboratories or the material that they store out there," at Los Alamos nuclear laboratory in New Mexico.

The same lackadaisical attitude prevailed in the Commerce and Defense departments during the Clinton years.

Hostility to security was coupled with a frivolity where "meetings would start late, there would be no agenda, and meetings would go on forever," which in itself can be attributed to bureaucratic inertia. But Trulock sees it as symptomatic of "a lack of seriousness" on security or counterintelligence.

Trulock does not want to be critical of the Bush administration. "I support the president, and I voted for him, but they were slow in addressing the legacy of the Clinton administration."

For one thing, there are just "way too many holdovers, too many Clintonites around," in Trulock's view. Recently, NewsMax.com reported on intelligence experts who called for the resignations of Jane Garvey at the FAA and George Tenet at the CIA.

"But the tragedy of September 11 has certainly shaken people and made them wake up."

It was Trulock's alertness to the Chinagate scandal that induced the "Clintonites" to force him out. At a subsequent House hearing, he and his Clinton-appointed supervisor gave conflicting accounts of what happened. Trulock agreed to take a lie detector test. His opponent declined to do likewise.

Hillary Clinton Tried to Stop Barbara Olson's Book

Inside Cover
Friday, October 12, 2001
Bill and Hillary Clinton reached new lows in the aftermath of September 11.

When news spread that Barbara Olson, the noted author and commentator, was among those who had died in the jet that struck the Pentagon, most Americans grieved for her and her family.

Not so with the Clintons.

Instead, they put their PR spin machine into high gear — to stop the publication of Barbara's newest book, *The Final Days*.

The Final Days — which is due out from Regnery this month and is anxiously awaited — details the sordid behavior of Bill and Hillary just before they left the White House.

In a mailing being sent by *Human Events*, the sister company of Regnery, editor Tom Winter reveals, "Within a week of the dreadful attack on September 11, powerful friends of Hillary Rodham Clinton tried to stop the publication of this book."

Winter reports that Hillary's friends worked feverishly to have Barbara's book "stopped before it was even printed."

He then asked, "What are they afraid of?"

Hillary's friends were even making threats, suggesting that "Barbara's reputation would be sullied if the book were printed."

Wonder who would sully Barbara's reputation?

Obviously, the Clintons have a lot to fear.

While everyone is aware of Clinton's cynical pardon of fugitive Marc Rich and Clinton's Whitewater partner Susan McDougal, how many Americans know that among those given last-second pardons were a convicted smuggler, a spy, a used car crook and even a drug lord?

And while many certainly heard about the lavish going-away gifts the Clintons' Hollywood cronies showered upon them, did they also hear how recklessly the Clintons looted the White House, shipping off 70 priceless museum pieces to Arkansas?

These and many more revelations will be revealed in this blockbuster new book.

Clinton in No Rush to Probe Past Intelligence Failures

Inside Cover
Friday, October 12, 2001

Ex-President Bill Clinton, who's been under fire lately for not going after Osama bin Laden aggressively enough during his own administration, said Friday that the U.S. should stay focused on the war on terrorism and not get distracted by investigations into past U.S. intelligence failures.

"There will come a time we can look back and say, 'Well, who should have done what when.' And it ought to be done," Clinton told ABC's *Good Morning America.*

"But now is not the time," he insisted.

Clinton's words appeared to be aimed at Connecticut Senator Joseph Lieberman, who called for a board of inquiry on Thursday into the attacks on the World Trade Center and Pentagon, saying the U.S. needs to find out why it was so vulnerable.

Since the September 11 attacks, Clinton has seemed obsessed with dodging responsibility for any U.S. intelligence lapses, and has even stopped passers-by on the street to describe his own efforts to get bin Laden.

How Clinton Turned U.S. Intelligence Into a Cash Cow

Charles R. Smith
Thursday, October 18, 2001

In 1993, terrorists linked to Osama bin Laden bombed the World Trade Center in New York City. In response, Bill Clinton turned the massive resources of the U.S. intelligence community away from national security and instead focused on commercial espionage.

The Clinton administration did not consider Russia, China or Osama bin Laden to be a threat against the United States. Instead, he considered the economic threat of losing global contracts to our allies in Europe to be the greatest evil.

The Clinton emphasis on commercial espionage became public in 1994 when then–CIA Director John Deutch announced that electronic intercepts of a Saudi prince gave Boeing a major contract.

According to Deutch, the National Security Agency had recorded phone calls between a Saudi prince and European aircraft manufacturer Airbus. The NSA intercepts suggested the Saudi prince was being bribed by Airbus over a multibillion-dollar airliner contract.

Deutch revealed to NBC news that the NSA recordings were provided to the Saudi government, which then promptly arrested the prince and awarded the billion-dollar contract to Boeing.

Boeing was not the only U.S. firm to take advantage of commercial espionage data provided by the Clinton administration. Another heavily documented case involves U.S. electronics maker Motorola and exports to China. This case, however, points directly at Bill Clinton.

USA vs. UK — The Battle of Bucks

In 1993, Motorola hired Clinton national security adviser Dr. Richard Barth to be a lobbyist inside Washington. Barth, who then worked alongside current CIA Director George Tenet, was a key member of the Clinton NSC White House staff. Barth was so important that Tenet wrote to him personally, trying to convince him to stay inside the White House.

"Barthman. Why are you leaving me?" asked Tenet in a 1993 White House e-mail. "Do you want my job? My wife? My 1974 Camaro? This place will suck eggs without you to keep me sane."

Despite the emotional appeal by Tenet, Barth left the White House to take a six-figure job with Motorola. In 1994, Barth returned to the White House, this time as a Motorola employee. Interestingly, Barth now sought to export sophisticated electronic-scrambling devices to China.

"European firms have for a number of months been able to market and sell encryption in China as a result of a decision taken by the UK intelligence agency, GCHQ," wrote Barth in a 1994 letter directed to the White House.

"I understand that our National Security Agency is aware of this change in GCHQ's position and would support our request for a change in US requirements for export licenses for China. The NSA has agreed that there should be a 'level playing field' in regard to China."

The Barth letter clearly illustrates that the Clinton administration was involved in an intelligence food fight with our allies in Europe. The UK intelligence agency GCHQ was now pitted against its U.S. counterpart, the NSA, in an export battle for bucks. Instead of cooperation in tracking known terrorists and global threats, the two agencies were now fighting each other at the behest of corporate profiteers.

NSA vs. GCHQ

Most Americans do not even know of the National Security Agency, much less the super-secret British GCHQ. I find it interesting indeed that the National Security Agency, well known for keeping its mouth shut, would spill its guts to an ex-NSC member employed in the commercial sector.

How did Barth know British GCHQ had changed its position? Who in the NSA told him there should be a "level playing field" for Motorola exports to China? How did Barth obtain this data for his company? No one in the NSA, GCHQ or Motorola will say, and Barth has so far declined to be interviewed.

The battle between Atlantic allies continued through 1994 and well into 1995. The documents from Barth clearly show that Motorola sought to export more than just scrambled radios to communist China. Barth's request included radiation-hardened electronics that are quite useful in nuclear combat.

Barth's correspondence also shows that President Clinton was directly involved.

"This is to request that your office initiate action to obtain a waiver from requirements for individual export license notifications to Congress for wireless mobile communications systems containing encryption for China," wrote Barth in a letter addressed to the State Department dated November 23, 1994.

"Such a waiver was issued by the President in September of this year for civilian satellite systems and encrypted products for use by American firms operating in China. Finally, while we now are not yet applying for licenses for encrypted systems for satellite positioning, we may within months be applying for such licenses for our IRIDIUM systems," noted Barth in his letter.

Barth's letter noted that Motorola sought to export sophisticated scrambled satellite control systems to Beijing, the same kind of hardened electronics that are now installed inside Chinese nuclear bombs aimed at America.

Yet Motorola had far more than Barth and the NSA inside the Clinton White House.

Motorola's CEO flew with Ron Brown on a Far East trade mission in 1994. Motorola's Hong Kong VP had coffee in the White House in 1996 with President Clinton.

In fact, Motorola's CEO had dinner with Chinese President Jiang Zemin and President Clinton inside the White House.

No small company could match the high-paying lobby jobs, the Commerce trips to China, the inside information from U.S. and British intelligence, the White House coffees or the state dinners.

Motorola played a game of musical chairs, with the players occasionally changing titles on six-figure jobs as they rotated from industry to bureaucracy to political staff and back again.

Presidential Waiver

Yet there is final proof that corporate profits overrode global national security inside the previous administration. The Motorola story ends on a classic Clinton note, with a single letter written to Commerce Secretary Ron Brown.

"Dear Ron," wrote Motorola CEO Gary Tooker in July 1995, "I am writing to thank you and some key members of the Commerce Department for your assistance in obtaining the Presidential waiver for encryption export sales to China."

The 1995 Motorola letter is proof positive that Bill Clinton is directly responsible for the present-day U.S. intelligence disaster. Bill Clinton turned America's spy network into a personal cash cow, aimed at pleasing big-dollar contributors instead of protecting the free world.

If any single person is responsible for the sad state of our NSA and CIA today, it is Bill Clinton.

Hillary Booed at McCartney's Twin Towers Relief Concert

Inside Cover
Saturday, October 20, 2001
New York Senator Hillary Clinton was roundly booed at former Beatle Paul McCartney's Twin Towers relief concert, held at Manhattan's Madison Square Garden Saturday night.

The embarrassing moment came as Senator Clinton introduced a short video clip from stand-up comic Jerry Seinfeld.

Though the former first lady has tried to capitalize on the Twin Towers tragedy, thrusting herself before one TV camera after another in an effort to connect with average New Yorkers and advance her 2004 presidential ambitions, McCartney's concert showed the effort still needed more work.

One eyewitness to the scene reported to the website FreeRepublic.com that Clinton "was booed so loudly, she had to yell into the mike to be heard."

Another estimated that "90 percent" of the crowd jeered the former first lady.

Her husband, the former president, who was also present, got a much warmer reception.

Hero Fireman Slams Phony Hillary

Inside Cover
Tuesday, October 23, 2001
Hero New York City firefighter Mike Moran, who thrilled a Madison Square Garden concert audience Saturday night when he taunted Osama bin Laden with the words "Kiss my royal Irish ass!" slammed New York Senator Hillary Clinton on Wednesday, saying she's a transparent phony.

"I think when times are good and things are going well, people will sit there and listen to the kind of claptrap that comes out of her mouth," Moran said in an interview with number one radio talker Rush Limbaugh.

Limbaugh had asked Moran why he thought the Garden audience booed Mrs. Clinton off the stage when she tried to introduce a video clip by comic Jerry Seinfeld. The hero fireman didn't hesitate to offer an explanation.

"When things are going like this, when it's serious times and serious men who actually suffered losses and she wants to get up and spew her nonsense — she doesn't believe a thing she says. She says whatever she thinks will fit the moment."

Moran told Limbaugh that Mrs. Clinton's phoniness is transparent. "I think it comes through. And in serious times, people don't want to stand for it."

Moran said he wasn't a hero. Instead, he praised the men of Ladder Company 3 in Manhattan, 12 of whom, including Moran's brother, perished while trying to rescue burn victims from the 40th floor of World Trade Center Tower One.

"The captain, Paddy Brown, gave a report from the North Tower that they had 30 to 40 severely burned people that they were trying to get down the stairs," Moran told Limbaugh.

"A few minutes later, he gave the most urgent kind of message a fireman could give — a Mayday that the building was coming down around him."

Moran said the building didn't fully collapse for another 10 minutes, more than enough time for his colleagues to escape certain death.

But, said the fireman, "they wouldn't leave those people."

"I can't allow myself to be compared to those true heroes," Moran told Limbaugh.

Bin Laden Terror Widow Blames Clinton

Inside Cover
Tuesday, October 30, 2001

In the wake of Osama bin Laden's murderous attacks on the World Trade Center and Pentagon, the widow of a sailor who died in the bombing of the USS *Cole* says she blames ex-President Clinton for not stopping the Mideast madman after he bombed other U.S. facilities in the 1990s.

"Each time these events happened, and it was all words and nothing ever happened," said Sharla Costelow, wife of Chief Petty Officer Richard Costelow, who died aboard the *Cole* as it refueled in Yemen on October 12, 2000.

Mrs. Costelow delivered the stinging indictment to WABC Radio's Steve Malzberg last week in a gut-wrenching interview that has been completely overlooked by the mainstream media.

The Navy widow listed the ways in which she thought the ex-president was partly responsible for her husband's death.

"I think I would start with the fact that Clinton downsized our military so much that we no longer had ships to come and fuel our ships. This is something that my husband and I discussed many times: relying on other countries to do it," Costelow told Malzberg.

She also blamed the ex-commander in chief for ignoring warnings that U.S. ships were on bin Laden's target list.

"I didn't realize this until after it had happened," she told the WABC host, "that bin Laden had given [a message] to bomb one of our ships in the year 2000, and we didn't heed that warning. Worse than that, we sent one of our destroyers all alone into a terrorist harbor with no protection, no security, no safety zones whatsoever."

The bin Laden terror victim said Clinton was also clearly wrong in removing Yemen from the list of nations that sponsor terrorism.

"This never should have happened when Yemen still had terrorist activity going on, and certainly knowing the connection that bin Laden had there."

Mrs. Costelow said she thinks the ex-president should be held accountable for such an egregious national security failure.

"My husband, a communications expert, worked for Clinton," she told Malzberg. "He was a very hard worker and dealt with White House communications and saved the government a lot of money. I know if my husband made a mistake that could have jeopardized President Clinton's security ... my husband would have been held accountable. I just expect the same of him [Clinton]."

"It was completely preventable and it never should have happened," she added.

Besides his wife, Sharla, Chief Petty Officer Costelow left behind three young sons — Dillon, 14, Brady, 6, and Ethan, 4. Contributions to the Costelow children's memorial trust fund should be sent to:

Memorial Fund
NFCU-Costelow Family
Patuxent River MSC
22598 MacArthur Blvd.
California, MD 20619

CIA Sources: Clinton Administration 'Didn't Want' Bin Laden Arrested

Inside Cover
Thursday, November 1, 2001

A U.S. intelligence official, speaking on condition of anonymity, this week called the Clinton administration's decision to pass up a chance to arrest Osama bin Laden in 1996 a "disgrace," saying "somebody didn't want this to happen."

A second intelligence official, also speaking anonymously, corroborated the charge that there was a deliberate effort to let bin Laden escape from the Sudan to Afghanistan, saying "somebody let this slip up."

The intelligence officials, both of whom were involved in secret negotiations between Washington and Khartoum to take bin Laden into custody, offered the damning accounts to New York's *Village Voice*.

The *Voice's* first source said the chance to arrest bin Laden should have been a no-brainer, despite FBI claims that it lacked the evidence to convict him in an American court. "We kidnap minor drug czars and bring them back in burlap bags," he told the paper.

The State Department may have blocked the wily terrorist's arrest to placate a part of the Saudi Arabian government that supported him, he speculated.

The second official lamented that the U.S. lost a treasure trove of intelligence on the elusive al Qaeda chief when it let him slip away. "It was not a matter of arresting bin Laden but of access to information," he told the *Voice*.

"We could have dismantled his operations and put a cage on top... That's the story, and that's what could have prevented September 11. I knew it would come back to haunt us."

Sudan's former defense minister, Major General Elfatih Erwa, agreed, telling the paper that he tried to warn the Clinton administration that letting bin Laden escape from Sudan to Afghanistan was a major blunder.

"We knew that if he went to Afghanistan no one could control him [but] the U.S. didn't care," Erwa said. "They forgot about human intelligence after the Cold War. The feeling of supremacy led them astray. Many think that. Now they're harvesting the thorns."

Clinton: I'd Run War Better Than Bush

Inside Cover
Friday, November 2, 2001

Disgraced ex-President Bill Clinton, who as a college student lied his way out of the Vietnam draft and then eviscerated the military as president, is reportedly telling friends that he'd be a better wartime leader than President Bush.

Paul McCartney's fiancée, Heather Mills, who met with Clinton during McCartney's October 20 disaster relief concert in New York, told Britain's Ananova News Service that she asked the ex-president, "Do you wish you were president now?"

His response? "I feel I would be better trained for it, more prepared," Mills claimed.

Asked to clarify the ex-president's remarks, Clinton spokeswoman Julia Payne did not return the *New York Post*'s calls, which carried Mills' quote in Friday editions.

Though McCartney's fiancée opposes the ongoing U.S. bombing and sympathizes with Clinton's "frustration" at being out of office, she backs the current commander in chief.

"I did not like Bush before this happened, but now I find him very human," she told Ananova.

Clinton Joins the Blame-America-First Crowd

Inside Cover
Thursday, November 8, 2001

Bill Clinton says that terror has existed in America for hundreds of years and the U.S. is "paying a price today" for its past sins.

This is what the millionaire speechmaker said Wednesday at Georgetown University, according to today's *Washington Times*.

"Here in the United States, we were founded as a nation that practiced slavery, and slaves quite frequently were killed even though they were innocent.

"This country once looked the other way when a significant number of native Americans were dispossessed and killed to get their land or their mineral rights or because they were thought of as less than fully human.

"And we are still paying a price today."

This is from the man who is causing a black heritage site in Little Rock, Arkansas, to be demolished so his presidential "library" can be built.

The impeached ex-president blames today's Muslim terrorism on Christians of long ago.

"In the first Crusade, when the Christian soldiers took Jerusalem, they first burned a synagogue with 300 Jews in it and proceeded to kill every woman and child who was a Muslim on the Temple Mount. I can tell you that story is still being told today in the Middle East, and we are still paying for it."

Fox News Channel tonight showed a clip of him sounding like a stereotypical Guilty White Liberal: "Those of us who come from various European lineages are not blameless."

Clinton's bizarre solution to terrorism: Make freeloading countries even more dependent on U.S. taxpayers. Despite the dismal failure of America's government schools to educate our own children, and despite the fact that Mideast nations send America-hating terrorist "students" to the U.S. for training, he thinks Americans should pay to educate students from foreign countries!

"We ought to pay for these children to go to school — a lot cheaper than going to war," he claimed.

Will Clinton's blame-America-for-terrorism comments spark even 1 percent of the criticism heaped on Jerry Falwell and Pat Robertson for their remarks that 9/11 was linked to America's immorality? Of course not; most media are not even reporting Slick Willie's not-so-bon mots.

Morris: Clinton Was Oblivious to Khobar Towers Terror Alert

Inside Cover
Tuesday, November 13, 2001

Former chief White House political adviser Dick Morris revealed Tuesday that his former boss Bill Clinton cared so little about global terrorism that his own assistant secretary of state had trouble getting him to pay attention to a bomb threat against the Khobar Towers Air Force barracks in Riyadh, Saudi Arabia.

"In 1996, I got a phone call from Dick Holbrooke," Morris told WABC Radio's Sean Hannity.

"He said, 'We're getting hard intelligence that terrorists are planning another hit on our guys in Riyadh... They're in the exact same building they were in when it was hit last time.

In June 1996, the Khobar Towers military barracks had been hit by a suicide bomber believed sent by Osama bin Laden, killing 19 American airmen.

Months later, after the barracks had been repaired, U.S. military personnel reoccupied it.

Holbrooke told Morris that the new U.S. Air Force tenants were "sitting ducks in that building," and then added:

"I've been trying to get hold of the president for two weeks about this and we're getting increasing reports about [the threat]. Can you call him?"

Morris said that when he reached Clinton about Holbrooke's warning, the president began cursing and complained, "You mean they're still in that building? I ordered six weeks ago for them to be dispersed."

Clinton said he would take care of the problem at a meeting with the Joint Chiefs the next day, Morris recalled.

"But he didn't follow it up," the top political strategist noted. "He didn't know whether they were in the buildings or not. He was inaccessible, so the guy who knew [about the threat] couldn't be in touch with him."

Morris told Hannity the oversight was typical of the way the administration worked.

"Clinton was a one-issue-at-a-time guy," he said, adding that the only foreign policy issue that seemed to engage him was Bosnia.

The reference to Bosnia prompted this exchange:

HANNITY: The only time he paid attention to foreign policy was when he had Monica working — who was he speaking to, what Alabama congressman?

MORRIS: Yeah, right. But the — well, he spoke to me on one of those ...

HANNITY: Ahhhwwww!

MORRIS: He did. No, no, I'm in the Starr Report. I'm one of the four conversations [where Clinton had sex with Lewinsky while talking to others on the phone].

Citing another example of Clinton's lax attitude toward terrorism, the former White House political guru noted that his boss never visited the World Trade Center after it was bombed in February 1993.

"When the bombing happened, he just issued a statement saying we'll fight them and all that. And then he gave it his Saturday radio address…It was never a big priority."

During Clinton's second term, Morris said, he was "terribly, terribly and totally distracted by impeachment. There was no way that he was going to pay enough attention to an issue like terrorism."

"In the second term," Morris said, "we didn't have a president. Now, was it his fault for Monica? Was it the Republicans' fault for impeaching? Was it his fault for not resigning? Who knows.

"But the fact is the United States didn't have a president for two years, and that's why."

Weinberger Blasts Clinton for Damaging Military

Inside Cover
Sunday, November 25, 2001
Former Reagan Defense Secretary Caspar Weinberger blasted ex-President Bill Clinton on Sunday, charging that his policies seriously undermined the U.S. military's ability to fight and win wars.

"I think Clinton basically did an enormous amount of damage to us during his eight years," Weinberger told WABC Radio's Steve Malzberg.

"He certainly allowed the military strength that we had at the end of the Gulf War to erode very seriously," the Reagan defense chief added. "And he also committed the military to all kinds of expeditions and impossible missions because it provided a little headline relief for him from time to time."

Echoing criticism in his new book, *In the Arena: A Memoir of the 20th Century,* Weinberger said that Clinton's strategic partnership with the Communist Chinese greatly enhanced their military power. "He was never above giving them various advantages that they wanted," even though Beijing was "very open in its opposition to everything we tried to do in the Pacific."

Meanwhile, as China's military grew stronger, President Clinton gave only lip service to the concept of missile defense for the U.S., Weinberger said. "He never did anything except block it in every way that he could during his whole eight years."

Asked about Clinton's recent speech at Georgetown University, where the ex-president suggested that America shared part of the blame for the 9/11 attacks because of slavery and U.S. mistreatment of the American Indian, Weinberger said:

"If it was the Unites States' fault, he has an awful lot of burden to bear, because he was there for eight years during a time in which we weakened ourselves substantially by a lot of his policies."

The former Reagan defense chief said Clinton "gave us, I'm afraid, about as poor a foreign policy and poor administration as I hope we'll never see again."

Clinton Paid 'Lip Service' to Terror Attacks, Expert Charges

Matt Pyeatt, CNSNews.com
Thursday, December 6, 2001

An increasingly bold series of terrorist attacks targeting American interests was met with tough talk from former President Bill Clinton but little action, according to terrorism experts asked to analyze the U.S. response to attacks between 1993 and 2000.

Larry Johnson, formerly with the CIA and the State Department and the current CEO of the Business Exposure Reduction Group, said he believes Clinton's weak response to the terrorist attacks that occurred during his presidency paved the way for the September 11 attacks on the World Trade Center and Pentagon.

"The Clinton administration paid lip service to the notion of combating terrorism through some money added, but generally kept it as a very low priority," Johnson said.

1993 World Trade Center Bombing

On February 26, 1993, a car bomb was detonated at the World Trade Center in New York City, killing six people and injuring thousands. The bomb caused extensive damage to the complex. Osama bin Laden is suspected to have been behind the attacks.

In reacting to the attack, Clinton urged calm.

"I would plead with the American people and the good people of New York to keep your courage up and go on about your lives. I would discourage the American people from overreacting to this," Clinton said.

Clinton assured Americans that he had put forth "the full, full resources of the federal law enforcement agencies — all kinds of agencies, all kinds of access to information — at the service of those who are trying to figure out who did this and why."

He also said he would implement a policy of "continued monitoring."

Clinton said the United States was "absolutely determined to oppose the cowardly cruelty of terrorists, wherever we can."

All Talk, No Action

Despite his rhetoric, Clinton made no changes in policy to prevent additional attacks, Johnson said.

"From the time President Clinton took office until May of 1995, a Presidential Decision Directive, PDD 39, sat in the National Security Council, in the In Box of one of the officials with no action taken. The significance of PDD 39 is that it was the document defining what the missions and roles were of combating terrorism," Johnson said.

"Despite what happened at the World Trade Center in 1993, the Clinton administration did not finally act on [PDD 39] until after the attack in Oklahoma City," Johnson said, referring to the 1995 attack in which an American, Timothy McVeigh, detonated a bomb outside the federal building in Oklahoma City, killing 168 people.

"The only reason for that is because in the two weeks prior to Oklahoma City, the front page of both *Newsweek and Time* magazine carried the question: 'Is President Clinton Relevant?'

Chuck Pena, senior defense analyst for the Cato Institute, agreed that Clinton's actions after the 1993 attack failed to match his words. But, Pena said, the circumstances were different than they are today.

"[Clinton's] actions were not necessarily 100 percent reflective of his rhetoric, nor were they effective." However, "there are some reasons for some of that. At the time, we were not looking at four or five thousand casualties as a result of a single terrorist act."

1996 Khobar Towers Bombing

On June 25, 1996, terrorists attacked the U.S. military complex and Khobar Towers in Saudi Arabia, killing 19 Americans and wounding hundreds more.

Shiite militant terrorists with connections to bin Laden are thought to have been responsible for the attacks.

In a televised statement, Clinton addressed the nation with news about the bombing:

"The explosion appears to be the work of terrorists. The cowards who committed this murderous act must not go unpunished," Clinton said. "America takes care of its own."

Johnson said Clinton did nothing of the sort.

According to Johnson, early indications were that the explosive used in the bombing of the Khobar Towers came out of the Becca Valley in Lebanon. A year later, however, Clinton restored full diplomatic relations with Lebanon including lifting travel restrictions and trade restrictions, Johnson said, "without requiring them to locate, arrest, apprehend or compensate U.S. citizens. He just let it go."

Pena said one must consider that terrorism was not the high-priority issue it is today.

"Part of it reflects, at that time, a certain tolerance for terrorism that was, compared to September 11, pretty small scale. I think the Clinton administration may have been overly cautious about not wanting to respond disproportionately to the terrorist acts that were perpetrated."

1998 Embassy Bombings

On August 7, 1998, terrorists bombed the U.S. embassies in Nairobi, Kenya, and Dar es Salaam, Tanzania, killing 258 people. More than 5,000 were injured.

The attacks were blamed on bin Laden's terrorist group, al Qaeda, which by this time had developed into a worldwide network.

On August 20, 1998, Clinton ordered cruise missile attacks on suspected terrorist training camps in Afghanistan and a pharmaceutical plant in Khartoum, Sudan.

"Our target was terror. Our mission was clear: to strike at the network of radical groups affiliated with and funded by Osama bin Laden, perhaps the pre-eminent organizer and financier of international terrorism in the world today," Clinton said at the time.

He told Americans that U.S. intelligence had uncovered information tying the bin Laden terrorist network to the embassy bombings.

"With compelling evidence that the bin Laden network of terrorist groups was planning to mount further attacks against Americans and other freedom-loving people, I decided America must act," Clinton said.

"Afghanistan and Sudan have been warned for years to stop harboring and supporting these terrorist groups, but countries that persistently host terrorists have no right to safe havens," he added.

Johnson said Clinton's tough talk again yielded no results.

"Clinton was always good about biting his lip, tears welling up in his baggy eyes and talking about 'We're waging a new war on terrorism,' and yet also during this period he basically cut the heart out of CIA," Johnson said.

2000 USS Cole Bombing

On October 12, 2000, terrorists bombed the USS *Cole* as it sat in the Yemeni port of Aden. The bomb killed 17 U.S. sailors. American officials quickly linked the attack to bin Laden and al Qaeda.

Global News Wire reported Clinton's response:

"If, as it now appears, it was an act of terrorism, it was a despicable and cowardly act," he said.

"We will find out who was responsible, and hold them accountable. If their intention was to deter us from our mission of promoting peace and security in the Middle East, they will fail, utterly."

Clinton ordered U.S. Navy ships into the Yemeni region and directed ground forces to step up their security measures.

"They spent a lot of money but it was always a symbolic gesture without the substantive approach," Johnson said.

The Bush administration, according to Johnson, is handling the issue differently since September 11. However, Johnson is waiting to see if Bush will keep his promise to continue the war on terrorism even after the campaign in Afghanistan is over.

"Bush is now drawing the line in the sand and going after the terrorist camps in Afghanistan. The proof will be if he goes after the next terrorist camps, which are in Lebanon. Those are the largest terrorist camps," Johnson said.

Robert Maginnis, vice president of policy at Family Research Council, said, "There seems to be a willingness to confront the adversaries by Bush no matter where they may be and to keep everything on the table.

"This president has been serious. 'We are going to take everything that we have and whatever it takes will be available for the commander on the ground.' But Clinton seemed to have been so hesitant about using the power that was available to him to go after the bad guys. That, I think, sent the wrong sort of signal," Maginnis said.

COPYRIGHT 2001 CNSNEWS.COM   ALL RIGHTS RESERVED.

Aide: Clinton Unleashed bin Laden

Chuck Noe, NewsMax.com
Thursday, December 6, 2001

Bill Clinton ignored repeated opportunities to capture Osama bin Laden and his terrorist allies and is responsible for the spread of terrorism, one of the ex-president's own top aides charges.

Mansoor Ijaz, who negotiated with Sudan on behalf of Clinton from 1996 to 1998, paints a portrait of a White House plagued by incompetence, focused on appearances rather than action, and heedless of profound threats to national security.

Ijaz also claims Clinton passed on an opportunity to have Osama bin Laden arrested.

Sudanese President Omar Hassan Ahmed Bashir, hoping to have terrorism sanctions lifted, offered the arrest and extradition of bin Laden and "detailed intelligence data about the global networks constructed by Egypt's Islamic Jihad, Iran's Hezbollah and the Palestinian Hamas," Ijaz writes in today's edition of the liberal *Los Angeles Times.*

These networks included the two hijackers who piloted jetliners into the World Trade Center.

But Clinton and National Security Advisor Samuel "Sandy" Berger failed to act.

"I know because I negotiated more than one of the opportunities," Ijaz writes.

"The silence of the Clinton administration in responding to these offers was deafening."

Thank Clinton for 'Hydra-like Monster'

"As an American Muslim and a political supporter of Clinton, I feel now, as I argued with Clinton and Berger then, that their counter-terrorism policies fueled the rise of bin Laden from an ordinary man to a Hydra-like monster," says Ijaz, chairman of a New York investment company and a member of the Council on Foreign Relations.

Ijaz's revelations are but the latest to implicate the Clinton administration in the spread of terrorism. Former CIA and State Department official Larry Johnson today also noted the failure of Clinton to do more than talk.

Among the many others who have pointed out Clinton's negligence: former Secretary of Defense Caspar Weinberger, former Clinton adviser

Dick Morris, the late author Barbara Olson, Russian President Vladimir Putin, Iraqi expert Laurie Mylroie, the CIA and some of the victims of September 11.

And the list grows: members of Congress, pundit Charles R. Smith, former Department of Energy official Notra Trulock, former House Speaker Newt Gingrich, government counterterrorism experts, the law firm Judicial Watch, New Jersey gubernatorial candidate Bret Schundler, the liberal *Boston Globe* — and even Clinton himself.

The Buck Stops Nowhere

Ijaz's account in the *Times* reads like a spy novel. Sudan's Bashir, fearing the rise of bin Laden, sent intelligence officials to the U.S. in February 1996. They offered to arrest bin Laden and extradite him to Saudi Arabia or to keep close watch over him. The Saudis "didn't want their home-grown terrorist back where he might plot to overthrow them."

"In May 1996, the Sudanese capitulated to U.S. pressure and asked bin Laden to leave, despite their feeling that he could be monitored better in Sudan than elsewhere."

That's when bin Laden went to Afghanistan, along with "Ayman Zawahiri, considered by the U.S. to be the chief planner of the September 11 attacks; Mamdouh Mahmud Salim, who traveled frequently to Germany to obtain electronic equipment for al Qaeda; Wadih El-Hage, Bin Laden's personal secretary and roving emissary, now serving a life sentence in the U.S. for his role in the 1998 U.S. embassy bombings in Tanzania and Kenya; and Fazul Abdullah Mohammed and Saif Adel, also accused of carrying out the embassy attacks."

If these names sound familiar, just check the FBI's list of most-wanted terrorists.

The Clinton administration repeatedly rejected crucial information that Sudan had gathered on these terrorists, Ijaz says.

In July 2000, just three months before the deadly attack on the destroyer USS *Cole* in Yemen, Ijaz "brought the White House another plausible offer to deal with bin Laden, by then known to be involved in the embassy bombings. A senior counter-terrorism official from one of the United States' closest Arab allies — an ally whose name I am not free to divulge — approached me with the proposal after telling me he was fed up with the antics and arrogance of U.S. counter-terrorism officials."

This offer would have brought bin Laden to that Arab country and eventually to the U.S. All the proposal required of Clinton was that he make a state visit to request extradition.

"But senior Clinton officials sabotaged the offer, letting it get caught up in internal politics within the ruling family — Clintonian diplomacy at its best."

'Purposeful Obfuscation'

Appearing on Fox News Channel's *The O'Reilly Factor* on Wednesday night, Ijaz said, "Everything we needed to know about the terrorist networks" was in Sudan.

Newsman Bill O'Reilly asked how Clinton and Berger reacted to the deals Ijaz brokered to bring bin Laden and company to justice. "Zero. They didn't respond at all."

The Clintonoids won't get away with denials, he said. "I've got the documentation," including a memorandum to Berger.

"This was purposeful obfuscation," he asserted.

O'Reilly wondered why the White House didn't want information about the terrorists. Ijaz said that was for the American people to judge, but when pressed he suggested that Clinton might intentionally have allowed the apparently weak bin Laden to rise so he could later make a show of crushing him.

Concludes Ijaz in the *Times*: "Clinton's failure to grasp the opportunity to unravel increasingly organized extremists, coupled with Berger's assessments of their potential to directly threaten the U.S., represents one of the most serious foreign policy failures in American history."

Noonan: Clinton, No Reagan, Was 'Clever Slob'

Wes Vernon, NewsMax.com
Friday, December 7, 2001

WASHINGTON — Ronald Reagan has been vindicated in foreign and domestic policy, and tried to warn his countrymen to be ready for anything, including a terrorist attack, according to the new book *When Character Was King*.

In an interview with NewsMax.com, author Peggy Noonan, a White House speechwriter for President Reagan and the first President Bush, said Reagan "was the kind of sunny man who could [nonetheless] see trouble down the road."

Knowing history as he did, Reagan understood that, as an ancient philosopher once declared, "Only the dead have seen the end of war."

"He knew trouble was coming," Noonan said of the man who "won the Cold War without firing a shot," to quote Margaret Thatcher.

The author, whose recollections of the Reagan years were recorded previously in *What I Saw at the Revolution*, said "one of the biggest lessons Reagan would take from September 11" is not that terrorists will restrict their weaponry to suicide bombs and briefcase explosives, but are capable of firing missiles at the U.S. from offshore.

"The biggest lesson Reagan would have taken from September 11, and I assume Bush ... aken is anything can happen," Noonan believes.

"This [terrorist attack] has not quelled our desire to see it [a missile defense shield] done, developed and deployed."

Eighteen years after President Reagan urged Americans to support the development of a missile defense for America, leftists on Capitol Hill and in wealthy liberal think tanks are still dragging their feet on what respected national security analysts see as a pressing need.

Further, warned Noonan, "each year, each rogue nation and psychotic leader who has nukes has greater and greater ability to deploy them. So we'd just better watch it. You've got to see trouble coming down the road, and you've got to plan for it."

That was Reagan's gift, to plan ahead, to prepare for trouble. That's what led him to advocate the missile defense shield. Even after the September 11 terrorist destruction, millions of Americans go to bed at night either unaware of our vulnerability to missile attack or unaware that terrorist forces that killed thousands on our own soil can also fire missiles at us.

Rosty Admits Reagan Tax Cuts Worked

Remember "Reaganomics," the derisive term liberals applied to the Reagan tax cuts?

Now a prominent congressional liberal of that era, who fought tooth and nail against the Reagan economic proposals, acknowledges they were good for the country. Noonan got that out of one-time House Ways and Means Committee Chairman Dan Rostenkowski, D-Ill., in an interview for her book.

"Look, I thought the Reagan budget and tax cuts would cause rioting in the streets," Rosty told her. "But you know what? They didn't and it all worked, and people got off the welfare rolls. And frankly, I guess it was a success."

Of course, as Noonan observed to NewsMax.com, Rostenkowski offers this retrospective from the vantage point of retirement. House Minority Leader Dick Gephardt and Senate plurality leader Tom Daschle feel they cannot depart from the holy grail of class warfare.

The Reagan influence is evident in today's White House with the second President Bush. Or so the president told the one-time Reagan speechwriter not long before her book went to press.

"He told me that he thought Mr. Reagan would be well pleased at how he had done," she said.

Noonan told NewsMax that Bush confirmed her impression that he had watched Reagan carefully during the years his father had served as Reagan's vice president.

A president has to stand for and breathe in a nation's soul, the president told her, and "that's what Reagan did most of all."

The younger Bush met Reagan when he was just out of college working with a friend on the Florida campaign of a U.S. Senate candidate.

When you met Reagan, you knew you had met somebody big, according to the future president.

But when President Bush refuses to go into Virginia just across the river to campaign for a gubernatorial candidate who might have won with just a little push, isn't that more the "bipartisan" model of his father, rather than the Reagan approach?

His Own Man

Noonan, who has met all three men, doesn't think Bush is "patterning his presidency on anything but what George W. Bush thinks is the right thing to do."

Further, "One doesn't sense that he is bearing the burden of his father or the burden of the Reagan legacy. He senses he has observed history for 50 years and that now he is going to rock forth as himself."

As for Reagan's activism in the Screen Actors Guild, where he ultimately became its president, the then-actor proved his mettle as a mediator and negotiator. These qualities would serve him well later as president of the United States.

First of all, when communists and communist operatives were worming their way into influential positions in Hollywood, he assured the outside world that Hollywood would do its own housecleaning. And he made good on that, working to clean out communist influence in motion pictures, even in the face of threats on his life and plans to toss acid in his face.

At the same time, Reagan worked with those he believed had been unfairly accused and cleared their names.

The infamous "Hollywood Ten" lost their credibility. People such as John Howard Lawson and Dalton Trumbo "were stood up to when they tried to insert communist messages in films," Noonan pointed out.

In fact, the studio chiefs "ultimately came to agree with Reagan and his friends."

Secondly, the negotiating skills required as guild president enabled him, as U.S. president, to resist the wily Soviet President Mikhail Gorbachev's entreaties to abandon his pursuit of a missile defense shield.

Clinton the 'Clever Slob'

A book on Reagan with the title *When Character Was King* begs for an obvious comparison with an era when character meant nothing: the Clinton years.

"Bill Clinton didn't have a great presidency," the author told NewsMax.com. "He didn't have a meaningful presidency. The poor man didn't even have a good presidency" and was "able to do only one thing, and that was to sustain his own personal popularity. Well, you know what? A clever slob can do that."

And how do you do it?

"You luck out with history. And that's what Clinton did. He ignored history. He didn't make plans for the future. He never looked down the road.

"All he did was enjoy the current prosperity that Reagan and the Republican Congress put into place, and enjoy the relative peace that was only a vacation before war started again. Too bad he didn't do serious things. Too bad he didn't protect us from the fix we're in … or to protect and prepare America."

We all know who Clinton really was, declared Noonan. "He was a slob."

Hillary: Don't Blame Bill's Sexcapades for Bin Laden's Escape

Inside Cover
Sunday, December 9, 2001

New York Senator Hillary Clinton said Sunday that it's unfair to blame her husband's affair with Monica Lewinsky and the resulting impeachment for his administration's failure to pursue Osama bin Laden aggressively enough during the 1990s.

"I don't think it's fair. I don't think it's an accurate rendering of what did happen," Clinton told NBC's *Meet the Press* host Tim Russert.

"I don't know all the details," Clinton explained. "But what has already been reported in many other sources demonstrates clearly — and I know from personal experience — how absolutely focused the president was on this and the kind of action that was taken."

Russert had asked Clinton about a recent report in *USA Today*, from which he quoted:

"Even Clinton's defenders acknowledge that for much of his tenure fighting terrorism wasn't his highest priority… In his second term, when bin Laden emerged as a mastermind of plots against Americans, Clinton seemed enmeshed in the Monica Lewinsky scandal and impeachment."

Mrs. Clinton's reference to her intimate knowledge of "the kind of action that was taken" appears to be an allusion to her husband's August 20, 1998, decision to launch a cruise missile attack on a suspected bin Laden terrorist encampment in Afghanistan.

But White House aides told *The Boston Globe* two months ago that President Clinton's attention was at best divided as he tried to cope with the bin Laden threat, with the cruise missile strikes coming just three days after he informed the nation as well as his wife that he had lied about his affair with Lewinsky.

Part of the "personal experience" Mrs. Clinton alluded to in her comments to Russert reportedly included berating her husband for his promiscuity, with one account saying she screamed, loudly enough to be overheard, "You stupid f—-ing moron! How could you risk your presidency for this?"

Just two weeks after the 9/11 attacks, former White House political guru Dick Morris told NewsMax.com that Clinton was so distracted by his affair with the 23-year-old intern that he became "risk-averse" when it came to dealing with the terrorist threat.

"My sense is that the affair made him passive and risk-averse," the former top aide said. "As a result, I think he was reluctant to interfere with the military or to order long-term involvement."

But in her comments to Russert, Mrs. Clinton tried to shift the blame to Congress.

"Let's remember, we didn't even have support in the Congress for the money laundering that we finally got after September 11. We didn't have support for a lot of the intelligence sharing that we thought we needed. You know, we tripled the budget but it wasn't always focused the way it should have been."

Repeatedly employing the term "we" to describe the White House decision-making process, Mrs. Clinton further explained:

"You know, I think the biggest difference, Tim, is that, you know, we could launch a cruise missile and tell the Pakistanis that it was on its way to try to get bin Laden — and missed him by, you know, a few hours, apparently. But we didn't have the kind of cooperation [we needed]."

Russert did not press the New York senator on widespread reports that her husband's administration declined to accept an offer from the Sudanese government to extradite bin Laden to the U.S. in 1996.

Neither was she asked about recent criticism from Afghanistan's leading feminist, General Suhaila Siddiq, who chided Clinton for her comments on liberating the country's female population from Taliban chauvinism.

"She cannot defend her own rights against her husband. How can she defend the rights of my country?" Siddiq told the London *Times* last week.

Clinton: To Stop Terrorism, West Must Share Its Wealth

Inside Cover
Tuesday, December 18, 2001

Last month Bill Clinton told a Georgetown University audience that the 9/11 terrorist attacks were the fault of U.S. slavery and mistreatment of the American Indian.

Now he's changed his tune, downplaying the slavery angle in favor of a new justification for Osama bin Laden's 9/11 kamikaze hit squad: The West won't share its wealth with an impoverished Third World.

On Thursday Clinton appeared before the Richard Dimbleby Lecture Series in Warwick, Great Britain, to give an address he titled "The Struggle for the Soul of the 21st Century."

Some highlights:

"It was exactly a year ago today, near the end of my tenure as president, on my final trip overseas, that I went to Warwick University with Tony Blair to deliver a speech. ...

"On that day a year ago, I said 'we have seen how abject poverty accelerates conflict, how it creates recruits for terrorists and those who incite ethnic and religious hatred, how it fuels a violent rejection of the economic and social order on which our future depends.'

"The world has now witnessed a tragic, graphic illustration of that new reality, one that, as Mr. Dimbleby implied, has made a lot of people rethink their rosy projections for this new century. ...

"We in the wealthy countries have to spread the benefits of the 21st century world and reduce the risks so we can make more partners and fewer terrorists in the future."

Clinton continued:

"September 11 was the dark side of this new age of global interdependence. ... If you don't want to live with barbed wire around your children and grandchildren for the next hundred years, then it's not enough to defeat the terrorists.

"We have to make a world where there are far fewer terrorists, where there are fewer potential terrorists and more partners. And that responsibility falls primarily upon the wealthy nations, to spread the benefits and shrink the burdens."

A TRANSCRIPT OF CLINTON'S REMARKS WAS MADE AVAILABLE BY THE BBC.

Morris: Clinton Ignored Plan
That Might Have Deported Mohamed Atta

Inside Cover
Friday, December 21, 2001

Former White House political guru Dick Morris revealed Thursday that he repeatedly urged but couldn't persuade ex-President Bill Clinton to take specific action in the war on terrorism, including enacting a provision that would have deported Twin Towers kamikaze ringleader Mohamed Atta earlier this year.

"The president would normally do about two-thirds of what I recommended," Morris told Fox News Channel's *Hannity & Colmes*. "[But] he didn't do a single thing of the stuff that I recommended on terror."

Morris said that White House agenda schedules for 1995 and 1996 show that he repeatedly made anti-terrorism recommendations during weekly strategy meetings with the president.

One of Morris' proposals would have resulted in the deportation of Mohamed Atta, he said, an act that would have prevented the 9/11 World Trade Center disaster.

"I was urging very strongly in meeting after meeting after meeting for a federal law that says that if you're here on a visa, your driver's license has to expire the day your visa does."

Morris said he urged Clinton to order the FBI and Immigration and Naturalization Service to cross-check state motor vehicle records with their own records on suspected terrorists.

"Had that happened, Mohamed Atta would have been thrown out of the United States three months before 9/11," Morris told Fox.

The kamikaze-plot ringleader had been stopped by Florida police earlier this year, but because he had a valid driver's license they had no way of knowing his visa had expired.

Other anti-terror steps urged by Morris included sanctions against European companies that helped Iran build its oil reserves. "Congress passed it and Clinton waived those sanctions every single time there was potential to apply them," he said.

Clinton and Morris also discussed mounting an armed intervention against terrorists featuring U.S. ground troops, but the plan never materialized.

"In each of these areas he fell asleep at the switch," the former top Clinton aide said.

Rumsfeld Slams Clinton Military Cutbacks

Inside Cover
Sunday, January 20, 2002

While noting that U.S. armed forces remain the most powerful in the world, Secretary of Defense Donald Rumsfeld blasted the Clinton administration Sunday for defense cutbacks he said left the military in such a "run-down" condition that rebuilding could take up to a decade.

"The infrastructure had decayed and it is still decayed and it will take now probably six, eight, ten years to get it back to the place that it ought to be," Rumsfeld told [NBC's] *Meet the Press* host Tim Russert.

The Bush defense secretary then added, "It takes time to run down a great military, and it takes time to build one back up."

He suggested that the full dimension of the Clinton cutbacks were only now being felt. "During a president's term of office, what he does with the military has very little effect during that period of time. Each president inherits what was done in preceding periods."

Rumsfeld was responding to Democratic Party and media arguments that the U.S.'s success in the Afghanistan war shows that criticism of Clinton's military cutbacks is unjustified.

Separately, the *New York Post* reported Sunday that a full 89 percent of Clinton budget cuts under the president's "Reinventing Government" initiative came at the expense of the armed forces.

In his recent book *In the Arena: A Memoir of the 20th Century*, former Reagan administration Defense Secretary Caspar Weinberger contends that President Clinton had reduced U.S. military forces by approximately 50 percent during his eight years in office.

Clinton Protected Terrorist Charity From FBI Shutdown

Inside Cover
Wednesday, February 6, 2002

Five years ago the FBI wanted to shut down a Muslim charity that had been identified as a terrorist front group, but it was stopped by the Clinton administration.

In December 2001, federal agents seized the assets of The Holy Land Foundation, which bills itself as the nation's largest Muslim charity, after announcing it had been caught funneling funds to the notorious Palestinian terrorist group Hamas.

But, according to *U.S. News & World Report*'s "Washington Whispers" column:

"FBI veterans tell our David E. Kaplan that they were ready to move on the group back in 1997 but were stopped by top officials at Justice and the Clinton White House."

"They didn't want to come off as Muslim bashers," a source close to the investigation told the magazine.

Unnoted by *U.S. News*, then–first lady Hillary Clinton also feted Muslim supporters of Hamas at the White House.

Her Senate campaign repeatedly raised money from groups with ties to Middle East terrorists — sometimes in secret — and disguised one contribution from the American Muslim Council as a donation from the "American Museum Council" in a Federal Election Commission filing.

Clinton Diverted Billions From Pentagon to U.N. Peacekeeping

Lawrence Morahan, CNSNews.com
Tuesday, February 12, 2002

CNSNews.com — A draft report by the General Accounting Office reveals that former President Clinton contributed over $24 billion for U.N. peacekeeping missions around the world between 1995 and 2001, money that wasn't officially credited to the U.S. account by the United Nations.

The report shows that America's "debt" to the United Nations was more than compensated for by extra peacekeeping assistance that the world organization never gave the United States credit for, U.N. critics said.

"This new GAO report makes it absolutely clear that the U.S. debt to the U.N. was a complete fraud," said Cliff Kincaid, a journalist and president of America's Survival, who released a copy of the draft report.

"And remember that this report only covers the fiscal years 1996–2001," Kincaid added. "If the complete years of the Clinton administration were taken into account, the figure could rise by several more billions."

The Clinton era saw an explosion in the number of U.N.-sponsored peacekeeping missions carried out by U.S. forces that were not necessarily supported by Congress.

Those peacekeeping operations were the cause of heated disagreements over dues, including debates on whether the United States had accumulated sufficient back dues to be voted out of the U.N. General Assembly.

Between fiscal years 1996 and 2001, the United States directly contributed an estimated $3.45 billion to support U.N. peacekeeping, the report states.

During the same period, however, U.S. indirect contributions to U.N. peacekeeping amounted to $24.2 billion.

Of the $24.2 billion figure, the GAO found that the largest indirect contribution — about $21.8 billion — was for U.S. military operations and services. This meant military personnel and equipment had to be diverted from Pentagon operations to the United Nations.

The GAO defined indirect contributions as "U.S. programs and activities that are located in the same area as an ongoing U.N. peacekeeping operation, have objectives that help the peacekeeping operation achieve its mandated objectives, and are not an official part of the U.N. operation."

For example, estimated U.S. indirect contributions to U.N. operations in Kosovo and East Timor, which involved nation building and the training of local government agencies, "amounted to over $5.1 billion and included military operations to help provide a secure environment and programs to provide food and shelter for refugees and train police and court officials."

Congress Limits U.S. Contribution

The United Nations assesses member states a percentage share of the total cost of peacekeeping operations. The U.S. assessed share has historically been over 30 percent of total peacekeeping costs.

In November 1994, Congress limited the amount the United States could pay to 25 percent of peacekeeping costs, beginning in fiscal year 1996, the report noted. However, the United Nations continued to bill the United States at its historically 30 percent of total costs, leading to U.S. arrears.

In 2000, U.N. member states agreed to change the assessment formula and to drop the U.S. share of the peacekeeping budget over a three-year period to 27 percent, the report said.

Between fiscal years 1996, which began October 1995, and June 30, 2001, the United Nations conducted 33 peacekeeping operations in 28 countries, according to the report. As of January 2002, 15 of these operations were still ongoing in Europe, the Middle East, Africa and Asia, involving over 47,000 military personnel, civilian police and observers.

"When you're spending American taxpayer dollars you need accountability for American taxpayer dollars, and the procedure that the U.N. has of requesting donations and the practice of the Clinton administration to categorize expenditures as donations removes that accountability," said a senior official familiar with the GAO report.

Speaking at Heritage Foundation in Washington, U.S. Ambassador to the United Nations John Negroponte said of U.S. involvement in peace-keeping operations: "If there is a threat to international peace and security out there, and it needs to be dealt with, it is better that we do it where possible with other partners who are picking up part of the cost."

He added: "So I would say that while we always want to be careful about the costs and we always want to be careful about where it is that we decide to undertake U.N. peacekeeping operations, there are demonstrable benefits for the United States."

COPYRIGHT 2002 CNSNEWS.COM. ALL RIGHTS RESERVED.

'Axis of Evil' Country Topped Clinton Aid List

Inside Cover
Sunday, February 17, 2002

A country designated by President Bush as part of the "axis of evil" received more foreign aid under former President Bill Clinton than any other country in the Asia-Pacific region, a congressional study concluded two years ago.

House Republican Policy Committee Chairman Chris Cox, R-Calif., said the study conducted by his panel found that under the Clinton administration, North Korea became the "largest recipient of U.S. foreign aid in the Asia-Pacific region," CNSNews.com reported Friday.

"In an astonishing reversal of nine previous U.S. administrations, the Clinton-Gore administration, in 1994, committed not only to provide foreign aid for North Korea, but to earmark that aid primarily for the construction of nuclear reactors worth up to $6 billion," the Cox Committee contended.

Quoting the committee's findings, CNSNews.com reported:

"The U.S.-funded light water reactors in North Korea will accumulate plutonium in spent fuel at the rate of about 17,300 ounces per year, enough to produce 65 nuclear bombs a year.

"The Clinton-Gore policy, it is now clear, has severely worsened the threat that North Korea poses to the world by systematically rewarding Kim Jong-il for his most dangerous misconduct. It has provided North Korea with an increased capacity for the development of nuclear weapons and the long-range missiles to deliver them."

Cox, along with fellow congressmen Ed Markey, D-Mass., and Benjamin Gilman, R-N.Y., has sent a letter to President Bush calling for the U.S. to cancel the nuke deal and urging him to spotlight the North Korean threat during his visit to Japan, South Korea and China this week.

Beyond aiding North Korea's nuke program, the Clinton administration was providing 500,000 metric tons of fuel oil per year to the communist dictatorship's state-run military-industrial base, a figure that was "almost double what North Korea's civilian economy can use," the Cox Committee said.

In 1999, Representative Cox conducted a separate investigation into China's acquisition of U.S. nuclear secrets during the Clinton years, concluding that the People's Liberation Army had, for the first time in its history, acquired the capacity to strike the continental United States with nuclear-tipped ballistic missiles.

Bin Laden-gate Witness Dares Dems: Depose Me on Clinton 9/11 Cover-Up

Inside Cover
Friday, May 17, 2002

The man who negotiated a deal for Osama bin Laden's extradition to the United States six years ago is daring Senate Democrats to call him as a witness in the upcoming probe into the government's 9/11 intelligence failures, saying he can blow the lid off the Clinton administration's cover-up of the episode.

Mansoor Ijaz, a major Clinton financial supporter who hammered out the 1996 bin Laden agreement with the government of Sudan only to have the White House turn the offer down, issued the challenge Thursday during an interview with nationally syndicated radio host Sean Hannity.

"I'm saying this point-blank," Ijaz announced in impassioned tones. "Clinton, Berger, Albright, Susan Rice — any of them that want to come and take us on — I've got the paperwork to back up what I've said and they know it. And they know they can't run and hide."

Ijaz complained that since September 11 he has yet to be called by either the House or Senate intelligence committees to give sworn testimony.

"[Senate Intelligence Committee Chairman] Bob Graham is a friend of mine and he knows what I've got in my files. And they know where to find me if they really want to find out the truth about what was possible at that time."

Ijaz charged that Senate Democrats don't want to call him in order to protect the previous administration.

"I'm absolutely convinced," he told Hannity, "that the Democrats are desperately trying to find a way to deflect the attention from the complicity of the Clinton administration in letting this terrorism problem get so far out of hand."

The former Clinton negotiator described the missed opportunity to get bin Laden and fingered former National Security Advisor Sandy Berger and former Attorney General Janet Reno as having key roles in the deadly foul-up.

"By May of 1996 the Sudanese had decided to get rid of bin Laden because he was becoming a problem there as well. They called the Clinton administration one last time and said, 'If you don't want him to go to Saudi Arabia, we're prepared to hand him over to you guys directly.

"And the Clinton administration's response to that was 'We don't have enough legal evidence against him, Ijaz explained.

Besides Berger and Reno, "Clearly the president had to have had a hand in making that decision," he added. "There's no question in my mind that he was involved in those decisions as well. There's no question about that at all."

The former Clinton negotiator suggested that Congress depose other witnesses who could corroborate and expand upon his account.

"The American people should know that I have even persuaded a senior Sudanese intelligence official, who was later the intelligence chief, that if it became necessary he would come to the United States and testify in closed hearings about precisely what they were prepared to do," he said. "And he would bring the data with him."

Another witness suggested by Ijaz: former Clinton administration Ambassador to the Sudan Tim Carney.

"Frankly, [Carney] can take the American people a couple of steps further in terms of taking them inside the deliberations that went on and telling people precisely how the politicizing of the intelligence took place at that time."

Ijaz also charged that Clinton officials deliberately went out of their way to stifle FBI anti-terrorism probes.

"The FBI, in 1996 and 1997, had their efforts to look at terrorism data and deal with the bin Laden issue overruled every single time by the State Department, by Susan Rice and her cronies, who were hell-bent on destroying the Sudan," he said.

The Bush administration takes a different approach entirely, according to Ijaz.

"I can tell you personally that I have dealt with the Bush administration's national security team." he told Hannity. "These are people who immediately react to information that is brought to their attention that is necessary and important for people to know. ... There is no comparison to the Clinton administration."

President Clinton Could Have Prevented Twin Towers and Pentagon Attacks

Wilson C. Lucom
Saturday, May 18, 2002

President Clinton and the Democratic members of Congress in 1995 could have prevented the terrorist attacks on the Twin Towers and the Pentagon. Now they have the political brazenness to blame these attacks on President Bush when they were solely responsible seven years earlier.

In 1995 Philippine Police Chief Avelino Razon uncovered the plot called "Operation Bojinka" to plant bombs in U.S. airliners, and hijack others and crash them into buildings like the CIA headquarters. Razon said the plot was discovered on the computer of Ramzi Yousef, the organizer of the 1993 bombing of the World Trade Center.

Yousef had fled to Pakistan, but his laptop was found in the apartment he shared with his accomplice, Abdul Hamin Murad. Razon said both were agents of Osama bin Laden.

The Washington Post quoted a Filipino investigator who said that as he watched the attack on the World Trade Center on television, he exclaimed in horror, "It's Bojinka! Why didn't they pay attention?!"

Razon told the *Philippine Daily Inquirer* that after the Philippine intelligence report was compiled in 1995, it was passed on to the U.S. Embassy and the U.S. Joint Task Force on Terrorism. The Clinton FBI was in full possession of all the frightening facts on Bojinka but did nothing.

The FBI assured Congress that everything was under control when Dale L. Watson, chief of international terrorism operations, said the FBI had identified "a significant and growing organizational presence of foreign terrorists in the United States." He swore the bureau had them under control. There is no doubt that the FBI would not withhold such important information from the president and told Clinton, just as President Bush was informed.

President Clinton was negligent when he did not insist that the FBI and other concerned agencies create plans to prevent such an attack from occurring. He was too concerned with Monica.

If this had been done in 1995, the Twin Towers and Pentagon attacks probably would never have happened, with 3,000 American lives lost and billions of dollars' worth of buildings destroyed. But Clinton was too busy with his sex exploits to pay proper attention to his job of protecting the United States from terrorists.

The Democrats must stop attempting to make September 11 into a political issue. They must now work together with the Republicans on the best methods to protect the American people from terrorists.

Clinton Hushed Up Federal Report Warning of Hijack Attacks

NewsMax.com Wires
Saturday, May 18, 2002
WASHINGTON — The following article, excerpts from an exclusive story published by United Press International six days after the September 11 attacks, describes a 1994 federal report that warned of possible terrorist strikes, including how hijackers could use airliners to hit landmarks such as the Pentagon or White House.

The Clinton administration never released "Terror 2000" to the public, purportedly because of concerns in the State Department that it would cause panic.

The September 17 story by UPI Pentagon correspondent Pam Hess said the report, which was obtained exclusively by United Press International, not only outlined the changing face of terrorism but also seemed to predict the scope and timing of the attacks carried out against the World Trade Center and Pentagon.

"Targets such as the World Trade Center not only provide the requisite casualties but because of their symbolic nature provide more bang for the buck. In order to maximize their odds for success, terrorist groups will likely consider mounting multiple, simultaneous operations with the aim of overtaxing a government's ability to respond, as well as to demonstrate their professionalism and reach," states "Terror 2000."

The report was compiled in 1994 after the 1993 World Trade Center bombing, from research and interviews with 41 intelligence, government and private industry experts, including foreign governments such as Israel and Russia.

"Terror 2000" was distributed to the Defense Department, State Department, Federal Emergency Management Agency (FEMA), intelligence communities and members of Congress on June 24, 1994, according to author Marvin Cetron.

'Scrubbed' by Clinton's State Department

At the State Department's request, it was "scrubbed" of some details, including how to hit the Pentagon or White House by airplane, using the Washington Monument as a landmark. It was never publicly released, again at the request of State, according to Cetron.

"They said: 'You can't handle a crisis before it becomes a crisis. It scares the hell out of people, and they can't do anything. It's like a person with cancer; some people don't want to know. Others want to know everything so they can fight it.

'They Took the Ostrich Approach'

"I think they took the ostrich approach," Cetron told United Press International.

Cetron runs an economic and technological forecasting company in northern Virginia that produces reports for the U.S. government, 300 Fortune 500 companies and 17 foreign governments.

Whereas once most terrorists were politically motivated and sought achievable ends — safe passage out of a country or the release of political prisoners — "Terror 2000" predicted a more dangerous form was evolving in the wake of the collapse of the Soviet Union.

'Mass Casualties'

"We appear to be entering an era in which few, if any, restraints will remain. ... Unlike politically motivated terrorists, they do not shrink from mass murder. ... Mass casualties are not to be shunned ... but sought because they demonstrate to unbelievers the cataclysmic nature of divine retribution. And if innocents suffer, God will sort them out."

Ethno-religious terrorists would be motivated by "fierce ethnic and religious hatreds" bent on the "utter destruction of their chosen enemies."

The 1.5-inch-thick report was compiled by Cetron and Peter Probst, then with the Office of the Secretary of Defense, and 40 government and private-industry experts after the 1993 World Trade Center bombing. Though it seems to accurately describe the situation that is unfolding now, it makes only passing mention of prime suspect Osama bin Laden as a specific threat.

"The ethno-terrorist is defending his family and his community, the memory of his ancestors, his cultural heritage, and the identity of his people, most of whom have suffered and many of whom have died simply because they were Armenians, Bosnians, Basques, Irish, Quiche, Ibo or Kurds. His enemies seek the subjugation or annihilation of his people, if only in his eyes; it is his sacred [duty] to prevent this evil, not only for the sake of the living and future generations, but out of reverence for the dead."

COPYRIGHT 2002 BY UNITED PRESS INTERNATIONAL. ALL RIGHTS RESERVED.

Torricelli Calls for 9/11 Probe Into Clinton Intelligence Failures

Inside Cover
Sunday, May 19, 2002

Senator Robert Torricelli, D-N.J., said Sunday that any investigation into what the Bush White House knew before the 9/11 attacks on the World Trade Center and Pentagon should also include the Clinton administration's failure to deal with the al Qaeda threat.

Asked by WABC Radio's Steve Malzberg whether a 9/11 probe should cover the Clinton White House, Torricelli replied, "I think it goes back as long as is necessary to understand whatever this persistent problem is."

He then added, "For whatever failings there were in the Bush White House, there obviously are equal problems with Janet Reno and with FBI Director Louis Freeh."

The New Jersey senator continued:

"Indeed, many of the misallocations of resources, the failure to properly be tracking people who were involved in al Qaeda goes back to the mismanagement of the FBI under Louis Freeh."

Senator Torricelli's comments make him the first elected Democrat to call for a probe into the possible Clinton administration mishandling of the al Qaeda threat.

He said he envisioned such a probe as a nonpartisan inquiry "not for purposes of blaming anybody, but we just have to find out what went wrong."

New York Senator Hillary Clinton, who called for a 9/11 probe into the Bush White House Thursday, could not be reached for comment on Torricelli's call for a similar investigation into her husband's administration.

But she devoted most of a Friday night speech in Dix Hills, N.Y., to national security concerns and her own role in making them the nation's top priority.

However, Mrs. Clinton took only prescreened questions from the audience and cut short an autograph-signing session when NewsMax attempted to ask about intelligence failures during her tenure as co-president.

Giuliani: 9/11 Probe Should Include Clinton Administration

Inside Cover
Sunday, May 19, 2002

Former New York City Mayor Rudy Giuliani said Sunday that any investigation into what the Bush administration knew in advance of the 9/11 attacks should also probe the Clinton administration.

After an address to Georgetown University Law School graduates, Giuliani was asked about New York Senator Hillary Clinton's call for a probe into the possible mishandling of 9/11 warnings by the Bush White House.

"The information that we're talking about, a lot of it goes back to 1998 and 1999 when Mrs. Clinton's husband was president," Giuliani told The Associated Press.

The man who earned the title "America's Mayor" for his leadership in the wake of the World Trade Center attacks said that any 9/11 probe should look at both the Clinton and Bush administrations.

"Remember, the Bush administration, when this attack took place, was a very new administration and they had just inherited the intelligence apparatus put in place by the Clinton administration. So when you look at this, you're going to have look at both," he told the AP.

"We're looking at a continuous course of conduct here," Giuliani added. "I don't know that people should be playing that kind of game."

The ex–New York City mayor said he didn't think either the Bush or Clinton administrations had enough information to have prevented the 9/11 attacks.

Giuliani's call for a probe into Clinton's handling of pre–September 11 intelligence information on al Qaeda follows comments earlier in the day by New Jersey Senator Robert Torricelli, who recommended a probe into what he called a "misallocation" of counterterrorism resources during the Clinton years.

Clinton Nixed Plan to Infiltrate al Qaeda, Top FBI Whistle-Blower Says

Inside Cover
Saturday, June 1, 2002

A presidential executive order issued during the Clinton administration hamstrung the FBI so badly that bureau lawyers decided it would be illegal to infiltrate Osama bin Laden's terrorist training camps in Afghanistan, a senior FBI official during the Clinton administration said Saturday.

Former Deputy Assistant FBI Director Daniel Coulson fingered the Clinton White House in the decision to pass up what could have been an al Qaeda intelligence bonanza, during an interview on Fox News Channel's *Fox & Friends* morning show.

ALLISON CAMMARATA: This morning we've also been talking about this FBI mole who had an opportunity to go to an al Qaeda commando training camp but was not allowed to, because at that time the FBI did not want to deal in criminal activity and give the sort of go-ahead for somebody to go be trained as a terrorist.

Is that changing now? Will we get our hands dirtier with these sorts of criminal activity because we have to infiltrate those areas?

COULSON: Well, absolutely we will. I think you have to understand that part of that concern came from an executive order of the president of the United States, Bill Clinton. They didn't want people working for the government who, as you said, had dirty hands or were involved in criminal activity.

U.S. News & World Report reveals the FBI's decision not to infiltrate the al Qaeda terror camps in its latest issue, saying the episode took place just "months" before the 9/11 attacks.

But the magazine makes no mention of the role played by the Clinton restrictions, which also stymied CIA efforts to gather human intelligence.

Coulson predicted that the Bush administration would not allow the FBI to be hobbled in the same way.

"You can see a big change," he told Fox News Channel. "I think Attorney General Ashcroft has a different view of the world. ... So things like this need to be done. The rest of the world does it and we should be doing it too."

The former deputy FBI director first gained national attention during the late 1990s when he criticized his agency's overzealousness during the Waco and Ruby Ridge debacles.

Ex–Bush VP: Clinton 'Policy Breach' Left U.S. Vulnerable to 9/11 Attacks

Inside Cover
Tuesday, June 4, 2002

Former Vice President Dan Quayle said Monday night that the lack of a firm policy to deal with terrorism during the Clinton administration was more responsible for leaving America vulnerable to the 9/11 attacks than any FBI or CIA intelligence failures.

"I don't believe 9/11 happened because of an intelligence breach," Quayle told Fox News Channel's *Hannity & Colmes.*

"I think it was really a policy breach. It was the inaction of the previous administration, by and large, that al Qaeda — and bin Laden in particular — thought that they could hit the United States and there would be a retaliation maybe of a cruise missile but nothing more than that," he explained.

The comments make the former vice president, who served under President Bush's father from 1989 to 1993, the highest-ranking former U.S. official to suggest that the Clinton administration should get the lion's share of the blame for not preventing the 9/11 attacks.

Quayle also insisted that President Bush would have struck back more forcefully against Osama bin Laden after earlier terrorist attacks on U.S. interests, taking action that could have averted 9/11.

"I can assure you if a USS *Cole* or an American Embassy had been hit under President Bush's watch, there would have been a different response," he said. "And I really think that bin Laden ... thought that he could hit us [on 9/11] and that the response would not be that much."

The former vice president also suggested that political correctness played a key role in allowing the 9/11 hijackers to elude U.S. anti-terror watchdogs, even after valuable intelligence on al Qaeda suspects was forwarded to Washington from the FBI's Phoenix and Minneapolis offices.

"This was, clearly, a situation where the FBI headquarters in Washington, D.C., [said], 'Oh, well, we can't do that. We might be getting into racial profiling, Quayle said. "'We might be doing something else, getting into wiretapping, when we really don't have probable cause.'"

Appearing on the same show, former FBI Assistant Deputy Director Daniel Coulson blamed a Clinton executive order for the failure of U.S. intelligence agents to infiltrate al Qaeda terror cells.

"The first thing you have to remember is that [Clinton] issued an executive order that said ... you can't use an individual who has terrorist connections in order to develop information about terrorist organizations, which is a huge bungle."

Coulson said the Clinton executive order "defies reason, it defies logic, and it's not consistent with the law."

"Every day in a criminal case, we use unsavory characters," he explained. "We use people that are murderers to find other murderers. And that puts a great burden on the CIA, and it impedes their abilities to do their job."

Bin Laden-gate Accuser:
Ex-Clinton Officials Trying to Silence Me

Inside Cover
Wednesday, June 5, 2002

A freelance diplomatic operative who alleges the Clinton administration turned down three separate offers to extradite Osama bin Laden to the U.S. during the late 1990s said Wednesday that ex-Clinton officials have been working hard to discredit him before he tells his story to 9/11 congressional probers.

"They've been trying for the last seven months real hard, and the harder they try, the louder I get," Mansoor Ijaz told radioman Don Imus. "They haven't got a prayer of trying to keep this under the rug."

"We don't want to see you up in the park by the cannon," Imus said somewhat facetiously — a reference to the late Whitewater witness Vincent Foster, who was found shot to death in a Virginia park in 1993 just as that scandal began to unravel.

Last month, NewsMax.com reported exclusively the comments of former Clinton spokeswoman Jennifer Palmieri, who called Ijaz "a crackpot" and said his account was "a joke." Palmieri is now the chief spokeswoman for the Democratic National Committee.

Other Clinton administration officials have tried to suggest that Ijaz has exaggerated his story.

In a subsequent interview with Imus, *New York Times* reporter Judith Miller acknowledged that her paper hasn't covered Ijaz's allegations because her Clinton administration contacts have said they aren't true.

Despite the attempts to undermine his credibility, the former Clinton insider says he expects to testify before the Senate Intelligence Committee next month.

"That's probably the point when I'll be brought in, I would say within a month or month and a half," he predicted. "I've been contacted by the intelligence committees to find out what I have in my files. I've got a pretty good written record of exactly what we did at that time."

After talking to Ijaz, Imus repeatedly told his audience that he found Ijaz's account thoroughly credible.

"CIA Officer: Clinton Helped Saddam"

Christopher Ruddy
NewsMax.com magazine, July 2002

Now, that sounds more than far-fetched. Certainly President Bush would rather see bin Laden's head on a platter than to have him as a dinner guest.

But a senior former CIA agent, who served in the Middle East for almost two decades fighting terrorists, thinks bin Laden may believe that, like fellow terrorist leader Yasser Arafat, he may someday find himself a guest of a future U.S. president.

This former CIA officer, Robert Baer, recently wrote the explosive book *See No Evil: The True Story of a Ground Soldier in the CIA's War on Terrorism*. Baer writes that when he sees Arafat "standing in the Rose Garden at the White House or when I hear that a CIA director has met privately with him at some desert tent, I wonder sometimes if Arafat's example doesn't make Osama bin Laden consider that he, too, might become a statesman in time."

Today our liberal media prefer to describe Arafat as a freedom fighter. Baer's observations are deemed politically incorrect.

That may be one reason his book — with many important revelations, a foreword by Seymour Hersh and Random House as its publisher — has gotten such little media attention.

Here are just a few of Baer's key points:

- In 1991, the CIA closed up its activities in Afghanistan and Saudi Arabia. During the Clinton years, things got even worse. Agency operatives around the globe were directed away from spying on the bad guys and told to start worrying about "human rights, economic globalization, the Arab-Israel conflict."
- Iran remains a major player in the terrorist world. Baer says that in 1982, Arafat "had put his entire worldwide terrorist network at Iran's disposal." In 1996, bin Laden formed an alliance with Iran. The purpose of the alliance was simple: Attack America.
- The Clinton White House's gross negligence and malfeasance were demonstrated by its handling of Saddam Hussein. Baer states that in 1995, top staffers at the National Security Council prevented a planned coup by Iraqi military leaders against Saddam. Baer was the top CIA man in northern Iraq working with Iraqi dissidents.

In 1995, the CIA summoned Baer from Iraq back to Washington. When he reported to agency headquarters, a CIA superior told him why he was called home: "Tony Lake [Clinton's national security adviser] ordered the FBI to investigate you for trying to assassinate Saddam Hussein."

After months of investigation, the charges were found to be baseless and dropped. Like many other CIA veterans whose own government thwarted them from doing their jobs, Baer retired. Still, the agency gave him due recognition. He was awarded its Career Intelligence Medal.

But the coddling of Saddam Hussein was not isolated to just targeting Baer and removing him from Iraq. In fact, the Clinton White House clearly decided to keep and maintain the Iraqi dictator in power.

In one of the most important revelations in *See No Evil*, Baer writes that Saddam might well have been deposed by his own troops, especially if the economic sanctions had been rigorously applied. But with U.S. complicity, he was able to sell millions of barrels of Iraqi oil by shipping them overland through NATO ally Turkey.

During the mid-1990s, Baer says, the oil smuggled through Turkey "was a lifeline for Saddam, who used the money to fund his intelligence services and Special Republican Guards — the forces that kept him alive."

The pipeline of smuggled oil was no hidden, disputed fact. Baer reports the Iraqi oil trucks stretched back anywhere from 20 to 70 miles as they waited to cross into Turkey.

Baer was baffled. He writes, "What I couldn't understand was why the White House didn't intervene." He says the U.S. could easily have closed down the truck pipeline into Turkey.

"It was almost as if the White House wanted Saddam to have a little walking around money," Baer writes.

Baer concludes that the Clinton administration "helped Saddam pay for his praetorian guard, just what you'd expect of a clever superpower that was secretly supporting the local despot."

Nobody who has studied Bill Clinton should be surprised by his duplicity. The facts show, and future historians will discover, that Bill Clinton was no friend of the United States.

U.S. Ambassador to Sudan
Confirms Clinton Snubbed Bin Laden Deal

Inside Cover
Tuesday, July 2, 2002

Former Ambassador to Sudan Tim Carney confirmed Tuesday night that the Clinton administration refused an offer from the Sudanese government to hand over terrorist mastermind Osama bin Laden in the late 1990s — directly contradicting former Clinton administration officials who have attacked the story as baseless.

"In fact, what was offered [by the Sudanese] was to expel bin Laden to Saudi Arabia, and the Saudis, because he was such a hot potato, simply refused to handle him," Carney told Fox News Channel's Alan Colmes.

"Then, as I understand it, there was an offer to send him to us," Carney recalled. The Clinton administration rebuffed the overture because, Carney said, "we did not have an indictment [against bin Laden] at the time."

Carney's account corroborates the claims of Pakistani-American freelance diplomat Mansoor Ijaz, who has maintained for months that the Clinton administration blew a crucial opportunity to take bin Laden out of circulation and ultimately foil the 9/11 terrorist attacks.

While the press has largely ignored Ijaz's claims, former Clinton officials have launched a fierce campaign to undermine his credibility and keep him from testifying before Congress.

"He's lying," former Clinton spokeswoman Jennifer Palmieri said in May. "The guy has absolutely no credibility."

"It's a joke. He's a crackpot," added Palmieri, now the chief spokeswoman for the Democratic National Committee.

Asked to respond to Ijaz's account in January, Clinton National Security

Counsel adviser Nancy Soderberg told Fox News Channel's Laurie Dhue: "He's living in a fantasyland. There was no such Sudanese offer."

Ijaz has said that former National Security Advisor Sandy Berger and former Assistant Secretary of State for African Affairs Susan Rice, as well as former Attorney General Janet Reno and ex-President Clinton himself, all deserve blame for mishandling the Sudanese offer to turn over bin Laden.

He has dared the Senate Intelligence Committee to take his sworn testimony about the episode as part of its probe into pre–September 11 intelligence failures. But so far, Democrats who control the investigation have declined to do so.

Recently, Ms. Rice lashed out at former Ambassador Carney, painting him as a disgruntled Clinton-hater with an ax to grind.

"He was unfortunately very angry at the Clinton administration for the decision to close his embassy in Khartoum soon after he got there, and perhaps that anger colors his recollections," she claimed.

But Ijaz and Carney may have picked up a powerful new ally last weekend when Secretary of State Colin Powell seemed to endorse their version of events, which they detailed in a *Washington Post* op-ed piece on Sunday.

Alluding to Ijaz and Carney's account in responding to criticism from former Vice President Al Gore that the Bush administration had so far failed to capture Osama bin Laden, Powell told *Fox News Sunday*, "I notice the previous administration didn't even make a serious try to get him."

Clinton Audio Exclusive: Pre–9/11: Bin Laden Strike Wouldn't Have Worked

Inside Cover
Wednesday, August 7, 2002

Flatly contradicting *Time* magazine's claims this week that his administration turned over workable plans to capture or kill Osama bin Laden to the Bush White House, ex-President Bill Clinton confessed earlier this year that his administration's plans had a "high probability" of failure.

Clinton made the stunning admission during a February address to a New York business group, which, apparently, *Time* declined to cover.

But NewsMax.com was there.

As our exclusive audiotape of the Clinton speech makes clear, the ex-president decided not to implement his own administration's plans to attack al Qaeda — not because of the impending presidential election (as *Time* claims) but because he thought such an attack wouldn't work.

NewsMax has transcribed Clinton's pertinent remarks below.

Remarks of Ex-President Bill Clinton
to the Long Island Association, Woodbury, N.Y.

February 15, 2002

Now, if you look back — in the hindsight of history, everybody's got 20/20 vision — the real issue is should we have attacked the al Qaeda network in 1999 or in 2000 in Afghanistan.

Here's the problem. Before September 11 we would have had no support for it — no allied support and no basing rights. So we actually trained to do this. I actually trained people to do this. We trained people.

But in order to do it, we would have had to take them in on attack helicopters 900 miles from the nearest boat — maybe illegally violating the airspace of people if they wouldn't give us approval. And we would have had to do a refueling stop.

And we would have had to make the decision in advance that's the reverse of what President Bush made — and I agreed with what he did. They basically decided — this may be frustrating to you now that we don't have bin Laden. But the president had to decide after September 11, which am I going to do first: just go after bin Laden or get rid of the Taliban?

He decided to get rid of the Taliban. I personally agree with that decision, although it may or may not have delayed the capture of bin Laden. Why?

Because first of all, the Taliban was the most reactionary government on earth and there was an inherent value in getting rid of them.

Secondly, they supported terrorism and we'd send a good signal to governments that if you support terrorism and they attack us in America, we will hold you responsible.

Thirdly, it enabled our soldiers and Marines and others to operate more safely in-country as they look for bin Laden and the other senior leadership, because we'd have had to have gone in there to just sort of clean out one area, try to establish a base camp and operate.

So for all those reasons the military recommended against it. There was a high probability that it wouldn't succeed.

Now I had one other option. I could have bombed or sent more missiles in. As far as we knew, he never went back to his training camp. So the only place bin Laden ever went that we knew was occasionally he went to Khandahar, where he always spent the night in a compound that had 200 women and children.

So I could have, on any given night, ordered an attack that I knew would kill 200 women and children that had less than a 50 percent chance of getting him.

Now, after he murdered 3,100 of our people and others who came to our country seeking their livelihood you may say, "Well, Mr. President, you should have killed those young women and children."

But at the time we didn't think he had the capacity to do that. And no one thought that I should do that. Although I take full responsibility for it. You need to know that those are the two options I had. And there was less than a 50-50 chance that the intelligence was right that on this particular night he was in Afghanistan.

Now, we did do a lot of things. We tried to get the Pakistanis to go get him. They could have done it and they wouldn't. They changed governments at the time from Mr. Sharif to President Musharraf. And we tried to get others to do it. We had a standing contract between the CIA and some groups in Afghanistan authorizing them and paying them if they should be successful in arresting [unintelligible].

So I tried hard to — I always thought this guy was a big problem. And apparently the options I had were the options that the president and Vice President Cheney and Secretary Powell and all the people that were involved in the Gulf War thought that they had, too, during the first eight months that they were there — until September 11 changed everything.

But I did the best I could with it and I do not believe, based on what options were available to me, that I could have done any more than I did. Obviously, nobody has been successful. I tried a lot of different ways to get bin Laden 'cause I always thought he was a very dangerous man. He's [unintelligible], he's bold and he's deadly.

But I think it's very important that the Bush administration do what they're doing to keep the soldiers over there to keep chasing him. But I know — like I said — I know it might be frustrating to you. But it's still better for bin Laden to worry every day more about whether he's going to see the sun come up in the morning than whether he's going to drop a bomb, another bomb somewhere in the U.S. or in Europe or on some other innocent civilians.

Clinton Admits: I Nixed Bin Laden Extradition Offer

Inside Cover
Sunday, August 11, 2002
Mansoor Ijaz, the Pakistani-American businessman who says he was rebuffed by the Clinton White House after negotiating a deal for the extradition of Osama bin Laden to the U.S. in 1996, has gained an important new witness who backs his story — none other than ex-President Clinton himself.

Former Clinton administration officials such as senior National Security Council aide Nancy Soderberg have described Ijaz as an unreliable witness. Former Clinton spokeswoman Jennifer Palmieri recently slammed him as "a liar" and "a crackpot."

But a tape recording obtained exclusively by NewsMax.com shows Clinton himself confirming all the key points of Ijaz's story.

In never-before-reported comments to a New York business group last February, the ex-president never mentioned Ijaz by name. But the events he related paralleled the freelance diplomat's story exactly.

"Mr. bin Laden used to live in Sudan," Clinton explained to a February 15 Long Island Association luncheon.

"He was expelled from Saudi Arabia in 1991, then he went to Sudan. And we'd been hearing that the Sudanese wanted America to start meeting with them again.

"They released him," the ex-president confirmed.

"At the time, 1996, he had committed no crime against America, so I did not bring him here because we had no basis on which to hold him, though we knew he wanted to commit crimes against America.

"So I pleaded with the Saudis to take him, 'cause they could have," Clinton explained. "But they thought it was a hot potato and they didn't and that's how he wound up in Afghanistan."

Since last December, Ijaz has insisted that he negotiated the deal for bin Laden's release from Sudan. But, he maintained, the Clinton White House declined to take advantage of the offer because of legal technicalities — a detail now confirmed by the ex-president.

Former Clinton officials trashed the bin Laden extradition story as an exaggeration at best, a complete fabrication at worst.

Asked to respond to Ijaz's account in January, ex-NSC aide Soderberg told the Fox News Channel, "He's living in a fantasyland. There was no such Sudanese offer."

"He's lying," Palmieri, now chief spokeswoman for the Democratic National Committee, said of Ijaz's story in May. "The guy has absolutely no credibility. You'll see that you never see him on television anymore once he was outed as being a fraud."

Mainstream reporters, apparently unaware of Clinton's February comments, have also discredited Ijaz's account.

In May, both *New York Times* reporter Judith Miller and NBC newswoman Andrea Mitchell told radioman Don Imus they declined to cover the bin Laden extradition story because they didn't find it credible.

Chapter 3

The CIA Failed

Senator Torricelli Played Key
Role in Closing Down CIA Ops

Wes Vernon, NewsMax.com
Tuesday, September 18, 2001

WASHINGTON — Senator Robert Torricelli, D-N.J., led congressional efforts in the mid-1990s that handcuffed the CIA's abilities to recruit spies — a key policy that helped allow the attacks of September 11 to take place with no intelligence warnings.

Current and former CIA operatives say that Clinton administration policies, which forbade the CIA from recruiting known terrorists and other criminals, left the U.S. government bereft of all intelligence about such terrorist groups.

In 1995, then-Representative Robert Torricelli, D-N.J., made secrets public at the behest of left-wing activist Bianca Jagger, his girlfriend at the time, according to Newark *Star-Ledger* columnist Paul Mulshine in the January–February issue of *Heterodoxy*.

The secrets suggested that the CIA had on its payroll one or more unsavory characters who had been involved in murder.

Torricelli gave away secrets he obtained through his membership on the House Intelligence Committee.

This so outraged then-Speaker Newt Gingrich that he tried to have the New Jersey Democrat kicked off the panel.

Later, Torricelli was criticized in a committee report for having compromised American intelligence-gathering abilities around the world, adding that numerous CIA sources had decided to stop giving information for fear they would be outed by a congressman.

At the time, Torricelli's activities and leaks against the CIA garnered a large amount of press attention.

Mulshine's article showed how Torricelli's action in giving away the name of a CIA source in Guatemala was based not on fact but on a conspiracy theory of "the loony left," as *Heterodoxy* later characterized it.

The lawmaker was accused of having leaped to a number of inaccurate conclusions about the CIA's role in the deaths of an American hotel owner named Michael DeVine and a Guatemalan guerrilla named Efrain Bamaca Velazquez.

In its 1997 report, the House Intelligence Committee had this to say about the antics of Torricelli, by then a senator:

"None of the allegations raised by Representative Torricelli in the March 22, 1995 letter to the president [Clinton] or subsequent public statements concerning the involvement of the CIA in the DeVine and Bamaca deaths in Guatemala have proved true."

Still, Torricelli's efforts paid off with the Clinton administration, which moved to ban the use of spies or the recruitment of spies that had any involvement with criminals or terrorists.

Torricelli effectively blinded the CIA.

It was about the time of this well-publicized incident that the CIA's slide into a deteriorated human intelligence capability accelerated.

As a former CIA spy in the Mideast told NewsMax CEO Christopher Ruddy, Bill Clinton simply changed the rules of how spies are recruited. A former CIA official later confirmed this to Fox News Channel's Bill O'Reilly.

And it was done in such a way as to make it impossible to recruit effective human spies. The agency, then under Director John Deutch and his top assistant, Nora Slatkin, implemented a "human rights scrub" policy.

As Senate Intelligence Committee Chairman Bob Graham has noted since Tuesday's attacks, effective human spies "are not found in monasteries."

Torricelli did not respond to repeated efforts by NewsMax.com to get his comment for this article.

But he turned up Monday night on Fox News Channel's *The O'Reilly Factor* to defend himself. O'Reilly accused him of "tying the CIA's hands," although he did not let Clinton or then-CIA Director John Deutch off the hook.

Torricelli said the CIA could hire anyone it wanted to spy for the U.S. — as long as the station chiefs get permission from Washington.

That set O'Reilly off. The popular TV host said the CIA agents had no confidence in Deutch — "They hated him" — and they didn't want to bother that "extra layer of bureaucracy" in Washington, "where they're out to lunch half the day anyway."

"You don't know that, and I don't know that," Torricelli shot back. "But the point is, on the principle, the agency's hands are not tied. They can hire anybody they want. They've got to get permission."

"Here's the deal," retorted O'Reilly. "The terrorists can blow up the World Trade Center. They don't have to get anybody's permission, all right? They can just do it. But if we want to hire somebody as a quick tip that that may be coming down, you can't do that without permission from some pinhead in Washington."

"I'm not sure the terrorists should set the standard we want to follow," the New Jersey Democrat countered.

"We're just defending ourselves!" exclaimed the television journalist.

Torricelli ended up blaming the CIA, saying they "had the authority to do it under law. They just didn't do it."

O'Reilly said the station chiefs and field agents believed that Deutch "didn't know his butt from his elbow." He added that Torricelli had caused another layer of bureaucracy to be created "within an agency that needs to be nimble and brutal."

O'Reilly did not bring up Bianca Jagger.

Like Ruddy, O'Reilly has been talking to former CIA operatives whose opinion of Deutch is universally low.

Torricelli has been in the news recently because of a federal investigation into bribery allegations against him.

The Nicaraguan-born Jagger, ex-wife of Rolling Stones rock star Mick Jagger, has appeared on Fox News Channel and other media outlets to promote environmental and other leftist causes and rail against America's use of the death penalty. She has also been romantically linked to Senator Christopher Dodd, D-Conn.

CIA Let Us Down

John LeBoutillier
Friday, September 21, 2001

Wednesday I wrote of a "war inside our intelligence community" over the involvement of Iraq in the September 11 bombings.

This "war" is between those who 'know' the truth about Saddam's direct participation in this horrendous act of war against the United States of America and those who let him survive in 1991 at the end of the Gulf War.

That night, CBS News led off its evening newscast with the very same story!

And Thursday's *New York Times* front page featured a story about this "split inside the administration" — and how Secretary of Defense Donald Rumsfeld favored the targeting of Iraq. So, too, did Deputy Defense Secretary Paul Wolfowitz.

Day by day — thanks to a free press — the truth is emerging about Iraq's crucial role in the attacks.

Yet last night President Bush carefully avoided any mention of Saddam Hussein. While specifically targeting the Taliban and Osama bin Laden's al Qaeda organization, the president shied away from mentioning any other governments involved. This may be to preserve the advantage of surprise — or it may be because the administration doesn't have the stomach for another war with Iraq.

The head of U.S. intelligence is George Tenet, director of the CIA. Tenet is the lone holdover from the Clinton administration. At the urging of his father, George W. Bush decided to keep Tenet in his job at Langley, Va.

Lost in the middle of this unfolding story is the pathetic performance of our own government to protect us.

Yes, changes have been made in recent years in our HUMINT (human intelligence) requirements. But there have been nothing but **spending increases** on intelligence each and every year — *especially under Clinton's presidency.* That was something I noted each of his eight years: While he gutted the military, he always increased our intelligence budget. At the time, it was speculated that perhaps the CIA had something (or many things) on Clinton and was able to 'bargain' with him for ever-increasing budgets.

One thing you must understand: *The CIA is a government unto itself — a government within a government.*

Anyone who doubts this is naïve.

It is a fact of life.

The CIA spies on other departments of the U.S. government and places agents inside the House and Senate staffs and inside its rival intelligence agencies — the NSA, the DIA and the service intelligence agencies.

The CIA keeps tabs on our own government *much more effectively than it has spied on our enemies.*

Even Chairman of the House Intelligence Committee Porter Goss — charged with oversight responsibilities — is a former CIA agent. In the CIA, there is really no 'former'. Once in, you're in for life.

Mr. Goss oversees the CIA as chairman of that crucial committee. Do you honestly believe he is going to be objective about limiting, criticizing, cutting or rebuking the CIA?

One of the consequences of September 11 must be a top-to-bottom *honest* reassessment of our failed intelligence apparatus.

Heads need to roll inside our own government for its failure to protect us.

And many, many questions need to be answered. For example, how come *Jane's Foreign Report* already knows that the "operational master-minds of last week's attacks" were Imad Mughniyeh, a Lebanese head of overseas operations for Hezbollah, and Dr. Ayman Al-Zawahiri, an Egyptian who has been tried in absentia, convicted and sentenced to death for the 1981 assassination of Egyptian President Anwar El-Sadat.

Both men have been meeting regularly with Iraqi intelligence for the past two years.

Why wasn't our own intelligence aware of this? Or, if they were, why do they continue to steer the investigation away from Iraq?

Jane's also reports that Mughniyeh "personally" murdered Beirut CIA Station Chief William Buckley in 1984. That was 17 years ago! And he is still on the loose? Why — through four U.S. administrations — has the CIA not caught and killed this bastard?

In our enthusiasm for President Bush's speech we must not lose sight of a basic fact: *The September 11 attack could have been — and should have been — prevented.*

We have a massive, $60 billion per year 'intel community' designed to prevent this type of attack.

It failed us badly.

The thousands of dead could be alive today if we had gotten our money's worth.

As it now stands, the CIA and our other related agencies are *completely useless* when it comes to protecting the people of the United States.

Terrorists on the official watch list fly into and out of this country — *often using their real names* as they go through our airports — and nothing is done!

So-called surveillance is ordered on two USS *Cole* bombing suspects *who are in our country* — and nothing is done!

Our intelligence has grown complacent, cocky, fat, lazy, too rich — and not 'hungry' enough to remember the desperate days of World War II when our OSS performed heroically behind enemy lines to thwart Hitler and Japan.

We will not win this War on Terrorism until we rip apart and then rebuild our own very-lacking intelligence apparatus.

More CIA Revelations — Political Correctness Kills

Christopher Ruddy
Monday, October 1, 2001

When former Israeli Prime Minister Benjamin Netanyahu called the infamy of September 11 a "wake-up call from hell," he meant just that. His characterization demands repeating again — and again — because worse than September 11 will happen unless we heed the call.

I am not so sure the commissars of political correctness, who dominate our media, our government bureaucracies and other institutions, are willing to unshackle the will of the American people and allow us to destroy the terrorists and the nations that back them.

President Bush has done a remarkable job — especially in light of the hand he inherited from the previous administration. It is also important to remember that a hidden problem for the Bush administration is that the U.S. government, including our Pentagon, CIA and other agencies, is still largely run by appointees of Clinton-Gore or the career military and bureaucrats Clinton-Gore promoted through the ranks.

The same people who left us vulnerable to the acts of September 11 are now claiming they will solve our future problems.

I believe long-term good will come out of this catastrophe only if we learn from the events of September 11, hold accountable the people in our government who failed us, and make necessary reforms.

If we do not do this, it is doubtful we will exist as a great nation 10 years hence.

We should also heed the Roman statesman Cicero, who remarked that great nations are destroyed not from the barbarians outside but from the civilized people within.

The logic of this is simple: There will always be barbarians outside the gates. It is up to us to have the character and strength and will to defend against them.

Before September 11, P.C. thinking taught us that nothing we do mattered; character didn't count. It was the Age of Clinton. After September 11, the overriding lesson is that *everything* we do counts; character *does* matter.

Even the liberal *Boston Globe* recognized this. Breaking from the P.C. crowd, it reported that Clinton's sexcapades and scandals detracted from his ability to focus on hunting down Osama bin Laden. That story received almost zero national press coverage.

And the *Globe* and many media still haven't talked much about what happened at the CIA.

Political Correctness Ruined the CIA

Our loyal readers will remember that NewsMax broke the story, within hours of the attacks, about how P.C. thinking by Clinton and Sen. Torricelli had prevented the CIA and its many patriotic members from doing their jobs.

The CIA was effectively banned from recruiting unsavory characters to penetrate terrorist cells.

But that is just a small part of how P.C. thinking has undermined America and the CIA.

During the past decade, the CIA has been twisted from an intelligence-gathering organization with a mission to protect America and her citizens — and turned into a model of political correctness.

Under Clinton, the CIA was told to stop focusing on spying and start focusing on P.C. agenda items like global warming.

Worse, the CIA staff was to become a model of P.C. ideology.

One analyst retired in disgust after the agency had appointed a person to become a lead analyst for a particular country.

This person was qualified because she was black, a female, and had graduated from an Ivy League college with a high GPA. The CIA was not concerned that the young woman did not speak the language of the country she was to analyze, nor had she ever visited the country.

She did prove, however, that the CIA was diverse.

Diversity Defined the CIA

As anyone who worked at the CIA can tell you, "diversity" was the buzzword that animated the agency during the Clinton years.

Diversity was the mission and the goal.

A CIA operative close to the Middle East told me that the agency was even placing women in countries like Islamic ones, where the culture does not view women progressively.

While this policy demonstrated the agency's commitment to diversity, it effectively cut its female operative out of any serious interaction with the host country's political and military establishment.

P.C. thinking dominated all the activities of the agency. CIA employees were regularly hit with a barrage of Orwellian P.C. workshops and literature explaining how they needed to be . . . well, sensitive and open to diversity.

One analyst, still a CIA employee, told me about one CIA sensitivity training seminar he had to sit through. The presenter, an expert in diversity, gave a PowerPoint® presentation on the benefits of diversity.

One slide showed an American Indian sitting on the ground working with beads. The presenter explained: "American Indians have a long tradition working with beads. They are good with beads, and they have, in modern times, become good working with wires."

Another slide showed an African-American professional sitting at an office cubicle on the phone. The presenter explained: "African-Americans are particularly sensitive to being interrupted while on the phone. You should avoid doing this."

As the analyst explained, "They were creating new stereotypes as they were complaining about old ones." The CIA had become the Central Intelligence Agency for Diversity.

How sad. How dangerous.

No wonder that, with an annual budget of $60 billion, the CIA had no warning, no informant in the September 11 network that several experts say must have numbered 300 people working in several countries.

Commissars Won't Heed Wake-up Call

I could swallow the government's failures of September 11 if we heeded the wake-up call, exposed the problems of P.C. thinking at the CIA and elsewhere, and made reforms.

But the commissars of political correctness that control the major media will have none of it. Consider how there has been practically no criticism by the major networks of President Clinton's stewardship of our national security agencies.

The same commissars who were, in the middle of this horrific crisis, attacking President Bush will not utter any criticism of Bill Clinton.

In fact, Clinton was actually being praised! NBC's Andrea Mitchell, Alan Greenspan's wife, was on the air spewing her venom for Bush, complaining that he was not, like Bill Clinton, a "comforter in chief." You see, according to P.C. thinking, Bush's desire to stay up in Air Force One to ensure the continuity of government was less important than going to New York City to cry, hold hands and show how we "feel."

Criticism of Clinton is taboo precisely because the major media know that criticism of him is criticism of them. They supported him and the bizarre P.C. thinking that has possessed them and brought us to the point of September 11.

So, instead of heeding the "wake-up call," the P.C. commissars in the media are continuing to play old tricks.

Within hours of the attacks, I heard P.C. anchors and commentators spinning that these events proved America does not need missile defense. Don't they care that the very same countries behind the terrorists are feverishly building and developing long-range missiles capable of hitting many American cities at once?

No, the commissars never lose an opportunity to spin.

CIA Leak to NewsMax: More Bad News

Inside Cover
Thursday, October 4, 2001
More leaks to NewsMax from inside the CIA.

One official, we'll call him 007 for our purposes, said he was "impressed" by NewsMax's coverage of the agency.

NewsMax's Chris Ruddy first broke the story in the wake of the September 11 attacks that the CIA had stopped recruiting spies in terrorist networks — citing insider sources "Roger" and "Harry."

That report was followed by more revelations about how the agency had become a model for political correctness, the CIAD — the Central Intelligence Agency for Diversity.

Agent 007 agrees, revealing to us that our "points on CIA environmental analysis were right on the money. Under Clinton, CIA spy satellite imagery was used to write special environmental assessments for Gore on sand turtles, dolphin schools, and volcano eruptions."

But that's not the end of the story, reports 007.

He notes how the current leadership of the agency was blatantly negligent about dealing with terrorism.

007: "The CIA treated counterterrorism as a second- or third-tier assignment from about 1992 until 9/11/01. Bill Casey treated it seriously, but the old boys at CIA disagreed. Reflecting the liberal internationalist bent of the DI (analysis office), the most-prestigious analytic jobs were following Western Europe and Canada. (Why do we even have a Canadian intelligence analyst? Why can't State do that?)"

More on Tenet: "He recently created a huge counterterrorism office and several days after September 11 hundreds of analysts were assigned to it. This effort is an attempt to show that CIA is serious about the terrorism threat, but mostly to save Tenet's skin, as well as the many other senior CIA officials promoted under the Clinton administration."

Ronald Reagan's CIA director, Bill Casey, had made the counterterrorism office a top priority, but his successors, including current director George Tenet, didn't.

007: "Our terrorist office was a 'center' — the Counterterrorism Center (CTC). We have two other centers, Crime and Narcotics (CNC) and Counterintelligence (CIC). CNC and CTC were backwaters for years. When the FBI was about to arrest Aldrich Ames, they gave him a do-nothing job in CNC. This didn't help its already low morale."

End of communication, 007 out.

Experts: Hold CIA, FAA Accountable

Wes Vernon
Friday, October 5, 2001

WASHINGTON — A military counterterrorism expert Thursday said CIA Director George Tenet and FAA Administrator Jane Garvey are not up to their jobs in the new terrorist war, and should step down.

Speaking at a forum titled "The War We Are In" sponsored by The Committee for Western Civilization, Retired Marine Col. Ed Badolato, executive director of the Counterterrorism and Security Foundation, focused on the "homeland defense" and internal security aspects of fighting the war triggered by the terrorist attacks September 11.

He said Tom Ridge, recruited by President Bush from the governorship of Pennsylvania to head a new Cabinet position dealing with 'homeland defense," will do well in the job. He also praised Vice President Cheney, who will coordinate the upcoming battle, and other officials in key spots on the Bush team, but added he "would like to see a couple of resignations."

Currently, our leaders "have a policy, but [as yet] no strategy," he declared.

When pressed by NewsMax.com to "name names" in his call for resignations, Col. Badolato said CIA Director George Tenet and FAA Administrator Jane Garvey should step down.

Though Tenet is a Clinton holdover who appears to have ingratiated himself with President Bush, Badolato said the CIA chief carries the baggage of the failed policies of the man who originally appointed him, and appears stuck in that mindset.

He did not disagree with the assessment that Tenet is a nice man who would be a delightful dinner companion, but was not cut out for the task at hand.

At the FAA, the colonel said Garvey had done "an extremely poor job" in light of the professionals who could have been appointed, and considering the inadequate security at airports.

Dr. Stanley Bedlington, a former counterterrorism analyst for the CIA, added that the policy implemented in the mid-1990s of forbidding CIA station chiefs to hire undercover agents without "clean" human rights records was very poor judgment.

"If you go out and recruit choirboys to do undercover work, your information is going to dry up very quickly," he said.

"What's [Robert] Torricelli doing in the Senate?" asked an outraged Herbert Romerstein, a former investigator for the House Intelligence and Internal Security committees, and onetime intelligence analyst in the Reagan administration.

"You can just see a station chief saying, 'I don't want to wake up the DCI and have him tell me I can't do this. So we won't recruit these guys in the first place.'" That can cost lives, he added. He recalled that a vicious murderer had put Mafia boss John Gotti behind bars.

NewsMax.com last month detailed how the 1995 CIA "clean hands" policy in the Clinton years was the result of pressure brought to bear by conspiracy theorists of the "looney left" and left-wing activist Bianca Jagger, then Torricelli's girlfriend. The New Jersey Democrat was then a member of the House Intelligence Committee.

Bill Casey's CIA: Seek and Wreak

Phil Brennan, NewsMax.com
Saturday, October 6, 2001

Get back the hard edge. Go from defensive to offensive. In other words, the CIA should take a page from the late William J. Casey's playbook, says Herbert Meyer, a former top aide to Ronald Reagan's CIA director.

Meyer was a key lieutenant to William J. Casey during the latter's tenure as director of central intelligence. Writing in Tuesday's *Wall Street Journal*, Meyer explains that the heart of the CIA's recent failure to deal with international terrorism "lies in its very structure and design, and until that is altered the agency will never be able to pull its weight in the coming fight."

Casey, a top Wall Street lawyer with extensive contacts reaching into the highest levels of international and domestic financial affairs, got his start as an intelligence officer working under the late William J. Donovan, another Wall Street lawyer and the World War II chief of the OSS, the predecessor of the CIA as the nation's intelligence arm.

"Donovan's orders to his OSS teams were simple: Figure out precisely how our enemy works, and wreak havoc," Meyer recalls. To carry out that mandate, OSS officers, picked from the ranks of the nation's financial and social elite, used their extensive contacts among "bankers, business executives and scientists at the highest levels throughout the world — people that no regular government employees would ever have met, let alone socialized and done deals with — to whom they could turn for insight, and sometimes a quiet helping hand when they wanted something awkward to happen to someone. It was a hard-driving, hard-charging — and in some cases a hard-drinking — crowd."

At war's end and with the beginning of the Cold War, Congress created the CIA, which, unlike its predecessor, "was designed as a defensive intelligence agency."

Since the national objective at the time was to "not lose" the Cold War — "to somehow contain the Soviet Union and keep it from winning, the CIA's assignment was to 'monitor, analyze, report, and sometimes launch an operation whose purpose was to stop the Soviets from doing something.'"

President Reagan changed all that. His object was to win the Cold War — not merely to prevent the Soviet Union from being the ultimate victor. And he brought in Bill Casey to help him bring that about.

Casey, Meyer says, knew his job was to go on the offensive and fully understood that you cannot do that with an agency built for defense. "His solution was not so much to change the CIA, but to build within the CIA an 'OSS'," Meyer reveals.

Like Donavan before him, Casey looked to the corporate world, "Wall Street, academia and so forth for the kind of people he needed — people who thought fast, could spot a pattern with the fewest possible facts, get their point across to everyone else and hit the enemy hard."

His people sharpened the analysis, forced the rest of the national-security apparatus to see things before they otherwise would have been visible, and wreaked havoc among our enemies.

They smuggled weapons to freedom fighters throughout the world, smuggled bibles into the Soviet Union itself, and mined harbors in Nicaragua. They discovered how the Soviets were stealing U.S. technology and crushed their network.

They understood the connection between the two Soviet natural gas pipeline projects reaching into Western Europe and Moscow's approaching economic crisis, then gave that information to the State Department and the White House, which moved to block the pipeline project and thus dealt Moscow a crippling financial blow.

"By the time Casey collapsed at his desk in 1986, the Soviet Union was on its last legs and within five years had imploded. Although the CIA didn't win the Cold War any more than the OSS won World War II, it had much to do with the final outcome because Casey had transformed it into an effective offensive agency, rather than a defensive one," Meyer writes.

With the end of the Cold war, the CIA tried to find a new role, getting on the war on drugs and dealing with the intricacies of international terrorism, and gradually reverted to playing defense rather than offense. Meyer says that this was a natural posture, because the national leadership — read Clinton administration — "articulated no objective that required an offense."

With President Bush putting the nation on the offense in the war against terrorism, the CIA itself must revert to Casey's approach.

Two things that need to be done, according to Mayer, are an all-out assault on the source of terrorist network financing and an attack on the terrorists' communications networks, which would leave them operating in the blind.

"[O]ur financial geniuses are smarter than their financial geniuses. We need a team of the smartest, most well-connected money wizards in our country to figure out how the terrorists' finances work — and then wreak havoc. If we put our very best people to work on this, it won't be long before Osama bin Laden will have trouble paying for his lunch, let alone for complex attacks," he explains.

Moreover, the terrorist networks and the states that support them "rely heavily on computers for communication. Again, our computer geniuses — men and women who are not government employees and never would be except in wartime — are better than theirs. We need to put the best possible team together and set it to wrecking the terrorists' ability to communicate, or to communicate undetected."

" Turning the CIA into an offensive agency won't, by itself, win the war against terrorism," Meyer admits. "But it will help, and the sooner we get cracking the better."

The CIA Director Is an Egyptian

Christopher Ruddy
Thursday, October 11, 2001
I spoke by phone with a friend in Egypt.

As you know, Egypt is not fully backing the U.S. — as it has in the past.

My friend gave some excellent insight as to why not. He recounted a joke published in one of Cairo's major daily newspapers. It goes like this, one friend to another:

"Did you know that the American CIA director is actually Egyptian?"
"Egyptian?"
"Yes, Egyptian ... because he had responsibility for the disaster of September 11 and actually kept his job. *Only an Egyptian could do that!*"

Yes, in Third World countries like Egypt, America is not respected.

No doubt we lost respect as a great power because a handful of knife-wielding young men could humble us.

But that respect can only be regained if we act tough. As Reagan said time and again, we should strive to be respected, not loved.

It is difficult to demand respect around the world if we don't hold our own leaders accountable.

This failure is noted in the unusual treatment of the CIA director, George Tenet, which has generated little press ink in America but has gained the notice of ordinary people on the streets of Third World nations.

Clearly, Tenet is a responsible figure. Tenet was appointed to his post by President Clinton in July of 1997. For more than four years he has had significant time to make an imprint there — and to shape the agency in his image.

Yet Tenet's agency was not able to prevent September 11. Estimates suggest that hundreds of terrorists were part of a global network that enabled these 19 fanatics to kill thousands of Americans. The CIA found out about these plans when and where you and I did, on September 11 on television.

Since September 11, the CIA director has assumed no responsibility for the events of that day. Congress, which is charged with holding the executive branch accountable, has been strangely quiet.

The head of the House Intelligence Committee, Porter Goss, has even gone out of his way to *praise* Tenet in the aftermath of September 11.

Editorially, the press has been generally quiet in its criticism about Tenet's role. Nothing unusual here. The liberal media know Tenet is a Clinton appointee, and any criticism of him is criticism of their boy Bill Clinton.

But the Republican Congress? Even the president went out of his way to visit the CIA late last month and to praise Tenet as well.

President Bush said, "You know, George and I have been spending a lot of quality time together. There's a reason. I've got a lot of confidence in him and I've got a lot of confidence in the CIA. And so should America."

Perhaps the president knows something we don't.

I spoke to my friend Harry, a recently retired ranking CIA official, and asked him about the president's curious behavior.

He said, "Everyone wants national unity, no finger pointing. But there will be an accounting in the future. There has to be."

I'm not so sure. And holding someone accountable long after the fact defeats the main purpose of demanding accountability.

We hold people accountable to set an example for others. Accountability has to be applied in a time frame. Winners are promoted, losers are demoted or canned. Businesses that are unaccountable go bankrupt.

It's mean and tough, but that's what makes our whole political and economic system work.

Failure to apply the rule of accountability weakens the system. A system without significant accountability goes broke. I would argue that a breakdown of accountability during the '90s led to the events of September 11.

In banana republics, officials are rarely held to account. Officials keep their jobs despite their mistakes, hence the joke about Tenet being "Egyptian."

In America we are supposed to be different.

Frankly, I am not so worried about the terrorists, Osama bin Laden, or even nukes in the hands of maniacs.

I am more concerned that our system of accountability work. Because if it does not, we will not be able to prevent future 9/11s — or worse.

September 11 demonstrated a catastrophic failure of our national security agencies and their leadership.

Rightly, most Americans are not placing the blame on President Bush or his new FBI director. The Bush administration is in its infancy.

But somebody, somewhere, should be held to account.

Former President Clinton is one such person. The former FBI director is another. And, of course, the current CIA director.

Had this disaster occurred in Britain, ministers would have had to resign. If they didn't, they would have been sacked. The opposition would have demanded answers from the government — accountability in action.

But we have discovered that America has been seriously undermined in the past few decades as strange thinking has permeated our minds. Accountability has been tossed out the window.

Consider that since September 11, Congressman Gary Condit has actually been tapped by Democratic House leaders to the new and important select House Subcommittee on Homeland Security and Terrorism.

Congressman Barr has been the lone dissenter, calling the appointment a "joke."

Condit, who should have been the focus of a full-scale criminal probe for lying and misleading the police in a missing persons case, is now given an honor by his peers. Condit has even fired up his campaign to run for re-election.

Condit is not the problem, he is a symptom. So is Tenet. Some of the internal code that forms the program of American democracy is broken.

We need to fix it soon.

The stakes are high. We are at war, a war we can win if we hold to old standards and thinking that made us the great nation we are.

If we do this, we will not only beat the terrorists but also remove the chance that weapons of mass destruction will be used against us.

Rewarding CIA's Failure

John LeBoutillier
Friday, November 9, 2001

The pain of September 11 is still vivid. The anger at the terrorists and their sponsors is still white-hot. So, too, should be our disappointment and sense of betrayal at *our own intelligence community* for its massive failure to prevent those attacks.

The CIA is our lead intelligence agency and, as such, should receive the lion's share of the blame for this failure.

But in the eight weeks since September 11, there has been *virtually no blame* whatsoever. Instead, there has been:

A) A show of support by the president for CIA Director George Tenet — the lone Clinton holdover — by going out to CIA HQ in Langley, Va., and praising Tenet, a lifelong Democrat who just happened to name the CIA's main building the George H.W. Bush building in honor of the former CIA director, former president — and father of the present president. (Could this partially explain President Bush's retention of this Clintonite and former Democratic Senate staffer?)

B) An increase by the president of $1 billion to the already staggering — and secret — CIA budget, which is closer to $60 billion than the $30 billion often repeated in press accounts.

C) No talk whatsoever of congressional hearings exploring this massive intel failure. Where is the oversight? Who is checking the CIA and putting the heat on the agency to clean up its act?

Now comes one more inside-the-Beltway move that *expands* CIA's power — rather than limiting it and making it more accountable.

As *The Washington Post* wrote, "A high-level presidential commission plans to recommend that the Pentagon's three largest intelligence-collection agencies be transferred to the director of central intelligence in a major restructuring of the intelligence community, according to sources familiar with the panel's findings.

"Under the proposal, the National Reconnaissance Office, which develops, builds and manages intelligence satellite systems, the National Imagery and Mapping Agency, which handles imagery intelligence systems and mapping, and the National Security Agency, which is responsible for electronic intercepts, would each come under the control of the CIA director.

"The proposal, which will be delivered to President Bush this month, would constitute the largest overhaul of the U.S. intelligence community in decades and is aimed at helping consolidate programs and reducing rivalries within a massive intelligence-collection bureaucracy that involves 12 separate agencies."

In other words, the CIA — rather than have some of its power stripped or limited — is actually going to have even *more* power.

This is a terrible move. What should happen is something that, for a brief period in time 20 years ago, actually improved our intelligence capability.

Back in the mid-1970s there was a huge debate inside the CIA over just how large the Soviet military threat really was. Statistics, pictures, budget numbers all painted a hazy picture. CIA was not certain how large was the USSR's military capability. (We should not be surprised at CIA's ineptitude. They did not even know that the Berlin Wall was coming down until they saw it on CNN.)

Back in the mid-1970s they decided on a unique approach: Team B. CIA brought in an entirely new group of analysts and experts who looked at the very same data that the regular CIA had examined.

And guess what happened? Team B 'read' this Intel *entirely differently.* Team B saw that indeed the Soviet military was twice the strength and size that the regular CIA analysts had determined.

Of course, Team B was then disbanded.

What we need now is not a consolidation of power in one agency. Rather, we need creative cooperation and constructive competition to force out the best analysis possible.

In other words, we need a permanent Team B.

The Scowcroft recommendation is yet another move to put too much power in the very hands that have performed badly.

Why is it that in Washington you always get rewarded for your failures?

Director Tenet's Agency 'Failed'

Douglas J. Brown
Monday, February 11, 2002

In his State of the Union speech President George W. Bush stated bluntly: "As we gather tonight, our nation is at war, our economy is in recession, and the civilized world faces unprecedented dangers. Yet the state of our union has never been stronger."

When Director of Central Intelligence George Tenet appeared before the Senate Select Intelligence Committee, he forcefully asserted his right to speak directly to the American people. Addressing the senators, he stated: "You get to speak to the American people. So do I, and I think it's important that they hear us on this question."

The DCI visibly bristled at the use of the word 'failure' in reference to the U.S. intelligence community and September 11.

"It was not the result of the failure of attention and discipline and focus and consistent effort, and the American people need to understand that," the DCI argued. And he continued: "When people use the word 'failure,' failure means no focus, no attention, no discipline — and those were not present in what either we or the FBI did here and around the world. And we will continue to work at it."

Somewhat emotional and slightly incoherent (good qualities in a DCI), Mr. Tenet obviously takes offense at the suggestion that September 11 was an intelligence failure. Mr. Tenet also implied in his statements that to "paint" September 11 as a major intelligence failure would be an injustice to the "competent men and women who risk their lives and undertake heroic risks" to protect America.

Well, Mr. Director, September 11 was a *catastrophic* intelligence failure. It's a simple fact, get used to it. Just as the DCI rightfully claims that the attacks that have been prevented were major intelligence successes, September 11 was a major intelligence failure.

Furthermore, most critics who are labeling September 11 an intelligence failure are not blaming the rank-and-file members of the intelligence community. They're blaming the leadership and senior management of the community.

Is it so difficult for a director of central intelligence to understand or accept that a major defeat in a war is going to be partly due to major intelligence failure? If it is, then critics demanding a new DCI are right.

Someone unable to understand and accept reality is not going to be a good DCI, whereas someone who has simply failed is still more than capable of being a great leader, a great DCI. Dulles, Helms, Bush, Casey —

each had his failures. As Mr. Tenet suggested in his testimony, the art of intelligence work is not going to be 100 percent successful. Intelligence failures happen.

When a DCI demands his chance to speak directly to the American people, as Mr. Tenet did, he needs to be honest and straightforward in what he chooses to say to the public. Mr. Tenet wasn't.

Just as honest and straightforward as the president was, the DCI should have told the American people something to the effect: "We had a major intelligence failure. We will not always be successful, but the commitment and ability of our intelligence community has never been stronger."

While critics may argue with the latter part of the statement, at least, the DCI wouldn't have undermined the public's confidence in his ability to report simple facts either to them or to the president. He also would have avoided insulting the American public's intelligence by refusing to call the failure what it was: a failure.

CIA Still in 'Near Chaos'

Inside Cover
Sunday, March 31, 2002

NewsMax.com has previously reported that the leadership at the CIA has done little to change the P.C. culture that the Clintons created at the agency.

In the wake of 9/11, the agency's top management appears unwilling to allow operatives to do the job necessary to penetrate terrorist networks.

Recently, NewsMax.com spoke with a high-ranking CIA official who described the situation at the agency as being in a state of "near chaos."

Newsweek: CIA Could Have Caught Terrorists

PR Newswire
Monday, June 3, 2002

NEW YORK — Months before September 11, the CIA knew that two of the hijackers — men who were living in America and taking flight lessons — were al Qaeda terrorists, but Washington did nothing, according to an exclusive *Newsweek* investigation in the June 10 issue of *Newsweek*.

Investigative Correspondent Michael Isikoff and Washington Bureau Chief Daniel Klaidman reveal what some U.S. counterterrorism officials say may be the most puzzling, and devastating, intelligence failure in the critical months before September 11.

A few days after a pivotal, secret planning meeting of al Qaeda in Kuala Lumpur, Malaysia, in January 2000, *Newsweek* has learned, the CIA tracked one of the terrorists, Nawaf Alhazmi, as he flew from the meeting to Los Angeles.

Agents discovered that another of the men, Khalid Almihdhar, had already obtained a multiple-entry visa that allowed him to enter and leave the U.S. as he pleased.

Yet the CIA did nothing with this information. Agency officials didn't tell the INS, which could have turned the men away at the border, nor did they notify the FBI, which could have covertly tracked the men to find out their mission.

Instead, during the year and nine months after the CIA identified them as terrorists, Alhazmi and Almihdhar lived openly in the U.S., using their real names, obtaining driver's licenses, opening bank accounts and enrolling in flight schools — until the morning of September 11, when they walked aboard American Airlines Flight 77 and crashed it into the Pentagon.

While recent attention has been focused on the shortcomings of the FBI, all along the CIA's Counterterrorism Center — the base camp for the agency's war on bin Laden — was sitting on information that could have led federal agents right to the terrorists' doorstep, report Isikoff and Klaidman. Almihdhar and Alhazmi, parading across America in plain sight, could not have been easier to find.

Newsweek has learned that when Almihdhar's visa expired, the State Department, not knowing any better, simply issued him a new one in July 2001 — even though by then the CIA had linked him to one of the suspected bombers of the USS *Cole* in October 2000.

Lost Road Map

The two terrorists' frequent meetings with the other September 11 hijackers could have provided federal agents with a road map to the entire cast of 9/11 hijackers.

But the FBI didn't know it was supposed to be looking for them until three weeks before the strikes, when CIA Director George Tenet, worried an attack was imminent, ordered agency analysts to review the files. It was only then, on August 23, 2001, that the agency sent out an all-points bulletin, launching law enforcement agents on a frantic and futile search for the two men.

Why didn't the CIA share its information sooner? "We could have done a lot better, that's for sure," one top intelligence official told *Newsweek*.

CIA officials preparing to testify before the Senate intelligence committee this week seem at a loss to explain how this could have happened.

The CIA is usually loath to share information with other government agencies, for fear of compromising "sources and methods." CIA officials also say that at the time Almihdhar and Alhazmi entered the country, in January 2000, they hadn't yet been directly identified as bin Laden terrorists — despite their attendance at the Malaysia meeting.

"It wasn't known for sure that they were al Qaeda bad-guy operators," says one official. CIA officials also point out that the FBI agents assigned to the CIA's Counterterrorism Center were at least informed about the Malaysia meeting and of Almihdhar's and Alhazmi's participation. But FBI officials protest that they only recently learned about the most crucial piece of information: that the CIA knew Alhazmi was in the country, and that Almihdhar could enter at will.

'Unforgivable'

"That was unforgivable," said one senior FBI official. This led to a series of intense and angry encounters among U.S. officials in the weeks after September 11. Meanwhile, to bolster their case, FBI officials have now prepared a detailed chart showing how agents could have uncovered the terrorist plot if they had learned about Almihdhar and Alhazmi sooner, given their frequent contact with at least five of the other hijackers.

"There's no question we could have tied all 19 hijackers together," the official said.

The links would not have been difficult to make: Alhazmi met up with Hanjour, the Flight 77 pilot, in Phoenix in late 2000; six months later, in May 2001 the two men showed up in New Jersey and opened shared bank accounts with two other plotters, Ahmed Alghamdi and Majed Moqed. The next month, Alhazmi helped two other hijackers, Salem Alhazmi (his brother) and Abdulaziz Alomari, open their own bank accounts.

Two months after that, in August 2001, the trail would have led to the plot's ringleader, Mohamed Atta, who bought plane tickets for Moqed and Alomari.

What's more, at least several of the hijackers had traveled to Las Vegas for a meeting in summer 2001, just a few months before the attacks. "It's like three degrees of separation," insists an FBI official.

CIA Thwarted in Getting Saddam

Christopher Ruddy
Thursday, June 6, 2002
Osama bin Laden Invited to the White House!

Now, that sounds more than far-fetched. And certainly President Bush would rather see bin Laden's head on a platter than to have him as a dinner guest.

But a senior former CIA agent who served in the Middle East for almost two decades fighting terrorists thinks that bin Laden may believe that, like fellow terrorist leader Yasser Arafat, he may find himself someday the guest of a future U.S. president.

This former CIA officer, Robert Baer, recently wrote the explosive book *See No Evil: The True Story of a Ground Soldier in the CIA's War on Terrorism.*

Baer writes that when he sees Arafat "standing in the Rose Garden at the White House or when I hear that a CIA director has met privately with him at some desert tent, I wonder sometimes if Arafat's example doesn't make Osama bin Laden consider that he, too, might become a statesman in time."

Baer's point seems fantastic. However, we now know for a certainty that Arafat has masterminded and backed too many terrorist acts to count, from the Munich massacre to jet hijackings and worse.

A veteran of the Mideast, Baer knows Arafat. Baer writes that while "terrorist organizations operate like the most complicated interlocking directorate ever created," he discovered that many of the trails of these groups and their activities "converge at the feet of Yasser Arafat."

Yet today our liberal media prefer to describe Arafat as a freedom fighter. Baer's observations are deemed politically incorrect.

That may be one reason that his book, with many important revelations, with a foreword by Seymour Hersh and published by Random House, has gotten little media attention since it hit bookstores earlier this year.

Perhaps a companion book might have been titled *Speak No Evil: Why a Veteran CIA Officer Should Keep His Mouth Shut About How Bill Clinton Undermined America's National Security.*

While Baer fairly criticizes problems in the CIA and its handling of terrorism from the days of the Reagan and Bush administrations, he also clearly shows that the infrastructure of the CIA's ability to fight terrorism completely collapsed under Bill Clinton.

Here are just some of Baer's key points:

- In 1991, the CIA closed up its activities in Afghanistan and Saudi Arabia. During the Clinton years things got even worse, when CIA operatives around the globe were directed away from spying on the bad guys and told to start worrying about "human rights, economic globalization, the Arab-Israel conflict." By 1995, the Clinton administration thought spy operations were so unimportant that a CIA analyst who had never served as a spy or even overseas was made director of operations, the CIA's chief spy.

- Iran remains a major player in the terrorist world. Baer says that in 1982, Arafat "had put his entire worldwide terrorist network at Iran's disposal." Baer believes that the Iranians were clearly the culprits behind the bombings of the U.S. Embassy and Marine barracks in the early 1980s. In 1996, bin Laden formed an alliance with Iran. The purpose of the alliance was simple: Attack America.

- The Clinton White House's gross negligence and malfeasance was demonstrated by its handling of Saddam Hussein. Baer states that in 1995, top staffers at the National Security Council prevented a planned coup by Iraqi military leaders against Saddam Hussein. Baer was the top CIA man in Northern Iraq working with Iraqi dissidents.

Baer also reveals just how much the Clinton White House sought to protect Hussein.

In 1995 Baer was summoned by the CIA back from Iraq to Washington. Upon reporting to CIA headquarters, a CIA superior told him why he was called home: "Tony Lake [Bill Clinton's national security adviser] ordered the FBI to investigate you for trying to assassinate Saddam Hussein."

After months of investigation, the charges were found to be baseless and dropped.

Like many other CIA veterans who were thwarted from doing their jobs by their own government, Baer retired. Still, the CIA gave him due recognition. He was awarded its Career Intelligence Medal.

But the coddling of Hussein was not isolated to just targeting Baer and removing him from Iraq.

In fact, the Clinton White House clearly decided to keep and maintain Saddam Hussein in power. [Note: I suspected this back in 1998 and wrote about it in an article titled "Maybe Saddam Actually Likes Bill Clinton."]

In one of the most important revelations in *See No Evil*, Baer reveals that Saddam Hussein might well have been deposed by his own troops, especially if the economic sanctions had been rigorously applied.

But with U.S. complicity, Saddam Hussein was able to sell millions of barrels of Iraqi oil by shipping them overland through NATO ally Turkey.

During the mid-1990s, Baer says, the smuggled oil through Turkey "was a lifeline for Saddam, who used the money to fund his intelligence services and Special Republican Guards — the forces that kept him alive."

The pipeline of smuggled oil was no hidden, disputed fact. Baer reports the Iraqi oil trucks stretched back anywhere from 20 to 70 miles as they waited to cross into Turkey.

Baer was baffled. He writes, "What I couldn't understand was why the White House didn't intervene." He says the U.S. could easily have closed down the truck pipeline into Turkey.

"It was almost as if the White House wanted Saddam to have a little walking around money," Baer writes.

Baer concludes that the Clinton administration "helped Saddam pay for his praetorian guard, just what you'd expect of a clever superpower that was secretly supporting the local despot."

Why would Bill Clinton, our president, do such a thing? Why would he help Saddam Hussein at the very time his public rhetoric against him was so strong?

Nobody who has studied Bill Clinton should be surprised by his duplicity. The facts show, and future historians will discover, that Bill Clinton was no friend of the United States.

'Corrupt' CIA Ensures U.S. Vulnerability to Terrorism

Jessica Cantelon, CNSNews.com
Monday, July 15, 2002

CNSNews.com — The Central Intelligence Agency is "politicized" and "corrupt," the idea of a Cabinet-level Department of Homeland Security is a "ridiculous notion," and the September 11 terrorist attacks were "not an act of war" but "a terrible criminal act," according to a former CIA Soviet analyst.

Melvin Goodman, a current professor of international studies at the National War College in Washington, D.C., spoke recently at the Institute for Policy Studies (IPS) in the nation's capital.

According to Goodman, it's "unbelievable" the U.S. wasn't better prepared for 9/11, considering the "tremendous amount of information" available to intelligence agencies beforehand.

"One of the things I'm sure [Vice President Dick] Cheney is trying to put the lid on is the kinds of information we got from foreign liaisons — from foreign intelligence — the CIA had access to," Goodman said.

Part of the reason for the U.S. intelligence failures is the "pure arrogance" on the part of the Bush administration, Goodman alleged, which, combined with the "parochial view" of Americans, contributes to the "stunning contempt" many Muslims have for America.

And unless American intelligence learns how to separate "the smoke from the real signals" and recognize warnings, the country will always lack national security, he said.

The president's plan to improve the level of safety by creating a new Department of Homeland Security was also criticized by Goodman as "a Rube Goldberg scheme of putting 30 different capabilities and specialties and offices into one agency and [trying to] manage it." Rube Goldberg, the late Pulitzer Prize–winning cartoonist, increased his fame by inventing machines that "showed difficult ways to achieve easy results," according to an Internet biography of Goldberg.

According to Goodman, the Bush administration immediately misidentified the events of September 11, 2001.

"I think we got off on the wrong foot the first day ... when we called this the 'war on terrorism,'" asserted Goodman. "This was not an act of war, this was a terrible criminal act."

Goodman said he left the CIA after becoming disillusioned with the corruption at the agency. The CIA, created by President Harry Truman in 1947 and originally concerned only with intelligence, began to change for the worse, Goodman said, when covert actions were introduced in 1952.

Today, he said, the agency is too concerned with government policy.

"The CIA is not supposed to have a policy angle," Goodman said. "They shouldn't give a damn what the policy is. They shouldn't give a damn which party the president comes from."

J. Michael Waller, vice president for research and publications at the Center for Security Policy in Washington, said, "Some of [Goodman's] stuff is just off the wall, and some of it has a point."

Waller told CNSNews.com that he agrees the "state of our intelligence services is in terrible condition."

"While we have some first-rate people and unchallenged technology, the system itself is broken," Waller said.

But Goodman's criticism of the president's plan to reform the nation's security apparatus is wrong, according to Waller.

"The president's proposal is the most sensible one so far" because America is in need of "a coordinating body, and Homeland Security is meant to solve that because it takes intelligence collected by the CIA and the FBI, and it has its own analytical unit."

As for Goodman's allegation of "corruption" at the CIA and criticism of the agency's covert activities, Waller said simply: "That's crazy. And he should know better. If he was a Soviet analyst for 20 years and sees no value in covert action, then he's part of the problem."

"For a 20-year CIA veteran to say that covert action tainted the role of the intelligence services is completely nuts," Waller continued. "That's not even something to disagree on. I think that argument is just nuts."

COPYRIGHT 2002 CNSNEWS.COM ALL RIGHTS RESERVED

Chapter 4

The FBI Failed

FBI Ignored Warnings of Fanatical Student Pilot

NewsMax.com Wires
Friday, September 14, 2001

PARIS — The FBI apparently ignored warnings from French security sources that a French-Algerian with an avid interest in flight training was a known extremist linked to Osama bin Laden, France's Europe 1 radio reported today, citing French security sources.

Europe 1 reported the FBI arrested a Franco-Algerian near Boston last August after he was found with several passports. Most were false, according to the report, but one was real. The station did not identify the suspect, who reportedly is 31 years old, but he possibly had contact with the hijackers.

According to the radio, the FBI contacted French security agents. The French identified the man as a known Islamist militant belonging to an Afghan-Pakistani group affiliated with bin Laden.

"He was taking flying lessons," said Europe 1 reporter Frederic Helbert in a later interview with UPI. Helbert said he got the information from sources close to France's counterterrorism department.

"But his instructors thought there was something strange because he was asking so many questions of his instructors about the planes from the big companies, and so on," Helbert said.

The flight school — Helbert was unable to name it or locate its whereabouts in the United States — reportedly told the FBI about the man's suspicious behavior. U.S. investigators apparently found flight manuals at the man's apartment, Helbert said.

The man was jailed, Europe 1 said. But the American security "machine" failed to follow up on the case, Helbert said — at least not fast enough.

"There were no more calls, no more requests," Helbert said, citing French security sources describing the FBI's lack of follow-up.

Separately, anti-terrorism prosecutors in Paris have opened a preliminary inquiry into possible connections between Islamist extremist cells in France and Tuesday's terrorist strikes on the United States, *Le Monde* reported in its Thursday afternoon edition.

The inquiry follows a separate investigation opened in Paris Monday into "an association of wrongdoers" linked to the arrest of suspected militants in Germany last December.

France was hit in the mid-1990s by a wave of terrorist strikes by Algerian Islamist extremists, in retaliation for Paris' support of the Algerian government during that country's bitter civil war.

Some Algerian extremists appear to be narrowly focused on overthrowing the military-backed government in Algiers. But counterterrorism experts believe others are linked to shadowy international terrorist groups.

More recently, French investigators have been puzzling over the killing of a lawmaker in Beziers by Safir Bghioua, a 25-year-old man of Arab origin. Police are trying to figure out how the young man came to possess a stash of weapons, including rocket launchers. But they have reportedly found no evidence Bghioua has any links to Islamist extremists.

COPYRIGHT 2001 BY UNITED PRESS INTERNATIONAL. ALL RIGHTS RESERVED.

FBI Blocked Agents' Request to Probe Terrorist

Phil Brennan
Monday, October 8, 2001

Top officials of the FBI stopped local agents from an in-depth investigation of a suspected terrorist, now believed to have been slated to be one of the hijackers.

Had the agents been allowed to investigate the terrorist, it might have given them advance warning of the September 11 disasters in New York and Washington, *The New York Times* reported in editions over the weekend.

On August 17, FBI agents in Minneapolis arrested Zacarias Moussaoui, a French citizen, on immigration charges.

Their suspicions had been aroused when a local flight school reported that Moussaoui wanted to learn how to fly large jet aircraft, but had insisted he did not need to know how to take off or land.

Moreover, he had specifically asked for information about flying in New York air space.

After the arrest, the FBI asked both the CIA and French intelligence for any information they had on Moussaoui.

French intelligence officials reported that their anti-terrorist files showed him to be both an extremist and a man with some very suspicious connections to terrorist groups, having reportedly traveled to Afghanistan and Pakistan several times.

With Moussaoui in detention, agents asked FBI headquarters for permission to check the hard drive on his computer and to launch a full-scale criminal investigation of the man.

Superiors at the FBI's Washington office flatly turned down the agents' request. Only after the September 11 attacks did FBI headquarters finally give approval for agents to examine Moussaoui's hard drive and open up a broader inquiry.

Reportedly, the FBI discovered that that Moussaoui had compiled data on how wind patterns affect crop dusters, as well as a large amount of information on crop-dusting aircraft. That critical information led the government to ground all crop-dusting flights in the U.S.

Law enforcement sources told the *Times* that had the FBI leadership not stymied the Minneapolis probe of their local office, the information they could have unearthed, combined with other intelligence available to them, could have alerted the government to the coming disaster.

"The question being asked here is if they put two and two together, they could have gotten a lot more information about the guy — if not stopped the hijacking," one investigator told *Newsweek* magazine.

Clintonized FBI Fingers 'Right-Wing Hate Groups' in Anthrax Probe

Inside Cover
Saturday, October 27, 2001

In a move reminiscent of the botched FBI investigations of the Clinton era, the bureau is actively pursuing weak leads suggesting that "right-wing hate groups" are involved in the recent wave of anthrax attacks on the U.S.

Meanwhile, clear circumstantial evidence pointing to Saddam Hussein and Osama bin Laden appears to have been placed on the back burner.

Before the terrorist attacks of September 11, the U.S. hadn't suffered a single case of inhalation anthrax since 1976.

Still, probers continue to insist they see no connection between the events of that day and the anthrax-laden letters sent out the next week to every branch of the U.S. government, the CIA, the big three network news divisions and the headquarters of prominent newspapers from New York to Florida.

"Everything seems to lean toward a domestic source," one senior FBI official told *The Washington Post* Saturday. "Nothing seems to fit with an overseas terrorist-type operation."

For some victims, such a claim seems more than a little absurd.

Steve Coz, for instance, whose *National Enquirer* headquarters in Florida was the first to be hit with an anthrax attack, complained two weeks ago that al Qaeda terror kamikaze pilot Mohamed Atta had been spotted in a local drugstore with reddened hands — a condition he thought could be a symptom of cutaneous anthrax.

Another detail the FBI seems anxious to overlook: the widely reported visits by Atta and his co-conspirators to Florida airfields, where they inquired about renting crop dusters and the size of the chemical loads the planes could disperse.

The bureau seems none too interested in other potential evidence that could tie Atta to the anthrax assault.

"In Florida, agents haven't tested cars or residences used by some of the hijackers, including those of Mohamed Atta," reported *The Wall Street Journal* Thursday. "FBI officials said testing isn't a priority, because they assume that by now, the hijackers' cars and apartments would have been cleaned, removing any trace of anthrax."

Ken Alibek, who once headed the Soviet Union's biological weapons program, said the FBI's "assumption" is wrong. He told the *Journal* that investigators should be conducting extensive testing for anthrax traces in vehicles used by suspects and in all places that a suspect resided.

Alibek's advice notwithstanding, Special Agent Rene Salinas told the paper, "At this time, there are no plans to go back and check [Atta's car and apartment] for traces of anthrax."

The FBI's belief that so-called domestic terror groups are behind the bioterror scourge is also belied by Friday's reports that anthrax found in a letter sent to Senator Tom Daschle contained bentonite, a substance weapons experts say is Iraq's signature.

While some analysts point out that bentonite was also used in U.S. anthrax production, the *Journal* reported Friday that those stocks "were destroyed in the 1960s."

Dr. Khidhir Hamza, a former top official in Iraq's weapons of mass destruction program, also disagrees with the FBI's domestic-terrorism hunch.

"This is Iraq," Hamza told CNBC.

"This is Iraq's work. Nobody [else] has the expertise outside the U.S. and outside the major powers who work on germ warfare. Nobody has the expertise and has any motive to attack the U.S. except Saddam to do this. This is Iraq. This is Saddam."

Saturday's news that the Czech government now confirms several meetings between Atta and a top Iraqi intelligence official in Prague last June — combined with reports last week that bin Laden was able to purchase anthrax from a factory in the Czech Republic — add further legitimacy to suspicions of a foreign bioterror tie.

Still, as the evidence mounts of al Qaeda and Iraqi involvement, the FBI seems hell-bent on looking the other way.

"Ultra right-wing organizations — including a particular West Coast group — have become a key focus of the massive federal investigation into the murderous anthrax attacks," the *New York Post* reported Thursday.

"Our feeling is the anthrax does not point to an international terrorist group," an FBI source told the Post for its front-page report.

The sentiment was echoed by a *Washington Post* front-page report two days later:

"The FBI and U.S. Postal Inspection Service are considering a wide range of domestic possibilities, including associates of right-wing hate groups and U.S. residents sympathetic to the causes of Islamic extremists," reported *Post* star Bob Woodward.

What actual evidence does the FBI have of a homegrown anthrax plot?

Not much, at least if published reports are any indication.

Charges against suspected domestic bioterrorist Larry Wayne Harris, who was thought to be targeting Las Vegas with "weapons grade anthrax" earlier this year, had to be dropped after the "suspicious biological agent" he was carrying turned out to be a harmless anthrax vaccine.

At least 20 abortion clinics have been evacuated in the last three years after receiving anthrax threats — including powdered letters. All turned out to be hoaxes.

The only U.S. prosecution for domestic bioterrorism to date was for a man who had mailed out two suspicious vials along with the note "You have just been contaminated by anthrax."

Though the threat alone was a crime, the vials themselves turned out to contain nothing but tap water.

In fact, of the more than 300 homegrown anthrax scares investigated by the FBI in the last three years, all proved to be bogus — until bin Laden put the U.S. in his crosshairs on September 11.

Still, federal probers seem anxious to round up the usual suspects, no matter how unconvincing the evidence. One supposed hot lead currently being pursued: the gun show connection.

"The FBI has been making inquiries about a Nebraska man who for several years has been selling manuals at gun shows that provide information on making chemical and biological weapons," *The Wall Street Journal* reported Friday. If the FBI thinks the unidentified suspect actually possesses any anthrax, it isn't saying so.

Then there's the ever popular militia angle, which the bureau is reportedly following with little apparent reason:

"In Michigan, FBI agents have met several times since September 11 with Ann Arbor police to talk about the whereabouts and capabilities of local militiamen," the *Journal* noted.

"[There's] some concern that people in that element might see September 11 as a good way to get more notoriety and exposure," the local police chief told the paper, citing no other evidence.

Even the Southern Poverty Law Project, which monitors U.S. hate groups and is seldom reluctant to point fingers, told the *Post* they have seen no evidence of a domestic group capable of launching a sophisticated anthrax attack.

If these reports reflect the true thrust of the FBI's anthrax investigation, it's clear the bureau has yet to overcome eight years' worth of Clintonization, where the only leads pursued were the ones that supported predetermined outcomes.

In fact, the bureau's decision not to test Atta's apartment for trace anthrax seems like déjà vu all over again.

Recall the Vincent Foster death case, where FBI agents told Congress there was no need to analyze blond hairs found on Foster's body or carpet fibers on his clothing.

Or Flight TWA 800, where investigators were uninterested in talking to 300 witnesses who said they saw a missile strike the plane.

With blunders like these, it's no wonder Mideast terrorists thought they could get away with anything.

FBI Irresponsible in Ruling Out Terror in Airbus Crash

Judicial Watch
Monday, November 12, 2001

WASHINGTON — Judicial Watch, the public interest law firm that investigates and prosecutes government abuse and corruption, today watched, with horror, as yet another U.S. airliner exploded, apparently killing all passengers aboard.

Given the current state of affairs, obviously terrorism cannot be ruled out. Yet in an apparent attempt to deflect blame from its continuing dismal performance in protecting the American people, the Federal Bureau of Investigation waited no more than a half-hour before it proudly announced that "there is no evidence of terrorist activity."

"The present conduct of the FBI (which bears a large responsibility along with the previous Clinton administration for the current state of unpreparedness among government agencies to terrorist attacks) is consistent with its past 'cover your backside' government mentality," stated Judicial Watch Chairman and General Counsel Larry Klayman.

"This attitude effectively gave a green light to terrorists to attack the World Trade Center, the Pentagon and the U.S. mail system with anthrax. In short, the FBI does not want to see reality, but instead continues to paint a rosy picture of its performance.

"Judicial Watch is investigating the FBI and other government agencies, such as the Federal Aviation Administration, Immigration and Naturalization Service, Department of Justice as a whole, Department of Health and Human Services and others who have failed to do their jobs by preparing and protecting the American people from terrorism.

"Given the current reality, unless proved otherwise, government agencies should presume that this latest tragedy is the result of terrorism, and not continue to turn a blind eye from the threat that went unheeded for too long," he added.

FBI Whistle-Blower Says Bureau Bungled Terror Probes

Inside Cover
Wednesday, November 14, 2001

An FBI special agent currently assigned to the bureau's terrorism investigation has filed a complaint with the Justice Department charging that the bureau and the Justice Department have mishandled and interfered with certain aspects of the probe.

"Based on the evidence, the FBI Special Agent believes that if certain investigations had been allowed to run their courses, Osama bin Laden's network might have been prevented from committing the September 11, 2001, terrorist attacks which resulted in the deaths of nearly 5,000 innocents," announced Judicial Watch in a press release Wednesday.

The Washington, D.C.-based legal watchdog group is representing the special agent, who came forward on condition of anonymity. Also joining the case as co-counsel is former lead House impeachment prosecutor David Schippers.

Judicial Watch hasn't said which cases the FBI whistle-blower has singled out, but Justice Department critics have complained about the case of Zacarias Moussaoui, suspected to be the "20th hijacker," who was unable to join the September 11 plot because he had been jailed for violating U.S. immigration laws.

Suspicious flight instructors in Norman, Oklahoma, notified the FBI last summer after Moussaoui asked to learn how to fly a jumbo jet without any takeoff and landing instructions.

By August 28, French intelligence had informed U.S. officials that Moussaoui had ties to Osama bin Laden. But the FBI was unable to persuade the Justice Department to issue a warrant to search his computer, and Moussaoui sat in jail until September 11.

After the Twin Towers and Pentagon were attacked, the Justice Department allowed Moussaoui's computer and home to be searched. They found evidence indicating he had been studying wind dispersal patterns and crop dusters, much like 9/11 terrorist ringleader Mohamed Atta.

The FBI whistle-blower is also alleging that he has suffered on-the-job retaliation for speaking out.

Judicial Watch has asked the Justice Department to commence an independent investigation into its client's claims.

Congressman: FBI Ignored Repeated Warnings

Phil Brennan
Monday, December 24, 2001

The FBI ignored several specific and sometimes frantic warnings of a Minnesota flight instructor who told the bureau that an Arab man could be planning to use a 747 jumbo jet as a flying "bomb."

The flight instructor notified the FBI about the unusual behavior of Zacarias Moussaoui, now under federal indictment for his membership in the al Qaeda network and his alleged role in the September 11 attacks on the World Trade Center.

The flight instructor at the Pan Am International Flight Academy near Minneapolis became suspicious when Moussaoui said he wanted to learn how to fly large jet aircraft, but insisted he did not need to know how to take off or land.

In October, reports first surfaced about the flight instructor's tip-off to the bureau.

But *The New York Times* reported this weekend that the instructor's information was much more specific and serious.

Representative James L. Oberstar, D-Minn., and other officials were briefed by the flight school, and Oberstar's revelations paint a picture of the FBI's negligence.

Oberstar said he was told by officials of a Minnesota flight school that the instructor called the FBI several times "to find someone in authority who seemed willing to act on his warning that Moussaoui appeared to be involved in terrorist activity."

Oberstar said the instructor made a very blunt warning to the FBI. He quoted the instructor as telling the FBI, "Do you realize that a 747 loaded with fuel can be used as a bomb?"

He called the instructor "an American hero."

Oberstar's revelations raise new questions about why the FBI and other agencies did not act to prevent the hijackings.

The congressman's account of the incident confirmed an October 8, 2001, NewsMax.com story that despite ample indications that the man was dangerous, FBI officials in Washington ignored pleas by their agents in Minnesota for permission to check the hard drive on his computer and launch a full-scale criminal investigation of the man.

As we reported then, FBI agents on the scene asked both the CIA and French intelligence for any information they had on Moussaoui.

French intelligence officials replied that their anti-terrorist files showed him to be both an extremist and a man with highly suspicious connections to terrorist groups, having reportedly traveled to Afghanistan and Pakistan several times.

On August 17, FBI agents in Minneapolis arrested Moussaoui, a French citizen, on immigration charges.

With Moussaoui in detention, agents asked FBI headquarters for permission to check his computer's hard drive and to launch a full-scale criminal investigation.

Superiors at FBI's Washington office flatly turned down the agents' request.

Only after the September 11 attacks did FBI headquarters finally give approval for agents to examine Moussaoui's hard drive and open up a broader inquiry.

Reportedly, the FBI discovered that Moussaoui had compiled data on how wind patterns affect crop dusters, as well as a large amount of information on crop-dusting aircraft.

That was the critical information that led the government to ground all crop-dusting flights in the U.S. Law enforcement sources told the *Times* at the time that had the FBI leadership not stymied the Minneapolis probe of its local office, the information they may have unearthed, combined with other intelligence available to them, could have alerted the government to the coming disaster.

"The question being asked here is if they put two and two together, they could have gotten a lot more information about the guy — if not stopped the hijacking," one investigator told *Newsweek* magazine.

FBI Can Do Nothing About Terrorists in Our Midst

Wes Vernon, NewsMax.com
Tuesday, March 5, 2002
WASHINGTON — "Mubarak says beware of 'sleeper cells' in U.S.," proclaims the lead headline in Monday's *Washington Times*.

Terrorists in the U.S. are "waiting to strike out," Egyptian President Hosni Mubarak told the newspaper ahead of his planned visit to Washington today.

He called for "extreme vigilance and close international operation against the scourge."

There's just one problem: The FBI can do little or nothing to stop it.

Steven Emerson, in his book *American Jihad: The Terrorists Living Among* Us, says that after the Watergate scandal in the mid-1970s the Senate committee headed by the late Senator Frank Church, D-Idaho, spotlighted some abuses and then went to the other extreme. The end result was that Congress piously tied the hands of our intelligence agencies.

"I soon learned that the FBI could do little or nothing to monitor such groups," Emerson writes. The '70s restrictions "had long since prevented the FBI from performing 'blanket surveillance.' Investigations could be done on particular individuals and then only if these individuals appeared to be in the act of committing a crime." In other words, only after most, if not all, of the damage was done.

Emerson quoted former FBI official Oliver Revel as saying the FBI is forbidden even to compile newspaper or other publicly available clippings on such groups without receiving prior permission to open an "investigation."

In fact, individual FBI agents can be and have been sued for deviating from those guidelines.

Sued by the Enemy

"Even more significant," writes Emerson, an investigative reporter who quit his mainstream media job just so he could pursue information for his book, "the FBI was particularly hamstrung if these groups operated under the auspices of 'religious,' 'civic,' 'civil rights,' or 'charitable' groups. This has provided cover for recruiting and fundraising by jihad warriors in the United States."

Such designations were "more than enough to fool the public, the police, and especially naïve leaders of religious or educational institutions" who would then sponsor the organizations in the name of "multiculturalism" and "diversity."

The problem is exacerbated by the fact that even after the September 11 terrorist attacks, Transportation Secretary Norman Mineta, a Democrat leftover from Bill Clinton's Cabinet, insists that there be no ethnic profiling at airport checkpoints.

Don't Offend the Muslim Terrorists

As National Rifle Association Executive Vice President Wayne LaPierre told a C-PAC gathering last month, it's OK to take grandma's nail clippers, but we can't engage in profiling because that might offend some Islamic fanatic with a fake ID, two aliases and no job.

Nineteen out of 19 of the September 11 hijackers all fit the same profile: Young males of Middle Eastern backgrounds and half of them had the name Mohammed. Should people fitting that description be subjected to special attention?

"No, not on that basis alone," the secretary told CBS's *60 Minutes* in December.

Bear in mind that we were told last fall that federalizing airport security personnel would somehow "professionalize" them. Anyone who dared to question that was accused (in one case in a headline on the front page of *USA Today*) of blocking tightened airport security.

Emerson's book opens with a scene in which a speaker extends "greetings from the occupied land."

To the cheers of his audience, he describes in detail a series of bloody attacks in the Middle East, including "entering the building and stabbing all the people" and an instance where a suicide terrorist drove a bus off a ravine, killing 17, including one American.

"I call on my brothers to take up arms with us ... to take up arms and arms alone," he urges.

The date: 1989. The location: Kansas City.

But the FBI can't do anything about such threats. Thanks to lawmakers such as Church, and then Representative Don Edwards, D-Calif., law enforcement and intelligence agencies are stymied.

The abuses spotlighted by the Church committee provided cover for left-wingers to do what they had wanted to do for years: Put tough curbs on investigations of internal subversion.

They had always been critical of laws that cracked down on the Communist Party or other groups that advocated the violent overthrow of the U.S. government. They argued that such advocacy was protected speech, and the hysteria of the '70s gave them just the opening they were seeking.

As Emerson notes, post–September 11 America is reaping the bitter fruit of that legacy.

FBI Missed Pre–September 11 Warning

Inside Cover
Thursday, May 9, 2002

FBI chief Robert Mueller said yesterday at a Senate hearing that the bureau all but ignored a 2001 memo written by an FBI field agent in Phoenix who detected a disturbing pattern of Middle Eastern men attending American flight training schools.

The New York Times reports that the agent noted there were a disturbing number of Arab men in the schools who might be linked to terrorist groups, and he recommended a national investigation of the situation.

Mueller stated that to investigate all of the Middle Eastern men in U.S. flight schools would have been "a monumental undertaking," and that even though the memo "was received at headquarters … it was not acted on by September 11. Even if we had followed those suggestions at that time, it would not, given what we know since September 11, have enabled us to prevent the attacks of September 11."

While admitting his agency's failure, Mueller further defended the FBI by saying that the agent mentioned several students by name, but that none were found to have had any ties to the 19 hijackers, so it might not have mattered had the agency indeed investigated the individuals named.

Senator Dianne Feinstein, D-Calif., in a brilliant flash of visionary hindsight, remarked that the memorandum was "much more consequential than many of them that I read on almost a daily basis now, much fuller, much more descriptive. … It was something that perhaps should have gone right to the director of the FBI, and perhaps he should have even sent it to the president."

John Edwards, D-N.C., stated more reasonably, "The American people are entitled to know why red flags were ignored, and I think the FBI has a lot of explaining to do."

Clinton's FBI Terror Probers Were Tipped on 9/11 Hijacker

Inside Cover
Thursday, May 23, 2002

As far back as President Clinton's first term, FBI investigators were aware that a suspicious group of young Arab men — including 9/11 kamikaze hijacker Hani Hanjour — were taking flying lessons in Phoenix, Ariz., an ex-FBI informant now claims.

Still, even though Hanjour and other would-be hijackers popped up on the FBI's radar screen in 1996, crucial information that could have prevented the worst terrorist attacks in U.S. history wasn't pursued by the Clinton-era Justice Department, the 9/11 tipster charges.

Aukai Collins, a paid informant, was asked by the FBI to monitor Arab and Islamic communities in the Phoenix area, ABC News reported Thursday night.

When they contacted him in 1996, the FBI already knew that Hanjour and the others were attending flight school, the network says.

Collins contends that he began supplying investigators with additional information on Hanjour two years later, in 1998.

In his upcoming book, *My Jihad*, Collins outlines the key intelligence he says he expected the Justice Department, then under the direction of Janet Reno, to act on.

"When I said there's this short, skinny Arab guy who's part of this crowd, drives such-and-such a car, I assumed that they would then, you know, start tracing him and see who his contacts were," he told ABC News.

"They all lived in an apartment together, Hani and the others," Collins said. Among other details he shared with Clinton-era terror watchdogs: Hanjour's Phoenix home address, his phone number and even a description of the car he drove.

"They knew everything about the guy," the informant told ABC News. Still, he complained, the FBI never saw the would-be hijacker, who would later slam American Airlines Flight 77 into the Pentagon, as a threat.

The network describes Collins as "a self-styled Islamic holy warrior" who was born in the United States but eventually went to fight for Islam in Chechnya, where he lost a leg to a land mine.

FBI sources acknowledge that Collins worked for the bureau — but emphatically deny he ever provided agents with any intelligence on Hanjour.

FBI Reprimands Agents for Consulting With CIA

NewsMax.com
Friday, May 24, 2002
Agent Coleen Rowley, general counsel in the Minneapolis FBI office, was reprimanded for trying to warn of Osama bin Laden's agents and their plans to attack the U.S.

Agent Rowley believes that the FBI paid little attention to the warnings being pieced together from around the country, including the letter from a Phoenix, Arizona, FBI agent warning of a disturbing pattern emerging at U.S. flight schools.

Minnesota agents felt the growing body of evidence should have been a warning sign that triggered a full investigation of Zacarias Moussaoui, but agents were told to back off.

Frustrated, they went to the CIA for help, but the FBI, instead of working together with other agencies to protect America and its citizens, chose to reprimand the agents for 'going behind the backs of their superiors,' which is a 'breach of bureau protocol,' according to a *New York Times* report.

Memo to FBI Director Alleges Interference

NewsMax Wires
Monday, May 27, 2002

WASHINGTON — The memo to FBI Director Robert Mueller, disclosed in snippets last week, was published in its entirety by *Time* magazine's website Sunday, and it accused headquarters staff of "almost deliberately thwarting" efforts to raise an alarm about so-called 20th hijacker Zacarias Moussaoui prior to the September 11 attacks.

The memo was written by FBI veteran Coleen Rowley, the FBI's chief lawyer in Minneapolis.

While Washington officials told the Minneapolis division to hold off examining Moussaoui's laptop and pursuing possible terrorist connections, Rowley told of repeated and futile attempts to get the cooperation of headquarters.

The 13 single-spaced pages were duplicated in an edited version on Time.com and excerpted in the magazine itself, explaining in detail the way the Minneapolis FBI crew was blocked.

She wrote to Mueller that had the investigation been allowed to proceed as requested, "it's at least possible we could have gotten lucky and uncovered one or two more of the terrorists in flight training prior to September 11th, just as Moussaoui was discovered," the memo said.

FBI officials, she said, were "consistently, almost deliberately, thwarting the Minnesota FBI efforts."

The memo criticized Mueller for never publicly disclosing the Minneapolis suspicions of Moussaoui, while headquarters personnel "almost inexplicably" threw up "roadblocks" and attempted to "undermine Minneapolis'" by now desperate efforts to obtain a ... search warrant, long after the French intelligence service provided its information and probable cause became clear."

In addition, FBI supervisors were allowed to make changes in affidavits filed from Minneapolis, a practice Rowley said was "fundamentally wrong."

"We faced the sad realization that the remarks indicated someone, possibly with your approval, had decided to circle the wagons," she wrote.

Crowley aimed some of her criticism directly at Mueller, writing, "I think you have also not been completely honest about some of the true reasons for the FBI's pre–September 11th failures."

She wrote that she had never before written to an FBI director in her more than two decades as an FBI agent and asked for the protections afforded by federal "whistleblower" provisions.

"I feel that certain facts," she wrote, "have up to now been omitted, downplayed, glossed over and/or mischaracterized in an effort to avoid or minimize personal and/or institutional embarrassment on the part of the FBI."

COPYRIGHT 2002 BY UNITED PRESS INTERNATIONAL. ALL RIGHTS RESERVED.

Reno Reprimand Prompted FBI's
Caution on Moussaoui

Inside Cover
Tuesday, May 28, 2002

Misleading FBI affidavits submitted during the Clinton administration to a secret Foreign Intelligence Surveillance Court resulted in the court's sharp reprimand of Attorney General Janet Reno, in an episode that likely contributed to the FBI's later reluctance to approve a search warrant application for the laptop computer of "20th hijacker" Zacarias Moussaoui.

In the fall of 2000, the seven judges on the surveillance court ordered Reno to appear in their secure courtroom, *The New York Times* reported Monday.

"The judges, in a letter signed by Chief Judge Royce C. Lamberth, had complained to her of a serious breach. Misleading affidavits had been submitted to the court, which approves warrants to eavesdrop on people suspected of being foreign agents or international terrorists."

Attorney General Reno acknowledged to the judges that the problem was "serious," the *Times* said.

The problem affidavits had been prepared by Michael Resnick, who is described by the paper as the FBI supervisor in charge of coordinating the surveillance operations related to Hamas.

Resnick's track record with affidavits in terrorism cases was so bad that the court told Reno it would no longer accept applications for search warrants and other surveillance requests that he prepared.

The court's reprimand in the Hamas cases prompted then–FBI Director Louis Freeh to review surveillance applications for various al Qaeda suspects, where he uncovered similar problems.

As a result of the affidavit problem, Reno turned Resnick's case over to the Justice Department's Office of Professional Responsibility, short-circuiting his career at the FBI, where he had previously been described as a "rising star."

The episode prompted the bureau to adopt a "play it safe" approach when it came to seeking information on terrorists like Moussaoui, according to intelligence sources interviewed by the *Times*.

In a 13-page letter delivered last Tuesday to FBI Director Robert Mueller and the House and Senate Intelligence Committees, Minneapolis agent Coleen Rowley complained that a mid-level manager at FBI headquarters in Washington blocked her office's attempts to secure the Moussaoui search warrant.

"She said that the headquarters supervisory agent had perceived that pressing the application for the warrant was an unnecessary career risk," the *Times* reported, drawing a parallel with the Resnick case.

While Rowley has not specifically named the person who she says blocked the Moussaoui warrant, Senators Patrick Leahy, D-Vt., Charles

Grassley, R-Iowa, and Arlen Specter, R-Pa., have identified David Frasca as the bureau official responsible.

Safire Blasts FBI Director Mueller for Cover-up

Inside Cover
Tuesday, May 28, 2002

Why, asked *New York Times* columnist Bill Safire, did FBI Director Robert Mueller "desperately stamp 'classified' on last week's memo to him from the Minneapolis agent and counsel Coleen Rowley?"

In a scathing column in today's *Times*, Safire answers his own question: "Because he is protecting the bureau's crats who ignored warnings from the field before September 11, and because he is trying to cover his own posterior for misleading the public and failing to inform the president in the eight months since."

Those are serious charges, but they are backed up by the contents of Rowley's 6,000-word memo.

In that memo, Rowley, a 21-year veteran of the FBI who was stationed in Minneapolis, wrote that Mueller is flat-out wrong in his insistence that even had the bureau acted on information in the so-called Phoenix memo and the information forwarded to Washington from her field office, it could not have prevented 9/11.

She wrote that Mueller's excuse was "an apparent effort to protect the FBI from embarrassment and the relevant FBI officials from scrutiny."

In the now-celebrated Phoenix memo, the FBI's Washington headquarters was alerted by the Phoenix field office of the presence of radical Islamists attending flight schools, with the field office recommending that the bureau take a hard look at flight schools all around the nation for potential terrorists. Nothing happened as a result of that memo.

In the case of the Minneapolis field office, bureau headquarters was told that agents had arrested one Zacarias Moussaoui for overstaying his visa, and it was asked for permission to examine his laptop computer. In spite of the fact that the bureau had information from French intelligence agents that the man was involved in terrorism, the agents were refused permission to check the computer.

Had they been able to look at the laptop, they would have discovered that it contained the telephone number of 9/11 terrorist Mohamed Atta's roommate, a fact not learned until after 9/11.

In her memo, Rowley charges that "discovery of other terrorist pilots prior to September 11th may have limited the attacks and resulting loss of life" and "your statements demonstrate a rush to judgment to protect the FBI at all costs."

Wrote Safire, "This is an unprecedented indictment not only of the time-servers at Justice and FBI headquarters last summer, but also of the director who has been insisting that the bureau is blameless ever since."

He wrote that he was "struck by déjà vu in [Rowley's] account of head-quarters' dismissal of the warning from French intelligence about the suspect detained in Minneapolis."

Incredibly, Washington FBI officials told the Minneapolis field agents that "maybe it was another Zacarias Moussaoui — just as the spooks at CIA told reporters that the Arab photographed meeting an Iraqi spymaster in Prague was another man with the name of Mohamed Atta."

FBI Lawyer: Bureau Official 'Deliberately' Thwarted Investigation

Dave Eberhart
Tuesday, May 28, 2002

The now-infamous memo written by FBI veteran Coleen Rowley, the FBI's chief lawyer in the Minneapolis field office, to her boss, FBI Director Robert Mueller, reveals that bureau officials may have engaged in a massive cover-up to hide their malfeasance and negligence that apparently led to the events of September 11.

In another sensational claim, she says that a senior bureau official continued to block the investigation of an al Qaeda terrorist after his cohorts had made their attacks on the World Trade Center.

In Crowley's 13-page memo, she recounts how the Minneapolis agents became desperate to search the computer laptop that had been taken from the arrested "20th hijacker," Zacarias Moussaoui, as well as to conduct a more thorough search of his personal effects.

In her memo to Mueller, Crowley took exception to claims that the events of 9/11 could not have been prevented and that any argument they could have was a result of "20-20 hindsight" rationale.

In fact, Crowley says, on September 11, "after the first attacks on the World Trade Center had already occurred," the Minneapolis office telephoned Washington and "the FBI Supervisory Special Agent [SSA] who was the one most involved in the Moussaoui matter and who, up to that point, seemed to have been consistently, almost deliberately thwarting the Minneapolis FBI agents' efforts."

Crowley said her office was shocked when, "Even after the attacks had begun, the SSA in question was still attempting to block the search of Moussaoui's computer, characterizing the World Trade Center attacks as a mere coincidence with Minneapolis' prior suspicions about Moussaoui."

In her opinion, even well before September 11, "reasonable suspicions quickly ripened into probable cause within days of Moussaoui's arrest when the French Intelligence Service confirmed his affiliations with radical fundamentalist Islamic groups and activities connected to Osama Bin Laden. ..."

However, says Rowley, she and her field office were thwarted at every turn as they tried to deal with FBI headquarters policy, which had to approve any motion by the field agents to present to a federal judge their affidavit of probable cause to search.

Headquarters peppered the Minneapolis agents with ridiculous questions and concerns, says Rowley. "For example, at one point, the supervisory special agent at FBIHQ posited that the French information could be worthless because it only identified Zacarias Moussaoui by name and he [the SSA] didn't know how many people by that name existed in France."

Compounding the nitpicking on the warrant, Rowley notes that FBI headquarters elected to very narrowly interpret the "public safety" exception to the Miranda arrest warnings, which allows law enforcement officers to question a suspect outside normal constitutionally permitted parameters if, by doing so, potential imminent harm to others might be avoided.

On the day of the attacks, when it was clear to the Minneapolis agents that Moussaoui desperately needed to be questioned (whether he consented or not, after being advised of his right to silence, attorney, etc.) about the potentially deadly plans of fellow conspirators, headquarters did not allow the agents in the field to go near the prisoner.

An exasperated Rowley figuratively throws her hands into the air in her memo: "Apparently no government attorney believes there is a 'public safety' exception in a situation like this!"

'Hindsight Is 20-20'

That exasperation swells further when she lambastes the FBI party line that no one should be hard on the bureau because "hindsight is 20-20."

Her take on this is to explain a very fundamental fact with regard to the key search warrant, which was quashed originally — not by any judge or magistrate, but by timid folks at FBI headquarters:

"The only main difference between the information being submitted to FBIHQ from an early date, which HQ personnel continued to deem insufficient, and the actual criminal search warrant which a federal district judge signed and approved on September 11th, was the fact that, by the time the actual warrant was obtained, suspected terrorists were known to have hijacked planes which they then deliberately crashed into the World Trade Center and the Pentagon.

"To say then ... that probable cause did not exist until after the disastrous event occurred, is really to acknowledge that the missing piece of probable cause was only the FBIHQ's failure to appreciate that such an event could occur."

Denied Key Information

Another point she hammers home is that as they scrambled to collect and articulate probable cause to search the terror suspect's computer, FBI headquarters denied the Minneapolis field agents key information:

"In all of their conversations and correspondence, HQ personnel never disclosed to the Minneapolis agents that the Phoenix Division had, only approximately three weeks earlier, warned of Al Qaeda operatives in flight schools seeking flight training for terrorist purposes!"

What is her remedy to insure that such things do not happen again?

Certainly, it is not the remedy being touted by the FBI chief — more bureaucracy in the form of a "super squad."

"FBI agents, especially in terrorism cases where time is of the essence," she suggests, "should be allowed to go directly to federal judges to have their probable cause reviewed for arrests or searches without having to gain the United States Attorney's approval."

In her opinion, "the Phoenix, Minneapolis and Paris Legal Attache Offices reacted remarkably exhibiting keen perception and prioritization skills regarding the terrorist threats they uncovered or were made aware of pre–September 11th.

"The same cannot be said for the FBI Headquarters' bureaucracy, and you want to expand that! Should we put the counter-terrorism unit chief and SSA who previously handled the Moussaoui matter in charge of the new 'Super Squad'?"

One anecdote she shares with her chief in her memo concerns one of many phone calls and e-mails exchanged with headquarters:

"I took the call. I said something to the effect that, in light of what had just happened in New York, it would have to be the 'hugest coincidence' at this point if Moussaoui was not involved with the terrorists.

"The SSA [supervisory special agent] stated something to the effect that I had used the right term, 'coincidence,' and that this was probably all just a coincidence and we were to do nothing in Minneapolis until we got their [HQ's] permission because we might 'screw up. …'"

At one point in the memo she confesses to her chief that "jokes were actually made that the key FBIHQ personnel had to be spies or moles, like Robert Hanssen, who were actually working for Osama Bin Laden to have so undercut Minneapolis' effort."

FBI Ignored 1998 Warning of Arab Pilots

Inside Cover
Wednesday, May 29, 2002

Phoenix memo redux: The FBI admitted today that it ignored one of its own pilots who expressed concerns in 1998 about Arab men seeking flight training in Oklahoma.

The FBI pilot told his supervisor in Oklahoma City "that he has observed large numbers of Middle Eastern males receiving flight training at Oklahoma airports in recent months," according to the memo. The pilot warned that "this is a recent phenomenon and may be related to planned terrorist activity." He "speculates that light planes would be an ideal means of spreading chemical or biological agents."

The FBI memo, dated May 18, 1998, was marked "routine" and never forwarded to headquarters.

FBI Director Robert Mueller also disclosed a second clue today that he said might be relevant to the investigation into the September hijackings: A Middle Eastern country where U.S. shipments are restricted sought unsuccessfully before September 11 to buy a commercial flight simulator.

The FBI refused to identify the country but claimed it was not one publicly connected to September 11. It said the information came from another U.S. agency that it would not identify.

Asked whether investigators might discover more clues already in their possession hinting at suicide hijackings, Mueller said, "There may be others out there."

He expressed regret about FBI headquarters bungling a warning from its Phoenix office about the large number of Arabs seeking pilot, security and airport operations training at U.S. flight schools. He said midlevel FBI bureaucrats should have immediately given the memo to top officials.

"There were a number of things that organizationally should have happened," Mueller said.

He said he did not learn about that memo until after September 14, when he asserted at a news conference: "The fact that there were a number of individuals that happened to have received training at flight schools is news, quite obviously. If we had understood that to be the case, we would have — perhaps one could have averted this."

The Coup d'état at the FBI

Christopher Ruddy
Thursday, May 30, 2002

This week I heard author Ron Kessler say the FBI "disintegrated" under former FBI Director Louis Freeh.

I happen to agree with Kessler.

But I would like to ask, where was Kessler all these years? And the Washington press corps? And Congress?

During the '90s they mostly hid under a rock, timid to challenge the political takeover of the FBI by the Clinton White House.

Any reasonable person knows that September 11 didn't happen in a vacuum.

Current FBI Director Robert Mueller claims that nothing could have been done to prevent 9/11 and that the FBI has no culpability. He also has tried to suppress criticism of the bureau.

All of this proves that Mueller is the wrong man to head the FBI at this critical juncture. An honest person needs to take the helm and begin fixing the FBI's problems.

And the FBI's problems began when President Bill Clinton, for the first time in American history, fired the sitting FBI director, William S. Sessions.

Clinton took this act on July 19, 1993, the day before his deputy White House counsel, Vince Foster, was found dead with a gunshot wound to the head in Fort Marcy Park.

In a written statement to me soon after the death of Foster, Sessions explained the reason he was fired: He opposed the White House's politicization of the bureau.

For decades the FBI had jealously guarded its independence from the White House and political parties. But Clinton abruptly ended that independence.

Remember when the Clintons got caught illegally and improperly using the FBI to investigate their perceived enemies in the White House Travel Office, in an attempt to justify their takeover of the office staffed by career civil servants?

The Clintons had little remorse using the FBI as a weapon. As Mrs. Clinton said at the time of the Travelgate affair, if the Clinton White House was opposed, their enemies would have "hell to pay."

And such was the case of Billy Dale, the head of the White House Travel Office, who was hounded by FBI agents, indicted on trumped-up charges and then had to spend millions to defend himself. Later, a jury would take minutes after his Soviet-style trial to declare him innocent of all charges.

The Travel Office and the Vince Foster case were just the tip of the iceberg.

During the '90s the Clintons turned the FBI into a veritable Gestapo. It became their protection squad, helping them to cover up a litany of scandals and controversies: FBI Filegate, TWA 800, FBI Labgate, Ruby Ridge, Whitewater, Waco, Chinagate and a litany of smaller scandals that should have led to Clinton's removal from office.

Certainly the rank-and-file members of the FBI were never in bed with the Clintons. The field personnel, as we have witnessed with people like Gary Aldrich, Coleen Rowley, Frederic Whitehurst and Robert Wright, have demonstrated the great bravery of our G-men.

But the leadership of the FBI has indeed been corrupted.

It began with the firing of Bill Sessions and the installation of Judge Louis Freeh as Clinton's FBI director.

Freeh, a Republican, was also an ambitious yes-man who would do anything to appease his masters at the White House.

He spent eight years playing a Mutt-and-Jeff routine with the Clintons, bad-mouthing them all over town to keep credibility with the Republicans, but acquiescing to their every wish at the bureau.

Within a year of Freeh taking the helm, he had removed, fired or transferred almost the entire senior leadership of the bureau from the FBI's executive committee.

At the same time, and for the first time, he brought in political appointees to run the FBI. A veritable coup had taken place in our government. As a senior prosecutor on the staff of Kenneth Starr told me, "Control the FBI and you control the country."

The Clintons had their hatchet man at the bureau. Freeh quickly moved the FBI away from its traditional investigative law enforcement role to one that reflected the Clintons' politically correct agenda.

For example, veteran agents who were catching white-collar criminals and terrorists were transferred to the District of Columbia's police precinct to help solve murder cases. Still others were placed on cases involving carjackings.

Freeh believed that veteran FBI agents, with decades of investigative experience, were a waste. He had hundreds of the bureau's most senior agents and FBI teachers transferred from their posts back to field offices. The chain of FBI expertise handed down from one generation to the next had been broken.

All of this and more was known to those journalists who covered the FBI during the Clinton years. But no one uttered a peep.

And the destruction of the FBI was apparently mirrored by almost every other law enforcement agency in Washington.

The media can't stop slandering and bashing J. Edgar Hoover, as great an American as there ever was one, but I am still waiting to hear about what happened to the FBI under Bill Clinton and Louis Freeh.

Agent: FBI Could Have Prevented 9/11

Wes Vernon, NewsMax.com
Friday, May 31, 2002

WASHINGTON — A veteran FBI agent Thursday charged that corruption inside the bureau derailed investigations that could have averted the terrorist attacks on America on September 11. His lawyers said the FBI had evidence that the World Trade Center was a possible terrorist target.

In a memo written 91 days before September 11, Special Agent Robert G. Wright Jr. warned that Americans would die as a result of the FBI's failure to investigate terrorists living in this country.

Wright went public at a press conference even though FBI Director Robert Mueller ordered him to stay in Chicago and threatened him with criminal prosecution if he spoke publicly about the agency's wrongdoing.

"The FBI is not protecting the American people," declared Wright at a conference sponsored by his attorneys at the public interest law firm Judicial Watch.

Judicial Watch Chairman and General Counsel Larry Klayman termed Mueller's comments Wednesday, that open criticism of him and other top FBI brass was welcome, were nothing more than "politically convenient statements."

'They Got Caught'

"They said that because they got caught with their hands in the cookie jar," declared Klayman, referring to a memo written by FBI legal counsel Coleen Rowley. She alleged in a memo that the FBI could have prevented the 9/11 attacks and that Mueller, though new to the job, has covered up for senior FBI officials.

Klayman said Mueller's reorganization plan announced this week was nothing more than "icing over a stale cake."

Wright produced a sworn statement about an FBI agent who refused to record a telephone conversation during the meeting with a suspect in an FBI criminal investigation related to terrorism.

Muslim Agent 'Does Not Record Another Muslim'!

The agent in question is quoted in two sworn statements, one by Wright and the other by retired agent Barry Carmody, as refusing to record the conversation because "a Muslim does not record another Muslim."

Carmody's statement said that refusal "may have negatively impacted the conduct of the FBI's investigation. I informed FBI headquarters twice about this incident in 1998 and again in 2000, but I am aware of no disciplinary action being taken against him in this matter."

Wright, whose whistle-blowing was first reported by NewsMax.com over two months ago, urged the Bush administration and Congress to "consider removing terrorism investigative matters from the hands of the FBI. For reasons of consistency, reliability and national security, these responsibilities should be assigned to a new federal anti-terrorism agency."

The assets of the Drug Enforcement Agency could be used to fund an anti-terrorism agency, he said. "Simply switch the terrorism responsibilities of the FBI with the nation's illegal drug responsibilities."

FBI's Gross Incompetence

"Knowing what I know," Wright continued, "I can confidently say that until the investigative responsibilities for terrorism are transferred from the FBI, I will not feel safe."

The agent, stationed in Chicago and now demoted to "meaningless paper-pushing" work, according to Klayman, charged the that FBI "cannot identify and prevent acts of terrorism against the United States and its citizens at home and abroad."

Even worse, he said, there is "virtually no effort on the part of the FBI's International Terrorism Unit to neutralize known and suspected terrorists residing in the United States. Unfortunately, more terrorist attacks against the American interests, coupled with the loss of American lives, will have to occur before those in power give this matter the urgent attention it deserves."

By phone from his law office in Chicago, Wright's lead attorney, David Schippers, who represented the House Judiciary Committee in its impeachment of Bill Clinton, chided the FBI for dropping the ball in dealing with domestic and international radical Islamic "charities" that were laundering money on American soil through U.S. financial institutions and other channels.

Stopping Muslim Terrorism Isn't P.C.

Had the bureau not been cowed by "political correctness," Schippers said, the money for much terrorist activity "would have been cut off."

In his opening statement, Judicial Watch's Klayman said the FBI had threatened Wright with his job if he were to go ahead and tell his story either in media statements or in a book he has been writing.

When Wright attempted to travel to Washington on his own time during the week after September 11, to meet with members of Congress about the FBI's incompetence and dereliction of duty regarding terrorism, his attorneys were threatened by the Justice Department, which oversees the bureau.

Klayman says Attorney General John Ashcroft should be required to answer for that interference. Moreover, the FBI informed Wright that he could not travel outside the Chicago division without the express permission of the bureau.

The Judicial Watch counsel said the FBI did have intelligence about terrorist activity planned against the World Trade Center and "other monuments."

Wright listed several major failures of the FBI. They include:
- lack of high-quality managers and modern computer technology;
- failure to modernize investigative objectives to deal with the new terrorist threat;
- too many investigative violations;
- incompetent managers not held accountable for their mistakes;
- an internal affairs unit that was "bias[ed] and unfair" to whistle-blowers and others;
- criminal conflicts that have "contributed to the preventable deaths of American citizens";
- FBI duplication of the investigative jurisdictions of other federal law enforcement agencies such as the DEA and the Bureau of Alcohol, Tobacco and Firearms.

"I love America, and likewise I love the FBI, particularly its purpose and mission," Wright told reporters at the National Press Club. "However, the mission has been seriously jeopardized to the point where American lives have been needlessly lost."

At the news conference, in answer to questions from NewsMax.com, Klayman said he hoped Congress would use its subpoena powers to require Wright and responsible officials to testify.

He also told NewsMax that if the FBI tries to drive Wright out of the bureau by isolating him and passing him up for promotions, "he will be a rich man" because Judicial Watch will take necessary legal action to see that the powers that be do not get away with this familiar bureaucratic tactic of retaliation.

The Disintegration of the FBI

Phil Brennan, NewsMax.com
Friday, May 31, 2002

The destruction of the once great institution of the FBI began with the election of Bill Clinton in 1992.

During the Clinton years, the FBI became a political tool and servant of the Clinton White House.

Case in point: the Clinton Pardongate scandal. In August 2000, the Atlanta field office of the FBI sent a memo to bureau headquarters in Washington. In that memo was information supplied by an informant regarded as reliable by local FBI agents.

According to the source, arrangements were being made to have then-President Clinton pardon two international fugitives, Marc Rich and Pinky Green. The pardon, the source told agents, would be granted in the final hours of the Clinton administration. Along with that tip were "detailed allegations of financial payoffs to ensure the presidential actions," wrote investigative reporter and editor Paul Rodriguez, who broke the story in *Insight* magazine.

"At the time the FBI received this information in mid-August 2000, Rich and Green were well known to the bureau as indicted tax cheats and lavishly rich fugitives on the lam. Rich's ex-wife was a close friend of Clinton and a big-time contributor and fund-raiser for Democrats. But even to casual observers the two fugitives were not plausible candidates for presidential pardons," Rodriguez wrote.

"In Washington, the bureau simply sat on this explosive tip, which included the allegation that millions of dollars were alleged to be deposited in secret bank accounts for Clinton and others identified as involved in securing the pardons."

As NewsMax.com reported on September 5, 2001, even after the actual pardons were granted on Clinton's last day in the White House, just as the informant had reported, the FBI failed to act on the explosive report. In fact, it wasn't until March, some two months later, that the bureau admitted the existence of the memo, and then only because the courageous agent who had written the memo refused to allow its cover-up to go unchallenged.

To this day, the bureau continues to stonewall on the matter, frustrating the efforts of congressional investigators to probe the buried scandal, Rodriguez told NewsMax.com.

As shocking as it is, this was simply another instance of the bureau covering up information and activities apparently deemed damaging to President Clinton and his administration.

In case after case, the bureau's prestige as the world's most efficient crime-fighting agency was trotted out to bestow official credence to stories cooked up to justify the Clinton administration's version of controversial incidents — versions that strain the credulity of even the most naïve observer.

In the end, the bureau's prestige as a reliable investigative agency whose word could be taken as gospel truth has vanished into the same black hole into which any information inconvenient to the Clinton administration also vanished.

Here is part of the sorry record of a once valued crime-fighting agency.

The Downing of TWA 800

- The FBI wrested control of the investigation into the destruction of TWA Flight 800 on July 17, 1996, from the National Transportation Safety Board (NTSB), the agency with the authority and responsibility to assume the role of lead investigative body in the matter.

  One NTSB investigator complained that "overbearing" FBI agents "immediately took control, and hampered a lot of things we did." NTSB officials portrayed the FBI as "aggressive beyond propriety" and described an atmosphere of suspicion and distrust, believing that the FBI routinely withheld crucial information.

- As NewsMax.com reported on May 16 last year, "This failure to share information was particularly focused on the FBI laboratory in Washington, which was characterized as a "black hole."

- According to another report on NewsMax.com, New York FBI Assistant Director James Kallstrom told a high-ranking New York state official that the FBI would not find that a missile shot down the plane because the American people couldn't handle it.

- Kallstrom also noted that several shoulder missiles went missing during the Gulf War.

- The official said the FBI also put the brakes on a speedy investigation, fearing it might hurt Bill Clinton's 1996 election chances.

- Veteran naval aviator and crash investigator Commander William Donaldson said he had witnesses to a statement by George Gabriel, the senior FBI agent on Long Island and personal friend of Kallstrom, and who had closely witnessed the downing of TWA 800 from his boat, that he believed what he had observed was a missile.

- The FBI knew that a crewman on a fishing boat had dredged up an object that he later said nearly perfectly matched photos of a MAN-PAD firing mechanism agents showed him. He said he examined the object, which resembled a tin can and had wires protruding from one end. After looking at it, he threw it overboard.

- The bureau fought tooth and nail to cover up the fact that testimony given by hundreds of eyewitness all but proved that TWA 800 was downed by a missile. And many witnesses said FBI agents badgered them to change their testimony.

- When the NTSB scheduled public hearings into the crash in Baltimore for December 8, 1997, the FBI pressured the NTSB to exclude those highly credible eyewitness reports and ban their live testimony from the hearings.

- The FBI influenced the content of the NTSB hearings by pressuring the NTSB chairman to exclude any evidence of an external explosion by banning all discussion, reports, test results and eyewitnesses that supported such an event. The absence of laboratory results of explosive residues from the hearings placed total reliance on the word of an FBI crime lab with a history of inadequate scientific checks and balances.
- On July 21, 1996, a safety board report states that Assistant U.S. Attorney Valerie Caproni informed Norm Weimeyer, head of the Flight 800 probe's operations group, "that no interviews were to be conducted by the NTSB." Safety board investigators could review FBI-supplied documents on the witnesses, "provided no notes were taken and no copies were made."
- The FBI gathered and controlled those statements as part of its criminal investigation of the crash.

The Death of Vincent Foster

Then there is the matter of the death of Vincent Foster on July 20, 1993. His death was quickly ruled a suicide by U.S. Park Police and, later, the FBI and two Special Counsel reports.

But few people remember that the controversy over Foster's death began on July 19, the day before, when President Clinton abruptly fired then–FBI Director William Sessions. Sessions would later say he was fired because he tried to stop the politicization of the FBI.

Though the high-ranking death should have meant FBI involvement, the White House ordered the FBI out of the death investigation and the inquiry into what happened in Foster's White House office. Later, the FBI was used by the Independent Counsel investigations to rubber-stamp the Park Police inquiry.

After years of investigation and the altering of key forensic evidence, the FBI was able to claim that Vince Foster had driven to Fort Marcy Park and shot himself there.

Veteran homicide detective Mark Fuhrman told *Details* magazine: "If he killed himself, he didn't do it there. If he committed suicide, then someone moved him to Fort Marcy Park."

"Someone tried to stage a crime scene that is not believable in the least, and to make it work they gave it to an investigative body like the Park Police who can be ordered around and bullied," Fuhrman told *Details*.

But the facts didn't add up. As Christopher Ruddy noted in *The Strange Death of Vincent Foster*, it was difficult to believe that Foster, a man who showed no signs of depression, did not leave a suicide note; killed himself in the back of an old park (original microscopic inspection found no evidence of grass stains or dust on his shoes); shot himself with a 1913 handgun that he didn't own and that left little evidence of blood loss and no spent bullet; and managed to neatly arrange his body, with gun in hand, after he shot himself.

Also, a key eyewitness, who came on the Fort Marcy Park scene before the discovery of Foster's body, reported that Foster's car was not in the parking lot at the time. The witness would later claim that FBI agents doctored his testimony to make it less suspicious. He sued the FBI after suffering harassment before testifying at a grand jury.

Another witness, Arkansas State Trooper Larry Patterson, testified that FBI agents badgered him to change his story: that he had learned of Foster's death *before* the body was found in Fort Marcy Park.

The Waco Affair

- The standoff between the FBI and the Branch Davidian sect headed by David Koresh ended in a conflagration on April 19, 1993, that incinerated some 80 members of the group along with many of their children. A controversy still rages over the actions of FBI agents on the scene.
- There is evidence that FBI snipers fired at the compound while it was being consumed by flames. A filmmaker has videos shot at the scene that he and other experts say prove that agents were shooting into the compound. The bureau insists that what they interpret as weapons being fired into the compound is actually sunlight glinting off broken shards of glass.
- Critics insist that the FBI ignited the holocaust when it sent tanks crashing through the walls of the compound building.
- The FBI ignored some of its own people, who insisted that Koresh and his followers could be convinced to surrender, and went ahead with the assault that killed the Davidians.
- The FBI ordered the destruction of the ruins, thereby forestalling any attempts by critics to examine evidence that would have indicted the bureau for its wrongful actions at Waco.

Ruby Ridge

On August 22, 1992, on a remote ridge in northern Idaho, a week-long standoff between white separatist Randy Weaver and federal agents ended in a shootout in which an FBI sniper shot and killed Weaver's wife, Vicky. The Ruby Ridge confrontation began a week earlier, when federal marshals tried to arrest Weaver for failing to appear in court on minor weapons charges.

It was later shown that Weaver's failure to appear was the result of an error by the court. When heavily armed authorities arrived, a gun battle broke out between marshals and Weaver's 14-year-old son, resulting in the deaths of the boy and a U.S. marshal.

- The FBI was called in and a standoff developed, during which time

Weaver's wife was killed by an FBI sniper.

- In 1994, a Justice Department investigation report of the incident revealed that the FBI's Hostage Rescue Team overreacted to the threat of violence and instituted a shoot-on-sight policy that violated bureau guidelines and Fourth Amendment restrictions on police power.
- In late October, FBI Headquarters Manager E. Michael Kahoe pleaded guilty to obstruction of justice. He had shredded an internal FBI critique of the agency's disastrous 1992 siege.
- Kahoe, court papers charged, did not merely destroy all copies of a report that he himself had prepared; he also ordered a subordinate "to make it appear as if the Ruby Ridge after-action critique never existed."
- The FBI disciplined 12 agents and employees, including Larry Potts, then the head of its criminal division. Incredibly, in the face of Potts' shoddy behavior at both Ruby Ridge and Waco, Freeh named Potts deputy director of the criminal division. After a scandal erupted over the appointment, Potts was forced to retire.
- In statements given before the Senate Subcommittee on Terrorism, Technology, and Government Information, two commanders who were at Ruby Ridge fingered Potts, at the time of the siege head of the FBI's criminal division, as the man who authorized agents to shoot on sight — a practice that, according to an earlier Justice Department inquiry, "departed from the FBI's standard deadly force policy ... [and] contravened the Constitution of the United States."

Politicization of the FBI

The outright politicization of the FBI began with the firing of then–FBI director William Sessions. In a written statement to Chris Ruddy soon after the death of Vincent Foster, Sessions explained the reason he was fired: " ... at the time I left the Bureau [I stated] that I would not be part of politicizing the FBI from within or without."

Sessions was replaced by Louis Freeh, who for the next eight years danced to the tune played by Bill Clinton, using the FBI as a tool to cover up the scandals of the Clinton administration.

- The FBI turned over to Clinton gumshoes confidential bureau files on top Republicans, allegedly to be used to blackmail them. The action was illegal, but no one at the FBI was punished for breaking the law in the so-called Filegate scandal.
- Freeh allowed the FBI to investigate innocent employees of the White House Travel Office who the Clintons wanted to replace with their own cronies. The employees were terminated although no evidence of wrongdoing on their part was ever produced by the bureau.
- Billy Dale, the longtime Travel Office head, was harassed by FBI agents, indicted on phony evidence and fully exonerated by a jury that acquitted him minutes after retiring to consider its verdict.

- It was shown that the legendary FBI crime laboratory had faked evidence and otherwise mishandled it. The agent who disclosed the scandal was harshly treated by his bureau superiors.
- In 1997, when the Clinton administration came out against Americans having the right of encryption — sending e-mail by code to protect the privacy of their messages — FBI Director Freeh quickly fell into line, making speeches supporting the Clinton-Gore policy.
- Freeh opposed the whole idea that Americans should be allowed to have private conversations. He told the Senate Committee on Commerce, Science, and Transportation that encryption poses a "threat to public safety," and said he wanted to forbid the use of encryption products unless they are "socially responsible," i.e., have key escrow built into them (a key held by a third party — in this case the feds).
- Freeh asserted that there was now an "emerging opinion throughout much of the world" in favor of key escrow. Al Gore called it a "consensus." But there was no such consensus; nobody was pushing it except the Clinton administration.
- FBI misbehavior so appalled two United States senators that they introduced legislation in June 2001 to create an inspector general post to oversee the bureau.

  Responding to national concern over the lack of FBI accountability, Senators Richard J. Durbin, D-Ill., and Arlen Specter, R-Pa., charged that the FBI had mishandled evidence and misbehaved in a series of public scandals, including Ruby Ridge, Waco, spies, fabricating crime lab evidence, withholding documents and imprisoning innocent men on false charges in order to protect "sources."

  Wrote columnist Paul Craig Roberts: "These scandals have cost the FBI credibility with the public. The two senators are trying to refurbish the FBI's image with an inspector general."
- Richard Jewell, an Atlanta security guard, was suspected by the FBI of planting the bomb in Centennial Park during the 1996 Olympics. Although they had not a scintilla of evidence, FBI agents convinced themselves they had the right man.

  They persuaded a friend of his to have dinner with him while wearing a wire to record all of Jewell's private conversation. They tried to trick him into waiving his rights. And they apparently leaked their suspicions to the press, stigmatizing him brutally through public accusations and innuendoes, without ever arresting or indicting him. In the end, the bureau had to write him a letter fully exonerating him of having any connection with the bombing.
- In 1998, the FBI decided that the Atlanta bomber was one Eric Rudolph, a fugitive they conveniently haven't been able to apprehend despite years of trying, spending millions of dollars and tens of thou-

sands of man-hours, offering a million-dollar reward and harassing residents of the North Carolina mountains where Rudolph was believed to be hiding.

The changes in the bureau announced yesterday will do nothing to rid the FBI of the moral rot that exists at the top rungs of the agency. Only a thorough investigation of FBI misconduct in the above cases can identify the problems that exist in the bureau's top echelons.

The real truth about TWA 800, the death of Vince Foster, the vanishing memo about the Marc Rich pardon and the facts about Waco and Ruby Ridge must be told, no matter who gets hurt. Let the chips fall where they may.

When Director Mueller was first appointed to his job, NewsMax.com called on him in an open letter to do just that. To date he has not.

At the time, NewsMax charged that "the FBI has become an agency that views its principal function as being the guardian of the federal government. And its principal weapon in protecting the interests of the government and its top executives has been the cover-up. These are the earmarks of a police state. A police agency that allows itself to become the servant of government becomes an enemy of the public it is sworn to serve and protect."

"Whatever else is wrong with the bureau — investigative sloppiness, corruption among its top executives and agents, even betrayal of country — all of this and more is a side effect of the agency's willingness to prostitute itself to protect corrupt officials of the federal government. That's where the rot began. If you really want to reform the FBI, that's where you have to start," NewsMax editorialized.

Ditto on that request today.

Wall Street Journal: **Mueller Should Resign**

Inside Cover
Friday, May 31, 2002

The Wall Street Journal on Friday became the first major newspaper to call for the resignation of FBI Director Robert Mueller in the wake of his announced shake-up of the bureau, saying that his response to reports that his agency bungled pre–September 11 intelligence shows he "isn't willing or able to change the FBI culture."

Arguing that Mueller's plans to hire hundreds of new agents and buy new computers may look good on paper, the *Journal* complained that he had given no indication he was ready to implement the one reform the FBI desperately needs: accountability.

"If Mueller had wanted to send a message to change the FBI mindset he would have fired the supervisory special agent who ignored the Minneapolis warnings on ['20th hijacker' Zacarias] Moussaoui."

Instead, according to FBI whistle-blower Coleen Rowley, that agent was promoted.

"All of this suggests that Mr. Mueller isn't willing or able to change the FBI culture," the paper contended.

"After Waco, Ruby Ridge, the Hanssen spy case, and now September 11, the lesson is that mistakes will go unpunished or be covered up, especially if they're committed close to the top. Specifically, this goes to the heart of the credibility of Mr. Mueller."

Noting that Mueller on Wednesday dropped his previous claims that the FBI had no way of knowing that anything like September 11 was coming, the *Journal* advised that he should complete "this week's mea culpa with an honorable resignation."

Report: FBI Nixed Chance to Infiltrate al Qaeda Terror Camp

Inside Cover
Saturday, June 1, 2002

Months before the September 11 attacks, an FBI informant was invited to attend an al Qaeda terrorist training camp in Afghanistan, but bureau anti-terror probers declined to give their approval for the undercover operation because it violated FBI guidelines.

U.S. News & World Report speculates that the decision not to infiltrate the al Qaeda camp may have blown a chance to learn about Osama bin Laden's plans to attack the World Trade Center and Pentagon.

The al Qaeda invite was reportedly passed to a supervisor, who in turn forwarded it to FBI headquarters. But the bureau's bin Laden investigative unit turned thumbs down on the idea because it involved "otherwise illegal activity" — participating in terrorism — a source told the magazine.

U.S. News does not give a date for the al Qaeda training camp invite — nor does it name the location of the FBI field office that generated the intriguing lead.

When contacted by the magazine, the FBI declined to comment on the report.

On 9/11, It Was Still Freeh's FBI

Dave Eberhart, NewsMax.com
Wednesday, June 5, 2002

No matter what their politics may be, many will agree that on September 11 it was still essentially Louis Freeh's FBI.

In the aftermath of September 11, Freeh has been almost an anonymous figure as far as the media are concerned.

Still, Freeh, a former bureau agent, prosecutor and federal judge, has been the most influential FBI director since J. Edgar Hoover.

And it was Freeh who had been at the helm of the nation's premier law enforcement agency for more than eight years, compared to the mere days of tenure for newcomer Robert Mueller by September 11.

But what kind of FBI was Louis Freeh's?

What might surprise some is that — remember, this was after the first bombing of the World Trade Center — it was well-funded and clearly understood terror pre-emption as job number one.

Bill Clinton's 'Best Possible Person'

Freeh had been launched as director in 1993 as Bill Clinton's golden boy, "the best possible person to head the FBI as it faces new challenges and a new century."

Clinton critics noted at the time of Freeh's appointment that former U.S. Attorney Robert Fiske had put forth Frech's name to Clinton legal counsel Bernard Nussbaum.

That Fiske was later appointed by then–Attorney General Janet Reno as the special counsel to investigate Clinton, Nussbaum and the Clinton's Whitewater dealings made some Republicans jittery about Fiske's and Freeh's impartiality.

At the time of Freeh's 1993 installation, Clinton emphasized that the FBI "operates in a new and challenging world. Terrorism once seemed far from our shores, an atrocity visited on people in other lands. Now, after the attack on the World Trade Center, we know that we, too, are vulnerable."

Brave new beginnings for a brave new FBI, but a refrain that is now all too similar to the latest promised renaissance of the bureau.

Today, Freeh heads personnel and security for the Delaware credit card company MBNA Corp., a prosaic position for the former top G-man.

Spurned by New Jersey

Surprisingly, Freeh missed the cut to be head of New Jersey's homeland security task force, a post made all the more sensitive because of the unhappy fact that some of the 9/11 plotting and recruiting went on in the Garden State.

Despite Freeh's infamous computer illiteracy (he never used e-mail) and the introduction of an expensive but faulty computer system on his watch that contributed to the Timothy McVeigh file debacle and a one-year backup at the FBI's crime lab, the bank security executive now sings the praises of those same magic computer boxes as the key tools of the anti-terror trade.

Last month at a speech in Cleveland, for instance, Freeh chortled over the digital age, as if enthralled with a new toy. He noted with wonder that the Internet was an amazing resource for bomb recipes, some made with easily obtained ingredients.

"We know that the potential for use of these weapons is enormous," he confided.

The USA PATRIOT Act is a "mild" response to the terrorist threat, considering the country's mood, he added.

Just a month after the September 11 attacks on the WTC and the

Pentagon, Freeh lamented in a speech to security industry executives that investigators lacked the ability to decipher encrypted messages on the Internet and needed legislation to compel software companies that manufactured encryption programs to unlock the messages' secrets.

Freeh and Zacarias Moussaoui

In a choice of anecdotes now sublimely ironic because of the recent Zacarias Moussaoui laptop tale of bungled opportunities, Freeh described how Ramzi Ahmed Yousef, convicted in the 1993 bombing of the WTC, disclosed to the FBI a plot to place bombs aboard 11 U.S. air carriers flying over the Pacific Ocean, plans to assassinate the pope, and a terror attack scenario featuring poison-laced explosives planted in the WTC.

Yousef's maniacal blueprints for the attacks were on an encrypted file left behind in a computer found in a Manila apartment, the director noted, decrying the fact that it had taken agents weeks to decrypt the plan.

"We don't have a computer, nobody has a computer, that will break it down in real time," he complained.

Yet just months later, it was Freeh's FBI that balked at examining the contents of Moussaoui's laptop, that magic black box coveted by a guy who had a keen interest in learning to fly planes without the benefit of instruction in taking off and landing.

Plenty of Money

And if there was a dearth of hardware and software to swiftly crack the nettlesome Yousef code, was it for lack of funds or resources flowing to Freeh's FBI?

No, according to the agency's hefty receipt books. From 1994 to 2001, Congress increased the FBI's counterterrorism budget from $79 million to $372 million — a nearly 500 percent windfall.

And Freeh effectively lobbied for the largesse by consistently preaching about the rigors of fighting the nation's first undeclared war on terror.

"In the aftermath of the World Trade Center bombing," he testified in 1994, "the U.S. must maintain credible defenses and constant vigilance against those groups who would terrorize the citizenry of this country."

But on his watch, in 1995, a laboratory built with counterterrorism funds was being used to augment the standard forensics operation.

Funds Diverted

That same year, many of the 1,000-plus agents that the FBI hired via $83 million in counterterrorism funds were trained and put on duty as regular street agents.

Also in 1995, about half of a $5 million pot for counterterrorism intelligence analysts was moved over to a computer crime center.

Through it all, Freeh oversaw his bureau as legislation and executive proclamations moved it ostensibly to center stage, where it was to serve as the salient tool to foil domestic terrorist attacks.

And to some extent that evolution brought forth worthy developments, perhaps the most noteworthy being the establishment of legal-attaché offices in 44 countries.

To this day, these well-conceived mini-bureaus garner valuable intelligence for FBI analysts and maintain liaisons with foreign law enforcement agencies.

Glorified Secretaries

Unfortunately, in Freeh's FBI too many of those analysts were glorified secretaries, according to former FBI agent and 30-year veteran I.C. Smith.

"They were paid as intelligence analysts," he notes, "but many times their actual function was more clerical in nature."

Also on the good side, Freeh established "joint terrorism task forces" designed to bond the famously insular FBI with state and local police and local prosecutors.

But Freeh critics are quick to point out that old bureau habits died hard. While laboring with the Department of Justice to frame a five-year national counterterrorism plan, drafters managed to exclude any role for state and local governments.

By the beginning of the end of the Freeh directorship, despite all the money and good intentions, the bureau's inertia as a Hooveresque cops-and-robbers institution prevailed.

In 1999, Freeh gamely admitted that his intelligence analysis capabilities were "deficient."

And the rest is history.

FBI Whistle-Blower Rowley Slams 'Ever-Growing Bureaucracy'

NewsMax.com Wires
Friday, June 7, 2002
WASHINGTON — An "ever-growing bureaucracy" at FBI headquarters hurts the ability of field agents to investigate terrorism, a whistle-blowing agent told a Senate panel Thursday.

Special Agent Coleen Rowley said these "roadblocks" contributed to her feeling that the FBI could have done more to prevent the September 11 terror attacks.

"Mistakes are inevitable," Rowley told the Senate Judiciary Committee. "But a distinction can and should be drawn between those mistakes made when trying to do the right thing and those mistakes made due to selfish motives."

Rowley, general counsel of the Minneapolis field office, became a key actor in the post–September 11 dramas when she accused the bureau's leadership of misleading the public about what could have been done to prevent the terror attacks on New York and the Pentagon.

"I feel that certain facts have, up to now, been omitted, downplayed, glossed over and/or mischaracterized in an effort to avoid or minimize personal and/or institutional embarrassment on the part of the FBI and/or perhaps even for improper political reasons," her memo says.

Rowley says that interference from headquarters frustrated the Minneapolis field office's investigation into possible terrorist connections of Zacarias Moussaoui, arrested almost a month before the attacks, and prevented the agents from searching his possessions.

"Some of the entities don't see their job as assisting the agents in the field, but see their jobs as a gatekeeper function, or a power thing," she said. "There are limits installed by managers, but the worst problem is micromanagement."

'Foolish, Endless Reports'

Much of the field agent's time is spent on "Paperwork. Writing foolish, endless reports."

FBI Director Robert Mueller had previously told the panel that the war on terrorism poses new challenges for federal law enforcement that require the FBI to change its structure, a need highlighted by the agency's failure to prevent the September 11 terror attacks.

COPYRIGHT 2002 BY UNITED PRESS INTERNATIONAL. ALL RIGHTS RESERVED.

Aldrich: Media Conceal Freeh's FBI Failures

Wes Vernon, NewsMax.com
Friday, July 12, 2002

WASHINGTON — Gary Aldrich, who blew the whistle on shocking security breakdowns in the Clinton White House, says the media are covering up former FBI Director Louis Freeh's role in the intelligence meltdown during the Clinton years.

He also warns that past FBI abuses from that era should serve as a caution signal regarding a willingness in some quarters to sacrifice liberty in the name of security.

In all of the uproar over who knew what and who fell down on the job before September 11, Freeh's name is rarely mentioned, even though he was the top cop during that entire period, until just shortly before the terrorist attacks on America last fall.

"I don't see any efforts at all to hold Louis Freeh accountable," Aldrich told NewsMax.com after a speech sponsored by Accuracy In Media.

He noted that security-minded writers and leaders were making the case for the ouster of Clinton holdover George Tenet as CIA director. But hardly any word about Freeh has turned up in any media discussion of the intelligence failures before 9/11.

There's "a deeper story here" with respect to the FBI "that people just won't talk about in this town," Aldrich said. "And that is the misuse of the FBI resources during the Clinton administration."

Pursuing Abortion Foes and Movers of Dirt

FBI agents' activities were micromanaged by Clinton's attorney general, Janet Reno, the FBI whistle-blower charged. They were told to "investigate such amazingly violent groups as abortion clinic protesters or to have FBI agents going around with camera equipment photographing piles of dirt that had been moved from point A on somebody's property to point B because this was a major EPA violation."

Continuing to add up this Clinton-Reno misuse of the FBI, with no apparent protest from then-Director Freeh, Aldrich ridiculed the pattern of "getting agents involved in this organized crime we call deadbeat dads."

"You realize there's an organized group of dads around this country who are running this cartel designed only for the purpose of avoiding child support payments. Did you know that?" he mockingly asked.

"We've had FBI agents chasing these guys all over the country. Of course, the guys we're talking about here were on the back of garbage trucks or in the lawn care business, where they get paid [under the table] cash and are going city to city, as transients always do."

It is this kind of "nonsense that went on during Louis Freeh's watch," charged Aldrich, whose book *Unlimited Access* blew the lid off the entire lackadaisical approach to White House security under Clinton.

"You people," he said, addressing his audience of conservative activists, "you people were the people that the Clinton administration wanted to look into to see if you had some plan to drive a truck up to the White House."

What's Bad for Slick Willie Is Bad for America

In a demonstration of what he called "very self-serving paranoia," Aldrich alleged that "the Clinton administration decided that anything that was negative to the Clinton administration was a threat to national security."

"Watch out for that in the current administration," he added. "Watch out for them using that rationalization to do what they do" in the post–September 11 environment, "because mere protest by citizens is as American as apple pie."

The veteran FBI agent faults the Bush administration for getting "poor political advice" to avoid raising issues concerning the damage the Clinton people did, because "there are some matters and principles that should not be ignored," among them, the previous administration's abuse of power, such as nearly 1,000 FBI files being given over to a political party for partisan purposes.

It is the Clinton-Reno-Freeh era of abuses that causes Aldrich to view with skepticism part of the Bush-Ashcroft plans for expansion of government power in the wake of 9/11. Many of the problems those proposals attempt to remedy could better be dealt with by applying laws already on the books, he believes.

"We have law on law on layer on layer," he said in answer to a questioner who stated that he was more concerned right now with whether he and his family would just survive the war on terror than with concerns about abuse of power.

Aldrich responded that laws already on the books are not being adequately enforced in the fight against terrorists. Nor, he said, is it necessary to add a lot of legislation to deal with corporate corruption.

'Take More of Your Liberty'

We have laws "where any one of those executives can be prosecuted and put away for 20 years," he said. But in fighting terrorists, instead of going after those who pose a danger to us, too many are ready to say, "Let's go over here and take more of your liberty."

He cited the GOP congressional primary in Georgia as a classic case of the split between privacy-minded and security-oriented conservatives. Aldrich strongly backed Representative Bob Barr, who has been redistricted into a race with fellow incumbent John Linder, whom the whistle-blower described as "a fine man," but one with less emphasis on the crucial privacy issues than is evident with Congressman Barr.

In cover-ups and bias, former Clinton aide George Stephanopoulos is "a classic case of what we're talking about" and "doesn't even bother to try to hide his politics" in his broadcasts with ABC News, as Aldrich sees it. He recalled that from the time Clinton began his quest for the White House, Stephanopoulos and "Ragin' Cajun" James Carville "set up a group to do nothing but spin the truth and hide the truth and lie."

ABC's 'Professional Liar'

Prior to the election, as well as after he went to the White House, Stephanopoulos was "a professional liar," declared the FBI whistle-blower, whose appearance on ABC's *This Week* after his book's publication in 1996 was allowed over the former Clinton aide's protest. And when Aldrich did appear, Stephanopoulos put up his colleagues to blindside the author with accusatory questions that attempted to discredit him.

Stephanopoulos is "as good an example as any" of what is wrong with the media today, the former FBI man and current think tank (Patrick Henry Center) executive said.

And yes, he added, you could say he is a living metaphor for the media's refusal to hold Louis Freeh accountable for what went on at the FBI on his watch.

Congress Fears Blackmail by FBI

John O. Edwards
NewsMax.com *magazine, August 2002*
The crisis America finds itself in can be explained by the bombshell revela

tion made this week to *The New York Times* by a senior aide to Senator Charles Grassley.

Kris Kolesnik, Grassley's chief investigator for almost two decades, explained why only two senators out of 535 congressmen and senators in Congress have criticized the FBI.

As Kolesnik put it, "they think the FBI will find dirt on them, and it will wind up in the public domain."

Perhaps these timid members of Congress are thinking of Congressman Jim Traficant. He was perhaps the most vociferous critic of the FBI, and he's now heading for jail.

For many of us who believe September 11 did not take place in a vacuum but was caused by years of abuses at the FBI, CIA and other agencies where no accountability was demanded of them, Kolesnik's comments only buttress our fears.

Those comments are quite significant.

Though his view that the FBI blackmails top lawmakers is widely held, it is the first time such sentiments have made it into the major press. (Remember, according to the liberal media, nasty government abuses are supposed to have taken place only under J. Edgar Hoover or during the Nixon administration.)

The Kolesnik revelation also means that the key branch of government — the one that most directly represents the people of this great country — has been held hostage by the nation's law enforcement agencies.

This also explains how President Bill Clinton could receive $10 million in illegal campaign cash from the Chinese and then transfer America's most guarded nuclear and ballistic missile secrets to them — with practically no complaint from Congress.

Now our adversary China has the design of every nuclear weapon in our arsenal, as well as the missiles capable of hitting our cities with pinpoint accuracy.

Before Clinton, China was lucky if it could get a missile off the ground without having it explode on the launch pad.

As egregious as Clinton's treason was, Chinagate was just the tip of the iceberg.

But Congress was silent about most of the Clinton abuses, and scattered criticism was always extinguished in short order. Perhaps the FBI had a role in that.

We know that after September 11 — the most catastrophic failure of intelligence by the FBI and CIA in our history — for months practically no one in Congress had any criticism of either agency.

In the days after September 11, some in Congress, including Congressman Porter Goss and archconservatives like Congressman Ron Paul were falling over themselves to actually praise the CIA Director. It was an amazing sight.

It took some five months for the CIA director even to be summoned before Congress to testify. And when he did, many of the senators questioning him spent most of the time kissing ass.

Since then, two senators have been critical of the FBI and CIA. Senator Richard Shelby has called for CIA Director Tenet to resign. Senator Grassley has been critical of the bureau.

But frankly, even their criticism has been late and tepid. And beyond them in Congress, there is just an abyss. No one wants to utter a peep.

This is why America has entered the danger zone that began with the events of September 11.

During the '90s our system of checks and balances — the ideal of accountability — was subverted by the Clintons.

Despite seeing the results of that on September 11, no one on Capitol Hill really wants to fix the problem. What does all this mean for the future?

Chapter 5

The Media Spin

Vile Media Make Snide Remarks About Bush

Inside Cover
Wednesday, September 12, 2001

Now more than ever, Americans need to support our president.

The big media apparently don't think they are U.S. citizens.

Mancow, the major morning drive-time host in Chicago, expressed outrage this morning on his show about Peter Jennings' comments on ABC.

Mancow noted to his audience Jennings' outrageous introduction of the president just before he addressed the nation in the middle of this emergency.

Mancow paraphrased Jennings as saying that "some presidents are articulate and some are not."

A NewsMax reader was similarly shocked and e-mailed us about CBS anchorman Dan Rather's introduction yesterday to President Bush's speech.

The reader quoted Rather as introducing Bush by saying, "No matter how you feel about him, he is still our president."

And NBC's Tom Brokaw has already started the media's blame game, blaming — guess who — George Bush!

A NewsMax reader watched Tom Brokaw interview General Schwarzkopf.

The reader paraphrased Brokaw's question:

"We don't want to blame anyone, but do you think the Bush administration was negligent in not getting actively involved in the Mideast peace process while all the violence was going on?"

Our reader said he was "outraged that NBC would even consider such a statement let alone broadcast it!"

Other NBC talking heads have made comments about Bush's lack of eloquence.

NBC's Campbell Brown just this morning broadcast in front of the White House and said people had complained about the president's lack of confidence when he spoke. She went on at length, saying that people hoped the president could give us a sense of confidence. She did not say Bush was giving Americans confidence.

Excuse us, Campbell. The president *has* been eloquent. He *has* been confident.

Real Americans support him 100 percent.

We are not so sure why the networks are spending time to analyze and criticize the president's speaking skills during a national emergency.

One thing for sure, Americans are fed up with the communication skills of elitists such as Jennings, Rather, and you, Campbell!

Stand for America, Stand With Bush!

Christopher Ruddy
Wednesday, September 12, 2001

I am as outraged by the American media elitists — supposedly on our side — as I am by our enemies.

NewsMax has been reporting on the snide, undermining and absolutely unpatriotic comments being made by the major media as the country faces one of its worst crises ever — with even greater potential dangers looming over the horizon.

How dare Tom Brokaw suggest that President Bush might have been "negligent" for not having been more involved in the Mideast peace crisis, as he did while interviewing General Schwarzkopf today.

A NewsMax reader said Brokaw's comments were very similar to ones made earlier in the day by NBC "foreign policy expert" Katie Couric, also complaining about the administration's handling of the peace process.

Another reader was similarly shocked watching NBC yesterday when correspondent Andrea Mitchell, the wife of Alan Greenspan, made "the snide comment that a president must not only be the 'Commander-in-Chief,' but also a 'Comforter-in-Chief.' "

Apparently, Mitchell then went on to say that she "questioned whether an inarticulate president" could accomplish this.

Mitchell "then praised Clinton for his comforting presence during the Oklahoma City bombing."

The reader expressed my sentiment: "That lady Mitchell is a disgrace."

And so are the other damn elitists running these big networks.

And let's remember that the big media — already making overt complaints that Bush didn't land Air Force One back in Washington immediately — can't let one complaint about Bill Clinton's culpability in this affair on the air.

Americans are not stupid. We know it was Clinton who left America weak and vulnerable to this attack — and perhaps worse.

Today the NPR crowd has led an orchestrated e-mail campaign against NewsMax, furious with my "Blame Clinton" article.

These phonies are feigning "shock" that I would criticize the man they supported as he worked to bring down America.

Reminding me that patriotism is the last refuge of a scoundrel, these complainers have claimed that I am un-American to reveal Clinton's responsibility. Instead, they say, we should "unite" the country and not "point fingers."

But let's take a step back and recall how Clinton and the media handled themselves in the immediate aftermath of the Oklahoma City bombing in 1994.

Rather than "comforting" the nation, I recollect how Clinton went on national TV, wagging his finger and lashing out at his political opponents for having caused this terrible bombing.

All the networks joined Clinton, along with the major paper — right in the middle of that terrible tragedy — blaming conservative Republicans, "Clinton-haters," talk radio, Rush Limbaugh, Jerry Falwell, the Internet — and anyone else who ever made a legitimate criticism of Bill Clinton.

Now when we have a real enemy, not just some nutcase, drug-using bomber such as Timothy McVeigh, the media don't want us to ask who led us to this situation.

They won't air any criticism of Bill Clinton, who is clearly responsible for the state of America's military and national security apparatus — we can't say a word.

It's clear the media are anxious to undermine Bush, to blame Bush, to hurt Bush.

They don't want Americans to recognize Clinton's role and the media's own complicity in giving him a free ride as he undermined America's national security.

We know better. That's why we will stand firmly with President Bush and for our country.

Newsweek, ABC, Newsday, Dowd Join Media's Anti-Bush Assault

Inside Cover
Thursday, September 13, 2001

The leftist media's shocking anti-Bush hatred in the face of national tragedy continues to grow.

Newsweek's Howard Fineman joined the media's pack mentality (i.e., lack of original thought) by moaning about Bush's flight on Air Force One. Of course, if Bush had immediately returned to Washington these same elitists would have complained about how he endangered himself.

Fineman, apparently referring to himself and his ilk, describes "a nation that harbors doubts about the president's ability." He pouts that "Bush has yet to find a note of eloquence in his own voice" and judges that the president "did not look larger than life at his Oval Office desk, or even particularly comfortable."

Then, referring to Al Gore's failure to steal the White House despite widespread nationwide Democrat vote fraud, Fineman continues to hammer at Bush:

"The tasks he faces now were made harder by the way in which he entered office, and by how he has conducted himself there so far. He got 500,000 votes fewer than his foe and needed a 5-4 U.S. Supreme Court ruling to seal the deal. As president he has avoided the bully pulpit; now he has to build one and speak from it at the same time. Leaders in Congress who know him like him, but some still quietly disparaged his ability even as they marveled at what, until that day, was his enviable string of good luck. 'Now he looks like a luxury we can't afford,' said one Democrat and likely 2004 rival.

"Nor has Bush built a consensus behind a foreign policy to justify the war he is about to make. To the contrary: the president, as some critics see it, has pursued a pull-up-the-drawbridges mentality that has only made matters worse. 'Our foreign policy for the past year has been too unilateral,' " Fineman quotes some Democrat senator as saying.

Anyone so unfortunate as to have *Newsweek*'s poison delivered to his home ought to cancel his subscription immediately — and say why he is canceling.

Then there's Ellis Henican, a Clinton idolater employed by the liberal Long Island newspaper *Newsday*.

"Mostly, George W. Bush has been keeping his head down, staying out of harm's way. He certainly hasn't shown his face around here.

"And really, isn't it about time? It's been two full days now since the first hijacked airplane slammed into the first twin tower, the start of the bloodiest terror attack in history. But since that very moment, the leader of the world's one superpower has been — where?

"Lingering for hours in the clouds. Nervously hopscotching across the country. From Florida to Louisiana to Nebraska. Unsure what direction to fly, while his aides bickered about where the president should land.

"And that first stilted statement from the president was released on videotape.

"Was Bush that frightened he'd flub the 'prompter read?

"Do we have a president too nervous to work live?"

And the hatred drones on and on.

Maureen Dowd, a fellow traveler at *The New York Times*, also wondered why Bush didn't make himself a target for terrorists. She and her like seem to think it's more important that they — and terrorists — know where the president is at all times.

"For much of the day we weren't sure where the president was. There were statements floating in from him from various secure zones in the air or underground. The vice president was out of sight. We didn't know where the first lady was. The secretary of state was in the air somewhere. The Capitol had been evacuated. Congressional leaders had gone off to a bunker somewhere. The Joint Chiefs of Staff could not be immediately accounted for," Dowd whined.

Maureen, take a Valium. Or two, or three, or 50.

Mark Halperin, in an "analysis" for ABC headlined "Bush Free Ride Won't Last," could think only of himself and his fellow media elites just one day after the bombings.

"Many senior officials in this administration have records suggesting they don't believe the press ought to be able to run terribly free during times of war," he cried.

"It's always hard and often tactless to question government statements during war, particularly while a war like this one commands significant public support. But this White House is secretive about the most routine of operations, thin-skinned about criticism and appeals for openness, and especially quick to assert the prerogatives of the executive branch.

"Neither the congressional opposition nor the press is likely — nor should they be expected — to show such deference for long."

Traitorous Media Work Leftist Agenda

Dan Frisa
Thursday, September 13, 2001

Even now, in the midst of the most vicious and horrific attack on Americans on American soil, the leftist media have shown themselves not only incapable of supporting the nation, but also capable of actually undermining the president, with *relish.*

The despicable traitors have made it their mission to undercut the authority of President Bush during America's darkest hour, proving themselves even more cowardly than the terrorist murderers who are the only beneficiaries of such contemptible conduct.

This morning's lead editorial in *The New York Times* is so replete with snide and cynical affect that it is tantamount to a declaration of support for those who murdered tens of thousands innocent Americans.

They slammed the president as they opined, "The administration spent much of yesterday trying to overcome the impression that Mr. Bush showed weakness when he did not immediately return to Washington."

Yeah, the very "impression" they and their leftist media comrades created all day Tuesday and Wednesday because they longed so much for their panty-waisted, lip-biting, teary-eyed hero — the very gutless wonder who lacked the ability and fortitude to destroy terrorist kingpin Osama bin Laden following other provocations, not the least of which was the assault on the USS *Cole.*

"The disturbing part of the administration's performance," they whined, "was the refusal of the president or any member of his cabinet to field questions. ..."

What? Field questions?

These ivory-tower juveniles are nothing more than spoiled brats and mindless, impatient fools. The time to provide information is when the very government under attack decides it is wisest to do so, and not a moment before. They tout the fact that the mayor and governor of New York did so and that it was so "reassuring" to see, even when they had no information to report.

Are we missing something?

The mayor and governor were involved solely with the rescue and recovery operations on the ground, and did perform a great service in *that* regard. There is, however, no comparison with the vastly different demands on the commander in chief during such a crisis. His responsibility is first and foremost to ensure the very stability of the national government as well as its successful conduct.

The president did his job, and it's reassuring that he did. There will be an appropriate time to answer questions, the important as well as the inane.

The *Times* further bashed the president by stating, "He must also show that he knows what he is doing. Mr. Bush came to the White House with as little preparation in international affairs as any modern president."

This is factually untrue. President Bush served as a close adviser to his father and was privy to the important decisions and the process of forging the allied coalition before and during the Gulf War. Compare that to Clinton's "expertise" in foreign affairs derived through protesting against the U.S. while in England and by "visiting" the Soviet Union, our Cold War enemy.

This same treasonous song is, of course, being sung by other leftist media egotists such as Canadian Peter Jennings, Democrat Dan Rather, society boy Tom Brokaw, sniveling Howard Fineman of *Newsweek*, pedantic Brian Williams of MSNBC and too-cute-by-half Katie Couric, among dozens of others.

They should be ashamed of themselves and would be well advised to drop their dangerous game of attacking the president when America itself is under attack.

They likely won't relent, as their misguided self-importance demands that their false and deadly carping continue, even if it provides more support to America's enemies.

This is war and such traitorous behavior is unacceptable.

Washington Post, Jennings, ABC Step Up Attack on President Bush

Wes Vernon
Thursday, September 13, 2001
WASHINGTON — Major media, including Peter Jennings' ABC News and *The Washington Post*, have launched a full-scale spin war against President Bush.

Already, liberal media outlets have been raising questions about the president taking a circuitous route back to Washington from Florida after being informed of Tuesday's terrorism.

The most direct salvo came from longtime liberal columnist Mary McGrory in today's *Washington Post*.

Building up to her attack on the president, McGrory praised New York Mayor Rudy Giuliani, Defense Secretary Donald Rumsfeld and British Prime Minister Tony Blair.

After noting that President Bush had not reiterated Giuliani's call for "tolerance for people who come from countries who are suspected of plotting the carnage" (a sentiment that has since been expressed by the administration through Bush and Attorney General John Ashcroft), the columnist went on to say the president "could not find the beat."

"He allowed himself to be hauled about the country like a fugitive to bunkers at Air Force bases in Louisiana and Nebraska."

She added that his security would want to protect him, but that the president "might have reflected that if Washington wasn't safe for him, it wasn't safe for the rest of us."

The columnist did not mention information from the White House since then that the president did in fact reject security recommendations that he not return to Washington at all the day of the terrorist attack.

As a predictable liberal opinion journalist, McGrory might be expected to fire away at President Bush as the country rallies around him. One might not be surprised that she would fail to mention that, at the time, there was good information that Air Force One was a target of the terrorists — "the rest of us" were not so precisely targeted — and that some unannounced detours might be logical to a Secret Service whose number one job is to protect the president. As has been said, you have to "consider the source."

But what to make of an exchange on ABC-TV between correspondent Claire Shipman and anchorman Peter Jennings?

In a transcript provided to NewsMax.com by the Media Research Center, Shipman (at approximately 9:40 a.m. Wednesday) said:

"Some people on Capitol Hill [she doesn't name them] and in the security community are wondering about why the White House was so quick and so open with the information today that the white House itself and Air Force One may have been a target. Not that they're suggesting that information is wrong, but there is a thinking among some [again, not named] that the White House was eager to put that information out in order to make it plain that President Bush had to spend his day yesterday flying around the country instead of coming straight back to Washington, that there may have been some politics involved in that decision..."

Anonymous sources conveying valuable information are a staple of good journalism. Anonymous sources firing cheap political shots, especially in a time of crisis, are usually regarded with a healthy dose of skepticism. Cheap political shots in an emergency situation could backfire on anyone identifying himself.

Jennings, a Canadian, noted that "we're all pretty skeptical and cynical about Washington" and that, of course, Shipman was not expected to reveal her sources. But the TV anchor asked if the correspondent was saying "people in the political establishment are saying what we're getting is a story from the White House today to explain why the president was traveling from Florida to Louisiana yesterday, under what we thought at the time was the pressure of his security detail."

Shipman's reply was that, again, "nobody is saying that what the White House and also the attorney general has said is not accurate — it looks plain from a number of sources that there may have been a plane aimed at the White House. People are just wondering" about why the information was put out so quickly and whether it is "something the white House is eager, obviously, to make plain."

"Nobody is saying" it, but by bringing up anonymous quotes implying it, the seed is planted. Even in time of crisis when Americans are rallying around the president of the United States, cheap-shot politics seems to live on in some quarters.

As is so often the case, an antidote to that comes from talk radio. On his show Thursday, Rush Limbaugh commented on those who sniped that President Bush's speech was not long enough. Those who voice that criticism, he noted, overlook the fact that any president, in order to make a long speech, would have to have the required "level of knowledge" justifying length, something then still being gathered.

"In the midst of a situation like this, we expect a man with a series of words to be able to somehow alleviate, or solve, or something short of that, the situation. That's not reality," declared the popular radio talkmeister.

"But these network anchors seem to desire somebody on television uttering words that have a calming influence and so forth, and that somehow solves the situation, or at least goes in the direction of solving it. It's totally unrealistic."

Jennings Still Calls Clinton 'President'

Inside Cover
Friday, September 14, 2001

Peter Jennings just can't hide his sneering disdain for President Bush — even in the midst of one of the worst catastrophes ever to befall America.

We note that during the National Prayer Service, Jennings referred to Clinton as "President Clinton."

When he observed President Bush's father, Gerald Ford and Jimmy Carter, he referred to them correctly as "former presidents."

A NewsMax reader also caught Jennings' Freudian slip and wrote:

"When will they learn that this nation's rightfully elected leader is

President George W. Bush?! I think Peter Jennings needs to find a new job where his left-wing views are needed. How about Afghanistan?"

L.A. *Times* Compares President to 'Little Boy'

Inside Cover
Friday, September 14, 2001

Readers have flooded NewsMax with reports of the left-wing media's sickening anti-Bush hatred during this national catastrophe.

From the notoriously leftist *Los Angeles Times*, TV critic Howard Rosenberg, who apparently has been watching television on some other planet this week, whined that "Bush has lacked size in front of the camera when he should have been commanding and filling the screen with a formidable presence as the leader of a nation standing tall under extreme duress."

"Even his body language is troubling, as when TV cameras captured him returning to the White House late Tuesday after being shuttled about on Air Force One after an alert that the presidential residence and plane also had been possible targets of that day's terrorism. The Bush we saw [who is this royal "we," Howie?], walking alone, appeared almost to be slinking guiltily across the lawn.

"Bush has seemed almost like a little boy at times — a kid with freckles wishing he were somewhere else — when instead a national anchorman was needed to speak believably with confidence about the state of the union during one of its darkest hours."

It's Howard Rosenberg who's "like a little boy" — a spoiled-rotten brat who needs a trip to the woodshed.

Newsday columnist Ellis Henican is still pouting that Bush didn't risk his life by coming to New York right away.

"Some people don't believe questions like that should even be asked. My e-mail and my voice mail are choked with people who think that way, spitting mad that I and a few other journalists even would open mouths at a time like this," Clinton idolater Henican moaned.

Why not urge him to close that big, spiteful mouth?.

Other readers have complained that ABC's Canadian anchorman, the snooty Peter Jennings, referred to Senator Joe Lieberman as "vice president" — wishful thinking on Jennings' part, no doubt. Others noted the disapproval of CBS news reader Dan "Buckwheats" Rather when New York rescue workers cheered our president.

New York *Times Still* Not Sure Bush Is 'Legitimate'

Inside Cover
Sunday, September 16, 2001

Most media and congressional leftists who attacked President Bush during our national emergency have backpedaled like crazy after an outpouring of rage from the public, but the dunce king of all media arrogance, *The New York Times*, is still at it.

Today it presents a "news analysis" by R.W. Apple Jr. And what a rotten Apple he is — the headline is "Bush Presidency Seems to Gain Legitimacy."

Even the worm-infested Apple admits, reluctantly, that the president has done well in the past week. But then, like other leftists who got their panties in a bunch over Al Gore's failure to steal the White House despite massive Democratic vote fraud nationwide, he has to get in his dig. He refers to Bush "easing the doubts about his capacity for the job and the legitimacy of his election that have clung stubbornly to him during his eight difficult months in the Oval Office."

What planet do these tiny-souled elitists live on? Bush's presidency doesn't "seem" to "gain" legitimacy, it was legit from day one. But what can you expect of a newspaper that deemed the genocidal communist dictatorship of Josef Stalin not just legitimate but praiseworthy?

CBS Covering for Clinton in Wake of Terrorist Attacks?

Inside Cover
Monday, September 17, 2001

As criticism of the Clinton administration's lax security policies continues to mount in the wake of last week's terror attacks in New York and Washington, CBS News reported Sunday that the ex-president actually ordered the assassination of leading suspect Osama bin Laden.

Reporting for *60 Minutes*, CBS's Leslie Stahl claimed:

"Following the attacks on the U.S. embassies in Africa in August 1998, President Clinton signed a directive authorizing the CIA to apprehend bin Laden and bring him to the United States to stand trial for his role in the bombings.

"The directive, which was modified several times, authorized the use of deadly force if taking bin Laden alive was deemed impossible. And in fact, according to government sources, non-Americans (we don't know what nationality) working on behalf of the CIA tried to kill bin Laden last year.

"These foreign operatives told the CIA they fired a rocket-propelled grenade at bin Laden as he drove in a convoy of cars through a mountainous road in Afghanistan, and that the grenade hit one of the vehicles — though not the one bin Laden was in."

The claim that Clinton authorized an assassination attempt on bin Laden comes just three days after The Associated Press reported that in December, the Pentagon presented the ex-president with information pinpointing the terrorist's whereabouts along with a plan to take him out.

But, according to the AP, Clinton reportedly took a pass on the proposal, leaving bin Laden in place while his apparent subordinates planned and executed Tuesday's devastating attacks.

On Friday, when questioned about the AP report by Fox News Channel's

Brian Kilmeade, Clinton himself made no mention of any so-called presidential directive authorizing the attempt on bin Laden's life.

KILMEADE: Mr. President, there's a report today that you had the best shot at [Osama bin Laden] in December, in the waning weeks of your presidency, and at the last minute you said, "No, too much of a risk." How true is that?

CLINTON: No, it's not true. The best shot we had at Osama bin Laden was when I bombed his training camp in 1998 and we missed him by just a matter of hours. Maybe even less than an hour.

KILMEADE: Do you feel somewhat responsible?

CLINTON: Well, let me say this. We tripled the intelligence budget for counterintelligence — for counterterrorism. Because I believed, as I said, that these kind of threats would be the most likely ones. (end of excerpt)

Beyond concerns that the ex-president failed to take firm action against bin Laden, security experts now say that Clinton-era restrictions hampered recruitment of the kind of spies that could have tipped the U.S. to Tuesday's attack.

Some also note that the sky marshal program, which had been strengthened by President Reagan after a wave of hijackings in the 1980s, was decimated during the Clinton years — making it easier for bin Laden's hijackers to simultaneously commandeer four airplanes armed only with plastic box cutters.

Jane Fonda: U.S. Must Understand 'Underlying Causes' of Terror Attack

Inside Cover
Saturday, September 22, 2001

"Hanoi Jane" Fonda advised Americans Thursday to "try to understand the underlying causes" of the September 11 terrorist attacks on the World Trade Center and Pentagon that killed thousands of her fellow citizens, adding that it would be a mistake for the U.S. to retaliate militarily against the perpetrators.

Discussing the attacks on an Atlanta radio station, the former actress and ex-wife of CNN chief Ted Turner said she was concerned about the emotional reaction to the disaster.

"It's hard to be hopeful, frankly," she told Mix 105.7 FM. "What concerns me very much is the saber rattling and the calls for vengeance."

"I think it has to be dealt with as a crime," the one-time exercise guru counseled. "And when there's a crime, you don't bomb a city or a country — you use very, very clever intelligence [and] undercover-type operations to get the criminals and punish them, and then you try to understand the underlying causes of the crime."

Fonda's comments have not been reported outside Atlanta, where they caused an uproar on talk radio station WGST on Friday.

She earned the moniker "Hanoi Jane" in 1971 at the height of the Vietnam War, when she traveled to North Vietnam, donned a Communist military uniform and pretended to shoot down U.S. pilots while manning an anti-aircraft gun in Hanoi.

ABC News Bans Flag Pins

Inside Cover
Tuesday, September 25, 2001

You won't be seeing the American flag on the lapels of Peter Jennings or his news colleagues at ABC News.

The Washington Post's Howard Kurtz reports this week that "ABC has barred its journalists from wearing lapel flags such as the one sported by White House correspondent Terry Moran."

"Especially in a time of national crisis, the most patriotic thing journalists can do is to remain as objective as possible," ABC spokesman Jeffrey Schneider told Kurtz.

"That does not mean journalists are not patriots. All of us are at a time like this. But we cannot signal how we feel about a cause, even a justified and just cause, through some sort of outward symbol."

Kurtz also dished out blame to Rush Limbaugh for airing claims that Jennings had "criticized President Bush for not returning directly to the White House after the attacks on New York and Washington."

The Limbaugh story, which was picked up by NewsMax.com, turned out not to be accurate. Limbaugh quickly apologized on air for the story.

Some Media Banning Use of the 'T' Word

Inside Cover
Friday, September 28, 2001

First it was a ban on wearing U.S. flag pins. Now some journalists are being told they can't call a terrorist a terrorist because they might appear to be judging the thugs who slaughter innocent people.

CNN, for example, says it wants to "define people by their actions," a spokeswoman for the cable network told *The Wall Street Journal*.

She said the kamikaze pilots flying the planes that hit the World Trade Center and Pentagon, for example, would be called "alleged hijackers," not "terrorists," because, she said, "CNN cannot convict anybody; nothing has been judged by a court of law."

Reuters has restated its policy of forbidding journalists to use the word "terrorist" in describing the attacks or their perpetrators, the *Journal* reports. Reuters reporters, however, can quote others using the term.

"We do not characterize the subjects of news stories but instead report their actions, identity and background," the company said in a written statement, adding that it has a similar proscription against the term 'freedom fighter.'

"The integrity of those accounts — and the safety of our journalists in hot spots around the world who provide them — depend on our adherence to these long-held principles," the statement said.

The Wall Street Journal, on the other hand, says it has told staffers they can use the word terrorist, but that "it should be used carefully, and specifically, to describe those people and nongovernmental organizations that plan and execute acts of violence against civilian or noncombatant targets, for example," not merely sympathizers with such people or groups.

The Associated Press refers to the Black Tuesday attacks as "terrorist attacks" because "we consider they meet the criterion," Managing Editor Michael Silverman said. Sometimes terrorists may call themselves freedom fighters, but "a lot of convicted murderers don't like the definition of themselves either," he added.

The *Journal* reported that the major broadcast and cable TV networks, including General Electric Co.'s NBC, Viacom Inc.'s CBS, Walt Disney Co.'s ABC and News Corp.'s Fox News, also said they have no new policies on such descriptive words or phrases.

The toughest response on the use of the word came from Bill Wheatley, vice president of NBC News, who told the *Journal*:

"A group of people commandeered airplanes and used them as guided missiles against thousands of people; if that doesn't fit the definition of terrorism, what does?" he asked. "We have no intention of changing."

Cronkite Compares Falwell to the Terrorists

Inside Cover
Saturday, September 29, 2001
The Rev. Jerry Falwell is in the same league as the terrorists who downed the World Trade Center and devastated the Pentagon, according to Walter Cronkite.

The one-time CBS News anchorman says the Rev. Falwell's controversial remarks about the September 11 terrorist attacks were "the most abominable thing I've ever heard."

Cronkite attacked Falwell for his September 13 statements on Pat Robertson's *700 Club* alleging that the terrorist attacks were divine retribution on America for tolerating "pagans, abortionists, feminists, homosexuals, the American Civil Liberties Union and the People for the American Way."

Although Falwell later apologized for the remarks, Cronkite ripped into him, telling *TV Guide* columnist Max Robins, "It makes you wonder if [Falwell and his host Pat Robertson are] worshipping the same God as the people who bombed the Trade Center and the Pentagon."

Nowadays remarks like that could get you busted on hate-crime charges, but it appears that the "most trusted man in America" is immune to that sort of thing.

So far, Cronkite has offered no criticism of press attacks on President Bush in the wake of the September 11 attacks or the way some media outlets have banned their news employees from wearing the American flag. No surprise here — Cronkite has long advocated the dissolution of the U.S. government and the creation of a one-world government.

Rather: Reporters Shouldn't Be Patriots

Inside Cover
Sunday, November 11, 2001

CBS Evening News anchorman Dan Rather cautioned Saturday that patriotism and journalism don't mix, saying that he thought reporters needed to set aside whatever feelings they have for their country while covering the U.S.'s war on terrorism.

"It's hard to be a patriotic journalist," Rather told NBC's *Access Hollywood*.

"Journalists need to be skeptical. Not cynical but skeptical. And they need to be independent. If necessary they need to ask the hard questions."

Though he thinks American journalists shouldn't overtly support the U.S. war effort, Rather argued that the Pentagon should grant reporters access to U.S. troops in the front lines.

Citing the advice of his CBS News predecessor Walter Cronkite, Rather told *Access Hollywood*: "Basically, Walter thinks that we, all of us in journalism, should be working harder to get the U.S. government and the military to install the kind of operations they had in World War II — that is, journalists in uniform, correspondent on their sleeve, but in uniform."

The CBS newsman said that reporters assigned to travel with military units should be "subject to censorship, but a legitimate censorship which takes the attitude: maximum information consistent with military security."

Rather's suggestion that quality journalism and patriotism are somehow at odds is a far cry from the position he took in September, when he pronounced himself ready to enlist in the U.S. war against Osama bin Laden.

"George Bush is the president. He makes the decisions, and, you know, it's just one American, but wherever he wants me to line up, just tell me where," he told late-night comedian David Letterman just days after the terrorist attacks on the U.S.

Goldberg Exposes Network Double Standard on Terrorism

Wes Vernon, NewsMax.com
Thursday, December 6, 2001

WASHINGTON — Among the many cans of worms former CBS newsman Bernard Goldberg has opened up with his new book, *Bias*, is a selective "connecting of the dots" when the establishment media cover terrorism.

When Timothy McVeigh was nabbed in the Oklahoma City bombing, the networks and the "prestige press" were quick to blame talk radio.

"What they found back then — or more accurately, what they convinced themselves they found — was a line stretching from Oklahoma City to the Republican Party to conservatives in general and finally to Rush Limbaugh," Goldberg writes.

More or less typical of the inside-the-Beltway media reaction at the time was a scribe for a Washington-based magazine who stopped just barely short of rubbing his hands with glee before telling this writer the bombing "changes the whole political landscape. The Republicans are now on defense. The so-called Gingrich revolution is now irrelevant."

That attitude was pervasive inside the Washington establishment, which saw the bombing that killed scores of innocent people as giving them a new political lease on life.

Goldberg quotes Dan Rather as telling his audience, "Even after Oklahoma City, you can turn on your radio in any city and dial up [anti-government] hate talk, extremist, racist and violent, from the hosts and those who call in."

The Washington Post, whose editors strive ever so diligently to make sure they are as authoritative with the liberal establishment as *The New York Times* is, "connected the dots" in an even more explicit manner.

Those Intolerant Liberals

A column by that paper's leading political writer, David Broder, singled out Rush Limbaugh and said, "I think there will be less tolerance and fewer cheers for that kind of rhetoric."

Put aside for the moment that some can remember a time when liberals denounced what they called "guilt by association." And put aside the fact that trying to link McVeigh with conservatives and talk radio is, as Goldberg says, "at best, a stretch."

The question the veteran broadcast journalist raises in his book is: Why don't establishment media types connect ALL the dots on terrorism?

On September 11, when "a band of fanatics declared war on the United States of America to punish us for not wanting to dwell in the fourteenth century, where they reside," almost no one in the major media made a connection to the "hate speech" heard throughout the Middle East, even in so-called moderate Arab nations.

How come there are no Christian suicide bombers, Jewish suicide bombers, Hindu suicide bombers or Buddhist suicide bombers?

"Was what happened on September 11 a subversion of Islam, as pundits and journalists on network and cable TV told us over and over again? Or was it the result of an h-o-n-e-s-t reading of the Koran?" Goldberg asks.

Of course, if taken literally and uncritically, "just about any holy book can lead to bad things." And for his part, Goldberg is willing to grant that Islam itself is a peaceful religion. Still, he says, it would be reasonable to raise questions about connecting t-h-e-s-e dots.

The 28-year CBS veteran puts it this way: "Why would journalists, so interested in connecting the dots when they thought they led to Rush Limbaugh, be so uninterested in connecting the dots when there might actually be dots to connect — from hateful, widely held popular attitudes in much of the Arab world straight to the cockpits of those hijacked jetliners?"

'I Hate Israel'

Examples? The book cites an article in *Commentary* magazine about a song called "I Hate Israel" that made an overnight singing sensation of a working-class crooner. The song apparently is wildly popular in Cairo, Damascus and the West Bank.

The *Commentary* piece tells of a series of articles in the leading government-sponsored newspaper in Egypt about how Jews supposedly use the blood of Christians to make matzo for Passover. A columnist for the same paper expressed his "thanks to Hitler of blessed memory who on behalf of the Palestinians took revenge in advance on the most vile criminals on the face of the earth. Still, we do have a complaint against [Hitler] for his revenge on them was not enough." (In other words, he did not kill enough Jews.)

Mentioning Arab extremism is not "politically correct," Goldberg notes. But suppose Israel had a hit song titled "I Hate Palestine"? *The New York Times*, he says, would put the story on Page One "and then run an editorial "just to make sure we all got the message — that the song is indecent and contributes to an atmosphere of hate."

Shortly thereafter, Peter Jennings, Tom Brokaw and Dan Rather would have fallen in line, because the networks get much of their news from that establishment organ. Mike Wallace might have landed in Israel, "looking absolutely mortified that those Jews would do such a thing."

If they're going to connect the dots for scapegoats, why not be consistent? Doesn't the refusal to do so, in and of itself, reflect bias? Goldberg thinks it does.

Though the media won't reflect on influences that led suicide bombers to ram buildings in the U.S. and kill thousands of people, some public officials are beginning to do just that in a more theological way.

"A spiritual attack" is what Senator James Inhofe, R-Okla., calls September 11. "An attack that was created in the mind and heart of Satan," he added in a Senate speech Tuesday. "A demonically inspired attack."

Inhofe, a born-again Christian, was, from his own perspective, discussing Goldberg's question as to why there are no Christian, Jewish, Hindu or Buddhist suicide bombers.

When it comes to making links to fix blame, media double standards abound, says Goldberg, who has caused an uproar in high media circles on the air and in print with his book on liberal bias.

For example, Goldberg asks, "Should we also accuse Americans who spoke out loudly and forcefully — including many journalists — of contributing to the 1972 bombing of the Pentagon, and to other sometimes deadly terrorism, perpetuated by fanatics on the left?"

To cite another case, this one not mentioned by Goldberg, recall the Unabomber, who was captured in Montana within months of the Oklahoma City bombing. This man, who had planted bombs around the country that had killed and maimed people, was found to have been influenced by extreme environmentalism. He had even heavily underlined passages in Al Gore's book, *Earth in the Balance.*

Dan, Peter and Tom did not connect those dots either.

No Way! Rudy as 'Person of the Year'

Christopher Ruddy
Tuesday, December 25, 2001

True to form, the Lexus Liberals who dominate *Time* magazine and the left-wing media have bestowed another honor on a fellow liberal Rudy Giuliani.

Don't get me wrong. Rudy Giuliani behaved admirably on September 11 and has given New Yorkers a sense of confidence in the wake of the worst disaster to hit America in peacetime.

But does he deserve to be named Time's Person of the Year?

Most certainly not.

But the left-dominated media didn't want to bestow the honor on the man who, according to their own litmus test, was the person who most affected the news for the better —George W. Bush.

The media were quick to take potshots at the president almost from the moment the terrorists slammed civilian jets into the World Trade Center and the Pentagon.

In its treatise on Mayor Giuliani, *Time* even puts in its digs at Bush.

Time says: "With the President out of sight for most of that day, Giuliani became the voice of America. Every time he spoke, millions of people felt a little better. His words were full of grief and iron, inspiring New York to inspire the nation."

How nice. The president was on Air Force One, running the country and making sure there was continuity of government in case of a nuclear attack.

But the media don't like that.

They wanted Bush to come, Clinton-like, and do some hugging in New York, hold a press conference, do some more hugging, and shed some Clinton-like crocodile tears. Then they would have been happy.

Because Bush is a Republican, a conservative one at that, they didn't support him *for* president and they won't support him as president.

Instead, they have been itching to score points against him.

Just weeks after September 11, all we heard were complaints that Bush had yet to retaliate.

When the bombing started, there was silence. But then complaints began again.

The dovish liberal pundits were saying this was no way to run a war — we needed a massive invasion of Afghanistan!

But now, as we have seen Bush's plan work and the Taliban crumble in short order, the left-wing media (and I separate them from the many liberals in this country who think Bush has done a great job) cannot name George W. Bush the Person of the Year. By any reasonable standard, George W. Bush was the person who most affected the news for the better.

Here was a man who inherited the mess of eight years of Clinton-Gore, eight years that left the nation bereft of an intelligence apparatus that should have prevented 9/11.

When Bush came into office, he surrounded himself with an incredibly strong team. As a sign of his remarkable leadership, he selected people who were more experienced and more able than he. Clinton didn't do that.

Almost every major player in the Bush administration is presidential timber and has openly considered running for the office: Cheney, Rumsfeld, Powell and Ashcroft.

It takes a special man to acknowledge that there are better men than he. Today, America is better off because Bush is a confident man who did just that.

Bush quickly rallied the nation as no other president has in modern times. He motivated a dispirited Pentagon to war.

He could have just as easily taken the Clinton-Gore road with a few cruise missile attacks at camel watering holes.

But he went to war instead. He told the American people it would be a sustained war. It would be a wider war. It would be a war of sacrifice and casualties.

This is Churchillian.

Bush then led the nation in war and sent his secretary of state to pull together an incredible alliance of nations. Even the Arab and Muslim world — despite great support for bin laden in the Arab street — supported the U.S. war on the Taliban.

Today the Taliban are finished and al Qaeda is in tatters.

And Bush's honor from the left-wing media?

Nowhere to be seen.

[Message to George: Take this to heart. The liberal media will not forget the 2000 election. They hate you. Do not make Dad's mistake and think you can ever win these miscreants over. Do what Reagan did: Confront the media and speak directly to the American people.]

Instead, *Time* honors Rudy Giuliani. Certainly Giuliani has been a good mayor in good times. Still, his time as mayor of New York can in no way be compared to the mayoralty of Edward I. Koch.

Koch was elected in 1977 and inherited a city teetering on bankruptcy.

The economy was in a recession. The feds told the city "drop dead" and crime skyrocketed as the city fielded just 22,000 cops.

Koch came into office and, remarkably, took on the very constituencies that elected him, including the city's all-powerful unions. That took courage.

He then went on to criticize fellow Democrat President Jimmy Carter, as he extended a welcoming hand to Republican Ronald Reagan. Talk about cojones.

Giuliani has never demonstrated that type of political courage.

He's been a good city administrator who surrounded himself with mediocre aides and yes men. He got away with it because, having inherited a police force of 40,000 and a city on the ascendancy during the biggest economic boom in history — well, of course he succeeded.

*The term "Lexus Liberal" was coined by Michael Savage.

Ted Turner Says September 11 Terrorists Were Brave Men

Jim Burns, CNSNews.com
Tuesday, February 12, 2002

CNSNews.com — Media mogul Ted Turner Monday praised the firefighters, rescue workers and police officers for their courage on September 11, but said he thinks the terrorists themselves were brave because New York's World Trade Center crumbled and the Pentagon in Washington was partially destroyed.

During a speech at Brown University in Providence, R.I., Turner, founder of CNN, said the hijackers were motivated by world poverty and "were brave at the very least.

"The reason that the World Trade Center got hit is because there are a lot of people living in abject poverty out there who don't have any hope for a better life," he said.

Turner added that he thinks the terrorists "also might have been a little nuts."

But the media mogul didn't stop there. He compared President Bush to Roman emperor Julius Caesar, and said America missed out by not electing Democrat Al Gore.

"A few more votes in Florida, and we could have had the best environmental president we ever had. Now we've got an oilman. He [President Bush] is another Julius Caesar. Just what we need," said Turner.

Leading media critic L. Brent Bozell III, president of the Media Research Center, parent organization of CNSNews.com, responded by saying, "I don't think Al Gore would agree with Ted Turner that Al Gore would make the best president.

"Clearly, America believes Bush as having done a magnificent job. It's in keeping with the craziness of Ted Turner that he is still campaigning for Al Gore," said Bozell.

The student newspaper, *The Brown Daily Herald*, also reported Turner as saying, "Since 1980, the three biggest problems facing the world have been the possibility of nuclear annihilation, the population explosion and the degradation of the environment. Nuclear war is the greatest threat to the world because of its possibility for instantaneous destruction."

He accused the United States of not following through on the 1968 Nuclear Non-Proliferation Treaty, which binds it to "cessation of the nuclear arms race at an early date and to nuclear disarmament."

"We lied," Turner said, declaring that the current administration does not have "any intention whatsoever" of doing away with the nuclear arsenal.

During the Cold War, Turner chose to make friends with Soviet leaders and asserted in his speech that international cooperation is the only way to avoid mutual annihilation.

"We're either going to live together or we're going to die together," Turner said.

He said he focused on what he had in common with international leaders and on inventive solutions like the Goodwill Games, and criticized former President Ronald Reagan for calling the USSR the "evil empire."

Calling other countries "dirty names" is "a great plan if you want to start a war with somebody," Turner said. He emphasized the similarity of Reagan's remarks to President Bush's recent identification of North Korea, Iran and Iraq as an "axis of evil."

"Ted Turner is an expert in dirty name calling," Bozell said, because that's what he's done "all his adult life against people he didn't like."

In recent years, Turner has become famous for frequently belittling Christians, and once said that America has "some of the dumbest people in the world."

In a statement, the Turner Broadcasting System reacted by saying, "Mr. Turner's remarks at Brown University on February 11, 2002, represent his personal opinions and in no way reflect the beliefs of Turner Broadcasting System."

COPYRIGHT 2002 CNSNEWS.COM. ALL RIGHTS RESERVED.

NewsMax Wins Victory for Firemen

Kevin Curran
NewsMax.com magazine, March 2002

They have earned the nickname "New York's Bravest" time and again. When a New York City firefighter climbs into a truck and heads to an alarm, there is the ever-present possibility it could be his last.

Firefighters stand by each other as guardian angels to stay one step ahead of the angel of death. As ordinary people flee danger, these extraordinary men and women run past them to face it head on. While modern technology has improved communications gear, breathing apparatuses and firefighting equipment, the one thing every firefighter knows will never fail is back-up from fellow firefighters.

So it was on that fateful morning of September 11, 2001. As the inferno roared from the windows of the World Trade Center, a parade of red trucks raced downtown. While thousands of people wrapped towels around their faces and ran from the plaza, hundreds of firefighters donned their oxygen tanks and marched into the towers. If they paused at all, it was to offer a quick prayer to St. Florian, the patron saint of firefighters.

As the sun traveled over Manhattan that day, the souls of 343 members of the Fire Department City of New York (FDNY) crossed its path on their way to heaven. One of every 18 New York City firefighters was lost.

In the aftermath of September 11, New York's Bravest returned to doing what they do best, saving lives and property. Mayor Rudolph Giuliani presided over the largest promotion ceremony in the department's history, but there was little to celebrate. Every new lieutenant knew he was replacing a fallen comrade.

Church bells tolled from Long Island to the Hudson Valley as husbands, sons and fathers were laid to rest. During his first seven years in office, Mayor Giuliani attended the funeral of every firefighter lost in the line of duty. With so many services, Giuliani could not get to them all and instead asked New Yorkers to show their support for the families by going in his place.

At the World Trade Center site that Edward Cardinal Egan dubbed "Ground Hero," firefighters continued their heart-wrenching search. When they came upon the body of a comrade-in-arms, they covered him with an American flag, paused for a prayer and carried him to a waiting ambulance.

Above the devastation, three firefighters fashioned a makeshift pole and hung from it the Stars and Stripes.

It was an event reminiscent of the raising of the colors on the island of Iwo Jima during World War II. History repeated itself as the image of firefighters Dan Williams, George Johnson and Billy Eisengrein was captured forever by photographer Thomas Franklin of *The Record* of North Jersey.

As the weeks passed, department officials considered ways to commemorate the spirit of those 343 fallen firefighters. They decided to turn Franklin's photograph, "The Flag-Raising at Ground Zero," into a life-size statue and install it at the department's headquarters.

Developer Bruce Ratner donated $180,000 for the design and construction of the artwork, and a clay model of the statue was unveiled for the New York media on December 21.

Some firefighters immediately noticed a significant difference between the statue and the event it depicted. Firefighters McWilliams, Johnson and Eisengrein happen to be white. Of the three heroes depicted on the statue, one was white, another black and the third Hispanic. In the media coverage that followed the unveiling, the only hint of the changing of the ethnicity of the firefighters was a brief mention in *Newsday*.

While New Yorkers may not have been completely aware of the difference between the reality of the flag-raising at the World Trade Center site and the fantasy of the FDNY's proposed memorial, New York's Bravest certainly did.

Some members of the department band that played at the ceremony stormed out after noticing the changes to the statue. They were persuaded to return, and none of the press present at the unveiling reported the musicians' protest. Retired Lieutenant Kevin O'Kane started a campaign to enlighten New York media outlets about the fraudulent alterations to the statue, but it seemed they preferred to remain in the dark. "I called one newspaper after another," O'Kane said. "Nobody wanted to cover this story."

More than two weeks after the unveiling, O'Kane was having no luck with Manhattan's journalists, so he contacted Carl Limbacher at NewsMax.com: "What Firefighters McWilliams, Johnson and Eisengrein did inspired the people of the United States in one of its darkest hours… The 343 firefighters [who] were killed at the WTC (54 of whom I knew personally) consisted of all races and creeds. But the fact is that the three firefighters who hoisted the flag on the afternoon of September 11th at the WTC were white and should be depicted as such."

NewsMax.com reported O'Kane's battle on January 8.

O'Kane's appeal for help was finally heard, but not initially in the canyons of midtown. On January 10, Al Rantel discussed the statue controversy during his program on KABC Radio in Los Angeles. The same day, *The Weekly Standard* produced its own version of the story on its website. Later that day, Brit Hume mentioned the story on the Fox News Channel.

O'Kane finally was able to bring his plight to a large number of New Yorkers on January 11. That's when he spent an hour with Sean Hannity on WABC Radio. The lieutenant had to share a microphone with civil rights activist Lawrence Guyot, who said changing the statue to reflect ethnic diversity was good idea. Hannity reunited O'Kane and Guyot on his Fox News Channel program, *Hannity & Colmes*, that evening.

O'Kane had finally succeeded. As he left the Fox studios on one side of Rockefeller Center, an Associated Press reporter on the other side of the plaza was preparing a story about the redesigned statue.

With the press of a button, that story headed for most of the newsrooms in the United States. Twenty-one days after the statue was unveiled and three days after NewsMax.com broke the story, the saga of the FDNY memorial had gone mainstream.

Why was the statue radically altered from a realistic portrayal to a politically correct vision? AP got the answer from fire department spokesman Frank Gribbon: "Given that those who died were of all races and all ethnicities and that the statue was to be symbolic of those sacrifices, ultimately a decision was made to honor no one in particular."

That explanation did not sit well with Bill Kelly, the attorney representing the three men who actually raised the flag: "It's become something political as opposed to historical." Kelly told AP the firefighters were "disappointed" about the department's decision.

In its 377-year history, the City of New York has seen the installation of hundreds of monuments. Some commemorate ideas, like the Statue of Liberty. Others remember people, such as Grant's Tomb. Many recognize historical events, from triumphs like George Washington's first inauguration to tragedies like the Triangle Shirtwaist fire.

Visitors to the Cathedral of St. John the Divine can view a memorial dedicated to the 12 firefighters killed in the 23rd Street Fire on October 17, 1966 (previously the worst one-day loss in the department's history). Although part of the cathedral was damaged by fire in December, the monument was untouched.

Travelers to the Big Apple can get a sense of how America became the enviable nation it is by visiting just a few of these landmarks. It is this legacy that troubles Kevin O'Kane the most. "My fear is that the word won't get out and that this fraud will be erected," O'Kane told Limbacher, "and future generations will come to regard this politically correct sculpture as a historic fact."

As the story moved into the public eye, some of the Bravest decided it was time to take action. On January 12, NewsMax.com learned that some firefighters were planning to raise funds on their own to place an accurate statue of "The Flag-Raising at Ground Zero." The piece would include a plaque naming the three firefighters.

A petition to halt construction of the altered statue circulated through New York firehouses, collecting almost 1,000 signatures. Many Americans apparently shared their outrage. Thirty thousand people responded to a CNN.com online poll taken January 13. Nearly 23,000 of them said a historically accurate monument should not be replaced with the politically correct model unveiled in December.

Firefighters McWilliams, Johnson and Eisengrein also moved to claim their roles in history. Kelly, their attorney, told the *New York Post* on January 13 that he had formally requested the department to halt the project. The next day Kelly told Fox News Channel he was considering seeking a court injunction to stop the memorial project.

One outspoken firefighter shared the outrage of O'Kane and the three flag raisers. Mike Moran told NewsMax.com: "I was infuriated when I found out. I couldn't believe it was true."

(Moran first came to public attention when he said a few choice words during an October benefit concert at Madison Square Garden. Taking the microphone from Paul McCartney, Moran told the crowd, "Osama bin Laden, you can kiss my royal Irish ass!")

Since it looked as if fire officials would not budge on their plan for the altered statue, another idea for a memorial emerged. On January 15, O'Kane suggested a monument to three fallen members of Ladder Company 118. Joey Agnello, Vernon Cherry and Peter Vega happened to be white, black and Hispanic.

O'Kane explained that a statue of these men would reflect the racial diversity department officials were seeking when they altered the statue of the flag-raising. "You could have a Ground Zero statue to those guys and you wouldn't have to change a thing," O'Kane said, "and then the first statue could go forward based on the guys who actually raised the flag."

The next day, New York's new mayor gave O'Kane and others upset about the statue a reason for hope. "It's unfortunate that we're in the situation that we are," said Michael Bloomberg.

Furthermore, Mayor Bloomberg ordered his new fire commissioner, Nicholas Scopetta, to meet with Bruce Ratner, the developer funding the statue, on January 17. Ratner was originally in favor of the politically correct but historically inaccurate statue, but he'd had a change of heart by January 17.

Reality scored a victory that afternoon when a fire department press release said Commissioner Scopetta "will consider new options for a fitting memorial to honor the members of the fire department who died and those who worked tirelessly at the World Trade Center following the September 11 attacks."

"I will support the fire department's decision on what constitutes a fitting and inspiring memorial," Ratner said after the meeting.

What will the official memorial look like? The department did not say if the flag-raising would remain the basis for the sculpture.

While department brass considers its next move, some of the Bravest will soon take that nervous ride to the next alarm reminded of the patriotism of their comrades. Three new fire trucks were delivered to the FDNY with a mural on each side showing a white firefighter raising a flag at Ground Zero. The art was not commissioned by the department; it is a gift from the company that made the trucks, Seagrave Fire Apparatus of Wisconsin.

NewsMax.com was the first to report the controversy. Our readers were aware of the daily changes in the battle against an inaccurate memorial.

In an e-mail to NewsMax.com and his supporters, Kevin O'Kane was grateful. "This change of heart on the part of FDNY administration and Bruce Ratner could not have happened without the outpouring of support from you and the hundreds of thousands of good people across America. Special thanks to Carl Limbacher who broke the story as a result of a simple e-mail I sent him. ... To you, the good people of America, you fought and won this battle. The victory is yours! God bless America!"

Secret Doomsday Hideaway
Compromised by Media Report

Inside Cover
Saturday, March 2, 2002

Wonder why the U.S. military doesn't trust the media?

Just ask the people who used to man the federal government's top-secret bunker underneath West Virginia's Greenbrier Hotel before their cover was blown by *The Washington Post* in 1992.

On Friday, the *Post* breathlessly reported as "breaking news" the story of the Bush administration's "shadow government" — a plan to keep federal operations going in the event of attack — that was first covered with much less hysteria by the Cleveland *Plain Dealer* last October as well as discussed in open congressional hearings.

But the *Post* itself blew the lid off classified plans to protect U.S. officials back in 1992, when it revealed to the world the top-secret location of Congress' doomsday hideaway.

The media's bright lights even gave the Posties an award for the security-compromising report, as the paper itself proudly announced at the time:

"The *Washington Post Magazine* has won first prize in investigative reporting in the 1993 Sunday Magazine Association awards for disclosure of the secret relocation center for Congress in the event of nuclear war," the *Post*'s May 14, 1993, edition proclaimed.

"'The Ultimate Congressional Hideaway,' by freelance writer Ted Gup last May 31, detailed construction of a bunker beneath the Greenbrier hotel in West Virginia."

Now anyone can take a virtual tour of the formerly secret Greenbrier bunker, which PBS makes available on its website while happily noting:

"Built under The Greenbrier, a luxurious Southern resort, the facility was designed to house the members of the House of Representatives and the Senate in case of nuclear attack. Compromised by an investigative reporter in 1993, the bunker is now open to the public."

Media Ignore It: Clinton Warned on
Bin Laden Hijack-Kamikaze Plot

Inside Cover
Thursday, May 16, 2002

If you don't recall seeing the blaring post-9/11 headline "Clinton Warned on Bin Laden Hijack-Kamikaze Plot," it's not because your memory is failing.

In fact, the big media mostly ignored the story — in marked contrast to today's wall-to-wall coverage of news that President Bush received a pre–September 11 CIA briefing on a possible bin Laden hijack plot.

And while the warning transmitted to Bush gave no inkling that bin

Laden planned to transform U.S. airliners into flying bombs and slam them into American office buildings, Clinton administration intelligence officials were in fact in possession of detailed information on an al Qaeda conspiracy to hijack several U.S. airliners — including a plan to crash one of the planes into the Pentagon or CIA.

It was called Operation Bojinka, a 1995 plot hatched by an al Qaeda cell in the Philippines with an eye toward blowing up 12 American airliners. Some would be booby-trapped with bombs, like Pan Am 103, others hijacked like the four U.S. jets commandeered on 9/11 and crashed into buildings.

Though the mainstream press never demonstrated much enthusiasm for the story, Accuracy in Media's Reed Irvine detailed what the Clinton administration knew — and when it knew it — for NewsMax.com last October.

Citing a September 13 Agence France-Presse report, Irvine noted that Philippine Police Chief Superintendent Avelino Razon had uncovered the plot to "plant bombs in U.S. airliners and hijack others to crash them into buildings like the CIA headquarters."

"Razon said [the plot] was found on the computer of Ramzi Yousef, the organizer of the 1993 bombing of the World Trade Center," Irvine reported. "He had fled to Pakistan, but his laptop was found in the apartment he shared with his accomplice, Abdul Hakim Murad. Razon said both were agents of Osama bin Laden."

A later Agence France-Press report noted:

"Among targets mentioned [in Yousef's computer files] was the World Trade Center in New York ... CIA offices in Virginia and the Sears Tower in Chicago."

Picking up where Irvine left off, *The Washington Post* quoted a Filipino investigator who said that as he watched the attack on the World Trade Center on television, he exclaimed in horror, "It's Bojinka. We told the Americans everything about Bojinka. Why didn't they pay attention?"

Razon told the *Philippine Daily Inquirer* that after the Philippine intelligence report was compiled in 1995, it was passed on to the U.S. Embassy and the U.S. Joint Task Force on Terrorism.

But, he complained, "It was not given credibility. Otherwise, it could have prevented the destruction of the World Trade Center."

The Clinton FBI was in full possession of all the frightening facts on Bojinka, but did nothing. Instead, as Reed Irvine revealed, the bureau assured Congress that everything was under control.

"In testimony before the Senate Judiciary Committee subcommittee on terrorism in February 1998, 'Bojinka' — which means 'big bang' — was described by Dale L. Watson, chief of the International Terrorism Operations Section of the FBI, only as a plot to blow up 'numerous U.S. air carriers.'

"He said that the FBI had identified 'a significant and growing organizational presence' of foreign terrorists in the United States. He swore the bureau had them under control."

The Clinton FBI counterintelligence chief told the Senate that as a result of the bombings of the World Trade Center in 1993 and the Murrah Federal Building in Oklahoma City in 1995, the FBI had developed an 'enhanced capability' to track terrorist activities.

Is it likely that U.S. intelligence possessed this much information on al Qaeda plans to slam planes into U.S. buildings — and didn't tell President Clinton?

Actually it is, if you believe the account of former CIA Director James Woolsey, who said Clinton never bothered to meet with him during his stint under Clinton as the nation's intelligence chief.

What about other administration officials, like Attorney General Janet Reno, who certainly should have known about Bojinka?

There Clinton may also have an alibi.

During all of 1998 — the same year FBI counterintelligence briefed Congress on the al Qaeda hijack plot — Clinton met with his Cabinet exactly twice: once in January to lie to them about his relationship with Monica Lewinsky, and again in August to come clean about the affair.

Dan Rather: Bush Issued Bogus Terror Alert to Cover Up 9/11 Bungle

Inside Cover
Wednesday, May 22, 2002

CBS Evening News anchorman Dan Rather accused the Bush administration Wednesday morning of issuing an unwarranted FBI terrorist alert to New York City yesterday primarily to distract from questions about its handling of pre-9/11 intelligence information.

Appearing on the *Imus in the Morning* radio show, Rather said he "believed" that his network's report a week ago that the White House received a CIA briefing before 9/11 on possible al Qaeda hijackings prompted the administration to issue the alert for political damage control.

"I can believe that the president and the people around him were surprised and peeved, to say the least," Rather contended, "that the information got out last week with [CBS's] report that President Bush had been briefed about some things that, in retrospect after September 11, would indicate that, well, maybe somebody should have done something."

The CBS newsman continued:

"And I can also believe that, as with every president, somebody's in the White House scratching their heads saying, 'How can we change the subject?' Now the subject has been changed, suddenly and very effectively, from 'How is it that the FBI and the CIA didn't move on the information they had? Where was the president briefed about what, when?'

"The subject's been changed," Rather explained, "from that, to suddenly one administration official after another, and each escalating it, [issuing] a new set of warnings."

The CBS anchor said he doubted the confluence of events was coincidental:

"Maybe these two things are not connected, but surely the people in the administration could forgive us for perhaps thinking, well, perhaps there's some connection here."

Prior to outlining his terrorist alert conspiracy theory, Rather sounded dismissive about the latest warning that had Manhattan in a virtual traffic lockdown Wednesday morning.

"We're on some kind of alert because somebody heard something that somebody may blow something up. [But] as a citizen, what are we supposed to do with that information?"

Rather also defended Democrat calls for a 9/11 investigation into the Bush White House, saying:

"We're not interested in just looking in the rearview mirror so we can nail somebody, you know: 'What did you know and when did you know it?'

"But this is pretty important stuff," he insisted. "Given the stories about intelligence failures that we already have heard about, who can argue that we don't need some kind of commission … led by professionals that goes into how the situation with al Qaeda was handled before September 11, what mistakes were made and what we can learn from that."

Rather insisted that curiosity about a possible Bush 9/11 cover-up had nothing to do with partisan politics.

"That's not playing partisan politics. There's already too much of that. That's trying to get information that can help us all in the future."

The CBS newsman also accused Attorney General John Ashcroft of taking advantage of insider information about terrorist warnings to fly on private jets while the public was kept in the dark about the secret alert, telling Imus:

"If the attorney general is given information that convinces him, 'Hey, I don't want to be on any commercial airliners just now. I'm gonna take government planes everywhere.' If the attorney general was told that … then it raises a question, Why wasn't the public alerted?"

"Some people probably would not have flown" had they also received the Ashcroft warning, he complained.

After the CBS news anchor's interview, NBC Pentagon correspondent Jim Miklaszewski called Imus to correct the record, explaining that Ashcroft's decision not to fly commercial aircraft last summer was prompted by threats against his life — and had no connection whatsoever to pre-9/11 intelligence information.

The Sum of All P.C. Fears

Inside Cover
Friday, May 31, 2002

The networks are giving a load of free publicity to Hollywood's new nuclear terrorism thriller, *The Sum of All Fears*, but most of the talking heads are ignoring the P.C. whitewash. In Tom Clancy's novel, the evildoers are Arabs, but the movie turns them into Tinseltown's favorite (in fact, only) villain: those awful white males.

Muslim terrorists? Naw, the audience would never buy that. Too unbelievable.

Reviewer Roger Ebert thinks money is at the root of Hollywood's evil. "The use of the neo-Nazis is politically correct: Best to invent villains who won't offend any audiences. This movie can play in Syria, Saudi Arabia and Iraq without getting walkouts," he writes in today's *Chicago Sun-Times*.

"It's more likely that if a bomb ever does go off in a big city, the perpetrators will be True Believers whose certainty about the next world gives them, they think, the right to kill us in this one," says Ebert.

As Robert Wilonsky says in his review for *New Times* Broward-Palm Beach, "When Affleck keeps getting work, the terrorists *have* won."

If you've seen the commercial with the charisma-challenged Ben Affleck mumbling about the evil Russian "neo-fascists," you might wonder why the movie didn't make the villains neo-communists, who after all are rearing their ugly heads again in Russia, as President Bush found out on his recent visit. But even though fascists and communists are two sides of the same totalitarian coin (Nazi, of course, stands for National *Socialist*), commie villains are also a no-no in La-La Land.

It's hard to think of a recent American movie whose villain isn't a white man. You might consider that strange, because nearly all the bigwigs in Hollywood are white men, but they're Guilty White Liberals who apparently are plagued by remorse over their inflated salaries.

Hollywood's Evil White Males, Part II

Ebert is an interesting character. A Bush-bashing, Clinton-loving leftist, he took gratuitous potshots at Attorney General John Ashcroft in his rave review of the critical and box-office bomb *The Majestic*, which was a tissue-thin piece of propaganda for Hollywood communists. Yet Ebert dared to make these comments in his pan of the awful Jennifer Lopez movie *Enough*, a "nasty item masquerading as a feminist revenge picture":

"The husband's swings of personality and mood are so sudden, and his motivation makes so little sense, that he has no existence beyond the stereotyped Evil Rich White Male. The fact that he preys on a poor Latino waitress is just one more cynical cliché. …

"Slim gets discouraging advice from a lawyer ('There is nothing you can do. He will win.'). And then she gets training in self-defense from a martial arts instructor. Both of these characters are African-American, following the movie's simplistic moral color-coding. The day when the evil husband is black and the self-defense instructor is white will not arrive in our life-times."

Targeting George Bush: The Media's FBI Blame Game

Inside Cover
Saturday, June 1, 2002

While Democratic Party leaders have largely backed away from their earlier criticism of President Bush for what they suggested was his failure to act on intelligence that could have prevented last September's terrorist attacks, a new strategy seems to be emerging: Blame Bush for 9/11 through the back door — starting with the FBI.

On Saturday, one of the Democratic Party's leading media organs attempted to move responsibility for the 9/11 attacks significantly up the Bush administration's chain of command, shifting the spotlight from FBI Director Robert Mueller to Attorney General John Ashcroft.

The New York Times report paints the Bush attorney general as asleep at the wheel while Osama bin Laden plotted to attack America.

"On September 10, Ashcroft rejected a proposed $58 million increase in financing for the bureau's counterterrorism programs," the *Times* said, juxtaposing that information with news that an internal FBI investigation had just concluded the bureau was woefully unprepared to deal with the threat posed by Osama bin Laden and other terrorists.

Though the dismal assessment was never shared with FBI budget officials, the paper notes that last August, then-acting FBI Director Thomas Pickard "met with Ashcroft on a supplemental financing request for counterterrorism, but was turned down."

While there's no question that the FBI and Justice Department were indeed caught napping by the bin Laden attacks — and even the conservative *Wall Street Journal* has called for Director Mueller's resignation — media coverage like Saturday's *Times* report has focused almost exclusively on intelligence failures during Bush's eight months in office.

And next week FBI critic Coleen Rowley is expected to testify publicly before the Senate Judiciary Committee about the bureau's Bush-era 9/11 intelligence failures, in a session that is certain to receive blanket media coverage.

Rowley has fingered Bush appointee Mueller in what she says was an orchestrated attempt to mislead the public about what the bureau knew before the 9/11 attacks.

In a scorching 13-page memo released to the press last week, she raked Mueller over the coals relentlessly, without offering so much as a negative word about his predecessor, Louis Freeh.

Meanwhile, neither the press nor House and Senate intelligence committees have shown any interest in deposing Clinton administration operative Mansoor Ijaz, who said the ex-president personally rejected three offers from the Sudanese government to "turn Osama bin Laden over on a silver platter."

As with Ijaz's claim that he can blow the lid off a Clinton-era 9/11 cover-up, Oklahoma Senator Don Nickles' call last week for a probe into the Clinton administration's inadequate response to al Qaeda terrorist attacks has fallen on deaf ears.

Though Nickles is the second-most-powerful Republican in the Senate, his recommendation for a 9/11 Clinton probe was reported only by his home-state newspaper *The Oklahoman* and NewsMax.com.

Morgan Freeman: 9/11 Not a National Trauma

Inside Cover
Monday, June 3, 2002

Actor Morgan Freeman appears intelligent in his movie roles. Appearances can be deceiving.

A co-star of Tinseltown's politically correct version of *The Sum of All Fears*, he's stirring up a fuss with comments made over the weekend about whether people want to see a movie about terrorism after the attacks of September 11.

"We had a trauma, but it's really not a national trauma," Freeman told New York movie reviewer Neal Rosen "If you were not in New York on September 11, what you saw was an event on CNN."

The New York *Daily News* today printed responses from victims' relatives.

"He's a star in the movie, so I figure he didn't want people not going to see it," said Bronx resident Ben Colon, whose wife, Sol Colon, was killed in the attacks. "But to say that September 11 was only limited to New York is an ignorant statement."

Gail Gottlieb of Manhattan said: "I think he's delusional. Was he on the moon that day?"

NPR Finally Apologizes for Slandering Christian Group

Inside Cover
Wednesday, July 10, 2002

Six months late, the boss of National Public Radio finally apologized today for what some congressmen call a "slanderous" report linking anthrax-laced letters to Traditional Values Coalition.

"We have made mistakes at NPR. One mistake was …our report about TVC," Kevin Klose, president of the taxpayer-supported radio network, said at a House subcommittee hearing.

"You have my personal apology for that mistake, and I hope to go on from there."

Andrea Lafferty, executive director of TVC, called the belated apology "theater" and said it could not undo the damage.

'Anti-Christian Bigotry'

"Clearly NPR employees graduated from the school of anti-Christian bigotry where their new math of two-plus-two-equals-four equates to Christian-organization-plus-speak-out-against-senators-equals-murder," Lafferty asserted.

TVC's lawyers continue to seek a retraction.

'Profiling' at NPR

In January, NPR falsely suggested that TVC was behind the anthrax letters sent last fall to Senate plurality leader Tom Daschle, D-S.D., and Senate Judiciary Chairman Patrick "Leaky" Leahy, D-Vt. It claimed the conservative Christian group "fit the profile."

After listeners objected, NPR broadcast a statement calling the reporting "inappropriate," but it failed to apologize or issue a retraction.

At today's hearing of the House Energy and Commerce Subcommittee on Telecommunications and the Internet, some lawmakers said they were "conflicted" about supporting more money sought by the Corporation for Public Broadcasting, NPR's parent outfit, because of its left-wing bias.

"Perhaps NPR cannot understand that members of TVC and members of the Christian community might be offended by this," said Representative Billy Tauzin, R-La. For these media elitists, "anyone outside that [liberal] circle is considered right wing, abnormal."

Fox News reported, "Some lawmakers question whether CPB [Corporation for Public Broadcasting], chartered in 1969 as an alternative to the three existing networks, is still necessary in the world of broad cable, digital and Internet information systems."

Representative Joe Barton, R-Texas, noted that the public was making CPB's relevancy apparent in its falling ratings.

"Put me down as one of the skeptics about the need for public broadcasting today," he said.

N.Y. Times Tries to Manipulate Public Opinion on Arming Pilots

Phil Brennan
Friday, July 12, 2002

Once again, *The New York Times* is using its news pages to manipulate public opinion — this time using a story about arming pilots in a blatantly obvious attempt to turn Americans against letting pilots have the right to carry guns against hijackers.

In a Page One story, the citadel of "mainstream" media once again proved just how biased it can be, especially in pursuit of the liberal agenda.

The "news" story was entitled "Armed Pilots? Many Travelers Are

Gun-Shy." Reading the *Times* story, one would be led to believe that most Americans oppose pilots being armed.

The *Times* never mentioned in the extensive article — one filled with shrill, anecdotal worries of fellow liberals — that several scientific polls taken since September 11 show that an overwhelming number of Americans want pilots to be armed.

After reporting that on Wednesday the House voted 311-113 to pass a bill backed by the Air Line Pilots Association that would allow commercial pilots to be deputized as federal flight deck officers and carry guns during flights, and noting the bill specified that guns were to be used only in the cockpit, the left-wing *Times* sought to show that the idea is unpopular with Americans.

Look Who's 'Extreme'

The *Times* claims that "the idea that those responsible for flying an airplane might also take on crucial security duties struck some travelers today as an extreme response, perhaps foolhardy."

Hmm, "some" travelers are opposed; better drop the issue right now. That line gives away the propaganda show to come.

"In nearly four dozen interviews in seven major airports, opponents of the idea outnumbered supporters by a ratio of roughly 3 to 2, and expressed deep concern about the consequences of using a gun on an airplane," the *Times* wrote. "People who favored the plan said the presence of an armed pilot provided an added layer of safety and confidence."

Among those quoted by the *Times*:

'Like Arming a Terrorist'

- "It's almost like arming a terrorist. I don't think any of them are highly trained in military combat. You're just basically putting a gun in the terrorist's hands," claimed Maryland college student Adam Dutko.
- Wine salesman Todd Ross of Gilbert, Ariz., featured in the story's first paragraph: "What if the pilot misses the assailant? Anything could happen. I think it's wrong. Absolutely wrong. It's not the way to go. If a pilot had a gun, I don't think I'd feel any safer."
- "They don't always know how to handle people, how to read people," said a woman who claimed to be a former stewardess but refused to give her name. "I flew for almost 20 years, and learned quickly that they couldn't deal with situations as well as we could."

'I'm Not Fond of Arms Anywhere'

- "I'm not fond of arms anywhere, so my initial reaction is, there has to be a better way," said Cynthia Shapiro, an eyeglass-frame designer.

     The paper ran Page One photographs of two of the anti-choice interviewees, complete with large-type quotations. It ran zero pictures of the pro-choicers but on Page A16 offered a photo of pro-choice pilots.

The article did include comments from a few people who dissented from the *Times'* party line.

- "I would feel more secure if they took a gun into the cockpit," said Elise Pryor of Phoenix.

'Splatter Them'

- "If you're going to hijack a plane and you know the pilot has a sawed-off 12-gauge shotgun, wouldn't that deter you?" asked Frank Nicholson, of Clemmons, N.C. "With a pistol they can miss. But with a 12-gauge, no way. It would splatter them all over the cockpit, and there's no way you can miss, either."

So, on the basis of its own interviews, with the anti-gun responses quoted extensively, the *Times* suggests that arming airline pilots, some of the most responsible human beings in the nation, already charged with safeguarding the lives of hundreds of passengers at a time, is a bad idea rejected by Americans by a 3-to-2 margin.

What Legitimate Polls Say

But the *Times* carefully ignored polls that show exactly the opposite — most of which indicate the public is 3 to 1 in favor of the proposal.

- A *Time*/CNN poll (two left-leaning outfits) taken just after the September 11 attacks revealed that 61 percent of Americans favored allowing pilots to carry guns.
- Two polls conducted more recently, one by the Winston Group and another by the Wilson Center, found that level of support had risen to 75 percent.
- A survey by Allied Pilots Association on October 9–10 found that 75 percent of respondents supported arming pilots. Apparently, those surveyed saw the issue as one of safety, not guns. Of those who advocated "some form of gun control," 77 percent also supported arming pilots, according to Rights Watch International in Raleigh, N.C.
- Other recent polls found by NewsMax.com indicate that 75 percent of all Americans as well as commercial pilots favor arming pilots.

But such statistics are inconvenient for the anti–Second Amendment rights *New York Times*, which not only doesn't want pilots armed but also opposes gun ownership by any and all Americans.

PART 2

New Dangers

❖

Chapter 6

Weapons of Mass Destruction

General Singlaub: Prepare for Biological, Chemical Attacks

NewsMax.com
Thursday, September 13, 2001

General Jack Singlaub, the former U.S. supreme commander of all U.S. forces in Korea, told NewsMax.com that additional, more significant attacks against the U.S. could take place in the next several weeks.

He warned that an escalation of terror — which might follow such an elaborate scheme as we have already seen unfold — might include the use of chemical or biological weapons of mass destruction.

General Singlaub said that he shared the views of NewsMax national security consultant Colonel Stanislav Lunev, who has also issued a similar warning.

"This is my view," he said. "There is a possibility of a biological or chemical attack."

The view that additional attacks are likely is shared by the U.S. government.

Fox News reported last evening that "lawmakers were told in classified briefings that additional attacks are 'possible if not probable' and they should not assume a false sense of security. This message has been conveyed with a very deliberate and serious level of magnitude."

"This is really war," General Singlaub told NewsMax.com. Singlaub himself witnessed the fireball explosion at the Pentagon;he lives just a quarter-mile from the military complex.

His analysis follows, with direct quotes in italic:

1. Go beyond the terrorists.
"This time we need to strike not only at the terrorists, but the c ountries that give them safe harbor, that finance them, that provide them sanctuary."

2. Russia and China are part of the problem.
"We need to remember that Russia and China continue to be in alliances with many of the nations that are supporting these terrorists."

3. President Clinton is largely responsible for this disaster.

"He decimated U.S. forces. He helped the very nations seeking to harm us, Russia and China. He claimed they were strategic partners. Russia and China have been backing these terrorist countries like Iraq."

"What Clinton did was get the good people out of these agencies, the intelligence agencies. They either quit or were fired. The people who supported Clinton stayed or were promoted.

"Look at the case of Notra Trulock [former head of nuclear weapons security at the Department of Energy]. He was fired because he complained about the lack of security. The people who agreed with Clinton and helped produce this current situation are still running these agencies in the U.S. government.

"Clinton policies also feminized the military. The promotion of feminization and homosexuality not only ruins morale, but to the rest of the world, our enemies look at that and think we are weak."

4. Don't tar Muslims.

"This is very similar to 1941, after Pearl Harbor, when the loyalty of Japanese were questioned. As it turned out, the Japanese-American were fiercely loyal. There are many good Arabs and Muslims in America. These are good Americans. Many, if not most, of the Arab countries have been good allies of the United States. We should not harm a lot of our good allies."

5. Missile defense is urgently needed.

"These defenses are needed for two different threats. First, from the threat of ballistic missiles, ICBMs, which still continue to threaten us. Second, we need theatre missile defense. We need also an expanded homeland defense. This might include upgrading the National Guard and expanding the Coast Guard."

Bush Warned Privately of Coming Nuke Terror Attack

Inside Cover
Monday, September 24, 2001

Hours before his rousing Thursday night address to a joint session of Congress, President Bush warned a congressional prayer meeting that there was credible evidence a second wave of terrorist attacks would strike the U.S., this time featuring chemical, biological or even nuclear weapons.

"It was quite a remarkable scene," *Newsweek*'s Howard Fineman told radioman Don Imus Monday morning.

"The president confessed to [the prayer meeting] his anxieties. He said, 'You know, I have to walk a fine line here. You know my problem.' "

Bush then explained:

"I don't want to alarm people, but there is evidence, there's enough evidence that we face further attacks."

The president's warning included the phrase "chemical, biological and plutonium —meaning the possibility of even nuclear terrorism," the *Newsweek* reporter said.

Shays Warns of Suitcase Nuke Terror Threat

Inside Cover
Tuesday, September 25, 2001

The chairman of the House Subcommittee on National Security, Representative Christopher Shays, R-Conn., warned Monday that the U.S. is vulnerable to nuclear attack by terrorists who may have access to as many as 60 briefcase-size tactical nuclear weapons now missing from the former Soviet Union.

Shays, who has held 18 hearings on terrorism over the last two and a half years, delivered the frightening warning in an interview with WABC Radio's Sean Hannity.

"We've known for years that the host countries have developed nuclear and biological agents and that they haven't been reluctant to share them with the terrorists. ... And frankly, the race we have right now is to make sure that [terrorists] don't get a nuclear device."

Shays warned that the impact of Russia's missing tactical nukes is so potentially devastating they would make an excellent weapon for geopolitical blackmail.

"I guess if you'd be willing to kill 50,000 people you'd probably be willing to use it. But they'd more likely want to blackmail us. More likely they'd say, 'There's a nuclear device somewhere in some city and if you don't do the following it's going to go off.'"

In 1992, NewsMax.com contributor Stanislav Lunev first outlined the threat posed by Russia's suitcase nukes in his book *Through the Eyes of the Enemy*. Lunev is the highest-ranking Soviet intelligence agent ever to defect to the U.S.

Shays said an adviser to Russian President Vladimir Putin had initially admitted to his committee that "out of 140 of [their tactical nukes], the Russians could only account for about 80 of them."

"Now the Russians are denying that and we don't really have a straight answer from our own government," he added.

U.S. officials believe that some of the missing Russian nukes have been sold to the highest bidder, Shays told Hannity.

"The problem we have with the Russians is they can't pay their employees. So some of this very sensitive, very expensive and very dangerous weaponry is being sold for ridiculously small amounts of money."

The congressional security expert said that the impact of a tactical nuclear blast on a crowded urban area would be devastating.

"They're like one-fifth of what was used in Hiroshima. ... It would be a disaster if it went off in any community. You wouldn't be able to go back for years. It would destroy a city. It would just be horrendous. It is our worst fear, obviously."

But the tactical nukes are small enough to make detection nearly impossible.

"They are literally the size of a large briefcase. They're not even the size of a big suitcase," he explained.

Shays said that as bad as the attacks of September 11 were, the worst may be yet to come - even without nuclear weapons.

"We have every reason to believe that terrorists have access to chemical and biological agents. ... It's not a question of *if* there will be a biological or chemical attack — it's a question of when, where and of what magnitude."

One particular threat that hasn't received much attention is smallpox, the congressman said.

"There are only two countries that basically have the germ — the United States and Russia. But the question is, Russia has been somewhat like a sieve in terms of some of their state secrets and some of their weapons - they're getting into the wrong hands."

The Connecticut Republican warned that the U.S. is woefully unprepared for a smallpox attack.

"Smallpox would be devastating. ... We only have about 12 million doses of the vaccine."

Shays said his committee ran a test to gauge the government's response to such an attack. Code-named *DARK WINTER*, the germ was theoretically released in Oklahoma.

"Frankly, we lost," he told Hannity. "We ran out of vaccine. ... We can't develop enough doses of smallpox. It would take five years."

A biological attack is harder to respond to than a chemical attack, Shays said.

"The challenge with a chemical is that it's instant and it's deadly, but at least it doesn't spread and you know about it right away. The problem with a biological agent is you don't know about it until about four days after the germ has been let out."

NATO Warned of Weapons of Mass Destruction

Inside Cover
Wednesday, September 26, 2001

London's *Daily Telegraph* reports today that U.S. officials are warning Britain and other NATO allies that the "war" against terrorism could mean conflict with nations possessing weapons of mass destruction.

U.S. Deputy Defense Secretary Paul Wolfowitz has told NATO delegates in Brussels there is a connection between states that shelter terrorists and those trying to develop nuclear, biological and chemical weapons.

Britain's Defense Secretary Geoff Hoon said: "The point has been made that there are some links between countries that harbor terrorists and those that allow the development of weapons of mass destruction."

Although no states were named, the comments appear to point directly to Iraq.

Wolfowitz has reportedly been arguing strongly within the U.S. administration that the war on terrorism should be extended to Saddam Hussein's regime.

Following their discussions, a somber NATO secretary-general, Lord Robertson, said the alliance would need to adjust its military thinking to cope with the new threat.

He told the *Telegraph*: "The campaign against terrorists will be long, arduous and will require radical new thinking. Adaptability, non-conventional thinking, patience and determination are key elements for this campaign."

Speculation that the U.S.-led coalition was moving closer to military strikes has been fueled by the announcement from Downing Street that Tony Blair has summoned a Cabinet meeting in the next 24 hours.

The prime minister's official spokesman sought to play down the news, insisting that nothing should be read into the timing of the meeting, which was "purely logistical."

Memo to Bush: A Plan to Prevent Weapons of Mass Destruction

Colonel Stanislav Lunev
Tuesday, October 16, 2001

TO: President George W. Bush
FROM: Colonel Stanislav Lunev
DATE: October 16, 2001
RE: Prevent the Use of Weapons of Mass Destruction

In September, just over a month ago, international terrorists used the "cheapest" way to attack America — hitting symbols of American financial and military power.

By doing this, the terrorists have demonstrated to the world just how vulnerable we are. Their success is now a powerful symbol to others — America can be hit by the "weak" at its very center.

The arrest of more than 600 people here in the U.S. over the last month suggests that terrorists number in the thousands or even tens of thousands.

Some "experts" have argued that we have seen the worst: Had the terrorists possessed nuclear, chemical or biological weapons, they surely would have used these first.

Such thinking is wrong and dangerous.

Remember, the terrorists of September 11 and their network members were no amateurs. They hatched their plan over years and trained well for it. They used "cheap" weapons not because they did not have "expensive" weapons of mass destruction; all evidence indicates they have such weapons.

The terrorists also have the resources to buy them. Even President Hosni Mubarak of Egypt told journalist Arnaud de Borchgrave that Osama bin Laden has as much $1 billion in assets from his opium trade.

Bin Laden also has the backing of one or more rogue nations, including Iraq.

It has been reported that Israel's Mossad has evidence that bin Laden's organization obtained several tactical nuclear weapons using Russian "mafia" intermediaries. For sure, Russian mafia actions would have the full backing of the Russian intelligence agencies and government.

So the answer is yes, these terrorists could have hit New York with a weapon of mass destruction, but they chose not to.

Why not?

I believe bin Laden, and perhaps his backers, want a much bigger war. They most certainly want to destroy America — at least its financial power and its military might.

Bin Laden wants a war between Islam and the West. Other nations, such as Russia or Red China, also want to see the U.S. brought to its knees — but for different reasons.

The terrorists and their backers understand that wars do not happen in vacuums or materialize out of nothing. These evil people are clever.

Bin Laden wants to win the hearts and minds of ordinary Muslims.

Of the 1 billion Muslims on earth, only 100 million are fundamentalists, and many of these don't agree with bin Laden's own fundamentalist views.

But to unite the Muslim/Arab world, to bring all fundamentalists together with the many secular Muslims, America must be perceived as the aggressor, victimizing Muslims.

To a degree, bin Laden has achieved this. He has shown to the rogue nations, the fundamentalists and others that by using nothing more than box cutters, he made huge strikes into the very heart of America.

Now, with America's justified bombing of targets in Afghanistan, bin Laden and his allies will try to turn the table on America.

No doubt our bombings, as strategic and surgical as they may be, will be played up in the Arab press as "America, the evil aggressor" — killing innocent poor people in Afghanistan for the actions of some crazy terrorists.

If that perception becomes strong in Arab and other countries, bin Laden has laid the groundwork for more "expensive" strikes against America.

Had bin Laden and his backers used a weapon of mass destruction on September 11, this act would have most assuredly backfired and led to his loss of support among the Muslim faithful.

But since September 11, the Arab press has been rife with reports of Americans mistreating people of the Muslim faith (which we know to be untrue).

With the advent of the bombing campaign, his al Qaeda network has released statements saying, through Al-Jazeera (the popular Arab satellite TV channel) that they will counterattack with bigger attacks against America because they are now justified, in their minds and the minds of many Muslims, in doing so.

How do we prevent such weapons from being used against us?

Right now, there is no way to assure America that such weapons will not be used.

We must be honest and admit that time may already have run out. The terrorists have had a huge time advantage over us. They had almost the whole past 10 years to move without sanction from the U.S. government.

For all practical purposes, these terrorists may have already deployed weapons of mass destruction here.

My experience in Russia's GRU (Russia's military intelligence agency) led me to believe that Russia had already deployed small suitcase bombs in the U.S. This is not so difficult and was even easy under the previous administration.

Already, you are doing many wise things. You understand it is important for America not to play bin Laden's game and not to go to war with Islam. You understand the importance of recreating America's intelligence capabilities.

Still, these are proactive measures that may not prevent a weapon of mass destruction from being used.

Already, I have encouraged you to warn all backers of al Qaeda, including any and all backers of terrorist groups and nations, including Iraq, Iran, Syria and others, that the use of weapons of mass destruction on American soil will cause the U.S. to use such weapons against any and all backers of these terrorists. You should tell them the U.S. will retaliate without investigation and go after "likely suspects."

As terrible as this sounds, it should be done, because the terrorists and their backers believe they can strike America with impunity because they have "distance" from these acts.

They don't believe that if they hit New York with a nuclear weapon, the U.S. will hit Baghdad or other centers.

America must quickly disabuse these nations of this idea. You should not just warn rogue nations, you must have your Pentagon begin to prepare to use such weapons against these nations.

If you do, the many spies in the U.S. government will report back to rogue nations that you are serious and if a weapon of mass destruction is used against America, you will respond with fury. Then no one will be safe.

I can assure you that this will be unsettling to America's enemies.

In the early 1960s, President John Kennedy was faced with a similar nuclear threat from rogue nation Cuba. Kennedy did not warn Castro that he would hit Cuba if the U.S. was so attacked.

Kennedy went right for the jugular. He warned Nikita Khrushchev in no uncertain terms that any nuclear attack by Cuba on the U.S. would require a "full retaliatory" strike at the Soviet Union.

When the Soviets heard the news that Kennedy was not going to be a pushover, weapons of mass destruction were immediately removed from Cuba.

You must emulate Kennedy now. You should do so sooner rather than later.

Bin Laden's Nuclear Weapons?

Inside Cover
Sunday, October 28, 2001

London's *Eye Spy* magazine reports on a secret operation at least 18 months ago whereby al Qaeda operatives acquired nuclear technology and hardware.

According to the Arabic language newspaper *Al Watan Al Arabi,* well-organized terrorists smuggled nuclear warheads, bought with opium and cash from the Russian mafia, overland out of Russian territory via secret routes through Uzbekistan.

There, former Soviet scientists removed the active uranium to be processed and placed it in backpack-size nuclear bombs ready for transportation to the West, undetected.

Sources say bin Laden has used two tons of Afghan opium and $30 million to buy over 20 nuclear warheads.

He has hired an international team of rogue nuclear scientists working in a secret underground base to convert warheads 'expropriated' from former Soviet republics into portable nuclear devices capable of striking targets around the globe.

The newspaper further states that bin Laden developed ties with the mafia of former Soviet republics during the Afghan War, which provided him with the key to obtaining nuclear missile warheads from the disintegrating USSR.

The magazine says MI6 and the CIA now have in-depth intelligence on this operation. Indeed, it is almost certain that when Colin Powell spoke with Pakistan, some of this information was divulged, prompting Islamabad to react.

Analysts believe bin Laden would have little hesitation in exploding a nuclear warhead, which many governments believe would lead to a frightening escalation in the war against terror.

Haig: Warn Rogue States of 'Devastating' Response if WMD Used

John Douglas Browne
NewsMax.com magazine, November 2001

EXCLUSIVE to NewsMax.com

Recent cowardly attacks have moved America from "an age of innocence into a new age of reality," General Alexander Haig, former NATO supreme commander, secretary of state and White House chief of staff, told NewsMax.com in a no-holds-barred interview. General Haig made several key points:

- President Bush is on the right track and doing very well.
- America should follow Israel's example by punishing nations that support terrorism.
- To prevent the use of weapons of mass destruction by terrorists, the president should give "a firm warning in advance that we would retaliate in kind and in a devastating manner."
- America should seek partners as it builds multiple coalitions to destroy these terrorists and their supporters.

Here's what the general had to say.

BROWNE: What did you think of the president's speech, and how is he doing?

GEN. HAIG: His speech was brilliantly crafted and superbly delivered. He has grasped the essential issues and is doing very well. Most importantly, he has set a clear plan for a broad strategy, based on coalitions, to be executed in a sequence according to priorities, based on intelligence. Unfortunately, some people find it hard to get their heads around this and urge a 'selective' response, confined merely to bin Laden.

BROWNE: Do you think he will succeed?

GEN HAIG: I'm very optimistic that he will succeed. His main challenge will be to maintain political support. We must give him credit and march in 'lockstep' support.

BROWNE: Until now, each country has had to deal with terrorism virtually alone. It appears that President Bush has changed that at a single stroke, by declaring a global war on terrorism, based upon coalitions of nations.

GEN HAIG: The success of his whole strategy will depend on this. It is said that "terrorism floats upon the fear of people." Now countries that were afraid to act will be emboldened. We must broaden our confidence in success and not be impatient.

BROWNE: So, this is a revolution in counterterror?

GEN HAIG: Yes, and it will prove key to success. The Israelis have said that they were successful only when they shared anti-terrorist sentiments with the populations of the countries in which the terrorists were hiding. In addition, the president's strategy is multifaceted. Its measures will include politics, economics, finance, psychology, culture, religion and military. It is very clear that military measures will not be exclusive.

BROWNE: How important was Great Britain in forming these coalitions?

GEN HAIG: Vital. If Britain and the 'special relationship' had not been right up front, the cost would have been immeasurable. In modern times, Britain has never let us down. Their support was a good guarantee that others would follow — even counties in central Asia, including Pakistan, which we have mistreated in the past. Progress has been remarkable.

BROWNE: Churchill said, about our alliance with Russia in World War II, that "adversity acquaints us with strange bedfellows." What do you think of the U.S. entering into coalitions with those who, until recently, it had branded as rogue states?

GEN HAIG: The 's' is very important. It is not a single coalition. One should never look a gift horse in the mouth, so we should not recoil at trying to deal with any state that agrees to help. However, we must assess their true commitment. Most importantly, we must ensure that no anti-terrorist alliance is used by certain countries (former rogue states) as an opportunity to brutalize certain other countries, such as Georgia. We must not allow them to represent us as intermediaries. We must deal directly.

BROWNE: Why do you feel that these Islamic terrorists are so anti-American?

GEN HAIG: I don't agree with those who say that it is because we support Israel. They are against democracy and the West. It is a throwback to a seventh-century philosophy in an area that was the cradle of modern terrorism, although Russia aided greatly in its evolution and development.

First, they (the Arab countries) tried feudalism and it failed. Then they tried Pan-Arabism, which also failed. After that, they flirted with the Western culture and were disappointed. Now, they (the extremists) are very frustrated and they (the terrorists) seize upon a seventh-century code that they feel justifies them in killing the 'infidel'.

BROWNE: Do you share the view of some that an imminent nuclear, chemical or biological terrorist threat now exists?

GEN HAIG: Speaking optimistically, I do not think that any terrorist organization yet has an effective means of delivery. But we should issue a firm warning in advance that we would retaliate in kind and in a devastating manner.

BROWNE: That should act as a serious deterrent to rogue states.

GEN HAIG: That's right.

BROWNE: Do you see the president's establishment of a Homeland Defense Department as a major move to strengthen America?

GEN HAIG: Yes, this is needed most urgently. I well remember when I was at the White House during our war on drugs. All the different government agencies, departments and even committees that had a finger in that war needed lashing together in order to get effective action. It was not done. Now the president has done what has been needed for decades. Don't forget that drugs have played a major role in the financing of terrorism. This lashing together is very, very critical, but it will be a very hard job and will require active support for the president.

BROWNE: It appears that, with consensus in Congress, President Bush could do much good for the long-term interests of the United States.

GEN HAIG: Yes. If he moves properly, he will achieve miracles.

BROWNE: From this, America could emerge much, much stronger?

GEN HAIG: They say "even an ill wind brings some good." I believe this latest outrage will result in America passing out of an age of innocence into a new age of reality.

BROWNE: As you say, the critical element will be the maintenance of political support.

GEN HAIG: It is this challenge that will dictate success, for in the past, the democracies have been found wanting. This time, we have been given a good and clear plan. Now, as Americans and allies, we must show patience, resolve and loyalty to President Bush in this global war on terrorism.

John Browne is a former member of Britain's Parliament and adviser to Margaret Thatcher when she was prime minister. General Alexander Haig Jr., former U.S. secretary of state, NATO commander and White House chief of staff, is a member of the international advisory board of NewsMax.com.

Report: Probers Suspect bin Laden Shipped Nukes to U.S.

Inside Cover
Sunday, November 11, 2001

A day after Osama bin Laden told a Pakistani newspaper that he had obtained nuclear weapons and is willing to use them against the U.S., another Pakistani paper claims investigators suspect he has pre-positioned the weapons inside America.

"Pakistani and American investigators believe that Osama bin Laden's al Qaeda network may have successfully transported several nuclear, biological, and chemical weapons of mass destruction to the United States," the *Frontier Post* reported Saturday.

A source with knowledge of the bin Laden nuke probe told the *Post* that the FBI, the CIA and Pakistani intelligence now believe that at least two briefcase-size nuclear weapons may have reached U.S. shores.

Investigators have traced at least one of the weapons to bin Laden's al Qaeda terror network.

"The weapon identified is a small 8-kilogram device that carries at least 2 kg of fissionable plutonium and uranium," the *Post* said. "The device, of Russian make, carries a serial number 9999 and manufacturing date October 1988."

The charging mechanism reportedly can be activated through a timer or even through a cell phone command.

In September, Representative Christopher Shay, R-Conn., who has chaired 18 hearings on terrorism since 1998 as head of the House Subcommittee on National Security, warned the bin Laden "suitcase nuke" scenario should be taken seriously.

"We've known for years that the host countries have developed nuclear and biological agents and that they haven't been reluctant to share them with the terrorists," Shays told WABC Radio's Sean Hannity. "And frankly, the race we have right now is to make sure that [terrorists] don't get a nuclear device."

Shays said an adviser to Russian President Vladimir Putin had initially admitted to his committee that "out of 140 of [their tactical nukes], the Russians could only account for about 80 of them."

"Now the Russians are denying that, and we don't really have a straight answer from our own government," he added.

On Saturday, Putin discounted the bin Laden nuke threat, saying he doubted al Qaeda had obtained a nuclear device from Russian sources.

The White House echoed the Russian president, saying the U.S. had no evidence suggesting bin Laden had obtained nukes.

Terrorist Nuclear Threat Real

NewsMax.com
Friday, February 1, 2002

The threat of terrorists acquiring nuclear material and building a dirty bomb is real, the *Chicago Tribune* reported Thursday.

A dirty bomb is a crude nuclear device that weds a traditional explosion with radioactive material, which could contaminate a wide area and cause heavy casualties in a densely populated area.

"As fears rise over terrorists trying to possess nuclear bombs, a disturbing trend is emerging in the shadowy world of weapons smuggling: More thieves are trafficking in plutonium and highly enriched uranium, the essential materials for a nuclear device," the *Tribune* reported.

The U.N.'s International Atomic Energy Agency in Vienna has confirmed "411 incidents of trafficking in nuclear material and industrial and medical radioactive sources."

Russia remains the main source of stolen nuclear materials.

The *Tribune* noted that "all the trafficking cases since 1999 have occurred in Europe or the countries of the former Soviet Union. In Paris, police arrested three men and seized 5 grams of highly enriched uranium inside a lead cylinder."

Osama bin Laden has sought to acquire nuclear materials to develop a weapon. U.S. intelligence is uncertain whether bin Laden has acquired nuclear materials or weapons of mass destruction.

Fallout Shelters Fall Short in U.S.

Dave Eberhart, NewsMax.com
Friday, February 15, 2002

Despite intelligence of homespun "dirty nukes" and the inevitable use by terrorists of nuclear device delivery via cruise missiles, the new federal Office of Homeland Security is not promoting fallout shelters, according to spokesman Gordon Johndroe. The reasoning behind the policy has the most to do with dollars and cents, with a little history and psychology percolating in the mix.

According to Commander Michael Dobbs, a policy planner on the Joint Staff, an effective shelter program would cost $60 billion, 30 times the cost of implementing a crisis relocation strategy in large cities.

"Evacuation is still the primary protective measure in the event of a nuclear incident," said Don Jacks of the Federal Emergency Management Agency (FEMA).

'Duck and Cover'

Edwin Lyman, scientific director for Nuclear Control Institute, has evaluated the state of affairs as nothing less than a return to the primitive Cold War ritual of "duck and cover."

"If there were a nuclear explosion of relatively small yield, people who are maybe tens of miles away would have something like a half an hour to shelter themselves," Lyman said. "Does this mean that the U.S. should reactivate a system of fallout shelters? I don't know."

According to Dobbs, civil defense programs have historically been on the government's back burner. Annual appropriations for civil defense never totaled much more than $1 billion (1962) and, from 1952 to 1986, varied between $200 million and $400 million.

In 1984, per capita federal expenditures for civil defense programs were 75 cents, contrasted with $6 for ballistic missile defense and $1,350 for the Department of Defense.

In 1957, with a bellicose Soviet Union flexing, President Dwight Eisenhower refused to initiate a fallout shelter program. Following through with his campaign promises of "missile gap" catch-up with the Reds, however, President John Kennedy was an exception to the rule, calling for "a fallout shelter for everyone as rapidly as possible."

In 1972 President Richard Nixon followed the lead of his former boss and refused to augment civil defense programs.

And it is not just the government that's been slow to get hot and bothered by the issue.

In a 1953 poll, Americans were asked whether they were likely to build an air raid shelter within the next year. Fewer than 3 percent said yes. True to the poll, 10 years later, fewer than one in 50 Americans had built any kind of shelter. And this was at the time of the Cuban missile crisis, when fears of nuclear holocaust were nearly pandemic.

According to Dobbs, the public apathy toward shelters during the Cold War was mostly grounded in a mind-set that such preparations were futile in the face of a large-scale nuclear exchange.

But that mind-set is changing and was well on its way to being recast, even before September 11.

In a 1999 survey by the Pew Research Center, 64 percent of those polled stated that they thought a major terrorist attack on the U.S. involving biological or chemical weapons would happen sometime over the next half-century.

The experts agree. They now see nuclear attacks from terrorists or a rogue nation as limited in scope and duration, making precautions for a WMD incident prudent. There is no more exaggerated fear of "nuclear winter."

The experts also agree that despite all that is being done by the states and the federal government, self-help will be the rule for many citizens during the initial hours of a large-scale nuclear incident.

The rub, according to Dobbs: "We are spending billions to train first responders and local leaders, but very little to train the general public." He suggested that FEMA provide citizens with information on how to protect themselves and their families from attack, just as the Home Front Command does in Israel. Another imperative: tax incentives for Americans who install a sheltered space in their home.

Dobbs also sees the nation's stockpiling of antidotes such as the controversial potassium iodide as a step in the right direction, but of limited utility for those who have to wait days after an incident until the medicines can be distributed.

Gimme Shelter

In the meantime, some Americans are voting with their pocketbooks and digging up their backyards just like the good old days of the Cold War. "They're treating me less like a crazy woman than they did before," Dr. Jane Orient of Tucson, Arizona, who promotes home shelters as head of Doctors for Disaster Preparedness, told NewsMax.com.

Fallout shelters are a good defense from radiation but are woefully inadequate in the U.S. and should become a government priority, she said.

Dr. Orient's favored example: "If that soot raining down in Brooklyn [from the World Trade Center] had been radioactive, there would be many thousands, maybe millions, of people dying slow, agonizing deaths from radiation sickness that could have been prevented had people had access to shelter."

If she had it her way, the U.S. would be more like the Russians, Chinese or Swiss. The Moscow subways double as shelters, equipped with blast doors. Much of the population of Beijing could be evacuated underground in about 10 minutes. And Switzerland has shelter for 110 percent of its population in private homes and public buildings.

In starkest contrast, companies such as Boeing that have contracts with the government are proscribed from preparing shelter space for emergency occupancy.

It all comes full circle, back to the dollars and cents. There are plans for basement shelters that cost as little as several thousand dollars. However, for really effective protection against biological, nuclear and chemical threats, prices jump to $40,000 and higher. The deluxe shelters are equipped with air filtration systems and hand-pump toilets, allowing people to hold out from 30 days to several months.

Canadian Intelligence: 'Axis of Evil' in Hot Pursuit of Nukes

Inside Cover
Wednesday, February 27, 2002

A report by Canada's intelligence service (CSIS) released yesterday said that "axis of evil" countries Iraq, Iran and North Korea are aggressively pursuing the acquisition of nuclear weapons and warned they may share them with terrorists who threaten the U.S.

"Iraq, with its demonstrated history of a large-scale program, appears determined to acquire a nuclear weapons capability at the earliest opportunity," the report said, according to Canada's *National Post*. "So do Iran and Libya, albeit being considerably less advanced."

While it's long been known that Iraq and North Korea were developing nuclear weapons, the prospect that Iran has the same ambition may explain why President Bush included the country in his "axis of evil" designation last month.

Iran has attempted to acquire the capacity to enrich uranium, necessary to produce nuclear weapons, by purchasing components piecemeal from suppliers in Western Europe, according to U.S. military and intelligence sources quoted in the CSIS report.

Dr. Khidhir Hamza, who ran the Iraqi nuclear weapons program during the late 1980s and early 1990s, said last week that the bomb his team built for Saddam Hussein was complete except for the key ingredient of enriched uranium. Hamza contended that Hussein is now working on a bomb that could have twice the explosive power of the one detonated over Hiroshima in 1945.

The former top Iraqi physicist said his scientists were in the process of obtaining enriched uranium from French scientists when the Gulf War interrupted the Iraqi nuke program.

Internal al Qaeda documents recovered during the U.S. war in Afghanistan show that Osama bin Laden had obtained designs for nuclear weapons, possibly from Pakistani nuclear scientists sympathetic to his cause, the *Post* said.

Representative Weldon Details Missing Soviet Suitcase Nukes

Inside Cover
Tuesday, March 5, 2002

National Security expert Representative Curt Weldon, R-Pa., detailed Tuesday night a chilling 1997 conversation he had with a former top aide to then–Russian President Boris Yeltsin, who revealed that scores of suitcase-size nuclear weapons had vanished from the old Soviet Union's nuclear arsenal.

"This goes back to May of 1997 when I took one of my delegations to meet with General [Aleksandr] Lebed, who had just stepped down as Yeltsin's top security adviser," Weldon told Fox News Channel's *Hannity & Colmes.*

"He was talking about the state of the Russian military and how generals and admirals were selling off technology they used to control because they felt betrayed by the motherland.

"It was then that he related a story to myself and six of my colleagues that he was assigned by Yeltsin to account for 132 small atomic demolition munitions. These are commonly referred to as suitcase nukes."

Weldon continued:

"He said, 'Congressman, I used all the leverage I have as the president's adviser. We could only locate 48.' Which meant that there were over 80 small atomic demolition devices with the capacity of one to 10 kilotons that they just could not locate.

"I came back and briefed the CIA and they said, basically, 'We have no way of knowing [if that's true],' " Weldon recalled.

Over the weekend *Time* magazine reported that a tipster had warned U.S. anti-terrorism probers last fall that one of the missing Soviet suitcase nukes had been smuggled into New York City by Osama bin Laden's al Qaeda terrorist network.

The tipster's information proved bogus, but the *Time* report has drawn new attention to accounts of missing Soviet nuclear weapons.

Scientists: Threat of 'Dirty' Nukes Is Real

NewsMax.com Wires
Thursday, March 7, 2002

WASHINGTON — The United States must accept that terrorists could use non-weapons-grade nuclear material to attack cities, scientists told a Senate committee Wednesday.

The Senate Foreign Relations Committee discussed radiological weapons that would involve not nuclear explosions but the spread of radioactive contamination among a civilian populace.

Senator Joseph Biden, D-Ill., committee chairman, noted that such weapons previously had been thought to be unusable, since the extremely radioactive materials needed would end up killing anyone creating such a device. The suicidal September 11 attacks, however, proved that theory wrong, he said.

"I just want us to look realistically at the threat and to make some realistic decisions, based on priorities and limited resources, after we have heard all the evidence," Biden said. "We need to know what has to be done to ensure that the threat remains exactly that: a threat and nothing more."

The witnesses, including Steven Koonin, a physics professor and provost of the California Institute of Technology in Pasadena, said radiological terrorism was more than just a fear, but a plausible occurrence with major consequences.

"Gram for gram, radioactive material can be at least as disruptive as weaponized anthrax," Koonin testified.

Casualties from an isotope-dusted conventional explosive or other attack likely would be light, Koonin said. Guidelines on radiation exposure, to say nothing of public misconceptions and fears, could prompt the long-term abandonment of highly populated areas, he said.

Witnesses estimated that cleanup costs from a sizeable radiological attack in a major city could easily exceed tens of billions of dollars.

"The danger presented is real and credible; it would not be a trivial undertaking by any means, but it is doable," testified Henry Kelly, president of the Federation of American Scientists.

If the Hart Senate Office Building in Washington had been contaminated with radioactive cesium instead of anthrax, Kelly said, the only way to meet Environmental Protection Agency safety guidelines would have been to abandon or demolish the building.

Kelly's testimony included a disturbing study by the Federation of American Scientists of possible radiological attack scenarios. If terrorists could manage the very difficult task of obtaining a rod of cobalt used in food irradiation, and were able to survive transforming that rod into a powderlike form, a bomb containing that material could contaminate hundreds of square miles.

An explosion at the southern tip of Manhattan in New York could spread the cobalt in an oval stretching into southwest Connecticut, the FAS study said. Strict EPA guidelines would require either decontamination or destruction of structures within the oval. Even if officials used the less-stringent rules Russia imposed after the Chernobyl accident, dozens of blocks in lower and midtown Manhattan would be permanently closed in the cobalt scenario.

The United States already has put several layers of defense in place to prevent such a scenario, said Harry Vantine, program leader for counterterrorism and incident response at Lawrence Livermore National Laboratory in Livermore, California, operated by the University of California for the Department of Energy. Weapons-grade material is under tight control, Vantine testified, but other radiological sources have lesser degrees of security.

The country should review all facilities using such sources to determine where defenses need to be strengthened, Vantine said. Lawmakers and agency heads should avoid the temptation to shortchange other programs to pay for moves such as this, he added.

"Programs in nonproliferation, proliferation detection, counterterrorism and homeland security are closely linked and must not be selected 'either/or' or conducted in isolation from each other," Vantine testified.

Several witnesses said expanding radiation sensor networks to put "one on every lamp post" would be another simple but very effective measure in preventing radiological attacks. Since shielding a weapon's radioactivity would be difficult, the sensors could provide enough advance warning to thwart an attack.

"The monitoring technology is well-established, the power and maintenance requirements are likely to be minimal, and the specificity and robustness will be high," Koonin testified.

COPYRIGHT 2002 BY UNITED PRESS INTERNATIONAL. ALL RIGHTS RESERVED.

Warren Buffett Sees Nuke Attack on U.S.

Inside Cover
Monday, May 6, 2002
Investment guru Warren Buffett says a terrorist attack on American soil is "virtually a certainty." Envy has fueled rage against the U.S. even as the ability to build a nuclear device has spread, Buffett said Sunday at the annual meeting of Berkshire Hathaway Inc.

"We're going to have something in the way of a major nuclear event in this country," said CEO Buffett. "It will happen. Whether it will happen in 10 years or 10 minutes or 50 years… it's virtually a certainty."

The top targets are Washington and New York because terrorists want to traumatize the nation and kill as many people as possible, Buffett said. Chemical or biological attacks are similarly high risks, he said.

Buffett, the second-richest man in the world, has holdings in Coca-Cola Co., American Express and the left-wing Washington Post Co., but his main business is insurance. The September 11 attacks cost his insurance companies billions.

Rumsfeld: Terrorists Will Use Weapons of Mass Destruction

NewsMax.com Wires
Wednesday, May 22, 2002
WASHINGTON — Terrorist nations will develop the capability to attack the United States with weapons of mass destruction, Secretary of Defense

Donald Rumsfeld told a Senate panel Tuesday.

"Let there be no doubt, it is only a matter of time before terrorist states, armed with weapons of mass destruction, develop the capability to deliver those weapons to U.S. cities, giving them the ability to try to hold America hostage to nuclear blackmail," Rumsfeld told a Senate Appropriations sub-committee.

"They inevitably will get their hands on them, and they will not hesitate to use them."

Iraq, Iran, Syria, Libya and North Korea are developing such weapons of mass destruction and will supply them to terrorists, to which they already are linked, the defense secretary said.

COPYRIGHT 2002 BY UNITED PRESS INTERNATIONAL. ALL RIGHTS RESERVED.

Potential Fallout From 'Dirty Bomb' Attack

Patrick Goodenough, CNSNews.com
Tuesday, June 11, 2002

Terrorists armed with "dirty bombs" might not be able to cause the devastation of a World Trade Center collapse, but they could trigger unprecedented panic, at enormous economic cost.

Experts with Jane's, the defense publication group, say the detonation of a "dirty bomb" — conventional explosives packed with highly radioactive material — in an urban area could have "catastrophic" results.

An entire suburb of Rio de Janeiro, Brazil, had to be evacuated in the early 1990s because of a radiation leak from a broken X-ray tube, according to a *Jane's Sentinel Security Assessment* report.

"A similar catastrophe in New York, London, Paris or Berlin could have major financial repercussions as well as a high human cost," it said.

"The longer-term effects could leave municipal areas uninhabitable for years and give rise to cancers and hereditary defects."

The Pentagon announced Monday that a suspected terrorist, Abdullah al-Muhajir, was arrested last month as he returned to the U.S. after receiving explosives training from Osama bin Laden's group.

Deputy Secretary of Defense Paul Wolfowitz said the man, who used to be known as Jose Padilla, was tasked to look for targets in the U.S. for a possible "dirty bomb" attack.

Jane's assessment of the potential effects of a "dirty bomb" terrorist strike echoes that of the global nuclear watchdog International Atomic Energy Agency.

The IAEA's Abel Gonzalez also sees the most serious implications being psychological and economic, rather than actual loss of life.

Experts generally cite another incident in Brazil when discussing the potential repercussions of a terrorist "dirty bomb" attack.

In 1987, scrap metal thieves stole a capsule of highly radioactive cesium-137 from an abandoned clinic in the city of Goiania, and handed pieces of it to associates around the city to sell.

Exposure to the radiation contaminated 249 people and cost four lives. Eighty-five houses had to be destroyed, and 125,000 drums of contaminated clothing and other items were collected. More than 110,000 people had to be monitored for possible exposure over the months that followed.

"A dirty bomb exploded in a major city could produce similar effects [to the Goiania incident]," says analyst S. Gopal of the South Asia Analysis Group (SAAG) in India. "While the death toll may not be high, the impact would be great with general panic and demoralization."

In the view of *Jane's Terrorism & Security Monitor*, "the mere threat of using a radiological weapon is a potent terrorist tactic, particularly in an urban center, given the likely terror induced by anything nuclear."

Similarly, Brigadier Gurmeet Kanwal, an Indian Army nuclear issues analyst, sees the potential result as the creation of "a fear psychosis that will add to the paranoia that has already got a deep hold over ordinary people the world over after the September 11 attacks."

And he adds that, depending on the radioactive ingredient used, the device could continue to spread radiation for many years.

Pakistan Concerns

According to the Pentagon, al Qaeda suspect Abdullah al Mujahir was arrested on his return from Pakistan.

Security analysts in South Asia and elsewhere point to Pakistan as a key potential source for the type of radioactive material necessary to make an effective "dirty bomb," also known as a radiological dispersal device.

Gopal argues that Pakistan's own nuclear program was born out of nuclear espionage and smuggling.

"It is therefore not improbable that some Pakistani official or scientist with sympathies for the [Islamic] fundamentalists would be tempted to supply nuclear technology or material."

The Washington-based Institute for Science and International Security has reported that it's not known whether all of the nuclear-grade material in Pakistan's possession has been used in actual nuclear weapons.

There is a possibility, it says, that some remains unused and, unless properly secured, could be vulnerable to theft by those motivated either by profit or ideology.

Bin Laden is strongly suspected of wanting to acquire non-conventional weaponry.

Last October, a leading Indian newspaper reported that customs officials earlier in 2001 had confiscated 10 packages of unspecified radioactive material on the Kazakhstan-Uzbekistan border. The report said they were bound southward for Quetta in Pakistan, and al Qaeda was suspected to be the intended recipient.

Dr. Rajesh Kumar Mishra, another SAAG analyst, recalls that testimony during the trial of terrorists involved in the 1998 bombing of U.S.

embassies in East Africa pointed to efforts by al Qaeda to acquire radioactive material as early in 1993.

Sudanese witness Jamal Ahmed Al-Fadl, a former close bin Laden aide, told the Manhattan court he had been approached back then by an al Qaeda representative about the possibility of buying uranium from Sudan. Al-Fadl could not confirm whether the material had actually been bought.

Common Sources

But the major concern about "dirty bombs" is that they do not necessarily need highly sensitive materials like enriched uranium or plutonium.

According to the IAEA, the required material could be stolen from low-security institutions like hospitals, laboratories and universities.

"The number of radioactive sources around the world is vast," it says, and include substances used in cancer radiotherapy treatment, in food preservation and in industry, for example, for checking structural quality.

"Security of radioactive materials has traditionally been relatively light," says the IAEA's Gonzalez.

"An undetermined number of radioactive sources have become orphaned of regulatory control and their location is unknown."

According to a Stimson Center report, the most prominent case of nuclear terrorism occurred in 1995, when Chechen separatists marked the first anniversary of the beginning of their conflict with Russia by placing a "dirty bomb" in a popular Moscow park.

The device, which contained cesium-137 — the same isotope that triggered the 1987 contamination panic in Brazil — was recovered before detonation and rendered harmless.

COPYRIGHT 2002 CNSNEWS.COM. ALL RIGHTS RESERVED.

'Saddam's Bombmaker':
'Dirty Nuke' Attack Worse Than Anthrax

Inside Cover
Wednesday, June 12, 2002

A "dirty bomb" attack on the U.S. would be both more lethal and easier to accomplish than the kind of widespread anthrax attack that panicked U.S. officials feared last fall, according to the one-time chief of Saddam Hussein's nuclear weapons program.

"If anthrax spores were used to terrorize the U.S., plutonium particles are more effective," reports Dr. Khidhir Hamza in Wednesday's *Wall Street Journal*. Hamza, who headed the Iraqi nuke program from 1987 to 1994, calls himself "Saddam's Bombmaker" in his book about those years.

"No high technology is needed to create plutonium dust and once tiny quantities of plutonium are lodged in the lungs there is no known cure," he says. "Most probably, the victim will not know he is afflicted till it is too late."

The Iraqi physicist spoke out as Democrats on Capitol Hill and sympathetic media organs like *The New York Times* accused the Bush administration of hyping the dirty-nuke threat for political reasons.

Hamza contends that Hussein actually tried to use dirty nukes in the Iran-Iraq war of the late 1980s but found them ineffective because the radiation dispersed too easily in the open desert.

However, he warns, "a contaminated building is a different story than an explosion in the desert sands." Any confined location or densely populated urban area is a ripe target for a dirty nuke, says Hamza.

The former Iraqi nuclear weapons chief says lax security in handling radioactive materials is rampant in the nuclear industries of Iraq, Iran, Lybia, Pakistan and the former Soviet republics.

"This creates an environment in which countries can claim lack of discipline of their workers as a cover for many missing radiation sources," he argues. "There are more sellers than buyers of nuclear materials in these countries."

"This environment is ideal for countries like Iraq to train and support a terrorist operation using radiation weapons with complete deniability," Hamza warns.

Experts Sum Up Their Fears of a Nuke Attack

Dave Eberhart, NewsMax.com
Tuesday, June 18, 2002

The screen dramatization of Tom Clancy's *The Sum of All Fears* features terrorists nuking the fans at the Super Bowl in Baltimore. This odd escape vehicle for a terror-warning-overdosed American public is raking in millions at the box office and graphically depicts the "inevitable" nuclear phase of the War on Terrorism described by such administration luminaries as Defense Secretary Donald Rumsfeld and National Security Advisor Condoleezza Rice.

"Hundreds of thousands" of Americans are potentially at risk of nuclear attack, no-nonsense Rumsfeld chillingly says. Rice, whose job it is to know about these things, grimly forecasts that the next terror shoe to drop will "make September 11 look like child's play, by using some terrible weapon."

But what do more neutral experts and institutions say — especially those that do not have to justify to taxpayers the expenditure of billions in a terror war?

And by neutral we don't mean folks such as investment guru Warren Buffett, who will gladly shock any sentient being within earshot with the unwelcome news flash: A nuke attack on American soil is "virtually a certainty."

Neither do we mean Graham Allison, Harvard egghead and an assistant secretary of defense in the Clinton administration, who predicts with the tools of a seer, "bin Laden's final act could be a nuclear attack on America."

Among the more benign experts, there is some general agreement on basics.

Homemade Nuke 'Can Be Ruled Out'

Starting with the good news, it's mighty unlikely that any terror group can build a nuclear weapon from scratch. One senior scientist at Los Alamos National Laboratory opines that the possibility of such an achievement is "so remote that it can be essentially ruled out."

To manufacture weapons-grade uranium, a terrorist would require thousands of sophisticated high-speed gas centrifuges, not to mention a safe haven in which to operate them. Even Iraq could not produce highly enriched uranium for a bomb after a 10-year, $10 billion program, which was eventually trumped by the Gulf War in 1991.

Basing a bomb on plutonium is just as onerous. Even with access to a reactor, the process to extract the plutonium necessitates a specially constructed plutonium extraction plant: chopping up radioactive fuel rods, dissolving them in acid and finally extracting the plutonium from the acid.

And it's not likely the terrorist group is going to find such a plant by rummaging through the newspaper classifieds as if scanning for flight training schools or rental crop dusters.

However, once one gets away from the scratch recipes, the experts agree that the probabilities increase exponentially.

Woeful Russia a Source

Our duty terrorist could certainly look to Russia for its supply of ready-to-rock-and-roll plutonium. The retired Evil Empire has tons of the stuff and, what's more, a poor accounting system, a tradition of smuggling and plenty of underpaid scientists to bribe and undermine.

The penny-pinching terrorist plotter could eschew plutonium altogether and go with buying or stealing the cheaper bomb-grade uranium, just like Uncle Sam used in "Fat Man" and "Little Boy" back in 1945.

One wrinkle: the usual requirement of uranium is a daunting 120 pounds a bomb. Experts say that such an amount is not available on the black market, and if it were, our crack intelligence agencies would know about it in a New York minute.

However, despite the dearth of atomic goods on the shelf, the terrorists are certainly out there trying their level best to steal some of the good stuff or buy it from some thief who has.

In 1993 about 6 pounds of weapon-grade uranium almost went astray in St. Petersburg. In 1998, another effort to steal about 40 pounds of former Soviet Union bomb-grade uranium was nipped in the bud.

Our frank Russian friends tell us that terrorists are now staking out their nuclear-weapon sites.

In any event, most experts agree that one day the terrorists will get their hands on that magic quantity of 120 pounds of bomb-ready uranium and lash it up with a so-called "gun-barrel" trigger where bullets of the fission-able stuff are fired at one another to crank up the runaway reaction that gives you the nuclear mushroom and fireball that figure in that sum of all our fears.

Like reactors and plutonium extraction plants, buying or stealing bomb-grade plutonium is improbable as well. If you believe Russian President Vladimir Putin, there just isn't the product out there to buy. Putin has guaranteed President Bush that none of his country's warheads are unac-counted for.

But some folks in the U.S. Department of Energy were of the opinion a decade ago that 603 metric tons of nuclear materials were stored in 53 sites in the former Soviet Union, where security was euphemistically rated "poor." That tonnage, some guarded mightily by locks and chains, is enough to crank out 41,000 nuclear weapons.

The atomic energy agency counts 18 incidents of trafficking in plutoni-um or uranium since 1993 — none, thankfully, involving enough material to make The Bomb.

There is more bad news about the poor man's uranium nuke. Makeshift as it may be, it works first time, every time. There's no need to ever test it, or for that matter to give away the fact that you have it.

While Swiss Have Shelters, Israel Preps for Nuke Attack Much Like U.S.

Dave Eberhart, NewsMax.com
Saturday, June 22, 2002

As the U.S. faces down the volatile "axis of evil" and Israel occupies a perennial ground zero for potential incoming nuclear missiles from Iran or Iraq, little neutral Switzerland leads the way in traditional civil defense.

Thousands of fallout shelters continue to be built in Switzerland, where the law of the land requires that every structure have space below ground for the number of people that occupy the building above.

"People might find it laughable that we built such rooms, but if we are ever under threat then we will be heroes to our people," said Kurt Grimm of the Swiss Civic Protection Authority.

Last year in the wake of September 11, the Swiss government conducted nationwide mock disaster exercises to test how its civil defense system would cope with a simulated nuclear event that contaminated a wide area of the country and forced millions of people into bomb shelters.

"The shelters were designed for all kinds of incidents, such as nuclear or chemical accidents, not just war," explained Juerg Balmer, also of the Civil Protection office.

Israel's Miserly Nuke Civil Defense

Meanwhile, back in embattled Israel, this past year the Cabinet allocated all of $110 million for preparations against not only nuclear, but chemical and biological attacks as well.

Also last year, in a move foreshadowing President Bush's quest to consolidate home security duties in a new department, the Israeli Cabinet singled out the office of the defense minister as overseer of the attack preparations. Previously, responsibility for domestic security was divided among the defense, public security and interior ministries.

The relatively minuscule attack preparations budget is earmarked for, among other staples, protective equipment for rescue troops, mobile (body) identification units, and medical stores.

When Prime Minister Ariel Sharon was last asked whether Israel was ready to protect its citizens against a nuclear attack by Iran, Sharon had no ready answer.

At least part of Sharon's discomfiture must be owing to the sad state of the shelters in his country.

Oops

Three months ago, a Jerusalem high school showed off to the city's mayor how efficiently the 550 pupils at the neighborhood school could move into a shelter if attacked. One key problem, however: The shelter at the ORT-Spanian school had room to accommodate only 200 pupils.

Recently, the Union of Local Authorities in Israel released a report indicating that 47 percent of the country's high schools and 44 percent of the secondary schools lack bomb shelter space for the students and staff.

Also in the report: 18 percent of the country's high schools and 24 percent of middle schools have no shelters whatever. Of those that do, only 35 percent of the high schools and 32 percent of the middle schools have shelters rated adequate.

The Union estimates the country lacks 295,000 square meters of bomb shelter space — the shortage owing simply to a lack of funds. Adding to the dilemma, the shelters that do exist are not necessarily appropriate as sustained protection from insidious nuclear fallout.

Relying on the Military

Like the U.S., which by the way features no fallout shelters for its non-congressional citizens, Israel looks to its military prowess and technological edge to hopefully keep the populace from having to dash to shelters in the first place.

Of course the paramount example of the Israel defensive formula is the June 1981 precision bombing of Iraq's reactor — at the time poised to produce fuel for a nuclear bomb. In a daring, nearly impossible raid, Israeli jets knocked out the target, knocking Saddam back at least a decade in his mad scramble for The Bomb.

Most impressive was the range to the target: about 560 miles, most of it over hostile Arab territory. In those days the U.S.-made F-16 had a combat radius of about 575 miles, giving the Israeli pilots little margin for error.

These days it's déjà vu for Israel, except that the rogue nation most dangerously playing with nuclear fire is Iran rather than Iraq.

Last year former U.S. Secretary of State Alexander Haig, always a big fan of the 1981 Israeli pre-emptive raid against Iraq, was warning Iran to expect a duplicate Israeli surgical strike against its nuclear reactor if Tehran pursued its reported quest for nuclear arms.

Such ominous saber rattling has not gone unnoticed in Iran.

"If Israel carries out any military action against Iran, it will face a response that will be unimaginable to any Israeli politician," Defense Minister Ali Shamkhani announced in February. Although denying that any retaliation would be nuclear, he reminded Israel and its American ally:

"Iran is not a small country like Iraq. Iran has a powerful artillery, a disciplined army, and skilled air defenses," Shamkhani said.

Jane's Intelligence Review has gone on record, writing: "[Israel] will almost certainly launch a preemptive attack on the Iranian nuclear and research and development infrastructure before it can generate enough weapons-grade material to make ballistic missiles with nuclear warheads."

Jane's added that Israel would more than likely get covert support for the raid from the U.S.

Beyond the Pre-emptory Strike: Deterrence

In addition to its manifest willingness to strike first and parley second, Israel has another key defensive tool in its arsenal.

Israel's launch in late May of its new "Ofec-5" military imaging reconnaissance satellite ramped up its ability to unilaterally detect missile threats originating in Syria, Iran and Iraq.

Israeli army Major General Yitzhak Ben-Yisrael said space vehicles such as Ofec-5 are of "utmost importance" to Israel for obtaining ballistic missile intelligence.

The launch of the spy satellite was not kept as a state secret because Israel wants its belligerent neighbors to know that by using its own space reconnaissance, it can retaliate for any detected mischief by launching a flurry of nuclear-capable Jericho II ballistic missiles — before incoming rockets even engage their targets.

About a week before Israel deployed its new eye-in-the-sky, Iran test-launched a 900-mile-range "Shahab-3" ballistic missile, fully capable of hitting Israel with a nuclear, chemical or biological weapon.

Meanwhile, stuck with an overabundance of shelters dating from the Cold War, the Swiss still build and refurbish their survival holes.

With the relative quiet that has followed 9/11, a few Swiss are regaining confidence or perhaps a sense of humor. Some of the more affluent seek a dual purpose for their mandatory shelters. Wine cellars and artists' studios are popular projects to modify the nation's 261,418 private shelters.

FEMA Preparing for Mass Destruction Attacks on Cities

John O. Edwards
Monday, July 15, 2002

FEMA, the federal agency charged with disaster preparedness, is engaged in a crash effort to prepare for multiple mass destruction attacks on U.S. cities — including the creation of sprawling temporary cities to handle millions of displaced persons, NewsMax has learned.

FEMA is readying for nuclear, biological and chemical attacks against U.S. cities, including the possibility of multiple attacks with mass destruction weapons.

The agency has already notified vendors, contractors and consultants that it needs to be prepared to handle the logistics of aiding large numbers of displaced Americans.

The agency plans to create emergency, makeshift cities that could house hundreds of thousands, if not millions, of Americans who may have to flee their urban homes if their cities are attacked.

Ominously, FEMA has been given a deadline of having the cities ready to go by January 2003 — in about six months.

A source familiar with the deadline believes the effort is related to making the U.S. prepared for counterattacks if the U.S. invades Iraq sometime next year.

FEMA is currently seeking bids from major real estate management firms, and plans to name three firms in the near future to handle the logistics and planning for these temporary cities.

FEMA officials have told these firms they already have tents and trailers ordered. The tents and trailers would provide shelter for displaced populations.

The real estate firms are expected to provide engineers and architects to lay the plans for emergency infrastructure needs, such as sewage and electricity.

FEMA's Plan for Mass Destruction Attacks:
Of Course It's True

Christopher Ruddy
Wednesday, August 7, 2002

Let me state for the record that FEMA is moving ahead with plans to create temporary cities that could handle millions of Americans after mass destruction attacks on U.S. cities.

Though the agency has denied the program to some of our readers and has made misleading claims about NewsMax's original story to members of the press, the basic facts of the story remain unchallenged.

In early July, NewsMax first reported in our e-mail news service, Insider Report, the story "FEMA Preparing for Mass Destruction Attacks on Cities," revealing that FEMA was seeking bids from three major real estate and/or engineering firms to help prepare for the creation of the emergency cities, using tents and trailers — if an urban area is attacked by NBC (nuclear, chemical or biological) weapons.

Since that report, several NewsMax readers and members of the press contacted FEMA and asked them if the NewsMax story was true.

These readers reported to us that FEMA has categorically denied the story.

For example, my friend Jonathan Kemp, who hails from an illustrious California family (his father was a director of Standard Oil of California), called FEMA's Washington office and was told by a public affairs officer, "The news report about FEMA building the temporary cities to house disaster refugees is totally bogus."

NewsMax, of course, told its readers it stood by the story.

In late July, I called FEMA and spoke with public affairs officer Chad Kolton.

I explained to Mr. Kolton that it was improper for the agency to claim that NewsMax had fabricated this story.

Mr. Kolton denied that there was any claim by FEMA that the NewsMax story was baseless, only that it was "factually inaccurate."

He made that claim without having read the NewsMax story, which he asked me to e-mail to him.

As I pointed out to Mr. Kolton, FEMA has put out a bid notice for the program to build the temporary cities (they call it "temporary disaster housing"). The bid is not only a matter of public record, it also is available on the federal government's website.

The Emergency Housing Cities

On June 19, FEMA posted a special bid notice offering contracting firms $300 million for a five-year contract to simply prepare plans to create temporary housing on a scale never before imagined, and then stand by.

This is reportedly one of the largest contracts ever awarded by FEMA for a disaster preparedness program.

The name of the program is entitled "Standby Technical Assistance for Disaster Related Operations."

The bid notice states, as NewsMax first reported, that three real estate/engineering firms will be selected for the program.

The firms will be required to provide "technical support, consultant and project management resources" with the specific duty to "provide project management resources and expertise to support the Disaster Housing Program."

According to the bid notice, the firms need to have professionals, including engineers, architects and other real estate-related experts.

According to a source familiar with the current bid, the program is a major expansion of a smaller program FEMA has had for temporary housing in case of disasters.

The Standby Technical Assistance program bid offering never mentions "mass destruction attacks" or terrorist preparedness.

Instead, the bid notice's "Statement of Work" sets out a broad mandate for the firms being contracted, stating that "The Contractor shall be required to provide support capability for all types of disasters with emphasis on riverine and coastal flooding, tornadoes, hurricanes, typhoons, earthquakes, and tsunamis."

The bid states: "… the firm must have at least one permanent and adequately staffed and equipped office located in the Washington Metropolitan area, and two (2) additional offices in other geographic locations within the United States with the capability supporting deployment operations in the event that one area is incapacitated."

The real purpose of the Standby Program was made clear to potential contractors at a meeting held on July 10 at the Department of Education headquarters in Washington.

FEMA officials met with the representatives of firms seeking the bids. Approximately 100 people attended the meeting.

FEMA officials made very clear that the purpose of one of the most massive undertakings in the agency's history was to prepare for potential mass destruction attacks on U.S. cities.

Sources who attended the meeting tell NewsMax that most of the meeting dealt with how the firms should handle biological, chemical and nuclear disasters.

After he had reviewed the NewsMax story, I again chatted with Mr. Kolton. He identified the factual "inaccuracies" in NewsMax's story.

One was that NewsMax reported the contracted firms need to be prepared for creating such cities by January of next year. Mr. Kolton said the firms only need be hired by January of 2003.

NewsMax reported that FEMA told contractors it had ordered tents and trailers for temporary housing. Mr Kolton said the tents and trailers have not been purchased yet. (That may be the case, but FEMA does currently possess tents and trailers for disaster housing.)

These are minor points — and a far cry from claiming the NewsMax story was "totally bogus" or "riddled with inaccuracies," as some members of the press have been told.

In fact, Mr. Kolton agreed that the program includes preparation for terrorist mass destruction attacks, though the FEMA bid notice specifically avoids using such language.

He stressed that the Standby Program is being implemented to prepare for "all types of disasters" including terrorist ones.

Asked why the bid notice conveniently forgot to mention the potential for terrorism, though it must be among the highest priorities for FEMA, he again stressed that the language does include that possibility — though the program's main focus, he said, is on natural disasters.

What natural disaster had caused such a need for the largest program of its kind ever in the history of FEMA?

In decades of emergency response, why, all of sudden, is FEMA set to spend $300 million just for architects and engineers over the next five years simply to be on "standby"?

This $300 million doesn't include the probable billions that would be needed for infrastructure and labor to implement the emergency cities.

What natural disaster would require FEMA to create emergency cities in different geographic areas of the U.S. at the same time?

Kolton responded that FEMA could foresee two Category 4 hurricanes slamming into two distinct parts of the East Coast at about the same time.

The evidence is clear that FEMA is preparing for mass destruction attacks. There is nothing wrong with this program, and in fact, the agency has a duty to disclose its plans to the public.

Far from panicking the public, I think the public would be happy to learn that the U.S. government — our government — is preparing for potential terrorist acts. FEMA should be applauded for thinking ahead. It has nothing to hide.

NYers Warned: Be Ready for Evacuation

Inside Cover
Wednesday, August 7, 2002
New York City's Public Advocate Betsy Gotbaum is preparing a report warning the city's residents that they need to be ready to evacuate in case terrorists strike again.

Gotbaum's disaster preparedness plan urges city dwellers to maintain a stockpile of basic survival gear like water and a flashlight — along with other more unusual items such as a compass, a map, a whistle and a particle mask, according to a draft of the Gotbaum report obtained by the *New York Post*.

"We're talking about getting out of the house or building or neighborhood," Gotbaum spokesman Stewart Desmond told the paper.

The disaster plan, a result of a yearlong study, is scheduled for release within the next few weeks, he said.

It's not clear whether Gotbaum's report is part of nationwide evacuation plans currently being formulated by the Federal Emergency Management Agency.

Chapter 7

Bioweapons

Don't Believe in Coincidences

John LeBoutillier
Wednesday, June 14, 2000
I don't believe in coincidences.

Here are two so-called coincidences — neither of which is anything but a deliberate act of malicious behavior against the United States.

I do not believe these "lost" or "stolen" computer hard drives at our Los Alamos laboratory disappeared "coincidentally" during the confusion from a calamitous fire *admittedly set by our own government!*

What is more likely is that our government has been dangerously penetrated — to the point where someone either set the fire with the intent to steal these valuable nuclear secrets or else used the fire as the distraction needed to steal these hard drives.

Amazingly, neither the media nor the congressmen and senators who grilled Energy Secretary Bill Richardson yesterday even raised the possibility of a *deliberate linkage* between the fire and the theft/loss of these secrets.

We have learned that under the Clinton administration **nothing should be ignored**. Anything is possible. The most innocent of explanations should be discarded; the worst implication should be drawn.

My guess is that the Chinese have deeply penetrated the Clinton administration. So deeply, in fact, that Clinton himself is not beyond suspicion. The Chinese military sees an invaluable "window of opportunity" closing when Clinton leaves office. So the time to strike is *now*.

Having learned what is where at Los Alamos, all that remained was a way to get those hard drives out of the lab.

The "controlled burn" was the *perfect distraction*.

Whatever happened will never be revealed. If suddenly in the next few days the Energy Department suddenly "finds" the lost hard drives, don't believe it. That will be a "cover story"; the truth is the lab's secrecy has been forever violated and we have to assume for security purposes that *all our enemies worldwide* may very well have total access to all our nuclear secrets.

A proper president would do the following: a) fire Richardson immediately; b) close Los Alamos permanently; c) investigate every single human being who works or has recently worked at Los Alamos — from the head of the lab down to the parking lot attendant; d) investigate everyone even tangentially involved in setting the forest fire — including upper-level bureaucrats who may have known of the "burn" before it was initiated.

Clinton, of course, is an **improper** president. He will do none of the above.

"Coincidence" number two is last fall's sudden appearance in the New York metropolitan area of an outbreak of West Nile fever.

Never before had this Middle Eastern virus been seen in the United States. Then it suddenly is found in people and in birds in the borough of Queens and then in other areas around New York City. Several elderly people died from West Nile; many others were severely ill and hospitalized because of this mysterious disease.

Again the media and the Congress were — and remain — lax in linking up two related facts. U.N. weapons inspector Scott Ritter has revealed that Saddam Hussein's Iraqi scientists were working on West Nile virus!

Why were Ritter and the United Nations inspecting Iraq at all? Because of evidence that Saddam was developing weapons of mass destruction and biological agents, as well. Thus, the United Nations kept severe sanctions on Iraq until Saddam could be proven to be in compliance with U.N. mandates on his government.

Saddam's country is suffering because of these sanctions.

And Saddam was so furious that the U.N. would not lift these sanctions that he finally threw out the inspectors.

Do you believe that this clever and devious madman would just sit idly by while the United Nations kept turning the screws on his regime?

Do you believe it is a "coincidence" that this virus suddenly then appeared **directly across the East River from U.N. headquarters?**

As I said, I do not believe in "coincidences" — at least not when it comes to cases involving liars and deceivers such as Clinton and Saddam.

West Nile Virus: I *Still* Do Not Believe in Coincidences

John LeBoutillier
Monday, September 25, 2000
Just imagine:

The motorcade arrived well past midnight at the back door of an unobtrusive middle-class Baghdad house. Guards leaped out of the front and back cars and quickly surrounded the middle car.

The back door of the house opened and two more heavily armed soldiers appeared. One nodded in the silence of the night.

With another furtive glance around the street the lead bodyguard opened the right rear door to the black limousine. Out stepped a familiar figure, who nodded and strode directly into the house.

Inside the former home of one of the regime's supporters the house had been transformed into the Iraqi equivalent of the White House Situation Room. Radio equipment squawked with military updates. A large electronic map of the Middle East showed deployments of military units, planes and mobile missile emplacements.

Taking a seat at the head of a long rectangular table, the Iraqi strongman Saddam Hussein removed his turban and brought the meeting to order. "Diplomatic update!" he barked.

The only man dressed in a civilian business suit pulled himself up to the table and replied: "Eminence, the news from New York and Washington is not good. Our people tell us that there is no chance the United Nations will even relax the sanctions. Our expulsion of the CIA spy Ritter has angered Washington, as we expected. Furthermore, Israel, the Saudis and the Americans are in agreement: No one will even talk of lifting or relaxing any of the strictures on our economy."

Saddam's mouth showed a cruel turn rarely seen in public photos. "The Saudis *and* the Israelis are working together on this?"

The diplomat nodded his silent assent.

Saddam then growled, "Research update."

Two nerdy-looking young men wearing military uniforms with a patch indicating a special 'scientific branch' of the Republican Guards nervously opened their file folders and passed papers around the table. The senior of the two addressed the head of the table: "Eminence, we have made progress in the delivery system. We can deliver the package — but we still have trouble with the potency of that package."

"How lethal?"

The other of the two nerds coughed once and nervously replied, "Occasionally lethal. But not a very high percentage yet."

Saddam scowled at this news. "What is the problem?"

"Eminence, we have been unable to pack a lethal dose into a mosquito and still have the mosquito able to deliver it. Such toxicity kills the messenger, so to speak."

The feared Iraqi tyrant actually smiled at this. "Understood." He swiveled in his chair and studied an electric world globe off to his left. Spinning it, he scanned both hemispheres and thought in silence. Then he looked at yet another military figure sitting at the table. "Targets?"

The senior military officer, his chest decorated with medals won during conflicts against neighboring Iran, slid a single sheet of paper across to the Iraqi strongman.

Saddam carefully read the document and then smiled. "Clever," he muttered.

Casually fingering the epaulet on his left shoulder, Saddam Hussein then ended the early morning meeting with a simple command, "Hit all four targets."

The meeting broke up. Saddam was escorted to yet another underground bunker for a safe night's sleep. Each of the other military contingents hustled off to their HQs to implement their leader's command.

Within days special teams of Iraqi scientists pre-positioned around the globe began a delicate — but deadly — process: releasing specially bred mosquitoes into the atmospheres of New York City; the Washington, D.C., suburbs; Israeli coastal regions and southern areas of Saudi Arabia.

The mosquitoes were loaded with the potentially deadly West Nile virus.

The goal: Inflict insidious damage to the civilian populations at the very centers of U.N. activity that were hurting the Iraqi civilian population through the continued imposition of sanctions against all aspects of Iraq's economy.

By this week it has been reported that in parts of New York City, the Maryland suburbs surrounding Washington, D.C., the mid-coastal region of Israel and the southern Saudi coastal areas have all seen a precipitous rise of the incidents of West Nile fever. Israel even calls it an epidemic.

Is it not odd that no such increase has been reported in, say, Seattle or Houston, or Paris or Moscow or Bangkok or Peking or Tokyo?

Is it just a coincidence these avowed enemies of Iraq have seen this sudden rise of West Nile, while no such increase has been reported anywhere else?

I don't think so.

Three months ago I wrote a column entitled "I Do Not Believe In Coincidences."

I still don't. Do you?

Anthrax Q & A

Kevin G. Briggs
Monday, October 1, 2001

The following question-and-answer sheet was prepared by Kevin G. Briggs, former president of The America Civil Defense Association and current director of the U.S. Disaster Preparedness Institute. His new book, *Preparing for Terrorism*, will be released shortly.

Due to recent concerns and the growing interest in biological/chemical warfare preparedness and mitigation, we have extracted the following article from a recent issue of the *Journal of Civil Defense* in an effort to assist you in your preparations for a potential biological attack on the United States.

Frequently Asked Questions About Anthrax

Question 1: Is the U.S. prepared for anthrax attacks?

Generally, no. An anthrax attack can occur very quietly without any bombs going off or any observable "clouds" being present. Our abilities to detect anthrax rapidly are very limited at present, so the first sign that an attack occurred could be thousands of people rushing to the hospital after a few days of exposure. Most states rate biological attacks as one of their weakest preparedness areas.

Question 2: Why worry about anthrax attacks?

Many are concerned that U.S.-based terrorists with ties to Iraq or Osama bin Laden might try to unleash a biological attack against the U.S. population in response to any major U.S. anti-terrorism initiative or military actions.

Question 3: Is this a credible threat?

This is an unknown. We know that Iraq has hidden and lied about much of its biological warfare program. We do know that Iraq has claimed to have produced, and subsequently destroyed (so it says), roughly 9,000 liters of anthrax.

In addition, it has admitted testing anthrax and other agents as part of its biowarfare program. As a result of this and other perceived threats, former Secretary of Defense Cohen decided to vaccinate all active duty and reserve personnel against anthrax. He shifted $500 million to new chemical and biological preparedness programs. Former President Clinton also added roughly $10 billion to the budget (in January 1999) into preparing for weapons of mass destruction terrorism — largely to help mitigate biowarfare attacks.

The bottom line is that Iraq has the technical expertise and demonstrated capability to support anthrax terrorism. Whether it or other terrorist organizations have successfully placed (or attempted to place) terrorists in the U.S. with anthrax is unknown — or at least unknown to the American public.

Many other countries have known or suspected biological warfare programs. Information and expertise from Russia's extensive biowarfare programs are likely to have leaked out to several other nations and terrorist groups.

Question 4: How big a problem is anthrax?

Anthrax weapons can be produced that can have the same killing capability as nuclear weapons for a fraction of the cost and expertise. For example, the Oak Ridge National Laboratory did a comparison of costs of various threats and came up with the following:

Weapon Lethality Versus Cost

From the late Dr. Conrad Chester ,Oak Ridge National Laboratory

Weapons compared to cost for

killing the most people within a square-mile area

Conventional cluster bomb weapons: up to millions of dollars

Neutron bomb: roughly $2 million

One ton of GB nerve agent: up to $100,000

1 kilogram of anthrax (2.2 lb): less than $50

Question 5: How deadly is anthrax?

According to Dr. Chester, cultured anthrax has roughly 2×10^5 lethal doses per gram. Anthrax in a slurry has roughly 10^7 lethal doses per gram. Powdered Anthrax has roughly 10^8 lethal doses per gram.

Former Secretary of Defense Cohen illustrated this point on TV by saying that a five-pound bag of anthrax, if properly dispersed, could kill perhaps half of the population of Washington, D.C.

Dr. Harold Strunk, who retired from the U.S. military and has extensive experience with anthrax, stated that a sugar cube quantity of anthrax could theoretically kill 100 million people. He pointed out that in reality, the number of people potentially killed by this amount of anthrax is much less because of the problems of dispersal within a population.

Question 6: How would an anthrax attack occur?

According to the late Dr. Chester, the best method of spreading lethal anthrax is through spraying the spores into the wind, where it is subsequently inhaled and begins to multiply. Dr. Chester, while at Oak Ridge National Labs, looked at many anthrax attack scenarios, which resulted, in part, with the following estimations:

Scenario 1: A single-operator terrorist with a truck-mounted 55-gallon drum of anthrax and sprayer could cause tens of thousands of deaths within a city.

Scenario 2: A sophisticated and well-trained technical terrorist group with four medium-sized planes (DC-3 size) were shown to potentially kill 35 percent of the U.S. population with one night flight spraying anthrax over key population centers.

Question 7: Some experts say anthrax is difficult to disperse through air and sunlight. Is this true?

Presumably the terrorists would be trained on what the best weather conditions are for dispersing anthrax spores and how to effectively produce an aerosol laden with anthrax spores. According to experts, this would typically be done at night or on an overcast day with a gentle breeze so that the sun would not kill off the spores before they are inhaled. Terrorists can certainly wait for the right weather conditions to exist. According to studies performed by the Oak Ridge Labs and the U.S. Congressional Office of Technology Assessment, a well-executed attack can kill thousands to many millions. The Defense Department has formally stated that a large portion of a city could be killed in a well-executed anthrax attack (see http://www.anthrax.osd.mil/.

Question 8: How vulnerable is the food supply to anthrax?

Anthrax spores can fall upon food in either a dedicated attack on the food supply or as a secondary effect of an airborne release. If ingested in a sufficient dose, then an intestinal form of anthrax can occur that can be lethal for somewhere between 25 percent and 60 percent of those infected — if it is conventional anthrax for which we have clinical data resulting from the few cases where people ate infected meat. However, if the antibiotic supplies are limited, or a more drug-resistant strain is used, then a higher percentage of deaths would likely be expected.

Question 9: What should be done at the governmental level?

Educate the public on the threat and how to counter it. This should include candid (but sanitized) information on any known attempted threats that have occurred in the past. The public deserves to know what is fact and what is fiction with the many rumors that have spread. (For example, *USA Today* and other news outlets reported a few years ago that there were several attempts by terrorists with biological warfare agents from Iraq who were successfully thwarted as they tried to enter our country — and some news sources said that some actually did enter.)

Public education should also include how to prepare in advance to limit your exposure during any future biowarfare attack, as well as instructing medical personnel on how to treat this disease (see the USPDI website for some practical recommendations: http://www.usdpi.org).

Learn more about the Russian and other strains of anthrax and develop new vaccines and antibiotics as required. Research on new non-drug-based antibiotics, such as the ASAP Solution being studied at BYU, should be accelerated. Expand the current vaccination program for people who live in high-threat areas or in high-risk professions. For example, a vaccination program similar to what is required of the military could be offered on a voluntary basis to medical personnel and first responders to blast/chem/bio/radiation scenes.

Encourage Congress to increase the vaccine production capabilities in the U.S. (currently only one company in the U.S. produces the vaccine) so that concerned citizens can be vaccinated, not just U.S. military personnel, and to allow for rapid mass immunizations should a large terrorist biowarfare attack occur.

Continue research on rapid detection devices for anthrax and other biological weapons and distribute these for real-time, 24-hour monitoring of major urban areas.

Increase the quantity of stockpiled antibiotics as well as the number of dispersal locations to respond to anthrax and other biowarfare attacks. Hours of delay in receiving antibiotics can translate to thousands or millions of additional deaths. Antibiotic stockpiles should be readily available to the medical community without having to wait 12 or more hours.

Low-cost disposable respirator masks and latex gloves should also be stockpiled, as the current supplies (especially of respirators) could be quickly depleted and lead to many unnecessary deaths and prolonged social disruption.

Train and immunize emergency services personnel on how to identify/treat/triage biowarfare victims and how to limit the further spread of anthrax and other biological agents.

Upgrade intelligence, customs and law enforcement capabilities to thwart potential biological terrorists without infringing on citizens' rights.

Question 10: What can the average American do to be prepared? Here are some practical steps to consider:

There is an extremely low risk of biological attack if you live far outside a major urban area. Hence, if you live tens of miles outside a major city, you probably do not need to do much to be prepared other than have food, water, power and medical supplies, etc., stored up in case of long infrastructure outages due to biological attacks. Some low-cost medical supplies, such as disposable HEPA or N95 respirators and some latex gloves, would be needed if a highly infectious biowarfare agent was used.

If you live in or near a large urban area, you should learn how to make bio-safe rooms at your home and place of business (see www.usdpi.org for details).

If you learn of an attack that is imminent or has occurred in your area:

Go inside your home or business and close your windows. Prepare a bio-safe room and don a HEPA or N95-style respirator mask, if available.

Monitor the radio or TV and seek medical advice immediately. The USDPI website provides information resources on what the military and others recommend for anthrax and other biowarfare agents.

If there is a known attack and you have previously been recommended to do so by your doctor, begin taking a safe dose of antibiotics. Be careful, because there is some wrong information out there produced by popular so-called biowarfare experts. This literature can be dangerous when it comes to dosages, especially as it pertains to mapping vet dosages of animals to humans.

If you really believe you've been exposed, you need to seek professional advice and antibiotic treatments immediately. If you wait until clear symptoms appear (normally after one to six days after exposure), in the case of anthrax, it will probably be too late to save yourself. However, be careful not to overreact to false warnings or rumors of attacks.

Dead animals or people who have died from anthrax should not be cut into but buried quickly and deeply or cremated to reduce spore spread, which occurs with exposure to air. Those treating suspected anthrax patients should wash their hands frequently and take preventive antibiotics [though sick human to well human transmission is unlikely].

Try to obtain vaccinations for anthrax if really concerned. (Note: These are not currently available to the general public, only the military and certain other fields, like veterinarians). You can write to your congressman to see if Congress can work to make this an option to the average American. There are a lot of issues surrounding the effectiveness of the vaccination program. One argument is that if an attack occurs with a genetically engineered special strain of anthrax (as with the Russian versions), the vaccine will not help much. The counter argument is that in many scenarios, especially one with a less sophisticated adversary, the vaccine may prove helpful in reducing your risk.

Butler: Saddam Hiding VX Gas

Inside Cover
Wednesday, October 3, 2001

Former chief U.N. weapons inspector Richard Butler warned late Tuesday that Iraqi dictator Saddam Hussein has been stockpiling deadly nerve gas for the last three years and may be planning to use it in a second wave of attacks against the U.S.

"When they threw our inspectors out three years ago, it was after I had presented him with evidence of large-scale manufacture by them of the vilest chemical substance, VX," Butler told Fox News Channel's Rita Cosby.

"And when they saw that we knew about that and wanted to take it away, they shut us down."

"I'll leave you to draw the conclusions," he added.

Butler pointed out that Hussein has used chemical weapons in the past.

"He has shown a distinct preference for those weapons — his weapons of choice, if you like."

And he noted that the Mideast madman has shifted his focus from Iraq's nuclear program to building up chemical weapons stockpiles.

"A nuclear factory is very visible," Butler explained, "where a chemical and biological [factory] aren't. He's putting all his efforts now behind biological and chemical weapons."

Meanwhile, the evidence that Osama bin Laden was the chief architect of the September 11 attacks on the U.S. continues to mount, Butler said.

"I was quite fascinated to see that the president of Russia has now said they know quite clearly that bin Laden did this," he told Cosby. "So a fundamental base of knowledge of who these perpetrators are is obviously coming in."

When asked if Hussein may have had a role in the September 11 attacks, Butler told Cosby, "I'm not prepared to say that I know [he had a role] because the evidence isn't in. [But] should it be investigated? You bet."

60 Minutes: Iraq Has Smallpox

Inside Cover
Sunday, October 7, 2001

60 Minutes reported Sunday night that Iraq has a strain of smallpox.

Smallpox is a deadly and highly contagious virus.

Only two countries were believed to have strains of the virus, the U.S. and Russia.

60 Minutes' Mike Wallace reported this evening that Saddam Hussein acquired some of the smallpox virus from a laboratory in Russia.

Russian scientists have also been helping countries like Iraq and Iran developed biological weapons.

Smallpox Is Ideal Weapon

Colonel Byron Weeks, M.D., Ret.
Wednesday, October 10, 2001

There has been intensive covert research in many countries, in an attempt to produce modifications in disease-producing viruses.

Russia and Iraq have been at the forefront of these researches.

There have emerged several major threats to mankind in the form of lethal viruses and bacteria.

Among these are smallpox (variola), hemorrhagic viruses such as Ebola, and the encephalitis viruses.

Ebola is extremely susceptible to sunlight, heat and drying. It is difficult to handle and deliver while still viable and infectious.

Nonetheless, it is highly lethal and effective in large enclosed spaces such as auditoriums and, probably, stadiums.

Most of the encephalitides are primarily mosquito- or insect-borne.

The ideal bioweapon should be highly lethal, hardy, easy to culture and not too complicated to deliver to the intended victim population.

Most of the weaponized viruses are difficult to deliver because they are fragile and especially vulnerable to exposure to air, sunlight, dryness and heat.

Russia is the principal nation conducting research on the nuclear polyhedrosis virus, an insect virus that secretes a protective protein crystalline coat around itself that renders the organism resistant to ambient effects of heat, cold and sunlight and also increases viability.

According to Dr. Ken Alibek, former head of Biopreparat, the bioweapons program for the Soviets, during the 1980s and 1990s the program experimented with the insertion of smallpox genes into the polyhedrosis virus, and may have succeeded in producing an even hardier killer virus.

I consider variola smallpox to be a likely biological weapon to be used against the United States, because those previously vaccinated have largely lost immunity.

Even in its original form, smallpox may be the ideal killer virus because it is readily cultured, highly contagious, and relatively resistant to environmental changes.

After a laydown from aircraft using aerosol suspension it will usually survive long enough in the aerosolized mist to be carried on the wind to reach, and eventually kill, a high percentage of human hosts. The airborne droplets are small (1-5 microns) and remain suspended long enough to spread over a 50-mile-wide area.

Smallpox: The Disease

Signs and Symptoms: Clinical manifestations begin acutely with malaise, fever, rigors, vomiting, headache, and backache. Two to three days later lesions appear, first on the face and arms, then later on the legs, quickly progressing from macules to papules (red spots) and eventually to pustular vesicles (blisters). They are more abundant on the upper extremities and face.

Diagnosis: Neither electron nor light microscopy are capable of discriminating variola from vaccinia, monkey pox or cowpox. The new PCR diagnostic techniques may be more accurate in discriminating between variola and other orthopox viruses.

Treatment: At present there is no effective chemotherapy, and treatment of clinical cases remains supportive.

Prophylaxis (Prevention): Immediate vaccination or revaccination should be undertaken for all personnel exposed.

Isolation and Decontamination: Droplet and airborne precautions for a minimum of 17 days following exposure for all contacts. Patients should be considered infectious until all scabs separate, and they quarantined during this period.

In the civilian setting, strict quarantine of asymptomatic contacts may prove to be impractical and impossible to enforce. A reasonable alternative would be to require contacts to check their temperatures daily and to remain at home. All bed linens and objects in contact with the infected person should be handled carefully [latex gloves, surgical masks] so as not to spread the virus. Disinfection of clothing, dishes and utensils with hypochlorite [bleach] should be carefully performed.

Any fever above 38°C (101°F) during the 17-day period following exposure to a confirmed case would suggest the development of smallpox. The contact should then be isolated immediately, preferably at home, until smallpox is either confirmed or ruled out, and remain in isolation until all scabs separate.

Although the fully developed cutaneous eruption of smallpox is unique, earlier stages of the rash could be mistaken for varicella (chicken pox). The smallpox blisters tend to all be at the same stage and size, whereas in chicken pox they are in different sizes and stages.

Secondary spread of infection constitutes a nosocomial hazard [spread by medical personnel in the hospital] from the time of onset of a smallpox patient's exanthem [rash] until scabs have separated. Quarantine with respiratory isolation should be applied to secondary contacts for 17 days postexposure. Vaccinia vaccination, with the attenuated [weakened] virus early in the disease, and vaccinia immune globulin both possess some efficacy in post-exposure prophylaxis.

References:

1. USAMRIID Manual of Biological Warfare.
2. *Biohazard*, Dr. Ken Alibek, former deputy commander of the Soviet Biopreparat for Research on Biological Weapons.

Dr. Weeks has had a distinguished medical and military career with the U.S. Air Force Medical Corps. He began military service as the youngest flight surgeon in the U.S. Air Force during the Korean War. After 15 years of military service, during which he served in senior posts, including Hospital Commander at Bitburg Air Force Base,

Dr. Weeks retired and entered private practice. For the past two decades, he has focused his studies on the threat of biological and chemical agents as weapons of war. Dr. Weeks has lectured and written numerous articles on infectious diseases and biological warfare.

Coz: Mohamed Atta Spotted With Possible Anthrax Symptoms

Inside Cover
Friday, October 12, 2001

In what could turn out to be the clearest indication yet that the terrorist hijackers who attacked the U.S. on September 11 are also behind the spate of anthrax cases diagnosed this week in New York and Florida, terrorist ringleader Mohamed Atta was allegedly spotted in a Florida pharmacy with possible symptoms of anthrax poisoning.

"We know that the FBI is now going to local pharmacies to see if [Atta] did in fact get Cipro," said Steve Coz, editor of *The National Enquirer*, in an interview on ABC's *Good Morning America*.

Cipro, the trade name for ciprofloxacin hydrochloride, is an antibiotic used to treat anthrax exposure.

"We know that he showed up at a pharmacy with red hands," Coz added. "There are people in this area who have very direct recollections of seeing him. He worked out in a gym where some of our employees were."

"We know Mohamed Atta was within three miles of the [American Media] building, we know he was within a mile of Bob Stevens' house," said Coz.

Stevens was the American Media employee who died from an anthrax infection a week ago. American Media's Boca Raton offices house *The National Enquirer*, *National Examiner*, *The Globe* and *The Sun*, where Stevens worked.

Thirteen out of the 19 suspected hijackers lived in different residences in South Florida in the weeks and months before the September 11 attack. Several reportedly inquired about renting crop dusters, in what investigators suspect was an aborted plot to spread biological or chemical weapons.

Alibek: Many Countries Have Smallpox

Dr. Kenneth Alibek
Monday, October 22, 2001

On October 12, Dr. Kenneth Alibek testified before a special congressional hearing entitled "Combating Terrorism: Assessing the Threat of a Biological Weapons Attack."

Dr. Alibek is the former head of Russia's biological warfare program.

Here are excerpts from Dr. Alibek's remarks before the House Subcommittee on National Security, Veterans Affairs, and International Relations, chaired by Representative Christopher Shays, R-Conn.

Representative Shays:

What I want you to know is that I believe, as many of you do, perhaps, that the Cold War is over and the world is a more dangerous place, sadly.

And I also want you to know that as far as I am concerned on the hearings that I have conducted and that the work I have conducted on this task force that it is not an issue of if there will be biological or chemical attacks, it is a question of when, where and of what magnitude.

And we are seeing that happen, we are seeing attacks occur, and while we can't be certain they are done by the terrorists, I suspect they are, I believe they are, and there will be many reasons why I think you will as well, but the issue is of what magnitude.

So, I believe that if they have the ability to deliver chemical and biological weapons, they will do it. If they have radioactive material, they will put it in a bomb and explode it. And if they have a nuclear bomb, they will use it. Part of my reason for believing this is from the very speaker that you are going to hear from, that will be introduced.

This is a gentleman who basically has the access, was the deputy director of the program within the Soviet Union, he had 30,000 employees, and he basically was in charge of their biological program, within the former Soviet Union, for offensive and defensive weapons. That was his responsibility.

In our hearings, he has made it very clear to us that the Soviet Union has done, and now the Russian Federation and their various independent republics have done, a pretty pathetic job of securing these weapons of mass destruction.

Dr. Kenneth Alibek:

Thank you. I am very honored. Of course, it is very difficult to cover the entire field of biological weapons threat and biological weapons defense in such a short discussion here, but I realize that today we are not going to cover everything.

We know now, everybody knows, what is going on here in the United States, what kinds of cases we are having using some biological pathogens. And you know, when I wrote my book *Biohazard* two years ago, I believed that something would happen in the future, but I didn't believe it would happen so soon.

And you know, in, I would say in the late '80s and '90s, I decided to spend more time analyzing biological weapons threat, not from the standpoint of biological weapons use in the case of war, but in so-called possible cases of biological terrorism.

But even analyzing this issue, developing medical defense, I couldn't imagine the first case we were going to see would be the cases using our postal system.

But we have got what we have got today, and we know that there are several cases of anthrax, and there are some cases of exposure to anthrax. What I would like to say in this specific case is maybe a couple words about anthrax. People don't know much about anthrax.

Anthrax

Generally speaking, anthrax is an infectious disease, it's a very unusual disease, it belongs to *Bacillus* species. Usually it doesn't cause significant outbreaks among humans. It usually causes the infection of livestock. Some people who work with livestock, who work with contaminated livestock, they can contract this infection.

Many countries, unfortunately, in the beginning of the last century, the 20th century, they started studying the probability to research and develop biological weapons based on this agent. This agent became very attractive because of some important reasons.

First, this agent is capable of forming spores; spores are a very dormant form of this agent's survival. They are very stable in aerosols, they are very stable in the environment, and they can survive in soil for years, or even for decades.

The second reason was it was infectious to humans and would cause a very significant level of pathology. Specifically, we knew if you are not able to start treatment of anthrax immediately after exposure, the probability of survival becomes lower and lower.

These factors led many countries to a conclusion to use anthrax as a possible weapon to conduct wars. And you know, when we talk about anthrax, we need to keep in mind many countries have been involved in these programs; some countries started these programs many years ago. ...

Anthrax has two clinical manifestations: so-called inhalation anthrax, sometimes we call it systemic anthrax; the second form of anthrax is called gastrointestinal form of anthrax; and the third form is cutaneous anthrax, or skin form of anthrax.

The cutaneous form of anthrax is not usually ... if it is treated, the number of casualties is unbelievably low, I would say less than 1 percent.

The second form, the gastrointestinal form of anthrax, usually results from consuming contaminated food, uncooked meat, something like this.

The most, I would say, threatening and dangerous form is inhalational anthrax. Inhalational anthrax usually results in a very high level of casualties if we are not able to detect this infection in time, and [by the time] we see the first signs of this infection the probability to treat it is getting very low.

Don't Focus on Anthrax Alone

But the general explanation of anthrax, why I decided to focus on anthrax, [is] because it has absolutely the same situation as all other infections. We know many other infections will be used for biological weapons. We know about plague, we know about others. We know about many viral infections, we discussed smallpox.

We know some governments, specifically the Soviet Union, [were] developing Ebola biological weapons, biological weapons based on Marburg virus and many others.

What I'd like to say is we shouldn't be focused just on this one infection.

Now, for today, it's anthrax, we need to study anthrax, we need to find solutions. And we will be able to find the solution, but the problem is this: If we just focus our attention on two or three infections/diseases, we are going to lose much.

What we need to do, in my opinion, our understanding of biological threat is still not complete. I would maybe say, even incorrect. A number of biological agents would be used in a biological attack. Dozens of agents, several dozens of biological agents would be used in biological weapons.

When someone says it is very difficult to deploy biological weapons, again, it's a matter of comparison. When we say difficult, we need to explain what we mean by difficult. You know, was it difficult to contaminate these letters? I don't think so. Would it be difficult to contaminate a salad bar? I don't think so. When we say that it's difficult to contaminate these agents, yes, you would say without some sophisticated techniques, it is difficult.

But when we talk about primitive techniques — and they're known — it's not so difficult. Another point, now we know about several cases of anthrax, we know that CDC and FBI are studying these cases.

We talk about what is the nature of the strain, some people say it was the Ames strain, originated from one of the universities in the U.S., I believe, … 50 years ago. But it doesn't mean this actual substance was developed here in the U.S.

For the last 50 years we've had a significant number of changes, you know; it was permitted to exchange strains. And let me say the actual origin of strain is not U.S., it could come from Malaysia or Middle East, it doesn't mean that it originated here.

Another issue, when we talk about these actual cases, whether or not these letters were prepared by professionals, we don't know and we can't answer this question until we start paying attention to completely different issues.

For example, we know that anthrax has several stages of development. We need to understand, first, what is the stage of development of the spores — for example, whether or not this powder contains vegetative cells and spore cells. Sophisticated methods would never use a combination of spore forms.

Another issue, what is the particle size of this powder? It would tell us what equipment they used, whether it was sophisticated or not.

What additives were in this powder? Because, for example, [if] it was just a simple powder, we can say it's not the work of professionals, sort of an amateur, let me say, attempt; but specific additives, we know what additives they use in these powders.

We can say at least whether or not it was done by professionals, amateurs, or we can say at least how to prepare for strains coming from this region.

In many things like this we need to study, many things we can do in the field of protection of our population.

When we see significant fear, people are fearful and they don't know what to do. They are scared to open the mail. Even some simple things would help people to understand that it's not something unbelievably scary.

For example, if we develop some sort of instructions for people, just how to deal with these letters, what is coming to my mind right away, we decided not to open letters.

But a simple technique to use, if you've got an iron and you're scared, just iron these letters before opening. They become harmless. There are many, many things we can do and things we need to do just to start explaining to people what can be done.

Soviets Developed Antibiotic-Resistant Anthrax

The Soviet Union developed several kinds of biological weapons, some were based on natural strains, and specifically… a hydrogen strain, it was not resistant to antibiotics. In '70s the Soviet Union started developing antibiotic-resistant biological weapons.

First attempts were not very successful in the '70s, then in the '80s there was a significant breakthrough. The Soviet Union started developing antibiotic-resistant biological weapons.

At first it was three, then five, antibiotics and then finally we developed a strain that was resistant to 10 antibiotics, including Cipro and quinolines.

If Russia or some scientists in the former Soviet Union don't sell this strain to terrorist groups or some rogue countries, it would take some significant time for them to develop such antibiotic-resistant strains.

Russia Shared Knowledge With Others

It's very difficult to say how much information was given to different countries, because nobody is advertising such information.

But when you read Russian scientific journals, that's what scares me to death.

If you take Russian scientific journals from 1992–1998, start reading what kind of articles they published throughout this period, you will be able to find everything.

How to create genetically engineered anthrax, antibiotic-resistant anthrax, how to develop protection of the virus using simple techniques, how to manufacture the virus using simple techniques, and so on and so forth. It is available, unfortunately, now.

I cannot and I don't want to accuse the country, but unfortunately one day many years ago a significant mistake was made when this information was permitted to be published. Now what you've got today, this information from the Soviet Union that in the '70s and '80s spent billions of rubles or billions of dollars on, … is now available for the cost of a translator. …

I would say that the number of publications is huge and if somebody is interested in finding some new ways to develop biological weapons, this information is available, you can go to any library in the U.S., and I believe any library around the world, and get this information.

Smallpox

It's not just vaccine; we knew for sure that North Korea was researching smallpox in the late '80s and the beginning of the '90s. This information was obtained while I was in the Soviet Union. It was published by the Russian Intelligence Services; in 1993 they again confirmed North Korea was involved in research of smallpox. ...

No, I would say that we shouldn't be naïve to think that there are just two depositories in the world stockpiling smallpox. In Russia, in the U.S. when this decision was made, it didn't mean that it was an obligatory requirement for all countries. ...

North Korea is a fact. You know, everything started in Iraq. We knew that Iraq in the '80s and early '90s was experimenting with [a virus related to] smallpox virus.

These viruses are from the same family.

Iron Your Mail

If you use a regular iron, steam iron, taking the mail, using a piece of fabric with high temperature and moisture would kill anthrax spores. ...

One of the possible ways [is using a microwave], but what we need to keep in mind is there is a problem. If you use some moisture and steam and high temperature you can kill the spores easily, but if you use just high temperature, in some cases the spores could survive.

The best way is to iron, with moisture and steam and high temperature.

Smallpox Is Highly Contagious

Smallpox is a highly contagious infection. We know that [with] somebody introducing smallpox we could see a very significant number of casualties, a very large outbreak, an epidemic.

Plague is not so contagious as smallpox, but if the number of people infected in pneumonic form of plague is high, it would start a significant outbreak. What we need to keep in mind, in these specific cases, it would be a completely different situation.

It comes back to our issue of lost knowledge. We need to retrieve this knowledge. We need to start analyzing what we knew in the '60s and '50s about these infections. It would give us a new understanding of what kind of protection we need to develop.

Saddam Connection: West Nile Virus the First Bioweapon?

Dave Eberhart
Thursday, October 25, 2001

Lost amidst the news about the bioterror use of anthrax is the growing menace of West Nile virus — and evidence it may have been the first bioweapon used by Iraq against the U.S.

This week the federal Centers for Disease Control and Prevention revealed that a Louisiana man had been infected, indicating the disease has spread far from its point of origin, New York.

West Nile virus, a mosquito-borne organism once completely foreign to the Western Hemisphere, has now spread from New York to Florida, Louisiana and Wisconsin.

The pathogen was first discovered in the United States in 1999 when it erupted in New York's Long Island City, the Queens community just across New York's East River from the United Nations. It killed seven people and caused serious illness in 62 others in New York and New Jersey. This year the virus killed an Atlanta woman, the 10th person to die from the illness in the U.S.

Though the disease has all but disappeared from media scopes since the anthrax scare, it has not gone away, and its possible terrorist origins have never been definitively ruled out.

At a news conference last week, New York Governor George Pataki said his state's health labs were running 24 hours a day to accommodate anthrax testing.

He noted in passing that New York state health authorities were moving workers dedicated to the West Nile virus to help test the flood of incoming samples.

Meanwhile, floating as invisible as a spore, was a recent notice that two elderly residents of New York's Nassau County became the ninth and 10th New Yorkers to receive diagnoses of West Nile virus in 2001.

Equally obscure: a recent article citing that Florida Department of Health extended warnings about West Nile virus to 12 more counties, placing 48 of the state's 67 counties on alert. The state confirmed seven human cases of encephalitis from West Nile virus in 2001.

Commenting on a recent outbreak of West Nile and the related death of one woman in Maryland, J.B. Hanson, spokesman for the Maryland state health department, said authorities have noted that the migration of the virus has roughly followed the Interstate 95 corridor.

"We haven't reached a consensus to explain that route," he said, adding yet another element to the mystery of the origin and processes of the disease. For if the Centers for Disease Control (CDC) is right and the virus's spread is owing only to the vagaries of Mother Nature, why does it seem to follow an interstate highway?

Iraqi Connection

And why has the disease broken out in the United States, Israel and Saudi Arabia — all primary targets for Iraqi dictator Saddam Hussein since the end of the Gulf War? (The disease has also broken out in Algeria in 1994, Romania in 1996–1997, the Czech Republic in 1997, the Democratic Republic of the Congo in 1998, and Russia in 1999.)

Experts agree that Saddam's bioweapons people might be brewing up God-knows-what in a French-built virology facility near Baghdad that has been closed to inspectors from the United Nations since Saddam threw them out years ago.

The facility, called the Foot and Mouth Vaccine Plant, was used for making botulinum toxin, or BTX — one of the most lethal biotoxins known.

In 1992, the United Nations tore down the buildings in which the BTX was made and destroyed equipment, but left standing the bulk of the facility, part of which was for virus research. (In 1985 the CDC sent samples of West Nile virus to a researcher in Iraq, stirring controversy in the media five years later, on the eve of the Gulf War, when reports came out that Iraq had a significant biowarfare program.)

All but missing in action on the front lines of the anthrax attacks: Controversial U.S. Surgeon General David Satcher told *The Jerusalem Post* last year that the genetic strain of the West Nile virus found in Israel was the same as the one found in New York.

And, of course, there remains the sinister shadow of *In the Shadow of Saddam*, the infamous book by Saddam's reputed former bodyguard and look-alike, Mikhael Ramadan. Published by a small press in the United Kingdom in 1999, the author's sensational allegations about Saddam's plans to wreak bioterror on the U.S. were featured that same year in *The New Yorker* magazine in "West Nile Mystery" by Richard Preston.

Preston quoted from the Ramadan account:

In 1997, on almost the last occasion we met, Saddam summoned me to his study. Seldom had I seen him so elated. Unlocking the top right-hand drawer of his desk, he produced a bulky, leather-bound dossier and read extracts from it. ... The dossier holds details of his ultimate weapon, developed in secret laboratories outside Iraq. ... Free of U.N. inspection, the laboratories would develop the SV1417 strain of the West Nile virus —capable of destroying 97 pc [percent] of all life in an urban environment. ... He said SV1417 was to be "operationally tested" on a Third World population centre. ..." The target had been selected, Saddam said, "but that is not for your innocent ears."

Author Preston questioned, "Why would a man presenting himself as an Iraqi defector predict that Saddam would unleash a virus just months before the same one broke out unexpectedly in New York? And, of all the thousands of viruses in the world, why West Nile?"

Adding another twist to the bizarre story, it turns out that, said Preston, "the fatality rate for West Nile is not remotely near ninety-seven per cent, and "SV1417" is not a standard designation for any known strain of West Nile virus."

At the same time that Ramadan was being discussed in the CIA, Dr. Ken Alibek, defector and former deputy chief of research for Biopreparat, the Soviet Union's main biowarfare program, spoke to lawmakers on Capitol

Hill, voicing his concern that the West Nile outbreak was "suspicious."

In his article Preston reported a conversation with an anonymous FBI agent, who told him that West Nile might be a good choice for a terrorist. He said, "If I was planning a bioterror event, I'd do things with subtle finesse, to make it look like a natural outbreak. That would delay the response and lock up the decision-making process."

An Army expert interviewed by Preston in the article told him that the military knew that Soviet biologists working for the Soviet Union's biowarfare program had evaluated the West Nile virus for use as a biological weapon.

Senator Specter: Smallpox Vaccinations Now

Wes Vernon, NewsMax.com
Saturday, November 10, 2001

WASHINGTON — Despite the health risks from smallpox vaccine, Senator Arlen Specter says he believes the risk of a smallpox attack is so great that he would immediately get his four grandchildren vaccinated.

Specter, the maverick Republican from Pennsylvania, said he also believes the government shouldn't stockpile the vaccine — current plans call for a 300-million-vaccination stockpile — but give citizens the right to decide themselves if they want to get the vaccination.

Specter made his comments before a Senate hearing with Dr. Anthony Fauci, director of the National Institute of Allergy and Infectious Diseases.

Fauci agreed with Specter's sentiments and said he, too, would want to be vaccinated now rather than wait.

Fauci says there needs to be an "open discussion" of the trade-offs in administering massive vaccinations before or after the disease has actually struck.

Specter is impatient with scientific concerns about the risks involved in pre-emptive vaccines. He says the parents or grandparents should make that decision.

Bonanza for Trial Lawyers

The odds are these. If there were a massive, nationwide vaccination program, estimates are that at least 300 to 600 Americans would die from the vaccination, or 1 to 2 out of every million. And that is a conservative projection.

This does not include the risk of side effects short of death, although these, too, are believed to be minimal. The elderly, babies under 1 year of age and pregnant women are believed to be especially vulnerable.

That sounds like a very small gamble, perhaps about as likely as winning the lottery. But if you lose the lottery, you go on to live your life. Not so if you take your chances with the smallpox vaccine and lose.

The benefit of vaccination, of course, is being immunized against the deadly disease.

Moreover, there are risks of doing nothing until the threat actually strikes.

Smallpox has a 20 percent to 30 percent mortality rate. Short of death, side effects of smallpox include encephalitis and permanent neurological damage.

There is no question that the risk of not doing anything is far greater than the risk of dispensing vaccine to the public.

Current plans call for stockpiling the vaccine until there is an outbreak. Not many health officials are calling for pre-emptive action. As of now, there are only 15 million doses on hand.

DARK WINTER

Part of the real fear of a smallpox outbreak is the panic that may ensue.

Smallpox is highly contagious, and a recent government exercise code-named DARK WINTER found that the outbreak would likely lead to martial law and a breakdown in civil order.

Widespread vaccinations could pull the rug from under the psychological terror involved in a smallpox attack.

Dr. Byron Weeks, a former Air Force colonel and biowarfare expert, said he believes the U.S. government should not delay and should begin using current stockpiles to vaccinate health workers and citizens.

He said as new stockpiles become available, vaccinations should continue.

Senator Specter believes that allowing people who are willing to take the small risk necessary to get vaccinated is just "common sense."

While government officials ponder the perceived dilemma of how to deal with a disease believed to be in the hands of terrorist countries such as Iraq, some Americans have considered going to Canada or Mexico to get vaccinated.

They are not willing to wait until this time next year, when it is expected that an additional 300 million doses will be available, even assuming massive vaccinations will be administered then.

Since Weeks' comments appeared on NewsMax.com, some health officials are resisting the idea, although health workers are being vaccinated.

This would lend credence to Weeks' fear that decision makers are behind the curve on the urgency of action now.

AMA: Smallpox Vaccinations Unnecessary

NewsMax.com Wires
Wednesday, December 5, 2001
SAN FRANCISCO — Despite the urging of several doctors, delegates to the American Medical Association declined to call for widespread vaccinations against a possible bioterrorist smallpox attack until, or if, an actual threat materializes and health authorities deem such action is necessary.

The delegates also tabled a measure that would have put the 290,000 member organization on record as advocating that doctors, their staffs and citizens who request the vaccination should be able to get it.

"We are the front line," said Dr. Joy Maxey, a pediatrician in Atlanta, Ga. She and others argued that doctors were likely to be the first to see a case of smallpox and they should be protected against the disease if it is used by terrorists.

There have been no smallpox cases in the world since 1979, and smallpox vaccinations — once a standard inoculation — have disappeared. Since September 11, government and private organization have worried that rogue nations or individuals might be planning to unleash the disease again. The only known stores of smallpox are believed to be in secured vaults in the United States and Russia.

Several doctors suggested that vaccination of the entire U.S. population with smallpox vaccine should be performed immediately, but AMA doctors disagreed that such a plan would be the right thing to do.

Dr. John Nelson, a member of the Board of Trustees from Salt Lake City, Utah, said mass vaccination would likely cause the deaths of as many as 300 people from the one-in-a-million risk from the vaccine itself, and controlling the disease through regional vaccination programs — if a case develops — has proven effective in the past.

He said the decision to hold off on recommending mass vaccination "must be based on science," not fears that may be unfounded or premature.

In other business at the AMA semiannual meeting in San Francisco:

—The AMA House of Delegates, the policy-making body of the organization, changed its stance on testing of pregnant women for infection with HIV — the virus that causes AIDS. Instead of advocating mandatory testing, the AMA urged that testing be universal but not mandatory.

Nelson said the change was made because of concerns that mandatory testing might frighten some women from undergoing any prenatal treatment to the detriment of her unborn child. By testing for HIV, and if the virus is found, treatment can prevent transmission to the child.

—The delegates asked the Board of Trustees to continue monitoring the supply distribution of influenza vaccine and report back on its findings at the House of Delegates' meeting in June. Members continue to report shortages in the vaccine which can prevent illness in the elderly and very young.

COPYRIGHT 2001 BY UNITED PRESS INTERNATIONAL. ALL RIGHTS RESERVED.

Chapter 8

New Threats

E-Bombs: Cheap, Easy, Extremely Destructive

Phil Brennan, NewsMax.com
Friday, September 21, 2001

A high-tech, low-cost electromagnetic weapon that can be put together by terrorist groups for a mere $400 could hurl U.S cities and towns back 200 years in the blink of an eye.

So writes Jim Wilson in a *Popular Mechanics* magazine story that explains in simple — and horrific — detail how terrorists could produce a weapon that could shut down a U.S. city, destroy all its electronics, its electricity supply, automobiles, computers, phone lines and just about all the modern technological devices and systems we now take for granted.

This is no secret technology, according to the magazine, but well known to the scientific community and the malefactors around the world who are already building weapons of mass destruction.

"You, however, will remain unharmed, as you find yourself thrust backward 200 years, to a time when electricity meant a lightning bolt fracturing the night sky," Wilson warns, adding that this "is not a hypothetical, son-of-Y2K scenario. It is a realistic assessment of the damage the Pentagon believes could be inflicted by a new generation of weapons — E-bombs."

Noting that the U.S. military is now building a generation of sophisticated E-bombs it will be ready to test next year, Wilson writes that the Pentagon is deeply concerned by the knowledge that smaller, hardware-store grade E-bombs can be built by any terrorist group for a mere pittance.

"Any nation with even a 1940s technology base could make them," Carlo Kopp, an Australian expert on high-tech warfare, told Wilson. "The threat of E-bomb proliferation is very real.

Popular Mechanics, Wilson explained, "estimates a basic weapon could be built for $400."

The technology behind E-bombs — electromagnetic pulse (EMP) devices — has been around a long time. According to *Popular Mechanics*, the idea can be traced back to 1925, when physicist Arthur Compton suggested it could be used to help study atoms.

Back during the Cold War, Russia used nuclear weapons to produce electromagnetic pulses created in the upper atmosphere to disrupt communications and electric power as an anti-ballistic missile weapons system.

According to NewsMax.com's Colonel Stanislav Lunev, a more sophisticated version of this technology provides Russia with its current ABM system.

Wilson writes that nuclear weapons experts set off H-bombs high over the Pacific Ocean, back in 1958, that created bursts of gamma rays that, upon striking the oxygen and nitrogen in the atmosphere, released a tsunami of electrons that spread for hundreds of miles.

As a result, "Street lights were blown out in Hawaii and radio navigation was disrupted for 18 hours, as far away as Australia." Since then the U.S. has taken the lead in developing EMP devices and the means to defeat them.

Popular Mechanics described the technology that would allow terrorists to develop what Wilson called "a poor man's E-bomb." It contains a tube filled with a chemical explosive inside a stator coil.

"To ignite an E-bomb, a starter current energizes the stator coil, creating a magnetic field. The explosion expands the tube, short-circuiting the coil and compressing the magnetic field forward. The pulse is emitted in high frequencies that defeat protective devices like Faraday Cages."

Adds Wilson, that pulse "makes a lightning bolt seem like a flashbulb by comparison."

During the 15 minutes after an E-bomb explodes, detonation electromagnetic pulses roar through electrical systems creating localized magnetic fields and causing electric surges to rip through the power and telecommunication systems.

"This string-of-firecrackers effect means that terrorists would not have to drop their homemade E-bombs directly on the targets they wish to destroy," Wilson explained.

Ordinarily secure sites, as telephone switching centers and electronic funds-transfer exchanges, could be destroyed through their electric and telecommunication connections.

He describes the result in chilling terms: "You will hear a sharp crack in the distance. By the time you mistakenly identify this sound as an innocent clap of thunder, the civilized world will have become unhinged.

"Fluorescent lights and television sets will glow eerily bright, despite being turned off. The aroma of ozone mixed with smoldering plastic will seep from outlet covers as electric wires arc and telephone lines melt."

Batteries in such devices as Palm Pilots and MP3 players will be overloaded. Computers will die, and the information they contain will simply vanish into dead cyberspace.

Internal combustion engines such as those in your car or truck will stop cold and never again start. Only diesels will still work, but the pumps that supply diesel fuel won't work because there will be no electricity to power them.

"Knock out electric power, computers and telecommunication and you've destroyed the foundation of modern society," he concludes. "In the age of Third World–sponsored terrorism, the E-bomb is the great equalizer."

In short, you'll find yourself back in what great-grandpa used to call "the good old days," when candles provided light, horses powered vehicles, and the only music you could hear at home came from single-sided 78 rpm records played on hand-cranked Victrolas (that's record players to you young whippersnappers).

Top Military Commanders Warn of Larger, Global War

John Edwards
Wednesday, October 3, 2001

Two of America's top former military commanders warn that America could quickly find itself in a global war.

In an exclusive interview with NewsMax, Admiral Thomas Moorer and General Jack Singlaub reveal several disturbing concerns about a major escalation in the months ahead.

Their interview, "America on the Brink of Global War," is part of NewsMax's Presidential Briefing series.

Both have unassailable credentials. Admiral Moorer served as chairman of the Joint Chiefs of Staff, the nation's highest-ranking military official, and helped bring the Vietnam War to an end.

General Singlaub is former chief of staff for U.S. forces in South Korea. In addition to serving as a field commander, he was also assigned to the CIA and is an expert on unconventional warfare.

Moorer and Singlaub have held combat command positions in World War II, Korea and Vietnam.

Both share the view that the likelihood of a greater war is strong, and fear that if several fronts opened up against the U.S. in hot spots like Taiwan and Korea, the results could be catastrophic for the United States.

"It's not like any war we have been in before, but we have got to have it," Admiral Moorer explains.

Moorer and Singlaub say the nature of this war will require several steps, with the first military moves aimed at eliminating terrorist cells.

But Moorer believes that the war will do the job only if we go after the nations that support terrorism, including Iraq, Iran and Syria.

"I think the war is going to broaden. I think that the president made it quite clear that this is a pure case of good versus evil and those who want to live in peace must unite and eliminate those who want to kill one another," General Singlaub says.

He adds ominously, "We just have to recognize that it's going to develop into a larger war and there are lots of people and nations involved."

In "America on the Brink of Global War," Moorer and Singlaub make several key points, the same ones they would tell the president if they were in the Pentagon today:

Focus on the Likelihood of a Bigger War. Both military commanders insist that while they would have Pentagon strategists working to deal with Osama bin Laden, the Pentagon's main focus should be to prevent and prepare for a major war.

Singlaub explains: "We have to be thinking along those lines and not get ourselves committed in one area."

Possible Flashpoints: Taiwan and Korea. Moorer and Singlaub see these as strong possibilities for the outbreak of a larger war.

Noting the diminished size of the U.S. military, now 40 percent smaller than it was just 10 years ago, a country like China may make a play for Taiwan while American military resources are so focused in the Mideast.

Worse, North Korea may launch its long-awaited invasion of South Korea. More than 30,000 American troops still sit near the Korean Demilitarized Zone, and General Singlaub, an expert on Korea, doubts U.S. forces could repel an armored invasion. The U.S. may have to use tactical nuclear weapons to stop an advance, he believes.

Moorer adds: "This is the whole point — if the U.S. focuses so much strength in one area," one or more of America's enemies may seize the opportunity to attack.

Oil Kingdoms, Kuwait and Saudi Arabia, at Risk. Despite the large U.S. buildup in the Middle East, both commanders believe there is little the U.S. could do to stop Saddam Hussein from invading and capturing Kuwait as he did in 1990. A similar threat exists to Saudi Arabia. Singlaub observed that during the Gulf War the U.S. had five divisions in Germany that were quickly moved to the region, with the air and naval support to move them there.

That isn't true today, he said. By the time we mobilize to prevent an Iraqi offensive, it will be "too late."

Moorer agrees. He thinks U.S. forces could eventually dislodge Hussein, but it would take much longer and the U.S. could expect heavy casualties this time.

Secure the Panama Canal Now. Both veteran military experts advise the U.S. to immediately secure the Panama Canal. Moorer says the U.S. has no troops in Panama now, and we need to make arrangements with the Panamanian government to ensure there is no interruption of Navy movement between the Atlantic and Pacific.

Singlaub notes that any interruption by terrorists, or by the Chinese company that controls the canal, could have catastrophic consequences for U.S. forces in Asia if, say, South Korea was invaded. Both commanders say in such a scenario even a matter of days could prove critical in preserving thousands of American lives.

"We cannot afford to lose the most strategic waterway in the world to our enemies," General Singlaub says.

8 Million Illegal Aliens Swarm U.S.

Phil Brennan, NewsMax.com
Friday, October 26, 2001

At a time when the U.S. faces an internal terrorist threat posed partly by illegal aliens, a shocking new report from the U.S. Census Bureau reveals that there could be 8 million illegal aliens — or more — in the U.S.

Incredibly, the number of illegal aliens living in the U.S skyrocketed by about 400,000 to 500,000 a year in 10 years, jumping from the 3.5 million estimated to have been here in 1990 to 8 million last year.

The new figure is at least a million more than previously thought, *The Washington Times* reported Thursday.

Steven Camarota, research director for the Center for Immigration Studies (CIS), said the new census numbers marked "the first time anyone in the government has said it is that big." Given that the 1990 estimate of illegal aliens was 3.5 million, Camarota said, "this number shows an inability to control the border."

Observers say this shocking revelation probably sounds the death knell for proposed amnesty programs and, moreover, will increase pressure on the administration to tighten control of the nation's borders to prevent illegal aliens from crossing into the U.S. and act to prevent those who have entered legally from overstaying their visas.

As *The Washington Post* reported Thursday (using P.C. euphemisms), before September 11 "support had been building for an amnesty program for undocumented workers, but that is now seen as unlikely. Not only is there less political support for regularizing undocumented workers, there is also less employer demand because the nation's economy is deteriorating."

According to Camarota, the Census Bureau's estimates clearly demonstrate that amnesties failed to solve illegal immigration.

A report issued by CIS shows that although 2.7 million of the estimated 5 million illegal aliens living in the country in 1986 were given amnesty (legal permanent residence), the newest estimates indicate that they have been entirely replaced by new illegal aliens and that by last year the illegal population was 3 million larger than before the last amnesty.

"These new estimates have enormous implications for the security of our nation," said Camarota. "If a Mexican day laborer can sneak across the border, so can an al Qaeda terrorist. While the vast majority of illegals are not terrorists, the fact that hundreds of thousands of people are able to settle in the United States illegally each year indicates that terrorists who wish to do so face few obstacles. We can't protect ourselves from terrorism without dealing with illegal immigration, and selective enforcement would be both immoral and ineffective."

Camarota's study noted that because the terrorist threat "comes almost exclusively from foreign-born individuals, immigration enforcement must be a central part of efforts to reduce the likelihood of future attacks.

"In fact," according to INS commissioner James Ziglar, "at least three of the terrorists who carried out the attacks of September 11 were illegal aliens, and the INS has no information at all on several others. In addition to concerns over terrorism, the huge number of illegal aliens living in the country also has significant implications for public services as well as for the job prospects of low-wage Americans in the current economic downturn."

Container Ships — The Next Terrorist Weapon?

Dave Eberhart, NewsMax.com
Monday, April 15, 2002

On September 11, Americans discovered that a civilian airline jet could be turned into a flying bomb.

Now the respected *Economist* magazine is warning that container ships could be the next terrorist vehicle.

Each year, more than 7,500 commercial vessels make approximately 51,000 port calls, off-loading 6 million loaded marine containers in U.S. ports. Current growth predictions indicate the container cargo will quadruple in the next 20 years.

One serious worry is that terrorists might use one of these ships to transport and then explode a nuclear device in a major U.S. port — perhaps crippling the U.S. economy as the nation's stream of commerce stops in a self-imposed protective embargo.

And the experts agree there is no silver bullet to prevent such a catastrophe.

Already, the U.S. Coast Guard is employing highly sensitive equipment to check ships for radioactive material. But such checks are not foolproof, nor can the Coast Guard scan all ships for the potentially lethal material.

Another concern is that the terrorists may use an oil tanker as a way to collapse the U.S. economy.

Noted journalist Arnaud de Borchgrave, in a special "Off the Record" briefing to NewsMax readers, warns that terrorists have already bragged about being able to explode a fully loaded oil tanker as it passes through the Strait of Hormuz.

Such a disaster, de Borchgrave says, would close the narrow strait and send the world economy into a tailspin..

But just how likely are such attacks?

Ominously, an al Qaeda manual discovered in the United Kingdom said seaport workers could make good recruits.

Furthermore, bin Laden is said to own a fleet of freighters, already used to smuggle explosives into Africa for the 1998 embassy bombings in Tanzania and Kenya.

Other unhappy factoids: The Philippines, home to more than one militant group, is the world's biggest crew supplier. And Indonesia, headquarters for many radical Muslim groups, comes in second at supplying crews for the nettlesome container ships.

But the worst news is that the vulnerability of the critical supply line has already been illustrated — in spades. Italian authorities recently found a suspected al Qaeda member inside a sealed container headed for Canada.

Only 2 Percent Inspected

With the stowaway were mobile phones, false credit cards, plane tickets and certifications identifying the man as an airplane mechanic.

Presently, only about 2 percent of containers arriving in the U.S. are inspected. And according to recent Hill testimony, even if that level reached 100 percent, the danger would not be neutralized, because if the infiltrated cargo even arrives at the U.S. port it may be too late.

One possible scenario: an electronic data system that would allow U.S. authorities to know in advance the origin, contents and shipper of each container — before it is ever loaded at the point of shipment.

This would allow U.S. authorities to target the most vulnerable or suspicious shipments, possibly rerouting and inspecting them before they arrive in the U.S.

One important fault in this plan is apparent, however, say the experts. Digitized or not, the maritime industry's present documentation is unreliable.

In one instance, U.S. Customs audited 181 ships and found 96 had more or fewer containers on board than identified. What's more, bills of lading describing the containers' contents also were incomplete or falsified.

And erroneous or not, the volume of paperwork is mountainous. The movement of each container is part of a transaction that can involve a score or more different parties: buyers, sellers, inland freighters and shipping lines, middlemen, financiers and governments.

A single transaction can crank out 30-40 documents, and each container can carry cargo for several customers, further multiplying the plethora of documents.

Expensive Gadgets

In the meantime, good intelligence and a handful of expensive gadgets are serving on the front lines of port security. The current mainstay: a $1.2-million-per-copy gamma ray machine.

Loaded on trucks, the machine's long white arm makes the device resemble an electric company's cherry picker. Dubbed "VACIS," the acronym for Vehicle and Cargo Inspection System, the machine sprays containers with gamma rays, producing a blurry X-ray-like image of what's inside. It takes skilled and experienced operators to make sense of the images.

But even with VACIS, the logistics of expanding the token inspections are daunting. According to the Charleston, S.C., customs office, its two dozen inspectors can't possibly keep up with the crushing volume of cargo pouring through the southern port's terminals.

"There are days when we have 10 ships coming in, and they might be spread across several terminals," explained one customs official.

The same hectic scene is duplicated at all the nation's ports, where staff levels have actually decreased over the years despite the fact that container volume has doubled since 1993.

So, what can be done to help make ports safe?

Part of the answer may rest with new technologies. Ancore Corp. of Santa Clara, Calif., for example, is making new machines that use laser-like beams of neutrons that can identify trace amounts of drugs or explosive residues.

Also being considered is having the U.S. push its borders out and screen containers in specially created security zones before they are loaded onto ships in foreign ports. Done with the cooperation of the foreign authorities, American inspectors would be on hand to assist local officials.

Robert Bonner, the head of the U.S. Customs Service, wants to kick off such a plan by focusing on the top 10 container ports that trade with the U.S. and funneling as many containers as possible through approved gateways. The top 10 would include Hong Kong, Rotterdam and Shanghai.

Ideas From Private Sector

Private enterprise has its own ideas. In recent congressional testimony, Wayne Gibson, senior vice president of Global Logistics for Home Depot, suggested that "a well-controlled supply chain can serve as a foundation upon which security measures can be built.

"While we source from over 40 countries and 268 vendors and 555 factories, 80 percent of that comes from five countries and 40 vendors. We had over 50,000 POs inspected in 2001. And 100 percent of our shipments were inspected."

And the Coast Guard is hard at work figuring out a solution. Captain Anthony Regalbutto, chief of port security for the United States Coast Guard, recently told Congress, "We're trying to establish two centers — one on the East Coast and one on the West Coast.

"In those fusion centers will be representatives from various government agencies, including Customs and INS and Office of Naval Intelligence and others, that will be able, then, to look at the information that's coming in and then pre-screen the information."

Regalbutto is also, for the first time, looking at or prototyping a canine program for the Coast Guard. "That's something that we want to prototype and we think that, again, with our marine safety and security teams as they go on board ships, particularly if we have intel information that we suspect on a ship, hopefully the dogs will be able to help us in that sensing ability."

Who's in Charge

One Hill witness, however, voiced concern that the salient issue must be a hammering out of just who is in charge. Christopher Koch, president and CEO of the World Shipping Council, has said:

"Customs is presently modernizing and adjusting its information systems, which will cost over $1 billion, and is planning on using [its] systems as part of the Container Security Initiative. Are the Customs systems what the government will use?

"The government should establish one system, not competing information systems. If the advanced cargo information system used for security screening is not Customs' job, the White House or the Congress should make that clear immediately, because Customs thinks that it is and is acting accordingly."

And, finally, who's going to pay the tab?

Basil Maher, president and CEO of Maher Terminals Inc., Jersey City, N.J., suggested to Congress that legislation must not assess fees or tax terminal operators or carriers for costs properly borne by the federal government.

"If any additional federal revenue needs to be raised for cargo transportation security purposes, it should come from existing federal revenue streams relating to cargo, which uses this system of ships, terminals, rails and trucks," Maher said.

One thing all agree on: Security procedures must be implemented in a manner that does not disrupt terminal operations and the $400 billion in commerce it supports.

Next Terror Target: Computer Networks?

Inside Cover
Monday, June 10, 2002
An attack on crucial computer networks, "unfortunately, is the future face of terrorism," says Dmitri Chepchugov, head of Directorate R, the communications security division of the Moscow police.

"After every terrorist attack, security is tightened up and improved," Chepchugov told *Time Europe*. "But these days you don't need to get a truck bomb into, say, a chemical plant or crash a plane into it. All you need is a group of hackers who get into the computerized control system, knock it out, and trigger a disaster."

Michael Vatis, former head of the FBI's National Infrastructure Protection Center, agreed.

"We have seen a clear decision by terrorist groups like al Qaeda to focus on critical infrastructures, financial networks and power grids," said Vatis, director of Institute for Security Technology Studies at Dartmouth College. "And they have developed expertise with computer systems for secure communications and planning attacks. The next step is to put the two together."

Probable targets would be power and water supplies, fuel facilities, telecommunications and banking networks, transportation and emergency services.

"Attackers could try to disrupt these systems during a conventional assault or, even worse, attempt to trigger a disaster by destroying them outright," reports *Time Europe.*

"Most government and many commercial organizations insulate the sensitive parts of their computer systems from the Internet. But it is harder to protect computerized systems from an inside job."

5,000 al Qaeda Members in U.S.

NewsMax.com Wires
Friday, July 12, 2002

WASHINGTON — U.S. intelligence agencies are watching several groups of Middle Eastern men thought to have links to al Qaeda, *The Washington Times* reported Thursday.

The groups are believed to be part of a setup of as many as 5,000 al Qaeda members and their supporters in the country, the *Times* said.

The FBI and other agencies are watching Seattle, Chicago, Detroit and Atlanta for small groups of about a half-dozen men thought to be al Qaeda members, the *Times* cited unnamed intelligence officials as saying. "One [intelligence] estimate is that there are up to 5,000 people in the United States connected to al Qaeda," the *Times* was told.

In Seattle, five men of Middle Eastern origin rented rooms and conducted activities that officials called unusual.

Intelligence reports sent to government policy-makers in the past month reported the 5,000 figure, which is higher than previous estimates. U.S. intelligence officials also said they detected signs of a plot against a cruise ship in Los Angeles in late May, the *Times* said. A dockworker at the Port of Los Angeles World Cruise Center in San Pedro, Calif., about 25 miles south of downtown Los Angeles, spotted two men videotaping and measuring the length of the pier near the cruise center, officials told the *Times.*

They left the area before being identified or questioned, however. Officials did not rule out that their activities might have been unconnected to terrorism.

But the information prompted the Coast Guard to issue a June 7 warning that terrorists were targeting U.S. ports, bays, rivers and shores, the *Times* said.

Another U.S. official told the *Times* that because of the secret nature of al Qaeda, it was difficult to determine how many of its members were in the United States.

"It depends on how you define an al Qaeda member," the official said. "There are hardened members and Muslims with sympathies to bin Laden."

COPYRIGHT 2002 BY UNITED PRESS INTERNATIONAL. ALL RIGHTS RESERVED.

Richard Clarke Prepares for Cyber 'Pearl Harbor'

Dave Eberhart
Monday, August 12, 2002

In the early morning hours of August 6, a series of electronic attacks were launched against U.S. Internet providers and websites on the East Coast. Insidiously, the attacks moved across the country to similar targets on the West Coast. Richard Clarke, the Bush administration's national coordinator for security, infrastructure protection and counterterrorism, watched anxiously, wondering if this might be the big one.

After a while it became clear to Clarke and his staff that the 700 percent spike in traffic that was jamming the cyber highways appeared to be coming from a relatively small number of computers, allowing Internet providers to protect their networks by filtering data from the attackers.

Just days before the disquieting attacks, Clarke was telling National Public Radio about his estimate of the worst-case scenario — that looming cyber "Pearl Harbor" he talks about as he travels the country pitching the virtues of security to private enterprise, the owners and overseers of 85 percent of the nation's fragile and vulnerable cyber infrastructure.

"Then there's the unknown. Have our enemies already penetrated our critical infrastructure successfully and we don't know it? Or are they in a position where — if there is a big conflict between us and them — they are already in a position to disable our critical infrastructure?"

Currently, Clarke and his second-in-command, Howard Schmidt, the former chief security officer of Microsoft, fall under the Office of Homeland Defense and occupy offices on the 10th floor of the old Secret Service building, two blocks west of the White House.

Clarke makes no secret of the fact that he is waiting with bated breath for the emergence of the giant Department of Homeland Security.

"It will have the National Infrastructure Protection Center, transferred from the FBI; the Critical Infrastructure Assurance Office, transferred from the Department of Commerce; the National Communications System, transferred from the Department of Defense; and [a federal security unit], transferred from the General Services Administration."

"It will concentrate our forces." Clarke enthuses. "It will concentrate the skilled staff that we have, and it will ensure added cooperation and added coordination both within the government and with the private sector."

In the meantime, Clarke and Schmidt must content themselves with badgering industry and cyber security vendors to get on the same dance card. Part of the rhetorical arsenal is a hefty collection of war stories designed to make the most lackadaisical cringe and crack open the company coffers to invest in those software patches, firewalls and other paraphernalia of the Internet security game.

'Door Locks'

"Fundamentally, cyberspace security is about buying and using door locks," advises Clarke. "Last year, it cost $15 billion to recover from virus-es, worms and denial-of-service attacks," he warns.

One of Schmidt's favored teaching anecdotes: "When the Melissa virus hit at one company ... it took about $14 million to bring that whole sys-tem up online after 10 days. When the Anna Kournikova virus hit the same company, they were able to contain it within 30 minutes with better processes, and that 30 minutes translated into about $12,000 worth of effort — quite a difference."

For his part, Clarke likes to hash over the invasions of Code Red and Nimda viruses that made the rounds last summer.

"We [the Critical Infrastructure Protection Board, of which he is chair-man] had Cisco, Microsoft and WorldCom all on conference calls, when we finally figured out this thing had infected thousands of servers. We were able to take apart the code and learn what it would have the servers do and when it would have the servers do it. At 4 p.m., we discovered that at 8 p.m. that night it would have all the servers attack one site — www.white-house.gov."

"What we were able to do ... was to get to the major [Internet service providers such as AOL, MSN, etc.], asking them to block the White House ... address on their edge servers. When you dial up on your AOL modem, the first place it hits on AOL is the local, or edge, server. Because we were able to act quickly, the tsunami [cyber attack] just fizzled. That's a classic example of how government and industry work together."

Clarke, 51, has experience at crisis management, having served as President Clinton's counterterrorism adviser for most of the 1990s. Although seldom dwelling on those days, he does draw an analogy between yesterday's unheeding aviation industry and today's sometimes dangerous complacency in that big hunk of the nation's privately owned infrastructure:

"There were many in the aviation industry who, knowing their vulnera-bilities to stop terrorism, nonetheless did not take care of them because they thought they would be inconvenient. They thought it would be costly. They thought it would raise questions about the goals and missions of the aviation industry. The aviation industry now wishes it had done otherwise. We — all the rest of us — still have an opportunity to take a look at our vulnerabilities."

When not beating the security drum, Clarke and Schmidt are busy edu-cating Congress. The big bogeyman in that department is the much-debat-ed exemption to the Freedom of Information Act (FOIA) that would ensure information given to the federal government about computer attacks would not be made public.

Security Flaws

CEOs are keen on the exemption because they are concerned about los-ing the confidence of customers and stockholders if it gets out to the world that their systems are vulnerable to hackers.

And it's not just systems at stake, but also the reputation of expensive software packages, the grist of the industry. Clarke notes that last year 2,000 security flaws in software were discovered in this country. He's looking for a figure closer to 3,000 this year.

"Our lawyers say the law, as currently written, would allow us to protect that information," says Clarke. "But that doesn't persuade companies to give us the information. Their lawyers believe they need additional protection; therefore, we need to get additional protection."

Amendments to the FOIA aside, Clarke would be happy simply to get the private sector to follow the lead of the federal government, which is moving toward spending 8 percent of its IT budget on IT security.

Clarke likes to quote a Forrester Research survey indicating Fortune 500 companies spend an average of 0.0025 percent of revenue on security — less than the budget of the coffee concession.

"If you spend more on coffee than you do on security, you will be hacked. And moreover, you deserve to be hacked," Clarke sums up.

Chapter 9

Freedoms

A Surveillance Superstate Looms

NewsMax.com
Thursday, September 20, 2001

It's been in the works for a while, but the World Trade Center cataclysm will move into high gear an assault on Americans' civil liberties and privacy that will shred many of the protections guaranteed by the Bill of Rights, some say.

According to *The American Sentinel*, "private sector inventiveness is being wedded to government intrusiveness to reap a disaster for civil liberties."

That was written before the WTC disaster. Now, under the guise of protecting Americans from future terrorist attacks, we can expect the U.S. to move quickly to implement a series of high-tech surveillance techniques now available that will put the day-to-day lives of all Americans under Big Brother's microscope.

Here's what lies in store for us as detailed by the *Sentinel* under the heading of "Anti-Freedom Mega-Trends":

- A capacity to track the movements of all automobiles. More than 50 U.S. cities have signed up with major companies such as Lockheed Martin for the installation of high-tech surveillance cameras at busy intersections, a first step toward a universal monitoring system capable of keeping tabs on citizen movements.
- Face-recognition technology that will allow Big Brother to pick John Q. Citizen's face out of a crowd and match it with those in a database. Using cameras such as those mounted around the last year's Super Bowl stadium, facial features of individuals are converted into codes and matched with faces in national databases. The Justice Department has spent $8 million toward development of this intrusive technology.
- Tagging and tracking gun owners. A collaborative effort between Big Brother and gun maker Smith & Wesson is developing a "biometric" device that won't allow a gun to be fired by anyone but its registered owner. The technology is just a step removed from allowing the government to set up a national database of gun owners — a high-tech form of national gun registration.

- A national ID system that will electronically "brand" youngsters before they reach the age of consent. According to *The Washington Post*, District of Columbia government schools have established a pilot program to set up a fingerprint/digital photographic ID database of all students ages 2 to 14. A similar program is being installed around the nation, including a K-12 system in Illinois.
- A whole slew of federal agencies maintain hundreds of databases on all U.S. citizens, and the Treasury's "Financial Crimes Enforcement Network" in collaboration with private financial institutions has the ability to tie all these records together into one huge database.
- Total federal control of all private medical records is possible under Clinton-era "privacy" rules now being pushed by the Bush administration. Under the system, all private citizens' medical records can be accessed by federal bureaucrats without requiring warrants, prior notice or consent of the individuals.
- Using the power sought by 42 of the nation's governors to tax Internet purchases across state lines, all such purchases could be monitored.
- The FBI's notorious "Carnivore" system (recently renamed) allows Big Brother to snoop on your e-mail. According to *The Washington Post*, Carnivore's capabilities are being expanded.
- "Suspicious Activity Reports" are being used against private citizens and their financial transactions. The U.S. Postal Service program known as "Eagle Eye," in which postal clerks file suspicious-activity reports to the IRS against people buying money orders the clerks regard as abnormal, is among such other snooping programs as banks' "Know Your Customer" system that monitors cash transactions and reports filed by hotels and transportation facilities when customers pay cash.

Carrying out these and other intrusive government snooping programs has been under heavy scrutiny by privacy advocates and thus has been somewhat curtailed in scope. But with the frenzy to combat terrorism now abroad in the land, thanks to the WTC attack, we expect the government will find it easier to put them to their full potential use.

In a statement issued in the wake of the tragedy, Representative Ron Paul, R-Texas, warned against just this eventuality.

"Times of tragedy and war naturally bring out strong emotions in all of us," Paul wrote. "Yet we must be careful to preserve personal liberty and privacy rights in the months ahead. Sometimes the people are only too anxious to sacrifice their constitutional liberties during a crisis, hoping to gain some measure of security. Yet nothing would please the terrorists more than if we willingly gave up some of our cherished liberties because of their actions."

In Terror War, Don't Surrender Personal Freedoms

Wes Vernon, NewsMax.com
Saturday, September 22, 2001

WASHINGTON — More than 150 organizations on the left and right, along with hundreds of computer scientists and law professors, are circulating a petition urging that personal freedoms not be sacrificed in the fight against terrorism.

At a news conference organized by the Free Congress Foundation's Coalition for Constitutional Liberties, the broad coalition recalled that in every conflict since the Civil War, the long-range pressures in the crisis of the moment have been aimed at greatly expanding the powers of the federal government to restrict our freedoms.

Anyone following much of the wall-to-wall TV coverage of the terrorist attacks on September 11 has heard the repeated mantra about how "we're going to have to give up some of our freedoms" if we are to succeed in fighting back.

That, of course, puts President Bush and Congress, as well as state and local officials, to a crucial test.

Bottom line: Can our lawmakers wage a war against terrorism in the name of protecting freedom and at the same time make sure that very freedom is not diminished at home by measures of our own government?

Free Congress Foundation President Paul Weyrich was among the first to warn of this dilemma within days of the attacks on the Pentagon and the Word Trade Center.

But it's not a case of either/or, the 150 co-signers warn. Pitting civil liberties against security is "a false choice," says their statement.

Among the groups in the coalition are the Association of American Physicians and Surgeons (AAPS) and the Rutherford Institute, generally considered conservative, and the American Civil Liberties Union and Common Cause, often in the forefront of liberal causes. All signed on to the statement titled "In Defense of Freedom at a Time of Crisis."

Dr. Jane Orient, AAPS director, says that while her organization "does not agree on every point or all wording of the statement," the potential for privacy violations is so great as to make this coming together of diverse groups "necessary."

Government efforts to make haste in destroying our enemy must be encouraged, AAPS believes, but it is also possible to make haste in destroying our country "just to keep our adversaries from doing it first."

The co-signers believe calm is required to determine where our intelligence and security failed.

Already there are reports that legislation is being sought on Capitol Hill to make it easier for law enforcement agencies to tap our phones, monitor our e-mail and check our voice-mail messages. Hopefully, such legislation won't see the light of day if it is formally introduced.

Reports are a dime a dozen in tense times such as what this country has experienced since September 11. But this diverse group hopes Americans will be able to keep their heads as they go about their tasks in countering the monstrous threat we face.

This group is in no way to be confused with a so-called peace movement that is beginning to gather and hold demonstrations around the country against President Bush's attempts to rally the country in this time of crisis. That is a coalition with a different agenda.

Analysis:
National ID — A Bad Idea That Won't Work

Phil Brennan, NewsMax.com
Friday, September 28, 2001

The idea of making Americans carry a national ID card bearing their photographs and fingerprints or other identifiers isn't just an assault on civil liberties, it would also be loaded with problems and take years to implement, experts say.

The most recent attempt to create a national ID system was contained in the 1996 Immigration Reform and Immigrant Responsibility Act, which mandated that the states incorporate information on driver's licenses that would allow them to serve as national ID cards.

Fortunately, this section of the act was invalidated by the Shelby Amendment to the appropriations bill, which in effect strangled the program in its crib.

Any revival of the system would of necessity employ the state driver's license method as the only practical means of implementing a national ID card program. And therein lies the rub — it probably wouldn't work.

Writing in Wednesday's *Wall Street Journal,* William M. Bulkeley noted the problems with issuing national ID cards using state driver's licenses as the identification credentials.

Here are some of the obstacles to putting such an idea into practice he listed in his article "Hijackers' Passports Highlight Issue of Rampant Fake IDs in U.S.":

- Driver's licenses are easy to forge. New technologies, such as color laser printers, have made forging driver's licenses child's play.
- There is no standardization between the 242 different types of state driver's licenses — including old and new designs, special licenses for young drivers, etc.
- Since most airport reservation agents are unfamiliar with out-of-state licenses, forgeries are seldom recognized.
- To work as national IDs, driver's licenses would have to contain either a photo or fingerprints, or both. Going to such a system in a nation of 280 million people would be a bureaucratic and technological nightmare to put into practice, requiring the states to spend

two and a half years to replace the driver's licenses of just half their people.

Editorial: Don't Federalize Airport Security

NewsMax.com
Monday, October 22, 2001

In response to tremendous fear of flying in the wake of the September 11 disaster, both the White House and Congress have been desperately searching for ways to beef up airport security.

Because of political correctness, the government has rejected the simplest, most effective method of securing planes: allowing the pilots to be armed. The pilots themselves have asked for this measure.

Other solutions are obvious, such as stronger cockpit doors and increased screening of luggage.

But one "solution" is no solution at all and may lead to weaker security. That bad idea, having the federal government take over airport security, should be rejected.

One need only look to the U.S. Postal Service to see what will happen with the federalization of airport security.

Would you be happy knowing the post office was running airline security? Jobs with the new airline security agency will be politicized and unionized.

It will be as difficult to fire an incompetent federal security officer as it is to fire an incompetent postal employee.

The federalization of airport security will not solve the problems.

Today, even with heightened security, knives and other weapon-like instruments still get through screening devices.

No screening service, federalized or otherwise, will be perfect.

That's why the U.S. should follow the example of Israel, which arms its pilots. Israel has not had a problem with airline terrorism in decades.

And the federalized security force won't solve the real, sleeper problem of airport security.

There are thousands of airport employees who work with airplanes in catering, maintenance and luggage. Many are not even citizens, some have never had a background check, and some are probably fifth columnists.

There is significant evidence that the terrorists of September 11 may have had knives and other weapons smuggled onto the planes, with the help of airport employees, before they boarded.

How would a federal takeover, creating a huge new $50 million bureaucracy, solve this problem?

The last time the terrorists took over a plane, they used knives. The next time it might be done with smuggled guns. Only arming the pilots will help prevent hostile takeovers of planes.

Clearly, the federal government does have an important role to play.

But we believe it's far better to have airports or private agencies responsible for security, and then have a separate federal agency responsible for compliance and dealing with breaches in security.

In 1993, both Congress and the American people overwhelmingly rejected Clinton's call for a federal takeover of health care as too expensive, too bureaucratic and disastrous for health care quality.

Today we should reject a federal takeover of airport security for the same reasons.

Voters across the country were swayed then with one powerful argument: Did they want their health care managed like the post office? Today we ask: Do you want your security on airplanes managed like the post office?

Be sure you let your representative and senators know you oppose federalizing airport security. Contact them today: Efforts to make this idea law will be decided this week.

Heston: Don't Let Terrorism Take Our Freedoms

Charlton Heston, America's First Freedom
December 2001

As I write these words, our nation is in a time of great grief and mourning. A vicious crime, an evil calamity, has been forced upon our union, and the true magnitude of our loss is only beginning to emerge from the destruction.

As president of this Association, on behalf of our millions of members, let me extend my heartfelt sympathy and sincere condolences to the countless American families touched by this horrible, heinous act of terror. Mere words cannot express the horror, sorrow or anguish you've endured — at best, mere words offer little salve or solace.

But take faith and fortitude in this: Grief has shaken us — but never before has our nation been so united or more resolved. Our freedoms are endangered by a truly sinister, insidious threat — but never before have more able or ardent allies come to freedom's defense.

As President Bush so tersely stated, the atrocious terrorist attacks that killed thousands of innocent Americans in New York, Virginia and Pennsylvania on September 11 constituted a direct attack on freedom. This is a war between fear and freedom. In defending her, we're united not just across America — but with much of the world. *And freedom will prevail.*

It wasn't just Americans who were killed in those attacks; among the missing are people from some 80 other countries, tourists as well as immigrants undoubtedly drawn here by the promise, genius, justice and freedom that, above all else, *define* America.

So I believe it's essential during this time of national crisis to remember who we are and what we believe. We are all Americans. And as Americans, we have a duty to protect the freedoms that make our union the example and the envy of the world.

In the weeks and months ahead, you can expect to hear a lot of proposals from lawmakers who seek to curtail our civil liberties in the name of feeling safe. Meanwhile, in the aftermath of the events of September 11, many Americans are allowing terror to trump reason.

The day after those terrorist attacks, a *Washington* Post/ABC News poll asked Americans whether they'd be willing to surrender some of their civil rights in order for the government to crack down on terrorism. Two-thirds of them — 66 percent — said yes. And less than 1 out of 4 said no.

A similar *New York Times*/CBS News poll put that number at 74 percent. A *Los Angeles Times* poll found that 68 percent of Americans approve of allowing police to randomly stop people who may fit the "profile" of suspected terrorists. Other polls found similar sentiments.

Meanwhile, pundits and politicians have spoken as if liberty and security were mutually exclusive, contradictory concerns. Former Secretary of State James Baker said, "We need to re-examine our civil liberties."

NBC's Tom Brokaw said, "We're going to have to reconsider a lot of our freedoms because of this attack." Former Secretary of Defense William Cohen said Americans will be forced to make "choices between security and civil liberties."

This is a road fraught with danger. I'm not talking about the inconvenience of longer lines, longer check-in delays and tighter security at American airports. What I'm talking about is the headlong rush to sacrifice liberty on the altar of safety.

As Benjamin Franklin said more than 200 years ago, "Those who would give up essential liberty, to purchase a little temporary safety, deserve neither liberty nor safety." And all too often, they lose both liberty *and* safety.

So before we allow a media-terrorized public to sacrifice more of our freedom, we should ask whether doing so could prevent any acts of terrorism in the future. Because, if we're not careful, we could be stampeded into surrendering freedom for no good reason.

As an editorial in Canada's *National Post* pointed out, "The lesson of this country's brush with terrorism in the October Crisis of 1970 was that widespread restrictions on civil liberties did not help to advance police work."

Representative Christopher Cox, R-Calif., warned, "The notion that we can reorganize every aspect of civil society to protect against terrorism is fool's gold." Representative Frank D. Lucas, R-Okla., said, "If we were going to be absolutely safe, we'd have to restrict people's freedoms to the point that it wouldn't be America anymore."

That, I believe, would hand the terrorists a prize victory — and would do more to desecrate the sacrifice of those Americans killed on September 11 than anything any terrorist could ever do to our nation.

Model State Bioterror Law Stirs Controversy

Dave Eberhart, NewsMax.com
Thursday, January 3, 2002

The Model State Emergency Health Powers Act (MEHPA) has come under fire for giving governors and state health officials broad power to involuntarily quarantine and vaccinate citizens, as well as authority "to control, restrict and regulate … food, fuel, clothing and other commodities, alcoholic beverages, firearms, explosives, and combustibles…"

Lawrence Gostin, a law professor at Georgetown University and professor of public health at Johns Hopkins University, wrote the draft bill, a blueprint for future state legislation, with grant money from the National Institutes of Health.

Although no state has yet enacted legislation based on the model, the American Legislative Exchange Council (ALEC), a bipartisan group of state legislators, has warned the plan would intrude on Americans' civil liberties.

Meanwhile, Citizens' Council on Health Care (CCHC), a Minnesota-based health lobby, is concerned that the proposal would provide intrusive authority for purposes far beyond bioterrorism.

But Gostin recently defended his draft bill. "The idea that we need it is very clear," he maintained, adding that when the next bioterror shoe drops, the states would be unprepared to counter the threat "without being able to plan, to conduct surveillance, to treat, to test, to vaccinate people, or if necessary, even to confiscate pharmaceuticals or vaccines."

Government Does Not Have Enough Power?

"Some states have far too few powers," Gostin explained. "Anybody who thinks we can fight a 21st century battle against bioterrorism with early 20th century legislation really just doesn't understand the sorry state of public health law in America."

But critics of the draft law, such as CCHC and ALEC, find fault with what they describe as its overbroad language. Jennifer King, a legislative expert with ALEC, pointed to the following language as troublesome:

- The term "property" is not limited to just land and buildings on that land, but also includes food, alcohol and even firearms.
- A "public health emergency" can be declared not only for bioterrorism attacks but also for epidemics, pandemic disease or natural disasters.
- The terms "epidemic disease," "pandemic disease" and "natural disaster" are not defined, leaving public health officials ample room for their own interpretation.
- There are no limits on the number or types of tests that can be performed on individuals, or on the bodily specimens that can be collected. DNA and genetic testing are not excluded.

'Due Process'

Gostin counters by insisting: "The prime responsibility of government should include a very careful attention to the health, safety and security of the population ... [I] have bent over backwards in writing the law to make sure that there was very careful attention to due process and checks and balances."

But Gostin's assertions have not mollified the critics, such as CCHC, which insists that due process could be trampled in the following examples:

- Although due process is allowed, the act permits state officials to identify and train personnel to serve as "emergency judges" to deal with citizen appeals of forced quarantine and isolation. Such training may be biased, said a spokesman for CCHC.
- Citizens are required to submit to medical examinations, vaccinations and quarantine against their will if a public health emergency is declared.
- Public health officials are given authority to "collect specimens and perform tests on any person" even if they are healthy with no history of exposure to disease.
- Health care professionals who refuse to provide forced medical examinations or vaccinations can be charged with a misdemeanor.
- Citizens who refuse to comply can be detained and charged with a misdemeanor.
- Police officers will be placed under the authority of health department officials.

But Gostin is quick to respond: "This is not anything to do with military tribunals or anything like that — there's a lot of due process. So, for those who say that there's not enough civil liberties in it, I think the only thing I could say is that for most of the provisions, the civil liberties protections are far greater than that which exists under current law."

Some states, including Minnesota, are already considering enactment in 2002. The Illinois State Legislature recently rejected a proposed bill modeled after Gostin's MEHPA.

Gostin forecast that his model legislation would be considered in "virtually every state" when the new state legislative sessions begin this month.

He said his model was designed to be adapted by the states as needed, to update their statutes. The proposal is not intended to be one-size-fits-all, he added.

Liberals, Strangely, at War With Freedom

Christopher Ruddy
Sunday, March 3, 2002

"The era of shrinking federal government has come to a close." — Senator Charles Schumer, D-N.Y.

In the wake of September 11, the liberal establishment, which once strenuously opposed increased state police powers, is reviving every imaginable, discredited, big-government attempt to squelch your freedoms.

Many of these ideas germinated in the Clinton era, and most of the federal government's hierarchy is still managed by Clinton-Gore appointees, who have been making a big push for this anti-freedom agenda.

After September 11, they have sought to wrap this power grab in Old Glory.

No doubt, public reaction after the September attacks helped the USA PATRIOT Act pass so quickly.

Obviously, the sweeping powers granted the government in this legislation had been well-baked long before September. The rush to approve the bill was so speedy, it's also clear that many in Congress did little to review its provisions.

Authoritarian programs and regulations that will take away your freedom and privacy, the same ones that in past years have been overwhelmingly rejected by the American people, are suddenly again on the fast track to passage.

In a recent edition of Lee Bellinger's respected *American Sentinel* newsletter, he outlined the left's power grab program:

National ID Cards

President Bush has opposed a national ID card, but lawmakers and bureaucrats are trying to create one using the back door.

The American Association of Motor Vehicle Administrators (AAMVA) is pushing hard for a scheme cooked up by Bill Clinton to convert your driver's license into a high-tech national ID card.

Under this scheme, all state driver's licenses would have to conform to new federal standards and include "biometric identifiers" such as your fingerprints or iris scans.

Even worse, all state DMVs would be linked in a new national database with comprehensive information on you — such as tax records and work history — which would be accessible to thousands of federal bureaucrats at the push of a button.

That won't do anything to stop foreign terrorists, since neither their "biometric identifiers" nor their personal information will be in the U.S. government database. But national IDs will give liberal power mongers the power to track everything you do and to have much more control over your life.

Trusted Traveler Cards

The Air Transport Association wants all travelers to carry trusted traveler smart cards containing detailed personal information such as criminal history, personal financial data, etc., etc., plus biometric identifiers.

Just like internal passports required to travel in the former Soviet Union, under this scheme you would have to show your trusted traveler

ID before boarding an airplane, cruise ship or train, or even renting a car.

The government would like to make the program "voluntary." This means that users of the card would have speedier access through airport security. Other law-abiding citizens who don't "accept" the card will be punished — they'll have to go through time-consuming and vigorous security checks.

Once these cards become widespread, trying to protect your privacy will make you instantly suspect and at a minimum subject to repeated police interrogations — if you are allowed to travel at all.

They also could be used to prevent you from traveling if the government claims you owe taxes, child support payments, or simply are "suspect," without asserting why.

Rest assured, once the system is implemented it won't be long before the card is required — especially if there is another terrorist attack that will give government officials an excuse.

Child Surveillance System

Schools across the country are starting to require students to carry high-tech ID cards, which track their every movement.

In the wake of 9/11, schools are also accelerating implementation of "Parents as Teachers" and "School to Work" programs. Under Parents as Teachers, government social workers will be assigned to every family of school-age children and visit them in their homes.

Will parents who are religious Christians, own guns or criticize big government be at serious risk of having their children taken away?

Under School to Work, detailed lifetime psychological files are being created for all children in government schools. Under this program, government bureaucrats will recommend what career your child, by the age of 8, should pursue — just as in the former Soviet Union.

Under this liberal scheme, now being implemented, Certificates of Initial Mastery will be required to work. These certificates will only be issued after children have performed many hours of mandatory volunteerism (much of which has nothing to do with education), given politically correct answers on their tests and submitted to invasive and very personal psychological testing and tracking.

In Washington, D.C., a model lifetime tracking program called Destiny, run by the D.C. Department of Motor Vehicles, is now being tested for future national implementation.

Mandatory Volunteerism

Another characteristic of totalitarian communist states, like Cuba and Communist China, is mandatory "volunteerism." Any free time people have after working, sleeping and eating is consumed by the state in the form of political lectures and assigned "volunteer" work — such as harvesting crops or working in hospitals. Those who don't volunteer are subject to harassment and even prison.

Under the name USA Freedom Corps, an unholy alliance of liberals and conservatives has revived Bill Clinton's AmeriCorps, expanding it fivefold to 250,000 paid volunteers. In the event of another terrorist attack, young people across the country may be drafted into the Freedom Corps.

Many of these "volunteers" may be used to spy on other Americans, including their parents. Quoting directly from the Freedom Corps' website, www.usafreedomcorps.gov/volunteer.html:

The new citizens corps includes initiatives to engage Americans in specific homeland security efforts in communities throughout the country. The volunteer initiatives, led at the local level by new Citizen Corps Councils, include a Medical Reserve Corps, a Volunteers in Police Services Program, a doubling of Neighborhood Watch, [and] a new Terrorist Information and Prevention System.

Militarization of America

Since September, National Guard troops and soldiers have become familiar sights at airports and even some sports stadiums. Now, under a $37 billion-plus Homeland Defense program, a military commander is being created for the U.S.

What's wrong with using troops as policemen?

In the first place, the military is trained to kill the enemy, not enforce laws, catch criminals or respect the rights of the innocent. Second, federal agents, including troops, have sovereign immunity from prosecution for any crimes they might commit, such as getting gun happy and shooting innocent civilians — making them much more of a potential threat to you than local police are.

Under the new Homeland Defense initiative, the federal government also plans to take much more control of your local police, "assisting" them with organization and intelligence and providing massive quantities of military-style weapons.

The Real Danger

The real danger of all these programs is not facing us today or even tomorrow.

The framework is being set up so in the not-so-distant future American freedoms will be tremendously curtailed and government will have unprecedented power over its citizenry.

In America, we have always rejected and feared increased state powers that give government officials the right to monitor and control citizens engaging in private activity.

But now, under the cover of the war on terrorism, many liberals who were once at the forefront of limiting government powers are now demanding these powers be increased.

The real question conservatives and liberals need to ask is why, in a war against terrorists, is there a demand for this massive increase in surveillance, militarization and regimentation being directed against the American people?

Shouldn't our energies be directed against terrorists?

Even with these new police powers, no one has yet to explain how they would have thwarted the September 11 terrorist attacks and others made against Americans abroad in recent years.

Instead of surrendering our freedom, we need to demand, again and again, that agencies like the CIA, FBI and INS fulfill their responsibilities, use the powers already granted them by the Congress, and root out terrorists before they make it to our shores.

President Hillary's Newly Empowered FBI

Inside Cover
Monday, June 3, 2002

When Hillary Rodham Clinton succeeds George W. Bush as the 44th president of the United States, as former top White House strategist Dick Morris predicts, will she abuse the FBI's expanded surveillance powers that were announced by Attorney General John Ashcroft last week?

That scenario — a newly empowered domestic intelligence agency placed at the disposal of a ruthless politician with a long track record of digging up dirt on her opponents — remains the most persuasive argument against allowing the FBI to freely snoop in mosques, temples, churches, public libraries and the Internet.

But a better question might be: What did the regulations that Ashcroft lifted last week do to keep co-president Hillary Rodham Clinton in line back when she had the old defanged FBI at her disposal?

The answer? Nothing.

It was under the pre-Ashcroft regime of Hillary appointee Janet Reno that the old straitjacketed FBI somehow managed to ship 1,100 FBI files over to the Clinton White House. Once there, Hillary's handpicked White House security chief, Craig Livingstone, pored through them while her ex–Rose law partner Bill Kennedy uploaded tidbits into his computer.

Of course, that was a "bureaucratic snafu," not an abuse of power, we were told by prosecutors years later.

After fired Travel Office chief Billy Dale had his FBI file placed at Mrs. Clinton's disposal, he suddenly found himself subject to a tax audit by the agency run by her old college roomie, IRS Commissioner Margaret Milner Richardson. Another unfortunate coincidence, investigators later explained.

Dale's audit would be the first of many similar IRS coincidences, with a multitude of Clinton scandal witnesses finding themselves similarly targeted. Paula Jones, Bill Clinton's most prominent accuser, even saw details from her confidential tax return turn up in the column of a Clinton-friendly reporter, the late Lars-Erik Nelson.

Neither were the pre-Ashcroft investigative restrictions enough to protect fellow Clinton accusers Gennifer Flowers, Juanita Broaddrick, Liz Ward Gracen — not to mention a myriad of conservative groups, all of whom eventually found themselves in the IRS's crosshairs.

Another such victim of coincidence was Linda Tripp, better known to the media as "the bad whistle-blower." Somehow the manacled FBI managed to leak details from Tripp's confidential FBI file — one of the 1,100 that had muddled their way over to the White House — to yet another Clinton-friendly reporter. Oops!

All this happened during the good old days, when the public was supposedly protected from the kind of FBI abuses civil libertarians are warning about now.

The truth is, when the American people turn over extraordinarily powerful agencies like the FBI to people with a clear record of abusing power, they shouldn't be surprised to learn that all the bureaucratic restrictions in the world don't make any difference.

The real danger isn't the FBI's new powers in the hands of good people. It's the lack of accountability in both the media and the courts for those responsible for orchestrating the bureau's old abuses.

Safire Warns of 'J. Edgar' Mueller

Inside Cover
Tuesday, June 4, 2002

The new guidelines governing FBI behavior are "an alibi" for Attorney General John Ashcroft's "nonfeasance," wrote *New York Times* columnist Bill Safire, who warned that Ashcroft "and his handpicked aide 'J. Edgar' Mueller" have used the new rules to gut the old guidelines designed to prevent the abuse of police power that once existed at the FBI.

Dubbing the FBI chief "J. Edgar" Mueller to call to mind the alleged abuses of police power by late FBI Director J. Edgar Hoover, Safire blistered Ashcroft and FBI Director Robert S. Mueller for needlessly exposing the nation and the American people to a civil liberties nightmare.

And, Safire charges, the two men "have done this deed by executive fiat: no public discussion, no Congressional action, no judicial guidance. If we had only had these new powers last year, goes their posterior-covering pretense, we could have stopped terrorism cold."

But, he adds, they already had the power to gather the intelligence needed to forestall 9/11, but "lacked the intellect to analyze the data the agencies collected," specifically such information as contained in the ignored Phoenix memo and the reports from the Minneapolis field office about arrested Zacarias Moussaoui being a known member of terrorist groups.

This "seizure of new powers of surveillance," the Times columnist asserted, is nothing more than a "smokescreen" to cover their failures to use the powers they already had.

Safire takes issue with Ashcroft's claim that all he is doing is making it possible for FBI agents to attend public events and surf the Internet like everybody else. But, Safire explains, they always could do such things — provided that they had "information or an allegation whose responsible handling required some further scrutiny."

That minor requirement is no longer in force: Under the new guidelines, the FBI can now run full investigations, lasting up to a year, without having any evidence whatsoever that a crime has been, or will be, committed. That, Safire wrote, is "aimed at generating suspicion of criminal conduct — the very definition of a 'fishing expedition.'"

The new guidelines open up a series of possibilities that imperil civil liberties:

- The enormous ability now available to government and private snoops to combine government surveillance reports, names on membership lists, and "data mining by private snoops" will enable them to create instant dossiers on law-abiding Americans.

- Every scintilla of data about Americans — the income tax returns they gave lenders to qualify for loans, their school and employment records, their credit card purchases, the money they give to charity and political parties, their charge accounts, insurance records, even their subscriptions to non-mainstream media publications such as NewsMax magazine, and every website they access, every book they ever bought, or even considered buying, on Amazon.com — everything about them can end up in FBI dossiers. And all of this without any hint that they have done a single thing wrong.

- "All your personal data is right there at the crossroads of modern marketing and federal law enforcement," Safire reveals. "And all in the name of the war on terror..."

"This is not some nightmare of what may happen someday. It happened last week," Safire wrote.

Chapter 10

New Dangers
New Responses

Representative Barr:
Allow Assassinations of Terrorist Leaders

Wes Vernon, NewsMax.com
Friday, September 14, 2001

WASHINGTON — The mass murders at the World Trade Center and Pentagon have revived the effort in Congress to override a Ford administration executive order banning assassinations sanctioned by the federal government.

On Thursday, Representative Bob Barr, R-Ga., sent out a letter urging his colleagues to sign on to his Terrorist Elimination Act, H.R. 19, "to repeal those portions of executive orders prohibiting the government from directly eliminating terrorist leaders."

In 1998, Barr wrote then-President Bill Clinton asking him to "consider lifting this ban and designing a new system so the threat posed by individuals proven to be directly responsible for the deaths of American citizens — such as Osama bin Laden or Saddam Hussein — can be eliminated in cases where it is simply impossible to capture them by ordinary means."

Three years later, Barr notes, "both of these terrorists are alive and well."

Former Representative Jack Kemp, R-N.Y., who favors a congressional declaration of war against the international terrorists, says he would favor the Barr measure only up to a point.

"I draw a distinction between assassination as a political effort. I do not favor attempts to assassinate leaders of governments that perhaps we need to see a change in," he said.

Appearing Thursday on the Sean Hannity radio talk show, the 1996 GOP vice presidential candidate recalled that under the Kennedy administration, the U.S. allowed the assassination of President Diem of South Vietnam, and there were attempts to get rid of communist Cuban dictator Fidel Castro as well. Often we end up with "something worse," he said.

However, "I agree with Israel," Kemp added. "Every time you find someone who's going to commit a terrorist attack, you take them out before they can attack unarmed men and women."

Under Kemp's distinction, Osama bin Laden would be a legitimate target. Saddam Hussein would not.

"Not if we're at war with Saddam?" Hannity asked.

Kemp hesitated and said the constant bombing of Iraq stirred hatred for the U.S. among innocent citizens and left Hussein in power.

"If we could've assassinated Hitler, we should've," Hannity commented.

In his widely circulated letter, Barr makes the argument, in effect, that a terrorist is a terrorist is a terrorist.

"When terrorist leaders, such as the ones who caused those attacks take the lives of Americans, I believe it is entirely appropriate for us to remove them by any means necessary, without arbitrarily limiting our options," he wrote. "The world has changed dramatically since" 1976 when President Gerald Ford signed the executive order.

"We are at war," the Georgia lawmaker reminded his colleagues.

Koch: Give Terrorist Nations Ultimatum

Wes Vernon
Monday, September 17, 2001

WASHINGTON — New York's beloved and outspoken former Mayor Ed Koch says countries that harbor terrorists — specifically naming Libya, Iran, Iraq, Syria and Afghanistan — should be given an ultimatum to surrender terrorists on their soil or face U.S. bombing.

Koch also praised the job President Bush is doing, calling his conduct "magnificent" — as he criticized some media outlets for sniping at the president.

In an interview with NewsMax.com today, New York City's leading elder statesman said the United States should say to each of those states: "Here is a list of terrorists that we've identified that you have in your country. You either deliver them to us for trial within the next five days, or get ready for us because we will destroy several of your major cities."

If it comes to that, Koch would say that if the terrorist states refuse the U.S. demand, "then tell your people to get out of those cities because we will be destroying them in the next five days, and we'd like to see the least number of civilian casualties."

The man who served as the city's mayor (1977–1989) and before that, a congressman (1968–1977) endorsed Vice President Cheney's statement on NBC's *Meet the Press* Sunday that the U.S. get back to the recruitment of human spies, an effort that was emasculated during the Clinton presidency.

Koch says the United States will have to pay people to betray their terrorist friends in the fundamentalist Muslim world. You can't fight that kind of intelligence battle any other way, he cautioned.

"It's very hard for us to infiltrate a cell made up of Muslims, who converse with one another, not only in Arabic or Farsi — and there are not too many Americans who can do that — but also joining in a cell [with people of that ilk] that they have known for years."

Some analysts have said effective, credible spies are not found among those whose revulsion goes to the question of "Who wants to get in a sewer with rats?"

If the answer to that question is "other rats," as Koch clearly believes, then we will have to "pay for the information, pay millions of dollars to people who would be willing to betray their cell members and give us the information. That's what I think we will ultimately have to do, and to use countries … to do exactly that."

While saying he hopes Pakistan keeps its word and cooperates with U.S. efforts to get at the terrorists, he adds, "There are questions about that."

As far as Koch is concerned, the mid-90s policies of not dealing with unsavory characters or those without a "clean" record on human rights were "stupid."

"That's all over with and people [now] realize how stupid that is. Wouldn't we be better off if we had assassinated bin Laden?"

Follow Menachem Begin's Example

Christopher Ruddy
Friday, September 21, 2001

President Bush last night was brilliant and emphatic: America is at war, a war we will win.

But what does this war really mean?

The significance of this war was explained earlier in the day when former Israeli Prime Minister Benjamin Netanyahu testified before Congress and said the acts of September 11 were a "wake-up call from hell."

As tragic as the events last week were, Netanyahu understands how dangerous our enemies are. Americans cannot fully absorb the horror of "hell" — if we believe it exists at all.

Of course, Netanyahu thinks "hell" is the eventual use of weapons of mass destruction by these groups and the nations that back them — that is, nuclear, chemical and biological weapons.

The use of such weapons by the bad guys is inevitable.

Iraq and Iran are both close to developing weapons of mass destruction, if they don't have them already.

In such a world, we need a leader who will lead by making tough, even unpopular decisions.

In the aftermath of the attacks, a friend in the Middle East called me and said, "Chris, we need leaders, but there are no leaders."

There is no Thatcher, Reagan, Sadat, Begin, Mitterand.

There is George Bush. He is our leader, and we believe he will be a great leader.

But to our allies, and to the rest of the world, President Bush is untested.

So far he has demonstrated great leadership. I pray that, like Lincoln, he will surprise many and rise to this occasion.

I also hope he will follow in the footsteps of Menachem Begin.

In 1981, Prime Minister Begin ordered the air strikes against Iraq's nuclear reactors at Osirak, destroying them.

Begin said Iraq was on the verge of having nuclear weapons. He was condemned by the Israeli press and the opposition within his own country. The whole world condemned him; even the Reagan administration condemned Begin — with the sole exception of then–Secretary of State Alexander Haig, who supported Begin's decision.

How the world thanks Begin today.

How the Arab states like Saudi Arabia must secretly be glad that Saddam was denied such nuclear weapons.

We need leaders who think like Begin, not for tomorrow but for many years ahead, and leaders who understand what Netanyahu meant when he said this catastrophe was just a "wake-up" call.

Begin's decision was a courageous one.

Courage is taking a stand when a majority opposes you. Courage is, as John Wayne once said, "When you're scared to death but you saddle up the horse anyway."

Right now, word out of Washington is that courage may be in short supply. The administration is reportedly divided between the bureaucrats led by Colin Powell, who want this "war" to be limited to Osama bin Laden and his motley crew, and the hawks in the Defense Department who want to clean house.

The hawks want to go after those countries, like Iraq and Iran, that have backed bin Laden.

The hawks understand Netanyahu. Next time, America may not be so lucky. Instead of thousands it could be hundreds of thousands of casualties.

The bottom line is that the wake-up call sent to us September 11 needs to be answered expeditiously and in the strongest terms.

Churchill Would Fight Tyranny of Terrorism

Jonathan Sandys
NewsMax.com
Wednesday, September 26, 2001

What is our policy? ... to wage war against a monstrous tyranny, never surpassed in the dark, lamentable catalogue of human crime.
— Winston Churchill, Hansard, May 13, 1940

Were Churchill alive today, his policy and advice then would, I believe, be the same as now. We as free democratic nations cannot afford to let ourselves be taken over by 'The Boneless Wonder.' War is inevitable; there is no backing away from our duty. There is no cowering behind the attitude of a conscientious objector. Either we fight to survive or we accept defeat and prepare for a fate worse than death where our right to choose will be taken from us. Where innocent men, women and children will be murdered for the pleasure of sport.

Were Churchill alive today, I believe he would have done as Prime Minister Blair has done, standing Britain shoulder to shoulder with America. Send troops in preparation of war. Visit the president and plan firstly to exhaust the 'jaw-jaw' solution, but should that fail, be prepared for 'war-war.' Sir Winston would no doubt have taken the view that although "No one can guarantee success in war, but only deserve it."

Terrorism is a serious problem, and although the enemy is unseen, masking himself behind a veil of religious fanaticism, we have no alternative but to fight.

No one wants to have a war; many feel that it is a useless solution. I have heard some people say, "World War II was different. We knew our enemy and we could see to fight them. These people are prepared to die for their cause; they care nothing for either their lives or the lives of those they murder." I agree.

I think there are not many people in the world who have not considered the above statement, but to those I must ask, what alternative is there?

Do we as democratic nations just sit and take everything we are given?

Do we as democratic people turn our backs on the freedom our parents, grandparents and great-grandparents fought for in the two world wars — our democracy, our freedom to vote, our freedom to live where we want?

Our freedom to exist was bought by those who fought, some of whom gave their lives in 1914–1918 and 1939–1945. We have to defend ourselves against the tyrannical power of terrorism that threatens us. We have to fight.

What is our aim? … Victory, victory at all costs, victory in spite of all terror; victory, however long and hard the road may be; for without victory, there is no survival.

— Winston Churchill, Hansard, May 13, 1940

Some in Britain (a small minority) are saying that this is an American war and why should we be drawn in? I remind that minority, without the support and help of America during The Second World War, we would have lost our struggle. Hitler would have taken the 'Island Nation' he wanted and this country — indeed, this world would have become a very different place.

Our American friends need us. We need them as well. Although Britain has not felt the anger of bin Laden and his motley gang or murderers, we are not unaccustomed to terrorism. For 30 years we have been fighting a war of our own against the evils of the IRA. If we don't join with America now in its struggle against terrorism and it loses, the IRA bombings will seem like a picnic to what bin Laden and his evil-minded fanatics will do to us.

The coming months will no doubt put a strain on all our lives. We must all focus on the aim of our cause, the aim of victory. We must put our faith in God. For some, we will have to take up the sword and fight for the good of mankind. This solution, although a last resort, may last for some years to come. We have to be strong. We fight not just for ourselves, we fight also for our children, grandchildren and great-grandchildren. "In war: resolution. In defeat: defiance. In victory: magnanimity. In peace: goodwill."

Churchill would have been proud to stand with us all and fight. He once said in a letter written in 1937: "Dictators ride to and fro upon tigers which they dare not dismount. And the tigers are getting hungry."

Perhaps the most compelling evidence that we have of Sir Winston Churchill's possible response to this attack can be found in a radio broadcast he gave in February 1941. "Here is the answer I will give to President Roosevelt. ... Give us the tools and we will finish the job."

Over these next coming days, weeks and months, let us be resolved to stand against those who would take the democracy that we have from us. Let us not be complacent. We must not take democracy for granted. We as a Free World are at war against a foe that, unlike Hitler, is not mad but desperate. When the bully is standing alone, there we will be. A bully is only a bully as long as he has people around him who agree with him. Should we weaken a link in the chain of terrorism, then the whole structure of terroristic violence will fall. Though odds may appear against us, we can win. We must fight. We must win.

Jonathan Sandys is the great-grandson of Sir Winston Churchill and the British political correspondent to NewsMax.com.

A New Kind of War

Donald Rumsfeld on www.defenselink.com
Friday, September 28, 2001
WASHINGTON — President Bush is rallying the nation for a war against terrorism's attack on our way of life. Some believe the first casualty of any war is the truth. But in this war, the first victory must be to tell the truth. And the truth is, this will be a war like none other our nation has faced. Indeed, it is easier to describe what lies ahead by talking about what it is not rather than what it is.

This war will not be waged by a grand alliance united for the single purpose of defeating an axis of hostile powers. Instead, it will involve floating coalitions of countries, which may change and evolve. Countries will have different roles and contribute in different ways. Some will provide diplomatic support, others financial, still others logistical or military. Some will help us publicly, while others, because of their circumstances, may help us privately and secretly. In this war, the mission will define the coalition — not the other way around.

We understand that countries we consider our friends may help with certain efforts or be silent on others, while other actions we take may depend on the involvement of countries we have considered less than friendly.

In this context, the decision by the United Arab Emirates and Saudi Arabia — friends of the United States — to break ties with the Taliban is an important early success of this campaign, but should not suggest they will be a part of every action we may contemplate.

This war will not necessarily be one in which we pore over military targets and mass forces to seize those targets. Instead, military force will likely be one of many tools we use to stop individuals, groups and countries that engage in terrorism.

Our response may include firing cruise missiles into military targets somewhere in the world; we are just as likely to engage in electronic combat to track and stop investments moving through offshore banking centers. The uniforms of this conflict will be bankers' pinstripes and programmers' grunge just as assuredly as desert camouflage.

This is not a war against an individual, a group, a religion or a country. Rather, our opponent is a global network of terrorist organizations and their state sponsors, committed to denying free people the opportunity to live as they choose. While we may engage militarily against foreign governments that sponsor terrorism, we may also seek to make allies of the people those governments suppress.

Even the vocabulary of this war will be different. When we "invade the enemy's territory," we may well be invading his cyberspace. There may not be as many beachheads stormed as opportunities denied. Forget about "exit strategies"; we're looking at a sustained engagement that carries no deadlines. We have no fixed rules about how to deploy our troops; we'll instead establish guidelines to determine whether military force is the best way to achieve a given objective.

The public may see some dramatic military engagements that produce no apparent victory, or may be unaware of other actions that lead to major victories. "Battles" will be fought by customs officers stopping suspicious persons at our borders and diplomats securing cooperation against money laundering.

But if this is a different kind of war, one thing is unchanged: America remains indomitable. Our victory will come with Americans living their lives day by day, going to work, raising their children and building their dreams as they always have — a free and great people.

Samson Option: Israel's Plan to Prevent Mass Destruction Attacks

David Eberhart
Tuesday, October 16, 2001

With American bombing raids into Afghanistan and a tough President Bush intimating more of the same for other terrorist-harboring nations, experts and armchair war watchers are inserting nuclear powerhouse Israel into the calculus of potential Armageddon in the Middle East.

Adding yet other variables, a defiant Saddam Hussein issued an ominous warning in late August, just weeks before the terror attacks on New York City and the Pentagon: "The battle [against the U.S.] continues on the economic, political and military fields. We are convinced we will be victorious."

All that the saber-rattling Iraqi dictator left out of this latest diatribe was a bold repeat of his 1991 pre–Desert Storm boast that if America attacked, the first to feel his wrath in the "mother of all battles" would be Israel.

After decades of living among hostile neighbors, Israel has yet to be attacked by an enemy using nuclear, chemical or biological weapons. One reason may be the horrific plan some claim Israel drew up to prevent such an attack. The plan was called the Samson Option. An astute investigative journalist and student of history chalked a dramatic potential solution to the volatile equation on the blackboard — a decade ago.

"Should war break out in the Middle East again and should the Syrians and the Egyptians break through again as they did in 1973 [Yom Kippur War], or should any Arab nation fire missiles again at Israel, as Iraq did [in the 1991 Gulf War], a nuclear escalation, once unthinkable except as a last resort, would now be a strong possibility."

Pulitzer Prize–winning author (*My Lai 4*) Seymour M. Hersh proposed this hypothesis in his 1991 best-seller, *The Samson Option*.

Captured and cruelly maimed, the book's biblical namesake uttered the ultimate fighting words: "Let my soul die with the Philistines."

That said, the divinely empowered Samson pushed apart the temple pillars — collapsing the roof and killing himself as well as his enemies.

In his exposé of Israel's clandestine nuclear arsenal, Hersh suggested that in the early days (late 1960s) of crude big-flash-and-bang nukes, one defensive option to counter an attack on Israel with weapons of mass destruction was for the beleaguered nation to mimic Samson and grimly trade holocaust for holocaust.

Hersh's 1991 prognostication of a "strong possibility" of the use by Israel of nuclear weapons rested on his knowledge that by the mid-1980s, Israeli technicians at the super-secret Dimona nuclear plant had produced hundreds of low-yield neutron warheads capable of destroying large numbers of enemy troops with minimal property damage.

Israel's ability to use nukes tactically and surgically, however, has evolved a great deal since the Samson Option was still realistically an option.

Israel's Military Might

In 1997, *Jane's Defence Weekly* examined satellite photographs of what it described as an Israeli military base at Kfar Zechariah, concluding academically, "Israel's nuclear arsenal is larger than many estimates."

According to *Jane's*, the site was said to house about 50 Jericho-2 missiles, believed to have a maximum range of about 3,000 miles with a warhead of about 2,200 pounds.

According to the report, the installation contained nuclear bombs, configured for dropping from bombers.

Furthermore, five bunkers at the site were cited as capable of safeguarding 150 weapons.

"This ... supports indications that the Israeli arsenal may contain as many as 400 nuclear weapons with a total combined yield of 50 megatons," the report concluded.

In 1998 *The New York Times* reported a Rand Corporation study commissioned by the Pentagon that opined Israel had enough plutonium to make 70 nuclear weapons.

More light was shed on the issue in February of last year when the Israeli Knesset (parliament) held the first public discussion on the country's nuclear arms program.

Issam Mahoul, an Arab Israeli MP and member of the Hadash (Communist) Party, petitioned that country's Supreme Court to force the government to permit a parliamentary debate on the forbidden subject.

The upshot of this bold and generally unpopular tactic was an unprecedented televised session of the Knesset at which Mahoul stated that, according to experts' estimates, Israel had stockpiled huge numbers of nuclear warheads.

This had increased to what he described as the "insane amount of 200-300." The weapons had been developed with the help of the South African apartheid regime.

Working up a head of rhetorical steam, Mahoul grandly alleged that three new German-built submarines just purchased by Israel were to be fitted with nuclear weapons.

Their stated purpose, he said, was "to cruise deep in the sea and constitute a second strike force in the event that Israel is attacked with nuclear weapons."

Mahoul also announced what was hardly a news bulletin — Israel was producing "biological warfare" weapons at the government's Biological Institute in Ness Ziona.

The obstreperous MP concluded that the government's official policy of "nuclear ambiguity" was the height of self-delusion. "All the world knows that Israel is a vast warehouse of atomic, biological and chemical weapons that serves as an anchor for the Middle East arms race," he said.

Despite the bristling inventory of nukes, the Israelis have a laudable history of restraint in brandishing, much less using, these most destructive of all weapons of mass destruction.

In fact, for most of the latter half of the 20th century, the Israeli Bomb remained invisible and unacknowledged. Israel's official position was to neither confirm nor deny its nuclear status, only pledging on the record "not to be the first to introduce nuclear weapons to the Middle East."

A Show of Restraint

According to Hersh, the best example of Israeli restraint in the face of great provocation came during the Gulf War.

On the second day of the American invasion, Saddam Hussein fired eight Scud missiles at noncombatant Israel. Two of the conventionally armed missiles landed on Tel Aviv. Then–Prime Minister Yitzhak Shamir responded by ordering mobile missile launchers armed with nuclear weapons moved into the open and deployed facing Iraq.

The Samsonesque strongman of the Middle East had stirred — and the world held its breath.

Promising Patriot missile batteries and loads of future aid, the United States pressured Israel to keep cool. After all, the allied coalition included a number of Arab nations, and the U.S. feared that dramatic Israeli retaliation could fragment the fragile alliance.

By the end of the Gulf War, Israel had dutifully absorbed 26 Scuds — none armed with biological or chemical weapons.

And therein lies the rub. What if the missiles had featured biochemical-agent warheads?

Israel's prime ministers have plenary jurisdiction over their country's nuclear activities.

The refrain used consistently by the Israeli leaders has been and remains an unqualified "Israel reserves the right to retaliate if attacked."

Traditionally, Israeli leaders have pigeonholed nuclear weapons as a psychological insurance policy for unthinkable contingencies, under the heading of "last resort."

The hope of those in the inner sanctums of national security is that the exigencies of America's New War send no such unthinkable contingencies in the direction of America's quiet ally.

Lucom Plan for Saving American Lives

Wilson C. Lucom
Thursday, November 8, 2001

President Bush should use the Lucom Plan, a two-step proposal that could end the war very quickly and save thousands of American soldiers from being killed in the war and thousands of you, American civilians, from being killed by terrorist attacks.

If the Lucom Plan had been used by President Bush when it was first submitted to him long before September 11, thousands of innocent Americans would not have been killed in the Twin Towers. Unfortunately, he did not use it.

Step One

The Lucom Plan's nonviolent first step is for the U.S. government to offer a $1 billion reward for the capture of Osama bin Laden. The U.S. would not have to pay one penny of the reward unless bin Laden is caught, *which would end the Afghanistan war.*

Not one soldier's life would have been lost nor one civilian killed in the United States by bin Laden's terrorist attacks if this plan had been implemented before September 11.

To an individual, $1 billion is a very large reward. It is, however, only 1/1,300 of the annual U.S. budget of $1.3 trillion, an insignificant amount to the U.S. government.

Even if all 28 terrorist leaders were caught, which would cost $12-14 billion, this is cheap compared with the $500 billion cost for war and, most important, saving up to a million American soldiers' lives.

The Lucom Plan is very cost-effective. The U.S. would let other people catch bin Laden without having to bomb anyone, to have aircraft carriers in place or to have bombing planes working regularly. All this immense cost would be eliminated.

It would have a great psychological impact on the terrorists. They would suspect almost everyone of betraying them for the $1 billion reward.

These are the reasons Bush should use the Lucom Plan at once to very possibly end the war and save hundred of thousands of American lives as well as billions of dollars of your tax money.

We cannot understand why President Bush will not try the Lucom Plan, because it is of no cost to the government unless the plan is successful and bin Laden is caught.

This war has already cost taxpayers over $4 billions in bombs and missiles, and bin Laden is nowhere near being caught.

Bush has the Air Force wasting billions of dollars bombing *empty* terrorist training camps. The terrorists knew they were going to be bombed and left long before the camps were bombed.

Clinton also wasted billions of dollars when he had bin Laden's empty training camps bombed. The terrorists will just establish training camps in other places.

It is the *terrorists* who should be bombed and killed so they cannot set up new training camps and continue attacking the United States.

It is very possible that bin Laden has already left Afghanistan and secretly set up terrorist activities in another country that harbors terrorists. The other country will deny he is in that country. Meanwhile, President Bush will have egg on his face.

Step Two

The second step of the Lucom Plan is as follows. It was and is the official policy of the Soviet and Russian governments, if attacked, to use nuclear weapons.

If Russia will use nuclear weapons if attacked, so must the United States use them if attacked, and it was attacked on September 11.

Before using nuclear weapons, President Bush must first warn all countries supporting or harboring terrorists that terrorism is evil and terrorists are evil. They must turn the terrorists over to the United States or the U.S. will use nuclear weapons against them.

If they do not do so, then it all depends on the courage, the 'guts', of President Bush. Does he have the courage of former President Harry Truman to end the war quickly, saving up to a million American soldiers' lives and also the lives of possibly a million people who would die from the atom bombs the terrorists will use on New York City?

On November 6, Bush said that Osama bin Laden was seeking nuclear weapons. On November 6, al Qaeda warned that terrorists were getting nuclear weapons. Israeli Prime Minister Netanyahu recently predicted that New York City would be bombed.

How many warnings does Bush need?

When the terrorists obtain the atom bomb, which may be sooner than anyone thinks, you can be sure they will drop it on New York City. If this is allowed to happen, President Bush's unacceptable excuse will be "we had no *direct* evidence the terrorists were going to use nuclear weapons."

The direct evidence will be only when New York City is hit with nuclear weapons, with hundreds of thousands or even millions dead.

The U.S. had no direct evidence the Twin Towers or Pentagon were going to be attacked. You cannot wait for direct evidence — you have to determine their intentions and then first kill them before they kill you.

This is the unpleasant, violent reality of war.

President Bush is horribly naïve if he waits for direct evidence before using nuclear weapons on the terrorists before they use them on the U.S. If this happens, Bush should be taken out and summarily shot for not having the courage of Harry Truman to drop the atom bomb on the terrorists before they kill thousands or hundreds of thousands of Americans.

President Bush should warn the nations harboring terrorists: If they do not comply, he should use nuclear weapons against them.

You do not need a coalition to make this decision. Bush must act as president of the United States, as President Truman acted. Just one bomb drop and these countries would get the message and stop harboring terrorists. It is suggested the first atom bomb be dropped on Saddam Hussein in Iraq.

If President Bush uses the Lucom Plan, either step could quickly end the war at a tremendous savings in the cost of the war and, most important, in saving thousands or even millions of American people from death and injury.

Write to your senators and congressmen, demanding that they tell Bush to use the Lucom Plan to save huge numbers of American lives. For further information on the Lucom Plan, go to endwar.com.

PART 3

The Axis of Evil

❖

Chapter 11

The Leaders: Russia and China

CIA Report Blames China, Russia for Massive Weapons Proliferation

NewsMax.com
Monday, September 10, 2001

The world is bristling with weapons of mass destruction and China has been the main supplier of nuclear, chemical and biological weapon-related equipment and missile systems to rogue states and unstable regions of the world, according to a new CIA report — a censored version of a more detailed report required by the 1997 Intelligence Authorization Act.

Bill Gertz, writing in *The Washington Times*, says the report shows that China supplied missile technology and related goods to Pakistan, Iran, North Korea and Libya.

Russia and North Korea are also listed as major exporters of these types of equipment and missile systems to the same regions, the CIA report added. "Chinese entities provided Pakistan with missile-related technical assistance," the report said. "Pakistan has been moving toward domestic serial production of solid-propellant [short-range ballistic missiles] with Chinese help."

According to Gertz, the report said Pakistan also needs continued support from China for its Shaheen-2 medium-range missile.

"In addition, firms in China have provided dual-use missile-related items, raw materials, and/or assistance to several other countries of proliferation concern such as Iran, North Korea, and Libya," the report revealed.

Gertz wrote that the CIA report also noted there are indications that China has continued to assist Pakistan in developing nuclear weapons in violation of a 1996 pledge to the United States not to do so. Moreover, China seems to have violated another pledge not to provide new assistance to Iran's nuclear program, which the CIA believes will be used to build nuclear arms.

There are also questions about China's continued nuclear cooperation with Iran in violation of its pledge, and "the administration is seeking to address these questions with appropriate Chinese authorities," the report said.

According to the report, China also supplied advanced conventional arms to Pakistan, Iran, Sudan and other nations. Russia and North Korea, along with China, were identified in the report as "key suppliers" of missiles and weapons of mass destruction to unstable areas around the world.

"During the second half of 2000, entities in Russia, North Korea and China continued to supply crucial ballistic missile-related equipment, technology and expertise to Iran," the report said. Russian firms "continued to supply a variety of ballistic missile-related goods and technical know-how to countries such as Iran, India, China and Libya."

Moreover, Russian missile assistance helped Iran in particular to accelerate its medium-range Shahab-3 missile development. The missile has been flight-tested three times, the report said, adding that continuing Russian missile assistance "likely supports Iranian efforts to develop new missiles and increase Tehran's self-sufficiency in missile production."

According to the CIA, Russia also supplies nuclear reactors for both China's and India's naval-propulsion systems. In addition, the report noted that India has discussed leasing nuclear-powered attack submarines from Moscow.

North Korea was identified as a supplier of missile goods to nations in the Middle East, South Asia and North Africa.

Gertz listed other chilling revelations in the report.

- Saddam Hussein is rebuilding a nuclear weapons program and in September called for "nuclear mujahideen" — holy warriors — to "defeat the enemy."
- Iran has a biological-weapons program and "limited capability for [biological-weapons] deployment."
- Iraq is converting Czech-made L29 jet trainers into unmanned aerial vehicles with the capability of delivering chemical and biological weapons.
- North Korea tried to purchase nuclear weapons-related technology last year.
- Libya is building missiles with help from Yugoslavia, India, North Korea and China, and may build a medium-range missile in the future.

Expert: Russia Knew in Advance, Encouraged Citizens to Cash Out Dollars

Dr. Alexandr Nemets
Monday, September 17, 2001

Russian press accounts and other activities by the Russian government this summer indicate that the Russian government knew in advance that something would happen to America, including a "financial attack" against the U.S.

During the past three months, Russian media and officials have encouraged citizens to cash out U.S. dollars pending an economic collapse there after an "attack."

Currently, the dominant view of the media is that the terrorist actions in New York City and Washington were just a "bolt from the blue."

Could it be? Yes, a well-organized group accomplished these dastardly acts. But just how well-organized was it?

Obviously, President Bush and Vice President Cheney are targeting the powers behind these terrorist groups, the states that give them safe harbor and backing.

Sponsors of state terrorism include Iran, Iraq, Libya, Cuba, North Korea, Sudan and Syria.

Did you know that all of these countries have very close ties with Russia and her military/intelligence agencies?

Could it be that the Russians actually expected this in advance and even counted on it, discussing the possible consequences?

My suspicions were raised this July and August as I scanned and sifted through all of Russia's major newspapers.

Considering Russia's close ties to these terrorist countries, Russian activities need close scrutiny.

Pravda *Wrote of Financial 'Attack' on U.S.*

Consider the July 12, 2001, Page One report in *Pravda* — still considered the establishment voice of Russia's old guard communists who control the military and intelligence agencies.

The *Pravda* article was entitled "Will the Dollar and America Fall on August 19? That's the Opinion of Dr. Tatyana Koryagina, Who Very Accurately Predicted the August Default in 1998."

This article struck me for several reasons. Major newspapers so closely aligned with the government do not attempt to create panic or fear in the public — unless the government wants this information to be publicly aired.

Also, a major newspaper would be reluctant to print a major prediction for which it could be held accountable.

This *Pravda* article was published about the same time as another strange event that took place in early July in the Russian State Duma.

The Duma held a conference titled "On the measures to provide the development of Russian economy in the environment of destabilization of the world financial system."

The chairman of the Duma Commission on Economic Politics, Dr. Sergei Glazyev, headed the hearings.

Some prominent foreigners, including Lyndon Larouche from the U.S. and Malaysian Ambassador in Russia Yacha Baba, were among the participants.

Tatyana Koryagina made a statement at the end of hearings — as a

Russian expert in the shadow economy, shadow politics and conspirology.

She is a senior research fellow in the Institute of Macroeconomic Researches subordinated to the Russian Ministry of Economic Development (Minekonom). The main theme of the Duma hearings was the rapidly approaching economic crash of the United States.

The hearings focused on preparing recommendations for President Putin as to what Russia should to do to soften the consequences of this coming catastrophe.

Pravda also detailed its own interview with Dr. Koryagina below.

Pravda: All the participants at the hearings stated that America is a huge financial pyramid that will crash soon. Still, it is hard to understand how this could happen in the first and richest country of the world — without a war, without missile or bomb strikes?

Koryagina: Besides bombs and missiles, there are other kinds of weaponry, much more destructive ones. ...

Pravda: Well, economic theory. But how it is possible for you to give an exact date [for the U.S. crash] — August 19?

Koryagina: The U.S. is engaged in a mortal economic game. The known history of civilization is merely the visible part of the iceberg. There is a shadow economy, shadow politics and also a shadow history, known to conspirologists. There are [unseen] forces acting in the world, unstoppable for [most powerful] countries and even continents.

Pravda: Just these forces intend to smash America on August 19?

Koryagina: There are international "superstate" and "supergovernment" groups. In accordance with tradition, the mystical and religious components play extremely important roles in human history. One must take into account the shadow economy, shadow politics and the religious component, while predicting the development of the present financial situation.

Pravda: Still, I don't understand what could be done to this giant country [the U.S.], whose budget is calculated in the trillions of dollars.

Koryagina: It is possible to do anything to the U.S. ... whose total debt has reached $26 trillion. Generally, the Western economy is at the boiling point now. Shadow financial actives of $300 trillion are hanging over the planet. At any moment, they could fall on any stock exchange and cause panic and crash. The recent crisis in Southeast Asia, which touched Russia, was a rehearsal.

Pravda: What is the sense of smashing just America?

Koryagina: The U.S. has been chosen as the object of financial attack because the financial center of the planet is located there. The effect will be maximal. The strike waves of economic crisis will spread over the planet instantly and will remind us of the blast of a huge nuclear bomb.

Pravda: Did Russia's crisis of 1998 have this religious-mystical component?

Koryagina: ... The Russian crisis of 1998 was preconditioned by internal factors. Yeltsin's policy enlarged its consequences. Now we have President Putin, and this is a good choice.

Pravda: What do we have to do now?

Koryagina: Recommendations, compiled by the Duma Commission of Economic Politics after the recent Duma hearings, offer instruction on what should be done to escape the consequences of a world crisis inspired by a financial catastrophe in the U.S. This document will be sent — or has already been sent — to President Putin.

Pravda: What should Russian citizens do?

Koryagina: They should start changing their dollars for rubles. President Putin and the Russian Central Bank are already taking the necessary healthy measures. There are high chances that after August 19 the ruble will become a very good currency.

Pravda: Why August 19, say, and not the 21st?

Koryagina: Some fluctuation in this date is possible. Serious forces are acting against THOSE WHO ARE NOW PREPARING THE ATTACK ON THE UNITED STATES [emphasis added]. August, with very high probability, will bring the financial catastrophe to the U.S. … The last 10 days of August have especial importance from a religious-sensible point of view.

[End of interview]

It is important to note that this story was not an isolated one or a cute, human interest story, as one may find occasionally on the cover of *The Wall Street Journal*.

It was a serious news report, and story, discussed widely in Russia, including on national TV programs. The thrust of the story was that Russian officials were strongly encouraging Russian citizens to cash out the U.S. dollar.

It is also important to understand that Dr. Koryagina is one of the leading economists in a Russian social group that, from the very beginning, has fiercely opposed "radical economic reform" in Russia. She is a firm supporter of President Putin.

She and her network actively support Putin, especially his foreign policy aimed at diminishing America's global role.

In particular, they support Putin's policy of engagement of Iran, Iraq and other nations of concern. Dr. Koryagina herself should be considered as an insightful, well-connected and well-informed person.

Dr. Koryagina says much about the invisible and unstoppable "international mystical-religious forces" preparing an attack on the U.S.

It looks like she knows the real nature of these forces and tries to disguise them in a "conspiratorial fog."

She is sure that such an attack or strike of some kind — sudden and effective — will soon take place and will cause panic and an ensuing crash of the U.S. financial system and the world financial system, already unstable. However, Dr. Koryagina evidently does not know the exact mechanism of the attack.

Duma Warned Citizens to Cash Out Dollars

The hearings in the Duma, which has become a rubber stump for President Putin, have been inspired, without doubt, by the Kremlin "taking the necessary healthy measures" in advance of a U.S. crash and world crisis.

The Kremlin clearly is thinking about how it should operate in the "new world" after the expected U.S. crash.

It is my belief that the Kremlin provided Dr. Koryagina with a very small part of its information on the forthcoming attack against the U.S.

Another article on this same theme was published by *Pravda* on July 17, 2001.

It was an interview with Chairman of the Duma Commission on Economic Politics Dr. Sergei Glazyev, one of the most prominent Russian economists.

The article was entitled "The Dollar and the U.S. Could Fall at Any Moment."

Dr. Glazyev, in his answers, did not mention the forces preparing an attack on the U.S. and its financial system.

He merely discussed the forms and scales of the forthcoming financial catastrophe in the U.S. and its consequences for Russia — mostly beneficial ones if the necessary measures are taken in advance.

In particular, like Dr. Koryagina, Dr. Glazyev advised the Russian public to change dollars for rubles and predicted that "the ruble will become the reserve currency for Eurasia, particularly in trade with China and India."

Third Article, More Media

Pravda published a third article on this theme on July 31–August 1, 2001. This article, "The Dollar and the U.S. Will Fall," was in the form of an interview with the Malaysian ambassador in Russia.

Other Moscow newspapers published articles of this kind also.

As a result, New York's Russian-language TV channel in early August was forced to state that "the Moscow rumors are ungrounded." Within a few days the public forgot all about this story.

The tone of Moscow economists predicting the crash of the U.S. financial-economic system is confident and somewhat delightful: "Finally, it is going to happen!"

They are not only discussing the future, they also are evidently trying to issue a self-fulfilling prophecy, transforming this future into the present. This is because the prospects described in the above articles are extremely attractive for the Russian elite for the following reasons:

1. It would become possible to pay off Russia's huge foreign debt with devalued dollars, which would be easy if oil prices jumped to $100 or more per barrel.

2. Russia would become equal among a weakened G-8 group of nations.

3. Investment conditions in Russia would become very attractive compared to the bleak global economy. Russia could become the recipient of huge foreign investments.

4. If U.S. military might is undermined (and it might be, if the financial system collapses), Russia would regain its control over the former Soviet republics, spread control to the Balkans and regain its former super-empire status.

Such a prize, such a temptation for the criminal Russian "elite"! One small push, and such great booty! While reading these articles, it is almost possible to visualize how they are licking their lips with excitement.

So, those in Moscow had very serious reasons not to share information with the U.S. about the coming attack — if they indeed had such information.

Very likely they did, and the maximum amount of information was concentrated in the Kremlin. According to numerous statements published by prominent U.S. economists after the tragedy, the times and places of the attacks were chosen — more precisely, very well calculated — as if the terrorists or those backing them had tried to do their best to undermine the U.S. financial and political systems and to cause a financial-economic crisis in the U.S.

There is some evidence that another targeted aircraft, a TWA plane at JFK airport, did not take off and perhaps another crash was thwarted. Was it intended for the New York Stock Exchange?

"It wasn't a healthy economy to begin with, and this could be just enough to push us into a mild recession and render a blow to consumer confidence," one of these economists told the UPI.

He continued: "There has been a complete disruption of passenger flights. Besides the airline industry, tourism, retail and the shipping sectors will feel the negative effects of Tuesday's attack. Tougher security measures now in place at the nation's airports will increase shipping and travel expenses that will be passed along to the consumer."

And the consumer confidence index, low already, declined additionally.

However, those in Moscow very probably waited for much greater effects.

Remarkably, immediately after the events in New York and Washington — at approximately 6 p.m. Moscow time — the dollar exchange rate in Moscow street exchanges fell from 29 rubles to 15-20 rubles — as if the Moscow financial experts had awaited the strikes or expected greater panic and collapse.

It is important to note that such a great fluctuation in the exchange rate happened in no other world capital. The next day, the dollar in Moscow gradually returned to its previous exchange rate.

U.S. Needs to Look at Source

A network of Arab terrorist groups — mostly in the U.S. and Middle East — merely provided the fingers to implement the terrorist strikes. These terrorist groups are supported by rogue nations — Libya, Syria, Iran, Iraq and Sudan — which are the "hands."

Now, if the U.S. and NATO forces carry out retaliatory strikes on Afghanistan, the "hands" will be punished.

And where are the body and heart of the beast?

And who provides the advanced military technology — including that needed for "special actions" — to these nations of concern? Who supports them in the U.N.? Who demonstrates daily the desire to diminish or undermine America's global influence?

Moscow and Beijing. And Moscow, probably, is even more evil and impudent. Let us consider the Moscow rulers.

Yes, of course, Putin immediately sent condolences to President Bush and the American people.

It should be taken into account here that in September 1999 Putin conveniently used the apartment explosions in Moscow and Volgodonsk (KGB-organized actions, in the opinion of most of the Russian media and in the opinion of the authors) to gain supreme power in Russia.

Now the Kremlin is making statements about a "joint struggle against world terrorism," about "the ties between the actions in New York and the actions in Moscow in September 1999."

Indeed, these events probably are closely tied to one another, the same forces behind both. But what is the actual name of these forces? The investigation should go all the way and provide the real answer.

Dr. Alexandr V. Nemets is an expert in Chinese-Russian strategic-military alliance development and has spent the last several years researching Chinese and Russian economic and military issues. Dr. Nemets immigrated to the United States in December 1994 and is co-author of Chinese-Russian Military Relations, Fate of Taiwan and New Geopolitics.

How Rogue Nations Aid Terrorism

Phil Brennan, NewsMax.com
Monday, September 17, 2001

President Bush and Vice President Cheney have made it clear that America's reaction to this terrorist attack will be different: America is at war and the U.S. will go after the nations that finance and support terrorist groups.

According to the U.S. State Department, several rogue nations are clear-cut state sponsors of terrorism.

Afghanistan, the shield and protector of ultra-terrorist Osama Bin Laden, isn't the only country accused of sponsoring terrorism. State sponsors of terror include Iran, Iraq, Syria, Libya, Cuba, North Korea and Sudan.

"The designation of state sponsors of terrorism by the United States — and the imposition of sanctions — is a mechanism for isolating nations that use terrorism as a means of political expression," according to the department's Office of the Coordinator for Counterterrorism in a report issued in April.

"Iran, Iraq, Syria, Libya, Cuba, North Korea, and Sudan continue to be the seven governments that the U.S. Secretary of State has designated as state sponsors of international terrorism," the report said, noting that Iran gave "support to numerous terrorist groups, including the Lebanese Hizballah, Hamas, and the Palestine Islamic Jihad (PIJ), which seek to undermine the Middle East peace negotiations through the use of terrorism.

"Iraq continued to provide safe haven and support to a variety of Palestinian rejectionist groups, as well as bases, weapons and protection to the Mujahedin-e-Khalq (MEK), an Iranian terrorist group that opposes the current Iranian regime. Syria continued to provide safe haven and support to several terrorist groups, some of which oppose the Middle East peace negotiations.

"In South Asia, the United States has been increasingly concerned about reports of Pakistani support to terrorist groups and elements active in Kashmir, as well as Pakistani support, especially military support, to the Taliban, which continues to harbor terrorist groups, including al-Qaida, the Egyptian Islamic Jihad, al-Gama'a al-Islamiyya, and the Islamic Movement of Uzbekistan."

In recent years, the State Department reported, "Notwithstanding some conciliatory statements in the months after President Khatami's inauguration in August 1997, Iran remains the most active state sponsor of terrorism. There is no evidence that Iranian policy has changed, and Iran continues both to provide significant support to terrorist organizations and to assassinate dissidents abroad."

Here is how the following countries are involved in state-sponsored terrorism:

Afghanistan

Islamic extremists from around the world — including North America, Europe, Africa, the Middle East, and Central, South and Southeast Asia — continued to use Afghanistan as a training ground and base of operations for their worldwide terrorist activities in 2000. The Taliban, which controlled most Afghan territory, permitted the operation of training and indoctrination facilities for non-Afghans and provided logistics support to members of various terrorist organizations and mujahideen, including those waging jihads (holy wars) in Central Asia, Chechnya and Kashmir.

The Taliban has continued to play host to bin Laden despite U.N. sanctions and international pressure to hand him over to stand trial in the United States or a third country.

Significantly, before the attacks on the World Trade Center and Pentagon, the United States repeatedly made clear to the Taliban that it would be held responsible for any terrorist attacks undertaken by bin Laden while he is in its territory. Afghanistan was thus already on notice that in the event of a terrorist act such as Tuesday's it would not escape severe punishment.

Intelligence experts believe that bin Laden was responsible for the a terrorist bomb attack against the USS *Cole* in Aden Harbor, Yemen, which killed 17 U.S. sailors and injured scores of others. The report notes that while no definitive link has been made to his organization, Yemeni authorities have determined that some suspects in custody and at large are veterans of Afghan training camps.

In August, Bangladeshi authorities uncovered a bomb plot to assassinate Prime Minister Sheikh Hasina at a public rally. Bangladeshi police maintained that Islamic terrorists trained in Afghanistan planted the bomb.

Pakistan

The United States has expressed its concern about reports of continued Pakistani support for the Taliban's military operations in Afghanistan. It is widely believed that Pakistan is providing the Taliban with materiel, fuel, funding, technical assistance and military advisers.

Pakistan has done nothing to prevent large numbers of Pakistani nationals from moving into Afghanistan to fight for the Taliban. Islamabad also failed to take effective steps to curb the activities of certain madrassas, or religious schools, that serve as recruiting grounds for terrorism. Pakistan publicly and privately said it intends to comply fully with U.N. Security Council Resolution 1333, which imposes an arms embargo on the Taliban.

After the attack on the USS *Cole* raised fear that the U.S. would launch retaliatory strikes against bin Laden's organization and targets in Afghanistan, Pakistani religious party leaders and militant groups threatened U.S. citizens and facilities if such an action were to occur, in the same way they did after the U.S. attacked training camps in Afghanistan in August 1998.

However, the government of Pakistan generally has cooperated with U.S. requests to enhance security for U.S. facilities and personnel and now appears ready to assist the U.S. in whatever action it takes against bin Laden and Afghanistan.

Cuba

Cuba continued to provide haven to several terrorists and U.S. fugitives in 2000. A number of Basque Fatherland and Liberty (ETA) terrorists who gained sanctuary in Cuba years ago continued to live on the island, as did several U.S. terrorist fugitives.

Havana also maintained ties to other state sponsors of terrorism, including Libya, Iraq and Latin American insurgents. Colombia's two largest terrorist organizations, the Revolutionary Armed Forces of Colombia and the National Liberation Army, maintained a permanent presence on the island.

Iran

Iran remained the most active state sponsor of terrorism in 2000. Its Revolutionary Guard Corps (IRGC) and Ministry of Intelligence and Security (MOIS) continued to be involved in the planning and execution of terrorist acts and continued to support a variety of groups that use terrorism to pursue their goals.

Iran's involvement in terrorist activities remained focused on support for groups opposed to Israel and peace between Israel and its neighbors. Statements by Iran's leaders demonstrated Iran's unrelenting hostility to Israel:

- Supreme Leader Khameinei continued to refer to Israel as a "cancerous tumor" that must be removed.
- President Khatami, labeling Israel an "illegal entity," called for sanctions against Israel during the Intifada.
- Expediency Council Secretary Rezai said, "Iran will continue its campaign against Zionism until Israel is completely eradicated."

Iran has long provided Lebanese Hezbollah and the Palestinian rejectionist groups — notably Hamas, Palestine Islamic Jihad, and Ahmad Jibril's PFLP-GC — with varying amounts of funding, safe haven, training and weapons.

This activity continued at its already high levels after the Israeli withdrawal from southern Lebanon in May and during the Palestinian uprising in the fall. Iran continued to encourage Hezbollah and the Palestinian groups to coordinate their planning and to escalate their activities against Israel. Iran also provided a lower level of support — including funding, training and logistics assistance — to extremist groups in the Gulf, Africa, Turkey and Central Asia.

Iran also was a victim of terror sponsored by Mujahedin-e-Khalq (MEK). The Islamic Republic presented a letter to the U.N. secretary-general in October citing seven acts of sabotage by the MEK against Iran between January and August 2000. The United States has designated the MEK as a Foreign Terrorist Organization.

Iraq

Iraq planned and sponsored international terrorism in 2000. Although Baghdad focused on anti-dissident activity overseas, the regime continued to support terrorist groups. The regime has not attempted an anti-Western terrorist attack since its failed plot to assassinate former President Bush in 1993 in Kuwait.

Czech police continued to provide protection to the Prague office of the U.S. government–funded Radio Free Europe/Radio Liberty (RFE/RL), which produces Radio Free Iraq programs and employs expatriate journalists. The police presence was augmented in 1999, following reports that the Iraqi Intelligence Service (IIS) might retaliate against RFE/RL for broadcasts critical of the Iraqi regime.

To intimidate or silence Iraqi opponents of the regime living overseas, the IIS reportedly opened several new stations in foreign capitals during 2000. Various opposition groups joined in warning Iraqi dissidents abroad against newly established "expatriates' associations," which, they asserted, are IIS front organizations.

Opposition leaders in London contended that the IIS had dispatched female agents to infiltrate their ranks and was targeting dissidents for assassination. In Germany, an Iraqi opposition figure denounced the IIS for murdering his son, who had recently left Iraq to join him abroad. Dr. Ayad Allawi, secretary general of the Iraqi National Accord, an opposition group, stated that relatives of dissidents living abroad are often arrested and jailed to intimidate activists overseas.

In northern Iraq, Iraqi agents reportedly killed a locally well-known religious personality who declined to echo the regime line. The regional security director in As Sulaymaniyah stated that Iraqi operatives were responsible for the car-bomb explosion that injured a score of passersby. Officials of the Iraqi Communist Party asserted that an attack on a provincial party headquarters had been thwarted when party security officers shot and wounded a terrorist employed by the IIS.

Baghdad continued to denounce and delegitimize U.N. personnel working in Iraq, particularly U.N. de-mining teams, in the wake of the killing in 1999 of an expatriate U.N. de-mining worker in northern Iraq under circumstances suggesting regime involvement. An Iraqi who opened fire at the U.N. Food and Agriculture Organization (FAO) office in Baghdad, killing two persons and wounding six, was permitted to hold a heavily publicized press conference at which he contended that his action had been motivated by the harshness of U.N. sanctions, which the regime regularly excoriates.

The Iraqi regime rebuffed a request from Riyadh for the extradition of two Saudis who had hijacked a Saudi Arabian Airlines flight to Baghdad, but did return promptly the passengers and the aircraft. Disregarding its obligations under international law, the regime granted political asylum to the hijackers and gave them ample opportunity to ventilate in the Iraqi government-controlled and international media their criticisms of alleged abuses by the Saudi Arabian Government, echoing an Iraqi propaganda theme.

While the origins of the FAO attack and the hijacking were unclear, the Iraqi regime readily exploited these terrorist acts to further its policy objectives.

Several expatriate terrorist groups continued to maintain offices in Baghdad, including the Arab Liberation Front, the inactive 15 May Organization, the Palestine Liberation Front (PLF), and the Abu Nidal organization (ANO). PLF leader Abu Abbas appeared on state-controlled television in the fall to praise Iraq's leadership in rallying Arab opposition to Israeli violence against Palestinians. The ANO threatened to attack Austrian interests unless several million dollars in a frozen ANO account in a Vienna bank were turned over to the group.

The Iraq-supported Iranian terrorist group, Mujahedin-e Khalq (MEK), regularly claimed blame for armed incursions into Iran that targeted police and military outposts, as well as for mortar and bomb attacks on security organization headquarters in Iranian cities. MEK publicists reported that in March group members killed an Iranian colonel having intelligence responsibilities. An MEK claim to have wounded a general was denied by the Iranian Government. The Iraqi regime deployed MEK forces against its domestic opponents.

Libya

In 2000, Libya continued efforts to mend its international image in the wake of its surrender in 1999 of two Libyans accused of the bombing of Pan Am Flight 103 over Lockerbie, Scotland, in 1988. Trial proceedings for the two defendants began in the Netherlands in May.

The court issued its verdict on January 31. It found Abdel Basset al-Megrahi guilty of murder, concluding that he caused an explosive device to detonate on board the airplane, resulting in the murder of the flight's 259 passengers and crew as well as 11 residents of Lockerbie, Scotland. The judges found that he acted "in furtherance of the purposes of ... Libyan Intelligence Services."

The court concluded that the Crown failed to present sufficient evidence against the other defendant, Al-Amin Kalifa Fahima, to satisfy the high standard of "proof beyond reasonable doubt" that is necessary in criminal cases.

In 1999, Libya paid compensation for the death of a British policewoman, a move that preceded the reopening of the British Embassy. Libya also paid damages to the families of victims in the bombing of UTA flight 772. Six Libyans were convicted in absentia in that case, and the French judicial system is considering further indictments against other Libyan officials, including Libyan leader Moammar Gadhafi)

At year's end, Libya had yet to comply fully with the remaining U.N. Security Council requirements related to Pan Am 103: accepting responsibility, paying appropriate compensation, disclosing all it knows and renouncing terrorism. The United States remains dedicated to maintaining pressure on the Libyan regime until it does so. Gadhafi stated publicly that his government had adopted an anti-terrorism stance, but it remains unclear whether his claims of distancing Libya from its terrorist past signify a true change in policy.

Libya also remained the primary suspect in other terrorist operations, including the Labelle discotheque bombing in Berlin in 1986 that killed two U.S. servicemen and one Turkish civilian and wounded more than 200 people. Although Libya expelled the Abu Nidal organization and distanced itself from the Palestinian rejectionists in 1999, it continued to have contact with groups that use violence to oppose Middle East peace negotiations, including Palestine Islamic Jihad and Popular Front for the Liberation of Palestine-General Command.

North Korea

In 2000, the so-called Democratic People's Republic of Korea (DPRK) engaged in three rounds of terrorism talks that culminated in a joint DPRK-U.S. statement wherein the DPRK reiterated its opposition to terrorism and agreed to support international actions against such activity. North Korea, however, continued to provide haven to Japanese Communist League-Red Army Faction members who participated in the hijacking of a Japanese Airlines flight to North Korea in 1970.

Evidence suggests communist North Korea might have sold weapons directly or indirectly to terrorist groups during the year. Philippine officials publicly declared that Moro Islamic Liberation Front had purchased weapons from North Korea with funds provided by Middle East sources.

Sudan

Genocidal, slavery-ridden Sudan continued to be used as a haven by groups, including associates of Osama bin Laden's al Qaeda organization, Egyptian al-Gama'a al-Islamiyya, Egyptian Islamic Jihad, Palestine Islamic Jihad and Hamas. Most groups used Sudan primarily as a secure base for assisting compatriots elsewhere.

Khartoum also still had not complied fully with U.N. Security Council Resolutions 1044, 1054 and 1070, passed in 1996 — which demand that Sudan end all support to terrorists. They also require Khartoum to hand over three Egyptian Gama'a fugitives linked to the assassination attempt in 1995 against Egyptian President Hosni Mubarak in Ethiopia. Sudanese officials continued to deny that they had a role in the attack.

Syria

Syria continued to provide haven and support to terrorist groups, some of which maintained training camps or other facilities on Syrian territory. Ahmad Jibril's Popular Front for the Liberation of Palestine-General Command (PFLP-GC), Palestine Islamic Jihad (PIJ), Abu Musa's Fatah-the-Intifada, and George Habash's Popular Front for the Liberation of Palestine (PFLP) maintained their headquarters in Damascus.

The Syrian regime allowed Hamas to open a main office in Damascus in March. In addition, Syria granted terrorist groups — including Hamas, the PFLP-GC, and the PIJ — basing privileges or refuge in areas of Lebanon's Bekaa Valley under Syrian control. Damascus generally upheld its agreement with Ankara not to support the Kurdish PKK, however.

Although Syria claimed to be committed to peace talks, it did not act to stop Hezbollah and Palestinian rejectionist groups from carrying out anti-Israeli attacks. Damascus also served as the primary transit point for terrorist operatives traveling to Lebanon and for the resupply of weapons to

Hezbollah. Damascus appeared to maintain its long-standing ban on attacks launched from Syrian territory or against Western targets.

Chinese Experts: Attacks Prove America Superpower Status Hollow

Al Santoli, China Reform Monitor
Thursday, September 26, 2001

Following the September 11, 2001, terrorist attack in the United States, the authors of the seminal 1999 Chinese People's Liberation Army text on 21st century "asymmetrical" warfare, titled *Unrestricted Warfare,* were interviewed in the September 13, 2001, People's Republic of China–owned *Ta Kung Pao* newspaper in Hong Kong.

The following are excerpts from the interview with the military theorists Senior Colonels Qiao Liang and Wang Xiangsui:

Hong Kong *Ta Kung Pao*: Qiao Liang and Wang Xiangsui foretold such a scenario of terrorists using high technological means to carry out attacks beyond the military scope in the 21st century to achieve military goals in their book *Unrestricted Warfare,* published in 1999. The large-scale terrorist attacks in Washington, D.C., and New York unfortunately were just like what they predicted.

Those carrying out the attacks were terrorists but not career military personnel, what they used were civilian airplanes but not military weapons, and what they attacked were international trade buildings but not military targets; however, the casualties and shock caused by the attacks were even more serious than those caused by a war. This is "unrestricted warfare" — it goes beyond the scope of military warfare but it achieves the objectives of fighting a war.

Colonels Qiao and Wang: The series of attacks taking place in the United States were very dreary and terrifying, but they must not be viewed from a single perspective. While the thousands of innocent people killed or injured in the attacks were victims of terrorism, they also were victims of U.S. foreign policy. September 11, 2001, very likely is the beginning of the decline of the United States as a superpower.

Ta Kung Pao: Qiao Liang and Wang Xiangsui show that it is impossible for weak countries to follow rules of strong countries in carrying out [military] actions. Although employing such [terrorist] means by them is completely not in line with basic morality of mankind, they do not think of whether it is honorable and just expect to achieve their strategic goals using various tactical means. Although the terrorists destroyed only two or three targets in their attacks, the effect was strategic. Such attacks will be one of the major forms of warfare in the 21st century.

Qiao and Wang: The attacks demonstrated the United States' fragility and weakness and showed that essentially it is unable to stand attacks. The National Missile Defense [NMD] system cannot save it.

The United States, a giant tiger, has been dealing with mice; unexpectedly, this time it was bitten by mice — it has been wielding a large hammer but has been unable to find the flea. From a short-term perspective, the attacks in the United States will very likely have some effect on China's economy — they might affect China's economic growth. However, from a long-term viewpoint, they could be favorable to China.

COPYRIGHT (C) 2001, AMERICAN FOREIGN POLICY COUNCIL

'Red Mafia' Operating in the U.S. — Helping Terrorists

Colonel Stanislav Lunev
Monday, October 1, 2001

I would like to reveal to you some "secrets" about the Russian Mafia.

Some background first. There are thousands of Mafia-type organized crime syndicates in Russia, including about 200 operating in Moscow alone, and more than 300 functioning internationally, according to Russian police estimates.

Total membership of these gangs, known to intelligence sources as the "Red Mafia," approximates almost 1 million "soldiers" — or the equivalent of all the Russian army's ground forces.

The Red Mafia is the continuation of Russia's Communist old guard. This is why the Russian Mafia is totally controlled and populated by "ex"-KGB and "ex"-GRU agents.

In reality, these men still work for Russian intelligence agencies and are still communist and still intent on destroying America — but today they have a new front and one that appears less menacing to the West.

The Red Mafia is up to all the same tricks the KGB engaged in, but now Western leaders dismiss the problems as simply a "Mafia" one rather than blaming the Russian government.

The Russians are providing nuclear technology to rogue countries like Iran — and the Americans and media here buy the excuse that "the Mafia" is doing it. As Russian leaders say, "We have no control over it."

This is the same organization that staged a series of apartment bombings in Russia, using — guess who — groups linked to Osama bin Laden.

Today, U.S. intelligence experts believe that almost two-thirds of all commercial institutions in Russia, some 400 banks (those in Moscow alone control more than 80 percent of the country's finances), dozens of stock exchanges and hundreds of large government enterprises are controlled by the Mob. About 40 percent of the GDP in Russia is in the hands of organized crime, working in concert with corrupt officials and businessmen.

These are striking figures, especially when compared to a range of 5 percent to 7 percent in the industrialized countries and up to 30 percent for some African and Latin American nations.

Of course this is Russia's domestic problem, but unfortunately now it is not only Russia's, because about 30 of the most powerful and dangerous

Russian gangs are already operating in almost all American states.

Using practically unlimited resources from Russia, these criminal syndicates are working independently and in close cooperation with local gangsters to establish control over America's profitable small and medium-size businesses.

In addition, Russian mobsters are penetrating the most sensitive areas of large U.S. companies and corporations, stealing their secrets to sell and using stolen data for their own illegal activities.

They are also very busy destroying local life by taking a very active part in contract murder, extortion and racketeering, money laundering, fraud, prostitution and other criminal "business."

Russian mobsters also pay very close attention to drug trafficking, considering this area as most promising and profitable.

In this activity Russian mobsters are using their international connections and expertise in cooperation with the most dangerous drug cartels of Latin American countries.

The seizure last May of 20 tons of cocaine from two "fishing boats" off the West Coast, manned by Russian and Ukrainian crewmen, has raised concerns in the U.S. intelligence community that Mexican drug cartels are doing business with the Red Mafia.

American experts believe that drug cartels in Mexico, considered to be among the world's most ruthless, have followed the lead of Colombian cocaine smugglers in forging alliances with the Russian mobsters and other Eastern European crime syndicates.

Led by the Arellano-Felix cartel in Tijuana, those alliances have been firmly established and involved in the shipment of both cocaine and heroin.

It is known that Colombian drug cartels established connections with the Russian Mafia as early as 1992. Russian mobsters, who operated from New York, Florida and Puerto Rico, moved quickly to help the Colombians import drugs into Europe through Italy.

Employing many former KGB agents, Russian criminal syndicates controlled almost all banks in Moscow and St. Petersburg and established others in Panama and the Caribbean to launder billions of dollars in illicit drug profits for themselves as well as for the Colombians.

As NewsMax.com reported, the partnership gave the Colombians a new market for their cocaine and heroin, nearly all of which previously had been destined for the U.S. It also provided the Colombians with an access to sophisticated weapons, intelligence-gathering equipment and other military hardware, including dozens of airplanes and helicopters, and special super-speedboats now being used to ferry drugs out of the country.

Chillingly, they almost got a Russian submarine for drug smuggling but the FBI destroyed the deal.

Russian criminals are also very busy in cyberspace, considering this area a most profitable one for their future profits and development. The Red

Mafia is working very carefully in cyberspace, and the real scope of this criminal activity is still little known by the American people.

Until now we have known only about some cases involving Russian criminals and small-crime groups, which were disclosed by the U.S. law enforcement agencies.

However, Russian hackers are blamed for a series of spectacular feats in recent years, particularly for stealing secret Microsoft source codes, ransacking the Pentagon's computers, hacking into NATO's military websites, posting thousands of credit card numbers on the Internet, and stealing millions of dollars from Western banks.

According to press reports, Russian hackers first captured the world's imagination in 1994 when a young mathematician, Vladimir Levin, hacked into the computers of Citibank and transferred $12 million to the bank accounts of his friends around the world.

He conducted the entire operation from his little one-room apartment in St. Petersburg.

Levin was arrested, but his case inspired other hackers — for example, Ilya Hoffman, a talented viola student at the Moscow Conservatory, who was detained in 1998 on charges of stealing $97,000 over the Internet. Another group of Russians stole more than $630,000 by hacking into Internet retailers and grabbing credit card numbers.

Some of the world's biggest Internet companies, including CompuServe and AOL, were forced to abandon Russia in 1997 because of the widespread use of stolen passwords.

Currently, Russian hackers are very busy in coordinated attacks on commercial and military computers in the U.S. and other members of NATO. When NATO launched its bombing campaign in Yugoslavia in 1999, Russian hackers retaliated with their own wave of attacks on NATO member countries, breaking into their websites, posting anti-war slogans and overloading them with floods of junk e-mails.

In October 2000, a sustained break-in of Microsoft's highest-security network was traced back to a computer address in St. Petersburg. In January of the same year, an unidentified Russian hacker calling himself MAXUS stole more than 300,000 credit card numbers from CD Universe in an extortion bid, but was never caught.

This list could go on and on; there is no surprise over the quality of Russian hackers, who are extremely well educated and talented. In fact, in Moscow there is a special training center for hackers named the Civil Hackers' School, which exists with the support of Russia's intelligence services and criminal syndicates.

Officially, the school is preparing specialists for legitimate jobs in computer security by shaping the new generation of computer whiz kids. But in reality it is providing high-level training for young Russian hackers, who have provoked fear and anxiety in the West.

Since 1996 this Civil Hackers' School, operating from a shabby little Moscow apartment, has trained several hundred highly trained hackers, who find jobs in the Russian intelligence community as well as in organized crime groups.

In the high-stakes game pitting fleet-fingered Russian hackers against the giants of American e-commerce and law enforcement, the Russians have been winning almost every time. All of these crimes, however, pale in comparison with the sheer size and scope of a hacking and extortion web that was so large that the FBI took the unusual step of warning the public about it in a March 2001 press release.

In this document, the FBI cited the ongoing danger from several organized hacker groups from Eastern Europe, specifically Russia and Ukraine, who were responsible for stealing more than 1 million credit card numbers and attacking the networks of over 40 businesses in 20 states of the U.S.

Nobody apparently knows, or perhaps even cares, how deeply the Red Mafia has already penetrated the American establishment. But the danger of this activity is already real in many American states and needs very close attention from U.S. law enforcement agencies, which until now have not been able to cope with this problem.

Russian Expert Who 'Predicted' Attacks Warns of New Ones

Dr. Alexandr Nemets
Thursday, October 4, 2001

The same Russian government expert who predicted last July that America was about to suffer a "financial attack" — and encouraged Russian citizens to cash out dollars and buy rubles and gold — has again surfaced to make more stunning forecasts.

Dr. Tatyana Koryagina gained some credibility in the Russian media because of her prediction of an unusual catastrophe that was about to hit the U.S.

She said it would take place on August 19 and would collapse the U.S. economy.

Koryagina is a senior research fellow in the Institute of Macroeconomic Researches subordinated to the Russian Ministry of Economic Development (Minekonom). She is reportedly close to President Putin's inner circle.

On July 12, 2001, *Pravda* published a Page One story on her predictions entitled "Will the Dollar and America Fall on August 19? That's the Opinion of Dr. Tatyana Koryagina, Who Very Accurately Predicted the August Default in 1998."

In her July interview, Koryagiuna told *Pravda*: "The U.S. has been chosen as the object of financial attack because the financial center of the planet is located there. The effect will be maximal. The strike waves of economic crisis will spread over the planet instantly, and will remind us of the blast of a huge nuclear bomb."

Late last month, *Pravda* re-interviewed Dr. Koryagina to get her take on the events of September 11.

Koryagina made the following key points in an article titled "Who Will Strike America in Its Back?"

New Strikes Will Come. In the near term, she said, "the powerful group" that masterminded the events of September 11 will make new strikes against America — of a financial nature and otherwise. She said they will "strike America in the back" and bring it down.

She noted that Americans are consolidating around their government and preparing retaliatory strikes against the "terrorists." However, Americans are nervous about spending. When they understand, after the upcoming new strikes, that their government can guarantee them nothing, they will panic — causing a collapse of their financial system.

Didn't Make Serious Mistake. About her forecast of July 12, Dr. Koryagina said, "I did not make a serious mistake. Indeed, between August 15 and 20, the dollar started trembling under the pressure of multiple bad news about the U.S. and the world economy. And within weeks, the Manhattan skyscrapers fell down. As a result, a significant part of the world financial network was paralyzed. This strike was aimed at destabilization and destruction of America and [in domino fashion] all the countries making countless billions of dollars."

The Powerful Group. Who is behind these strikes? Koryagina claims the U.S. is painting a false picture. She said the operation was not the work of 19 terrorists but a larger group seeking to reshape the world. She claimed a group of extremely powerful private persons, with total assets of about $300 trillion, intends to legalize its power and to become the new world government. The September 11 strikes showed that this group is afraid of nothing — human lives have zero value for them.

Koryagina again encouraged Russian citizens to cash out dollars. The Koryagina claims are not easily dismissed, especially her clear indications in the interview before September 11 that the attacks on America's financial system would be of an unusual nature. Her comments also mirrored similar warnings issued by Russian officials.

Still, this story raises other questions. Did the Russian government know in advance and what was its involvement?

On September 28 *The Washington Times* reported that "U.S. intelligence agencies have uncovered information that Russian criminal groups have been supplying Osama bin Laden and his al Qaeda terrorist network with components for chemical, biological and nuclear weapons."

Of course, the Russian Mafia has very close ties with Russia's intelligence agencies.

It is important to note that Russia is a significant backer of almost every state sponsor of terrorism, some with links to bin Laden's group. These include Iraq, Iran, Syria, Libya, North Korea and Cuba.

The Next Strike Could Come From China

Dr. Alexandr Nemets and Dr. Thomas Torda
Friday, November 9, 2001

The authors have learned that in September-October 2001, almost all federal money that had been assigned for studies of China's growing military potential and People's Liberation Army (PLA) modernization — as well as research on Sino-Russian military and defense-technological cooperation — was switched to financing the Afghan campaign.

This is probably the worst loss America suffered in the aftermath of the September 11 strikes, and even the terrorists could not have dreamed of such a success: The nation is blind and totally unprepared for a new, much more terrible strike.

The new official foreign policy concept — "now America has no enemies except for terrorists" — is dead wrong. In particular, the PLA in September-November continued its rapid march toward modernization. The U.S. is still considered in Beijing to be the "major future enemy."

And who is the major supplier of advanced military technology to the PLA? Russia, of course.

On September 12, Beijing newspapers published short reports on the terrorist strikes in New York and Washington. Most of these papers, such as *Jingji Ribao,* or Economic Daily, published on the same page — alongside the reports from America — much more detailed descriptions of new agreements concluded during the visit of Chinese Premier Zhu Rongji to Russia on September 7-11.

Some items of these agreements deserve special attention:

- By 2005, China and Russia will put into service the 2,500-km oil pipeline connecting the Eastern Siberian city of Angarsk, the easternmost terminal of Russia's oil pipeline network, with China's northeastern city of Daqing, Heilongjiang Province, the northernmost terminal of China's oil pipeline network. As a result, tens of millions of tons of Russian oil from the huge Western Siberian deposits will flow into China.
- Simultaneously, construction work on a high-capacity natural gas pipeline connecting China and Russia (with a route approximately the same as that of the oil pipeline) will intensify.
- Sino-Russian trade volume will rise significantly during 2001-2002. In particular, in 2001 it could rise about 30 percent from its 2000 level and surpass $10 billion, while Chinese imports from Russia would increase about 40 percent, to more than $7.5 billion.
- China is purchasing five TU-204-120 large passenger aircraft from Russia and will ramp up technological cooperation with Russia in

this area.
- China will increase the percentage of high-level machinery and high-tech products in its imports from Russia.
- China and Russia will expand cooperation in nuclear energy technology.
- China and Russia will greatly expand cooperation in the space area, including satellite development, satellite application technology, space science and technology (S&T), and development of basic modules for satellites and space launch vehicles (SLVs).
- China and Russia will step up cooperation in the aviation industry; Russia will provide China with next-generation aircraft technology.
- China and Russia are considering the ABM Treaty concluded by the U.S. and USSR in 1972 as one of the basic pillars of international stability; both countries are against the deployment of a U.S. National Missile Defense (NMD) system.
- Both countries will expand multilateral cooperation within the framework of the Shanghai Cooperative Organization (SCO), including China, Russia and four Central Asian republics.

In reality, this means the following:
- The Sino-Russian Alliance, formalized and codified in the 30-year "Chinese-Russian Good Neighborly Treaty of Friendship and Cooperation," signed during the visit of Chinese President Jiang Zemin to Moscow in July 2001, has been further buttressed by the pipelines connecting China and Russia.

    The laying of such pipelines will provide a solid foundation for large-scale bilateral cooperation for decades to come. Also, by late September China received permission to explore and develop oil and gas over most of Eastern Siberia and the huge Yakut Republic of the Russian Far East. This further solidified the cooperation and alliance between the two nations.
- Chinese imports of arms and related technology from Russia in 2001 will rise 50 percent to 60 percent from their 2000 level and will expand at about the same rate in 2002.
- In 2001–2002 China, aided by Russia, will dramatically boost development and production of advanced satellites, SLVs and related technology — for civilian and especially for military needs.
- The same holds true for the most advanced fighters, AWACS aircraft, military transports, and other modern technology for the PLA air force. PLA ground forces and the navy will also get their share of the new weaponry from Russia.

The publishing of the two aforementioned reports side by side on the same page is symbolic: Under the new world situation, China will increase economic and military-strategic cooperation with Russia, and the arms component could be the weightiest one in this relationship.

Some questions should be answered here.

1. Won't China have trouble financing these huge arms import deals?

By late September, foreign currency reserves in China's Ministry of Finance reached $195 billion; in addition, foreign currency deposits in state-owned banks approached $140 billion. And China's foreign debt obligations are comparatively low.

Moreover, the consequences of the September 11 strikes have brought China a real windfall: Chinese economists, including those of the People's Bank of China, expect that many billions of dollars — "scared money" from U.S. financial markets — will rush into China now.

Eventually, annual foreign investment in China could expand, under the direct impact of the September 11 events, from the present $50 billion to $100 billion. Therefore, China will have no financial problems with arms imports.

At the same time, Russia will suffer serious financial difficulties: The recent world oil price drop will cause — as early as 2002 — the loss of about $20 billion for Russia ($2 billion for every $1 per barrel of oil price drop); added losses related to falling prices for natural gas, chemicals and metals are comparable. Altogether, these losses could amount to over 10 percent of Russia's GDP.

That is why Russia is ready to deliver any amount of the most advanced weaponry and related technology to literally any nation, let alone such an experienced ally and close friend as China.

2. Why is China continuing its program of intensive military modernization in a period when all countries should be uniting to counter the terrorist threat?

In the opinion of the authors, supported by the conclusions of some Washington-based experts, China's leaders will deal with the great temptation to "solve the Taiwan problem" when major elements of the best U.S. troops and weapons are engaged in the Middle East and Asia — this despite the formal condolences sent by President Jiang to President Bush after the September 11 strikes and warm negotiations between the two leaders in Shanghai on October 19-21.

Moreover, according to the most recent data, China's leaders — just like those in the Kremlin — are very irritated by the U.S. military presence in Pakistan, Afghanistan and Uzbekistan. Deployment of several PLA divisions in October 2001 in Xinjiang, near the borders of Afghanistan and the Central Asian republic of Tajikistan, could become a prelude to military escalation in this area also.

3. Perhaps Russian President Vladimir Putin, widely hailed now as an American ally, will hesitate to supply China with powerful munitions that could be used against America?

It would be very naïve even to consider such a possibility. It is known for certain that during the two weeks between September 11 and September 25, Putin telephoned Jiang several times to discuss in detail all aspects of the present situation, and evidently got Jiang's blessing for a temporary alliance with Washington.

Jiang and Putin additionally promoted their cooperation in all areas during the recent APEC summit in Shanghai.

PLA Modernization

Let's look at the most important directions of current PLA modernization, based mainly on Russian assistance.

Development continued at a very high rate in September-October 2001 in the following areas:

1. Developing space warfare, which includes:
   a. Developing manned spacecraft and special heavy SLVs for their launch. The manned spacecraft will fulfill several important military functions.
   b. Developing and launching large- and mid-sized satellites for both civilian and military ends (reconnaissance, guidance and positioning, command and control for ground-based troops, military telecom).
   c. Developing, mass-producing and launching mini-satellites and even micro-satellites. These will form specialized low-earth-orbit satellite constellations or even networks, supporting military activities such as reconnaissance, missile guidance, command and control, and tracking and destroying of enemy satellites (specialized "Parasitic Star" satellites and "nano-scale" satellites are under development for this purpose).
   d. Constructing and upgrading ground-based stations for satellite command and control.

Russian assistance plays a decisive role in realizing almost all the above-listed items. A critical element here is a PLA program for establishing a Space Force — along the lines of the newly established Russian Space Troops.

2. Upgrading the air-defense network.

Just after the September 11 strikes, the PLA received an order to shoot down all aircraft approaching important facilities without permission. This means that mass production and deployment of advanced air-defense weapon systems in the PLA would additionally accelerate. This trend in PLA modernization has two objectives:
   a. Providing reliable air defense for critical military and infrastructure facilities all over China.
   b. Building from Beijing to Guangzhou a multi-level air defense network to protect the mainland coast from Taiwan and U.S. air strikes during any conflict around the Taiwan Strait.

New air-defense systems in this network include the following:
   • improved domestic 25-mm and 35-mm anti-aircraft artillery models;

- domestic QW-1,QW-2, HN-5, and FM-6 portable anti-aircraft missiles;
- domestic low-altitude FM-series air defense missiles (ADMs) and Type-95 combination missile-gun air defense systems (copied from Russia's Tunguska missile-gun system);
- mid-altitude ADM systems, including the Chinese-made HQ-7, Russian-made Tor-M1, and the latter's Chinese clone, the HQ-17;
- high-altitude ADM systems, namely, China's FT-2000, Russia's S-300 PMU1, and the latter's Chinese variant, the HQ-15. Units of the best Russian high-altitude ADM system, the 400-km-range Triumf S-400, were also delivered to PLA by September 2001.

Almost all these systems are largely or entirely based on Russian technology.

In the very near future, China's air-defense network will be enhanced by deployment of several Russian-made A-50 AWACS aircraft and launch of reconnaissance satellite constellations.

3. Copying Russia's "sixth-generation warfare" concept and technologies.

In practice this means the active and comprehensive use of Russian army expertise and technology necessary for fielding$wing:

- Constructing modern information warfare systems (advanced computer networks for troop command and control, as well as sophisticated tools for destruction of enemy networks).
- Broadly introducing precision-guided munitions (long-range guided missiles).
- Establishing a five-dimensional battlefield (with ground, naval, air, space and electromagnetic components or dimensions).
- Developing sophisticated "asymmetric warfare" techniques, extremely suitable for terrorist strikes against developed nations.

There is evidence that the PLA and Russian army are helping each other in implementing this sixth-generation warfare concept.

Realization of these three directions — definitely overlapping in some ways — will become a real force multiplier for the PLA. Already the PLA — and especially its "striking fist" concentrated near the Taiwan Strait and South China Sea — is much stronger than it was only two years ago. This "striking fist" will be further enhanced and upgraded in 2002.

In addition to the aforementioned three major directions, China and Russia in September-October 2001 accelerated the implementation of earlier concluded military-technological pacts: the delivery from Russia and production in China, with Russian technology, of advanced fighters and airborne missiles, new destroyers, diesel-electric and nuclear submarines, "super-advanced" missile craft, and state-of-the-art ordnance for the PLA ground troops. This should be considered as the most serious consequence of the Sino-Russian alliance.

China Buying Twin Towers Scrap Steel, Denies Souvenir Report

Inside Cover
Thursday, January 24, 2002

One of China's largest steelmakers, Bao Steel of Shanghai, has acknowledged the purchase of 50,000 tons of scrap metal salvaged from the World Trade Center disaster site in New York.

An initial report in Beijing's *Youth Daily* claimed that Bao Steel planned to turn the WTC steel into souvenirs, "taking into consideration the unique historical value and commemorative significance" of the wreckage. The souvenirs could be molded into the form of miniature Twin Towers, the paper said.

But a spokeswoman for Bao Steel denied the souvenir report, telling Agence France-Presse, "We have bought the scrap steel, but just for recycling and reprocessing because the quality is good. It was made in Japan. It's absolutely impossible to make souvenirs because that will affect the relations" between the U.S. and China.

A ship carrying the Twin Tower scrap metal is expected to arrive in China on Friday. Bao Steel paid $120 per ton for the WTC scrap metal.

It is the only Chinese company to have purchased steel salvaged from Ground Zero, AFP said.

China a Terrorist Threat to U.S., Dissident Wu Warns

Wes Vernon, NewsMax.com
Saturday, January 26, 2002

WASHINGTON — China is stabbing the United States and the free world in the back in the war on terrorism.

Harry Wu, the dissident who fought Chinese communist brutality on its home turf, told NewsMax.com in an exclusive interview that "China is a state terrorist country."

President Bush, before he visits China on February 21, would be well served if he is fully informed of freedom fighter Wu's dire warnings, and of the startling revelations in a new book that backs those warnings to the hilt.

The blockbuster Internet best-seller *Seeds of Fire: China and the Story Behind the Attack on America*, written by award-winning former foreign correspondent Gordon Thomas, is making a big splash in international circles.

Dr. Wu's charges against China, based on his foundation's studies and his own experiences, are further verified by Thomas' revelation that when those murderous terrorists slammed into the World Trade Center and the Pentagon, killing thousands on American soil, they were cheered on and supported by communist China.

Let no one think that China is somehow a real part of the "anti-terrorist coalition," especially when one considers the book's revelations of China's relationship with Osama bin Laden.

Ironically, China's largest publishing conglomerate — the Communist Party–controlled Xinhua Publishing Corp. — has bought the Chinese publishing rights to *Seeds of Fire*. This same publisher created a furor when it issued books, films and videos glorifying the strikes of September 11 as "a humbling blow against an arrogant nation."

China means to destroy the West, according to leading dissident Wu, the soft-spoken but determined anti-communist who spent years in Chinese prisons. While many of us may have been able to oppose communism from the relative safety of the greatest and most prosperous nation on earth, Wu fought it right up front, behind enemy lines so to speak, and spent years of torture and hard labor for his trouble.

Nuclear Attack 'Before 2015'

His warning that China means to do great harm to the West cannot be doubted by anyone who reads the never-before-published documents in *Seeds of Fire,* including briefing papers from the CIA that show how China may launch an all-out nuclear attack against America "before 2015."

One can only speculate whether Chinese willingness to openly publish its own evil deeds is a sign of confidence that it no longer needs to fear retaliation. It's as if they were saying: "This is what we're up to. What are you going to do about it? You're economically hooked to us."

That economic interdependence is the number one factor that bothers Wu, whose Washington-based Laogai Research Foundation has been working for 10 years to expose systemic human rights abuses in China's vast, secretive network of forced labor camps.

Wu argues that anyone who kids himself by accepting the huge communist nation as part of a Western-organized crusade to combat terrorism is dealing with a contradiction in terms.

Relatives Hostage in China

Right now about 100,000 Chinese living in the U.S. cannot speak openly about terrorist persecution behind the Bamboo Curtain for fear of what will happen to their families in China.

"Their families become hostages. This is terrorism," Wu told NewsMax.com. "This is state terrorism." Further, it is but one example of the terrorism the rogue state inflicts on victims inside and outside its borders.

The Thomas book delves into Chinese intelligence operations in the United States. In the earliest years of the Cold War, congressional committees would haul spies and homegrown Soviet sympathizers before their hearings to demand information on communist intelligence networks in the U.S. Today, revelations of Chinese communist spying in the U.S. get short shrift in the media and bungled official investigations.

Wu, twice imprisoned by the Chinese — the second time after he had actually become an American citizen — sees the international industrial commerce dealings with the his former homeland as fulfilling an old Lenin prophecy.

The Bolsheviks had said that when it comes time to hang the capitalists, they will be bidding against each other to decide who will supply the rope.

U.S. Says China, Russia, Cuba, Syria, Libya Abet Terrorism

Wes Vernon, NewsMax.com
Tuesday, May 7, 2002

WASHINGTON — China and Russia "are unquestionably the two largest sources of" weapons of mass destruction that end up in the hands of rogue nations dedicated to the destruction of the U.S.

That comment from Under Secretary of State John R. Bolton came in a Q&A session after a speech Monday in which he added Cuba, Libya and Syria to the list of rogue terrorist nations, second only to the "axis of evil" first described by President Bush in January when he bestowed that dubious honor on Iraq, Iran and North Korea.

"I only had a half an hour to give the speech," said Bolton when asked why he didn't come down equally hard on the two larger powers.

"I'd just like to hear from a single Russian who can say how a nuclear-equipped ballistic missile–capable Iran is in Russia's national interest," the under secretary told a group at the Heritage Foundation.

"Of course, there isn't any answer. And that's why we hope we can persuade the government of Russia to cease and desist."

His boss, Secretary of State Colin Powell, has referred to China and Russia as U.S. allies and has praised Cuban dictator Fidel Castro.

Though stopping short of including Russia and China in the "axis of evil" of rogue states, Bolton did say the U.S. expected them to abide by non-proliferation agreements.

It is not clear exactly when U.S. patience with these powerful nations will run out. But in his speech, the high State Department official said that those who do not become part of the U.S. effort against terror "can expect to become the target of it."

Bolton did say the U.S. was working with the Chinese and the Russians on arms agreements and other cooperative efforts.

As forecast by NewsMax.com, Bolton came down hard on Cuba as a nation that provides "safe haven for terrorists" from around the world.

Sorry, Clinton: Castro Is Not Our Friend

In so doing, he flatly rejected a Clinton administration report in 1998 that concluded Cuba did not represent a significant military threat to the U.S. He credited Cuba's "aggressive intelligence operations against these United States" for keeping this nation largely in the dark about threats from the communist island 90 miles from the U.S. Last year's arrest of a Cuban agent working for the Defense Intelligence Agency was cited as an example.

"The United States," Bolton went on, "believes that Cuba has at least a limited offensive biological research and development effort."

Biological and chemical warfare, along with harboring terrorists, pose a potential threat to the lives of millions of Americans. Castro has thumbed his nose at diplomatic initiatives for more than 40 years.

Castro "collaborates with other state sponsors of terror," Bolton said. Cuba has developed a sophisticated biomedical industry, and "analysts and Cuban defectors have long cast suspicion on the activities conducted in these biomedical facilities."

Last year Castro visited Syria and Libya, as well as Iran. The United States has called on Cuba to cease all bioweapons-applicable cooperation with rogue nations and to comply with all its international treaty obligations, Bolton said.

In answer to a question from NewsMax.com, Bolton declined to say when all diplomacy with Havana is likely to be exhausted. Any thought of military action, he reminded us, is a matter for the Defense Department.

Significantly, however, the under secretary of state for arms control and international security did say the U.S. would pursue diplomatic measures, international condemnation and uncover terrorist activities, "or otherwise bring a halt to their activities."

The U.S., Bolton said, was determined "to prevent the next wave of terror," and "will take whatever steps are necessary to protect and defend our interests and eliminate the terrorist threat."

Threat From Libya and Syria

Libya and Syria are pursuing development or have the capacity to develop weapons of mass destruction, sometimes in violation of international treaties to which they are signatories, he said.

"Beyond the 'axis of evil,' there are other rogue states intent on acquiring weapons of mass destruction, particularly biological weapons," Bolton said. "Given our vulnerability to an attack from biological agents ... it is important to carefully assess and respond to potential proliferators.

"As the president has said, 'America will do what is necessary to ensure our national security.'"

Bolton called the potential spread of weapons of mass destruction "the gravest security threat" the United States and its allies face.

"The attacks of September 11 reinforced with blinding clarity the need to be steadfast in the face of emerging threats to our security," he said. "The international security environment has changed, and our greatest threat comes not from the specter of nuclear war between two superpowers ... but from transnational terrorist cells that will strike without warning using weapons of mass destruction."

The United States suspects Libya has a "long-standing pursuit" of nuclear weapons, and since the lifting of U.N. sanctions in 1999, the regime of Moammar Gadhafi has been able to increase its access to dual-use technologies, Bolton said. It has been able to re-establish contacts with "illicit foreign sources of expertise, parts and precursor chemicals" for chemical weapons.

Libya, not a signatory to the chemical weapons convention, had produced at least 100 tons of chemical weapons at a facility that later closed but then reopened in 1995 as a "pharmaceutical plant." It is possible the plant could still be used to produce chemical weapons, Bolton said.

"Significantly for predictive purposes, Libya became a state party to the BWC [Biological Weapons Convention] in January 1982, but the U.S. believes that Libya has continued its biological warfare program," he said.

Just last week, Gadhafi, long a pariah, made overtures to the U.S.

Syria, meanwhile, is believed to have a long-standing chemical warfare program. It has stockpiled sarin gas and is engaged in the research to develop VX, a more toxic nerve agent than sarin, Bolton said.

Syria's missiles, the official noted, are within striking distance of Israel, Jordan and Turkey.

China Still Building Ties
With 'Axis of Evil'

Inside Cover
Tuesday, May 28, 2002

While the U.S. sees a significant warming of relations between itself and Russia in the wake of 9/11, this has not been the case with China.

China has given lip service in support of America's war on terrorism, at the very same time it has stepped up its relations with rogue terrorist states, including ones identified by President Bush as the "axis of evil."

The London *Economist* has recently expressed concern that China's "worrying friendships" with rogue nations such as North Korea, Iran, Libya and Iraq are a "flaw" that could undermine the alliance against international terrorism.

In Tehran, Jiang Zemin used a television interview to explain China's view of the Israeli-Palestinian conflict — one critical of "Israeli killings."

On April 24, during a stopover in Malaysia, Chinese leader Hu Jintao made a sideswipe at America, indicating that in Asia, China would oppose the "bullying superpower."

Since September 11, Jiang Zemin and Hu Jintao have played the "good guy/bad guy game" in diplomacy with the "axis of evil" in order to outmaneuver the U.S., reports the Hong Kong Chinese-language *Cheng Ming*.

The "11 September" incident disrupted communist China's overall diplomatic strategy. In response, overseas trips taken by Jiang and Hu this year signify a revision in its diplomatic emphasis — adopting a strategy of "joining hands with the axis of evil in defiance of the anti-terrorist center" — to counter U.S. dominance in global affairs.

China Continues to Arm al Qaeda

Inside Cover
Friday, June 21, 2002

Despite their own concerns about Islamic terrorism, Communist Chinese military officials have continued to arm Osama bin Laden's al Qaeda commandos with sophisticated surface-to-air missiles even after the 9/11 attacks on New York and Washington, D.C., according to U.S. intelligence reports.

"Late last month, U.S. Army Special Forces troops discovered 30 HN-5s, the designation for Chinese-made SA-7s surface-to-air missiles, in southeastern Afghanistan," reports *The Washington Times* in Friday editions. "Other intelligence reports indicated the Chinese shipped missiles to the Taliban after September 11."

Just last week a captured al Qaeda operative told interrogators that he had fired a surface-to-air missile at a U.S. military plane from a position just outside Prince Sultan Air Base in Saudi Arabia. The missile was a Chinese made SA-7, according to Pentagon sources.

Before September 11, the People's Liberation Army provided training for Afghanistan's Taliban militia and its al Qaeda supporters, the *Times* added.

"It was carried out in cooperation with Pakistan's ISI intelligence service," defense officials told the paper.

Though Beijing has denied supporting al Qaeda forces, reports indicate that Chinese dictator Jiang Zemin was so impressed with bin Laden's 9/11 attack that he sanctioned a domestic propaganda effort suggesting the U.S. got what it deserved.

"In the immediate aftermath of the attacks, workers at Beijing Television worked round-the-clock to produce a documentary they called *Attack America*," reported the London *Telegraph* in November.

In the video, Chinese film editors mixed real news footage of the two commercial jetliners slamming into the World Trade Center with scenes from a 1998 remake of *Godzilla* where the monster wreaks havoc on New York.

As carnage fills the screen, the film's narrator proclaims that the city had reaped the consequences of decades of America bullying weaker nations.

The anti-U.S. entertainment bears the imprimatur of the Communist Party–controlled media, the *Telegraph* said, with the most popular offerings produced by the Xinhua information agency, Beijing Television and China Central Television.

"Communist Party officials say President Jiang Zemin has obsessively watched and re-watched pictures of the aircraft crashing into the World Trade Center," the *Telegraph* said.

The Real Axis of Evil

John LeBoutillier
NewsMax.com magazine, July 2002

President Bush made headlines earlier this year with his "axis of evil" phrase in his State of the Union Address. It was probably inspired by former President Reagan's "Evil Empire" speech almost 20 years ago.

In both cases the squishy, softheaded diplomats whined about the "inappropriateness" of such a phrase, and the countries involved — Iran, Iraq and North Korea — squawked about their innocence.

Recently, Under Secretary of State John Bolton added more rogue states to the list: Cuba, Libya and Syria.

The real story here is that all six of these rogue states should be known as only the "Sub-Axis of Evil."

The really evil nations are — and have been for half a century — Russia and Red China. Period!

G.W. Bush can sit with Russia's president, career KGB man Vladimir Putin, and proclaim him a man "with a good soul." But KGB men are selected primarily because they do not have souls!

Putin's Russia is more dangerous than at any time since the fall of the Berlin Wall in November 1989. Russia is re-arming its own military and also manufacturing "weapons of mass destruction" for its allies — including Iran, Iraq and North Korea — to earn hard currency.

It is a plain fact that Moscow is helping Tehran build a nuclear facility from which the Iranians will eventually be able to extract the materials necessary to build a nuclear weapon. Russian scientists and military advisers are frequently dispatched to Iran to help guide this project.

Similarly, Moscow has long been a defender of Saddam's regime. Longtime Soviet/Russian leader and one-time Prime Minister Yevgeny Primakov is a great personal friend of the Iraqi strongman. Russia has equipped the Iraqi military — and re-equipped them after the 1991 Gulf War defeat. Russian military advisers frequently help their Iraqi counterparts. Soviet/Russian military doctrine is the order of the day in the Iraqi military.

North Korea has — since its inception — been a Soviet/Russian "client state." During the Korean War, the Soviets supplied Pyongyang with military technology, MiG jets and fuel. In return, the Soviets received access to U.S. prisoners of war for drug experiments, brainwashing practice and tortured "debriefings" about U.S. military technology.

In the 50 years since the Korean War, Moscow has kept a close relationship with Kim Song-il, the longtime dictator of North Korea, and extended it to his son, Kim Jong-il. (Moscow is not stupid; it wants allies next to its simmering archenemy, Red China, despite any short-term rapprochements that seem to occur from time to time.)

Beijing, too, has an equally close relationship with all three "axis of evil" countries. Chinese missile technology has been sent to all three. So, too, have Chinese scientists in hopes of expanding biological and chemical weapons programs.

It is a shame that the Bush administration cozies up to Moscow and Beijing at a time when those two nations are arming, supplying, supporting and encouraging the very terrorist activities we have declared war against.

We need to call a spade a spade. The "evildoers" Bush loves to lambaste are headquartered in Moscow and Beijing. They are not our friends. They are just evil.

American foreign policy should not be cowed by the angry rhetoric sure to come if we tell the world the truth about these two enemies of freedom.

That is not to say that Iran, Iraq and North Korea do not need to have their governments removed; they most certainly do.

But it is like fighting cancer. Until you remove the main tumors, the disease is still inside the body.

We have the unprecedented opportunity now, as the only superpower, to use our influence and might to force these evil governments out of business.

Through our economic power we can almost buy a change. Through our trade power we can induce a change. And through our military might we can demand a change.

This opportunity will not last forever. China is racing to become a military superpower. Moscow is rebuilding quickly.

Now is not the time to squander this opportunity with lowered goals and fear of a hostile reaction from the striped-pants diplomatic set.

Now is the time for America to attack the cancer of evil — wherever it may reside.

Chapter 12

Iraq

Did Iraq Hire Bin Laden?

Inside Cover
Wednesday, September 12, 2001
The *World Tribune* is reporting that Iraq may actually have *recruited* Osama bin Laden to attack the United States yesterday.

The *Tribune* reported Israeli officials as saying the horrible events of yesterday were too complex for one group to have planned and that Israeli intelligence "briefed the Cabinet of Prime Minister Ariel Sharon hours after the catastrophe ... telling the Cabinet that the most likely sponsor for such an attack is Iraq."

Iraqi television called the attack the "operation of the century" and made the following, proud statement in the face of thousands of innocent American deaths: "The collapse of U.S. centers of power is a collapse of the U.S. policy, which deviates from human values and stands by world Zionism at all international forums to continue to slaughter the Palestinian Arab people and implement U.S. plans to dominate the world under the cover of what is called the new [world] order. These are the fruits of the new U.S. order."

Saddam vs. the Bushes

John LeBoutillier
Thursday, September 13, 2001
This tragedy is becoming very understandable: It is payback from Saddam Hussein to the first George Bush team that ran the Gulf War 10 years ago.

Back then the American — and Coalition — team was run by Bush, Cheney and Powell.

Today our government — again busily assembling a new Coalition — is comprised of Bush, Cheney and Powell.

Saddam Hussein has been lying in wait to get back at the USA for our overwhelming victory over him back in 1991.

Indeed, he may have hired Osama bin Laden — as was mentioned in an Inside Cover item yesterday — to carry out the actual operational details of this massive act of terrorism. But all intelligence experts now seem to agree that a only state intelligence service could have provided the logistics, the 'inside information' — including White House codes mentioned by "White House sources" in the press today — to run such an effective operation.

And Saddam certainly has the motive.

Let us remember a few things:

1. In the early 1980s — while Reagan was president and G.H.W. Bush was vice president — we were allied *with Saddam* against the Iranians. We had a military alliance with Baghdad. We had very good and friendly relations with Saddam.

2. When Bush became president in 1989, his State Department dispatched a woman, April Glaspie, as ambassador to a Muslim country. (This in itself was a terrible misjudgment.) Ms. Glaspie had a communications failure with Saddam on the fateful days leading up to the invasion of Kuwait. (She was subsequently recalled.)

3. The invasion caused Desert Shield and then Desert Storm. Iraq's military was destroyed — but its weapons of mass destruction research capabilities remained somewhat intact.

4. Bush, Powell and Cheney had their foot on Saddam's jugular — but they let him get off the ground and rebuild himself.

This was a fatal error that led to this week's carnage in New York and at the Pentagon.

5. When Bush lost the election in 1992 Saddam was not finished with him. He tried to assassinate our former president by destroying a private jet that Bush was to use to fly to Kuwait to celebrate the anniversary of our victory.

6. The eight years of Clinton were wonderful for Saddam because Clinton withdrew our U.N. inspectors and relaxed some sanctions. Clinton also 'looked the other way' as Saddam began selling oil again to accumulate cash to finance suicide missions like this week's.

7. The election last year of his nemesis' son — G.W. Bush — was the perfect way for Saddam to close the circle against his enemy — the Great Satan.

8. Saddam most likely hired Osama bin Laden — or partnered with him — and selected as targets the very symbols he most despises: the White House, the Pentagon, the Capitol and the World Trade Center — the symbols of financial stability and wealth from which Saddam has been cut off by the first Bush's sanctions!

So Saddam ordered this diabolical plan.

Now comes the key question: Is W. Bush going to be satisfied with pinning all the blame on Osama bin Laden? Or will he and the very men who mistakenly allowed Saddam to survive 10 years ago — his father, Powell and Cheney — have the guts to admit their tragic error and now go get Saddam?

This is the key to this awful mess. This whole war is Saddam vs. the Bushes. Will the Bush team admit they made a mistake 10 years ago and now go correct it? Or will they once again let this son of a bitch live to terrorize us again?

Ex-CIA Chief Woolsey Sees Iraqi Fingerprints

NewsMax.com Wires
Friday, September 14, 2001

WASHINGTON — A former CIA chief sees the hand of Iraq behind Tuesday's attacks, and he warned the White House not to shirk the hard realities of possible state sponsorship.

"First of all we have to find out who did this thing," R. James Woolsey told United Press International in a phone interview Thursday.

But he said the Bush administration must "undo the mistakes of the Clinton administration and not just look at loose associations of terrorists or a terrorist group" such as that of Osama bin Laden's al Qaeda, but also consider the serious ramifications of possible state involvement.

Woolsey served as director of central intelligence in the first Clinton administration, from February 5, 1993, to January 10, 1995. He and Clinton were not close. In 1996 the hawkish Democrat endorsed GOP presidential candidate Bob Dole.

The Washington power lawyer told UPI that he is not sure that Iraq is involved in the attacks, but added: "What we don't want to do is what the Clinton administration did and put blinders on about state involvement by focusing just on a terrorist group."

To do so, he said, is to risk falling into a trap laid by bin Laden and Iraqi dictator Saddam Hussein.

"Why else would [bin Laden] issue fatwas [Islamic edicts] and put out videotapes and chant poems and have all his subordinates come up on networks where they know they're being listened to and all talk about how they're carrying out terrorist operations?" Woolsey asked.

He suggested that Saddam Hussein could be "sitting there grinning with bin Laden, saying: 'This is good for both of us. I don't get blamed, and you get the credit you want.'"

In criticizing the Clinton administration, Woolsey referred to a series of plots in New York City in the early 1990s, notably the initial bombing of the World Trade Center on February 26, 1993. Two factors were at work, he said.

The first was that the facts of the various bomb plots were unclear but prosecutors had blurred the distinctions for their own purposes. "It was easier for the prosecution to get convictions of all of the people who might have been involved in any of these plots in New York if they folded all the charges together under the Seditious Conspiracy Law and said it was all one conspiracy," Woolsey told UPI.

"If it's all one conspiracy inspired by the blind sheikh," he said, referring to so-called mastermind Omar Abd Al-Rahman — "that is, the World

Trade Center, and the effort to blow up the Holland Tunnel, the Lincoln Tunnel and the U.N., etc. — it confuses things for a jury to come in and say, 'And by the way, the Iraqi government was also involved.'"

The second important factor, Woolsey said, was that the Clinton administration "was less than enthusiastic about having confrontations with Saddam" in which American casualties might be incurred. "So I think there is a real chance that Iraqi government sponsorship was overlooked."

Woolsey commended Laurie Mylroie's opinion essay "Bin Laden Isn't Only One to Blame," which appeared in Thursday's editions of *The Wall Street Journal*, as well as "Getting Serious," the newspaper's accompanying editorial.

He said that his essay "The Iraqi Connection: Blood Baath," which appeared later Thursday on The New Republic Online, "takes off from some of Laurie's work on the '93 bombing of the World Trade Center, and suggests that the U.S. government now should go back and look hard at the possibility that there was Iraqi government involvement in that.

"And if the Iraqis were involved in '93 and have gotten away with it for eight years, and then launched another attack that has some real similarities both in target and in methodology to previous attacks against the World Trade Center and trying to blow up an airliner in the Pacific, we may have a modus operandi."

Woolsey said that Mylroie endorses the thesis of Jim Fox, who handled the FBI's investigation of the 1993 World Trade Center bombing for the first year and a half. Fox died in 1997.

Fox's theory, Woolsey told UPI, is "Ramzi Yousef is not just a random person we don't know, but is in fact an Iraqi government asset." In 1998 Yousef was sentenced to life plus 240 years for the 1993 bombing.

Woolsey expanded on the Fox-Mylroie theory in his New Republic essay.

According to this view, Ramzi Yousef was not the alias of a Pakistani named Abdul Basit, as it had been believed. Rather, Yousef was an Iraqi agent who had assumed Basit's identity when occupying Iraqi intelligence officers doctored police files in Kuwait, where the real Abdul Basit had lived in 1990.

Woolsey noted that Abdul Basit and his family disappeared during the occupation and have never been seen again.

COPYRIGHT 2001 BY UNITED PRESS INTERNATIONAL. ALL RIGHTS RESERVED.

CBS: Terror Pilot Met With Iraqi Intelligence Chief

Inside Cover
Tuesday, September 18, 2001

Investigators may have uncovered concrete evidence of an Iraqi connection to last week's terror attacks on New York's World Trade Center and the Pentagon in Washington, if a Tuesday afternoon CBS News report is true.

Mohamed Atta, the pilot of the first plane to slam into New York's Twin

Towers last week, met with the head of Iraqi intelligence in Europe earlier this year, according to an intelligence report discovered by U.S. probers, the network says.

"U.S. intelligence officials believe the report to be accurate, but do not know if it is 'smoking gun' evidence of Iraqi involvement," says CBS. "It is, however, the first solid indicator that a foreign state may have aided, abetted or had prior knowledge of Tuesday's attacks."

Atta is believed to be the ringleader of the band of 19 Mideast terrorists who hijacked four U.S. airplanes and slammed all but one into American landmarks last week.

After the attacks, as leaders worldwide roundly condemned the acts of Atta and his co-conspirators, only Iraq had words of praise.

Calling the attack the "operation of the century," Iraqi state-controlled television announced, "The collapse of U.S. centers of power is a collapse of the U.S. policy, which deviates from human values and stands by world Zionism at all international forums to continue to slaughter the Palestinian Arab people and implement U.S. plans to dominate the world under the cover of what is called the new [world] order. These are the fruits of the new U.S. order."

Israeli intelligence is said to believe that Baghdad may actually have recruited Osama bin Laden, who U.S. officials say is the leading suspect behind Tuesday's terror attacks.

Weinberger: Take Saddam Out

Inside Cover
Saturday, September 29, 2001
Saying retribution against Saddam Hussein is long overdue, former Defense Secretary Caspar Weinberger said it's time for the U.S. government to get him.

Weinberger made the comments in a taped interview with Al Hunt, co-host of CNN's *Capital Gang*, that was aired today.

"I'd like to see him taken out," Weinberger told Hunt, noting Hussein's buildup of weapons of mass destruction.

Weinberger, one of Ronald Reagan's key architects of bringing down the Soviet Union, had great praise for the Bush administration.

Weinberger said the Pentagon was moving "sequentially" — wiping out terrorist cells in Afghanistan before it sets its sites on Hussein in Baghdad.

Report: Iraq Behind Anthrax Attacks

NewsMax.com Wires
Monday, October 15, 2001
Britain's *Guardian* newspaper reported Sunday that American investigators probing anthrax outbreaks in Florida and New York believe they have all the hallmarks of a terrorist attack — and have named Iraq as the prime sus-

pect as the source of the deadly spores.

The *Guardian* notes that in liquid form, anthrax is useless — droplets would fall to the ground rather than stay suspended in the air to be breathed by victims.

"Making powder needs repeated washings in huge centrifuges, followed by intensive drying, which requires sealed environments. The technology would cost millions."

The London paper quoting CIA sources as saying that "Iraq has the technology and supplies of anthrax suitable for terrorist use."

One CIA source told the paper: "They aren't making this stuff in caves in Afghanistan. This is prima facie evidence of the involvement of a state intelligence agency. Maybe Iran has the capability. But it doesn't look likely politically. That leaves Iraq."

American officials have already revealed that anthrax bacteria used in the recent attacks is the "Ames strain" of anthrax originally cultivated at Iowa State University in the 1950s. Iraq is believed to have that strain.

Other sources indicate that al Qaeda members picked up vials of anthrax powder in the Czech Republic.

CIA sources believe that terrorist ringleader Mohamed Atta met with Iraqi intelligence officials twice in Prague, with the second meeting this past spring.

Already there are indications that Iraq may be part of the new war's "second phase." The first phase is under way: Closing down Taliban and al Qaeda operations in Afghanistan.

The *Guardian* reports that former CIA Director Jim Woolsey has recently visited London on behalf of the U.S. Defense Department to "firm up" other evidence of Iraqi involvement in the September 11 attacks.

COPYRIGHT 2001 UPI ALL RIGHTS RESERVED

Iraq Deadlier Than Ever, Saddam Boasts

David Eberhart
Wednesday, October 17, 2001

The Iraqi military has been able to reconstitute a considerable part of its pre–Desert Storm (1991) combat power, according to *Jane's World Armies* and the *National Security Studies Quarterly*.

Dictator Saddam Hussein recently corroborated the rehabilitation of Iraq's military prowess — despite the pounding of the Gulf War and continuing economic sanctions that embargo the importing of the tools of warfare.

"Our military capabilities are now bigger," Saddam announced confidently in late August. "Conditions in Iraq have this year become better than previous years, economically and in our capacity to face up to challenges and confront the Americans."

Other Iraqi officials simultaneously asserted that there would be a beef-ing-up of anti-aircraft defenses in a bid to wipe out U.S. and British war-planes, which patrol "no-fly" zones in the north and south of the country.

In the meantime, political leaders at home and around the world ponder and debate whether an attack on terrorist-harboring Iraq is the Bush administration's answer to a question often asked by the media and Arab leaders: "What's next after the Afghanistan campaign?"

Senator Joe Lieberman, D-Conn., said in an address Monday to New Democrat Network that he wanted President Bush to remove Saddam from power — now.

Meanwhile, National Security Advisor Condoleezza Rice deferred to her commander in chief, saying in a recent TV interview, "The president has said that his goal is to watch and monitor Iraq." So far, U.S. investigators have disclosed no firm link between Iraq and the terror attacks of September 11.

Bob Kerrey, former Democratic senator from Nebraska, recently voiced the concern of many political leaders that hitting Saddam in the midst of a controversial bombing campaign in Afghanistan could result in a fracture of the anti-terror coalition and "every American Embassy from Morocco to India set on fire."

If action against the Saddam regime does get under way, coalition attack-ers may confront a formidable foe.

According to a report published in the *National Security Studies Quarterly*'s spring 1998 edition, "assessments of the damage done to Iraq's military industry after the Gulf War stated that 25-30 percent of Iraqi mili-tary industrial capability had been destroyed or damaged."

"British wartime assessments indicated that all of Iraq's artillery and ammunition capability had been eliminated, and that restoration would take several years."

Ominously, however, the report qualified, "This estimate was optimistic."

'Significant Reconstruction'

By March 1992, according to the report, U.S. intelligence had found "significant reconstruction" at Iraq's estimated two dozen military-indus-trial sites, and that limited production of artillery and ammunition had been resumed.

According to Robert Gates, then the CIA chief, by early 1992 a resilient Iraq had restored limited production of artillery, munitions and possibly armored vehicles, and also claimed to have repaired nearly 200 military industrial buildings.

In a similar evaluation, *Jane's* reported that the Iraqi army ended the war — and subsequent uprisings — with as little as a quarter of its pre–Gulf War divisional strength, a quarter of prewar manpower and half of its equipment.

"The rebuilding has taken place against a background of political insta-bility, with numerous senior officers losing their lives in coup attempts and purges, and in light of the impossibility of obtaining new equipment or spare parts due to the UN embargo," said the report.

But the bottom line, according to the respected sourcebook for military hardware around the world: "Nonetheless, the Iraqi military has been able to reconstitute a considerable portion of its pre–Desert Storm combat power."

Saddam's career, since assuming power in 1979, has centered on domination of the Persian Gulf. By 1990, Iraq's military industry was enormous. It employed more workers than the Israeli defense industries, and the military-industrial labor force constituted at least 40 percent or more of Iraq's total industrial employees.

Iraq spent $14.2 billion between 1985 and 1989 on industrial technology, almost all of which had military applications. During congressional hearings, Senator John McCain, R-Ariz., provided even higher numbers, arguing that Iraq spent $27 billion on weapons technology and industrial supplies from 1980 to 1990.

After the Storm

According to *Jane's*, the rapid recovery of Iraq's military capability suggests that the reported two-day stockpile of ammunition remaining to Saddam in 1991 was rapidly replenished by local industry.

Postwar analyses of Iraq's military industry identified at least 33 military-industrial facilities producing conventional weapons alone, 10 of which could not be located. CIA estimates from 1990 stated that 25 military and at least 40 civilian facilities were involved in Iraq's military industrial efforts.

Forces on the Ground

The Republican Guard, Saddam's touted elite force, was — before Desert Storm — the best-equipped and best-paid unit in the Iraqi army.

In recent years, according to *Jane's*, the regime has concentrated its energies on reconstituting the Guard formations. By 1997 the country had reconstituted eight divisions. The sourcebook noted, however, that these units were undermanned and poorly equipped.

There has been no military equipment procurement from recognized sources since August 1990. However, qualified *Jane's*, Iraq made sure that a sizeable quantity of high-quality main battle tanks (MBTs) survived the Gulf War.

The MBTs, and much of the elite Republican Guard to which they were allocated, were moved well out of harm's way before the allies mounted their big push into Kuwait in February 1991.

Estimates of the total number of MBTs in the Iraqi army's arsenal vary. A recent Department of Defense estimate was in the region of 2,000. Even though this is a huge decrease from the pre–Desert Storm estimate of 5,800-7,000, it is still sufficient to give pause to hostile Third World neighbors.

Many analysts believe that Iraqi ground forces have retained a very strong capability in anti-tank warfare. While the army lost large numbers of anti-tank weapons during the Gulf War, it is still believed to retain quantities of good equipment, including man-portable guided missiles as well as other missiles mounted on helicopters and armored vehicles.

The army still has several thousand 85 mm and 100 mm anti-tank guns and heavy recoilless rifles. The DoD also estimates that Saddam commands 150 self-propelled artillery weapons (in comparison with an estimated 500 before the war) and perhaps 1,800 towed artillery weapons (compared with up to 5,000 before the war.)

According to *Jane's World Armies*, Pentagon estimates of Iraqi air force strength in April 1992 included about 350 aircraft with operational capabilities — although only about 150 were thought to be airworthy at that time. By mid-1993, it was estimated that the Iraqi air force had built its remaining operational strength to about 50 percent readiness.

Meanwhile, the debate goes on.

'Saddam's Bombmaker' on Anthrax Attacks: 'This Is Iraq!'

Inside Cover
Tuesday, October 23, 2001

A top Iraqi military scientist who defected to the U.S. in 1994 said late Monday that he's absolutely certain his former boss, Saddam Hussein, is behind the wave of anthrax attacks that have swept the U.S. in recent weeks.

"This is Iraq," said Dr. Khidhir Hamza, in an interview on CNBC's *Rivera Live*. "This is Iraq's work."

Dr. Hamza headed up Hussein's nuclear weapons research program in the early 1990s and has authored the book *Saddam's Bombmaker: The Terrifying Inside Story of the Iraqi Nuclear and Biological Weapons Agenda*.

"Nobody [else] has the expertise outside the U.S. and outside the major powers who work on germ warfare," Hamza told *Rivera Live*. "Nobody has the expertise and has any motive to attack the U.S. except Saddam to do this. This is Iraq. This is Saddam."

The Iraqi weapons expert told CNBC that his homeland had developed the capability to weaponize anthrax even before he defected to the U.S. seven years ago, and continues to maintain that capability.

"I have absolutely no doubt," he said. "Iraq worked actually even before the Gulf War on perfecting the process of getting anthrax in the particle size needed in powder form to disseminate the way it is being disseminated now."

After linking the Iraqi dictator to the U.S. anthrax attacks, the man familiar with Saddam's secret doomsday strategy said he thinks the anthrax contamination of America's postal system is just the opening salvo in Saddam's bioterror war on the U.S.

"Probably this is the first wave," Dr. Hamza told Rivera. "I'm not trying to frighten everybody in this, but probably this is the first wave."

While Saddam Builds Monuments, Babies Die

Phil Brennan, NewsMax.com
Sunday, November 4, 2001

Saddam Hussein squanders his oil billions on monuments to himself while untended babies abandoned by their starving parents die in the streets or waste away in grubby hospitals.

Last year, Saddam pocketed a staggering $11 billion from the U.N.'s oil-for-food program, which is intended to help alleviate the grinding poverty afflicting the Iraqi people. It was part of the $38.6 billion that has gone to Iraq under the program since 1996 — according to Western governments, more than enough to feed Iraq's people. The blame for the fact that it has not been employed for that purpose lies squarely at Saddam's door.

While Saddam builds magnificent edifices such as the multimillion-dollar Mother of All Battles mosque in Baghdad and lavish palaces for himself all across the nation, the majority of his people live on the brink of starvation.

In a gut-wrenching report in Britain's Electronic Telegraph, correspondent Hala Jaber reveals the hideous details of the effect on tiny infants abandoned in the streets of Basra by mothers who cannot feed themselves, much less their offspring. The babies who do not die in the filthy debris-filled streets wind up in the city's hospital.

"They look dead," she writes. "The seven babies, little more than bundles of torn sheets, lie malnourished and motionless in a bare, filthy back room of Basra's main children's and maternity hospital.

"The oppressive air, filled not with the usual antiseptic odour of medical facilities but the foul stench of human waste, is stirred only by the occasional entrance of the cleaner, who bustles in between mopping wards to quickly wash each infant in the basin. Otherwise, they are all but left alone. The doctors and nursing staff are already overwhelmed by the sheer numbers of seriously ill children in their care."

The helpless tots are the victims of Saddam's relentless assault on his nation's economy, which he has pillaged to build his monuments and his arsenals of weapons of mass destruction.

Under his merciless rule, Iraq's once thriving middle class has all but vanished, leaving the nation with a tiny class of super-rich and a huge underclass of poverty-stricken, slowly starving people.

Doctors at the hospital where Jaber saw the babies told her they are horrified by the number of abandoned infants who die on the streets of Basra, Iraq's second-largest and once prosperous city, before they can be taken to the hospital.

"Their mothers cannot take care of them," a doctor told Jaber. "They have no money and no means to feed them, so they are now dumping these children. Sometimes the babies are adopted; other times, like now, nothing happens and suddenly we have a roomful of them.

"It is heartbreaking and we really do our best for them, but we do not have full-time staff and the proper facilities to take care of them. I have seen good days and some beautiful days in this hospital, but these are really the bad days."

Critics blame the U.N. sanctions for the deaths of as many of 500,000 children since they were imposed, but Western leaders, who question the accuracy of that figure, insist that Saddam himself bears full responsibility for the tragedy of Iraq's suffering masses.

Said one British official: "We don't deny that there is a great deal of human suffering in Iraq, but the direct cause of this is the regime, not sanctions."

The piles of money Saddam has lavished on Baghdad show up in the scores of new boutiques, electronic retailers and marketplaces where, Jaber writes, "only foreigners and rich Iraqis can afford the exotic wares on display."

The rest of Baghdad's population has to get by with their monthly food rations of such basic staples as rice, sugar, tea, fat, grains, flour and soap.

"Red meat and chicken have become luxury items, with many families going for weeks without either," she adds. The once thriving middle class has all but been wiped out and become part of the underclass that makes up the majority of Iraq's population.

And while babies die in the streets, the rich enjoying Saddam's patronage haunt Baghdad's plentiful new restaurants and nightclubs. On the roads, the latest-model BMWs and Mercedes of Saddam's new elite compete with battered and ancient Volkswagens.

And in Basra, which was once the third-largest oil producer in the world, the poverty is now so bad that many families are selling the monthly food rations they get from the government to buy shoes for their children and bus fare to find work.

Mylroie: Saddam Is Behind the Terrorist Attacks

Jarret Wollstein
Thursday, November 8, 2001

NewsMax: Why do you think Saddam Hussein is behind the September 11 attack on America?

Mylroie: Just look at the evidence.

First, as I document in *Study of Revenge*, Saddam was behind the first attack on the World Trade Center in 1993, which was also designed to destroy both buildings. The mastermind of that attack was Iraqi intelligence agent Ramzi Ahmed Yousef.

Yousef arrived in the U.S. on September 1, 1992, on an Iraqi passport and left the country the night of February 26, 1993 — the same day the World Trade Center was first bombed.

Second, as we've documented at Iraq News, Hussein has also been involved in all major terrorist attacks on the West since the Gulf War.

Third, the leader of the September 11 attack, Mohamed Atta, met with Iraqi counsel Admed Samir al-Ani in the Czech Republic at least four times before the 9/11 attack.

There is also tremendous evidence that subsequent anthrax attacks are connected to Iraq. The cumulative evidence that Iraq was a key player in the September 11 attack and subsequent anthrax attacks is overwhelming.

Don't forget: The U.S. is still at war with Iraq. The Gulf War never really ended. The sanctions against Iraq are essentially a continuation of that war, and U.S. pilots bomb Iraq on a regular basis.

Saddam has far greater cause than any other party to attack the United States.

NewsMax: Why, then, is the Bush administration reluctant to name Iraq as a culprit?

Mylroie: Partly, it's genuine confusion about who is sponsoring terrorism that developed during the Clinton administration.

Ten years ago, U.S. authorities believed that major terrorist attacks on the U.S. were state-sponsored because only states had the resources to mount such attacks. That all changed under Clinton.

The Clinton administration maintained that with the first World Trade Center bombing, a new type of terrorism emerged, which the FBI called "International Radical Terrorism." In a 1994 report, the FBI's Terrorism Research and Analytical Center described International Radical Terrorism as follows:

"IRT ... is a trans-national phenomenon. Its adherents generally overcome traditional national differences by concentrating on a common goal of achieving social change, under the banner of personal beliefs, through violence. ... IRT adherents may not consider themselves to be citizens of any particular country."

This 'loose network of terrorists' theory is clearly the one the Bush administration is now operating under and is dead wrong. Only states have the resources to mount these attacks. Equipment to manufacture weapons-grade anthrax costs millions of dollars and requires skilled scientists. Common sense tells you that it's not a bunch of nuts living in caves.

A second reason why the Bush administration is reluctant to name Iraq: It means a much tougher war with potentially millions of American civilian casualties.

Iraq has literally tons of chemical and biological weapons, as well as lots of missiles and sleeper agents already in the U.S. to deliver them. No one wants to deliver that message to the American people.

The Pentagon is aware of Iraqi involvement, but the Bush administration is still in denial.

NewsMax: So, what is the role of Osama bin Laden and his al Qaeda network?

Mylroie: They're working together. Bin Laden provides the ideology and foot soldiers. He provides a smoke screen for Iraq. Iraq provides the direction and expertise for the attacks.

NewsMax: What is the evidence that Saddam is also behind the anthrax attacks?

Mylroie: ABC News reported on October 29 that at least two labs have concluded that the anthrax used in the U.S. was coated with two additives linked to Iraq's biological weapons program: bentonite and silica. These additives make anthrax particularly lethal by preventing spores from sticking together, enabling them to float and making anthrax easily inhalable.

Bentonite is a trademark of the Iraqi weapons program. Iraq is the only country in the world that uses it.

The German newspaper *Bild* also reports that according to Israeli security, Mohamed Atta, who organized the 9/11 attacks, was given a vacuum flask of anthrax when he met with the Iraqi counsel in the Czech Republic.

We also know that Saddam has enormous quantities of anthrax. In 1995, before U.N. weapons inspectors were expelled from Iraq, they estimated that he had produced 2,000 gallons of anthrax — enough to kill every person on earth. God knows how much he has now, in addition to his weaponized smallpox and other deadly biological weapons.

NewsMax: Why haven't we seen massive biological attacks on the U.S.?

Mylroie: Saddam know that the only way he can survive is if others are blamed for the terrorist attacks on America, at least for now. So initial attacks have been small, but much larger attacks are being planned.

The Iraqi newspaper *Babil*, published by Saddam's son, clearly spells out their strategy. The September 20 edition predicted a three-stage American war on Afghanistan: 1) air attacks, 2) escalating air attacks and ground troops, and 3) a Vietnam-style quagmire and growing Muslim counterattacks.

Babil says during the first two stages Iraq will not publicly involve itself in the war because "[Americans] will watch Iraq accurately and seriously. If we do anything, Iraq will be attacked, not just like the attack of 1998, but perhaps like the attack of 1991 [the Gulf War]."

However, once we reach stage 3 — a Vietnam-style quagmire — *Babil* warns, "At this stage, it is possible to turn to biological attack, where a small can, not bigger than the size of the hand, can be used to release viruses that affect everything."

Again, this is what an official Iraqi newspaper was saying on September 20 — before the first anthrax attacks.

Also consider that the anthrax attacks we've seen have been progressively more lethal. The first attacks didn't kill any postal workers, just people in the vicinity of the letter. Then postal workers and bystanders were infected, and we have a more sophisticated form of anthrax that floats around.

The next stage could be antibiotic-resistant anthrax, which Iraq can easily make. The attacks are getting more and more sophisticated. It's a clear progression, testing our defenses.

NewsMax: Does Saddam also have nuclear weapons?

Mylroie: He has everything he needs to make several nuclear weapons, perhaps more, with the possible exception of fissionable material — plutonium or U-235. And he's doing everything possible to get them.

NewsMax: Under what circumstances would Saddam use nuclear weapons?

Mylroie: If his back is to the wall. It's called the "Samson strategy." If Saddam knows he can't win, he will kill as many of his enemies as possible before he dies.

That's also when Saddam would attack Israel with his Jerusalem Army.

NewsMax: How would you respond to this threat if you were president of the United States?

Mylroie: First, I'd do everything possible to minimize casualties and risk. I'd ground all crop dusters and round up everyone who might be responsible. Then I'd go after Iraq.

I'd bomb the Special Republican Guard that keeps Saddam in power. I'd bomb his 40 palaces and anyplace else he might be. I'd work with the Iraqi resistance to get rid of his corrupt regime. I'd do whatever it takes to put Saddam in his grave.

The State Department doesn't want to do it. Bush doesn't want to do. But we have to do it, and the sooner the better. The only alternative is to wait until Saddam launches a massive biological or nuclear attack on the U.S. that kills millions.

Ritter: Iraq 'No Threat'

Inside Cover
Monday, November 19, 2001

NewsMax has reported before how former U.N. arms inspector Scott Ritter has become an apologist for Saddam Hussein's regime.

As the administration has pointed a clear finger at the Iraqi regime for building weapons of mass destruction, Ritter took to the airwaves today to pour cold water on the allegations.

Ritter said he had "no doubt" Hussein was building such weapons — but only up until 1993.

Since then, Ritter told Fox News Channel's John Gibson, Iraq's "determination to acquire such weapons isn't there." Saddam is "a threat to his own people but not the United States," Ritter said.

He claimed that Iraq does not have the "industrial infrastructure" to build such weapons, and that its number one goal is to have "sanctions lifted."

It all sounds good, but it diametrically contradicts what Ritter said in 1996, when he quit the U.N. team claiming the Clinton administration had not allowed inspectors to do their job.

Ritter's claims don't jibe with claims of the head of Iraq's nuclear weapons program, who now believes Saddam has built one or more nuclear devices.

If, as Ritter claims, the Iraqis had no interest in building such weapons, they would have allowed in U.N. inspectors, which would have automatically lifted sanctions.

Ritter of all people should know this.

Instead, Hussein has kept the inspectors out and has lost billions.

Hussein obviously believes the weapons are more important than money.

Laurie Mylroie is publisher of the online newsletter Iraq News and author of Study of Revenge: Saddam Hussein's Unfinished War against America. *She is convinced that Iraq is behind recent terrorist attacks on America, and that those attacks will continue and escalate until Saddam Hussein and his government are removed. NewsMax interviewed Laurie Mylroie.*

Iraq's Money Pipeline Wins Allies

Dave Eberhart
Monday, December 10, 2001

Follow the money.

That dictum may be the best way to figure out why so many countries oppose U.S. efforts to target Iraq in the next phase of the war on terrorism.

Press reports chalk up the rhetoric against U.S. military intervention in Iraq to the simple reluctance of Arab coalition members to war against a sister Arab country.

But the money trail may give a more complete explanation for their recalcitrance, as well as that of non-Arab states that oppose targeting Iraq.

In recent years, Iraq has been carefully channeling billions of dollars in trade to its neighbors and potential foes under the U.N.-mandated "oil for food" program.

Apparently, members of the U.S. coalition against terrorism may not be so anxious to upset this multibillion-dollar trade to a recession-strapped Europe and Middle East.

Iraq's U.N. Ambassador, Mohammed Douri, perhaps said it best: "Politics is about interests. Politics is not about morals."

A large part of the disincentive to war: Baghdad's oil revenue has leaped from $4 billion in 1997 to $18 billion last year.

Much of that windfall goes to buying goods in the marketplace; even the brokering of the Iraqi oil generates millions of dollars.

The U.N. Security Council voted in late 1996 to allow Iraq to sell oil to purchase food, medicine and other humanitarian goods under the "oil-for-food" program.

Over time, all limits on the amount of oil that Iraq could sell were removed, though the revenue is funneled to a U.N. escrow account and Iraqi purchases are monitored by a Security Council committee.

According to U.N. records, Egypt signed more than $740 million in contracts with Iraq in the latter half of last year alone. The United Arab Emirates did $703 million in business. Syria purchases about $1 billion in oil from Baghdad each year.

All three countries strongly oppose any U.S. intervention in Iraq.

Before falling into disfavor because of its posture regarding sanctions against Iraq, France was a huge beneficiary of trade with the outlaw nation, cutting deals for over $3 billion worth of such goods as mini-buses, garbage trucks and communications gear.

Russia has done more than $2 billion in business with Iraq under the program. Not surprisingly, Russia recently rejected a U.S. plan to modify the oil-for-food program. It has also warned the U.S. it will withdraw its support for the war on terrorism if Iraq is attacked.

Russian oil giants earn large profits by trading Iraqi oil on world markets.

If and when sanctions are lifted, Russia's oil interests look forward to more business with Iraq, which has huge oil reserves.

Iraqi Oil in U.S.

And despite Iraq's ostensible refusal to sell its oil directly to the U.S., Japan and the United Kingdom, Iraqi crude has become the fastest-growing source of U.S. imports as it flows into the U.S. through middlemen.

Nearly 40 percent of Iraq's oil exports end up in U.S. refineries.

Larry Goldstein, president of the Petroleum Industry Research Foundation, has identified traders in Russia, China and Europe as buying discount Iraqi oil, re-styling it, and selling it to U.S. companies at bargain prices.

According to Goldstein, U.S. oil companies make billions of dollars in profit from this cheaper oil difference every year.

Department of Energy figures indicate the companies receiving the oil are Chevron, Exxon-Mobil, Valero, Clark and Marathon Ashland.

Even perennial U.S. ally the Netherlands has been lobbying the Security Council to lift the ban on foreign investment in Iraq's oil sector.

The Netherlands wants to obtain commercial contracts for its own firms, including the powerful Royal Dutch/Shell Group.

For its part, Baghdad knows full well the financial clout it packs.

When France got too cozy with the U.S. sanctions policy, Baghdad slashed its imports of French goods to $310 million in the second half of 2000, down from $616 million in the first six months of last year, according to the U.N.

Baghdad also rattled its financial saber in the face of neighboring Turkey and Jordan to discourage them from backing a U.S.-British proposal to stop Iraqi smuggling.

Turkey and Jordan, of course, are significant beneficiaries of Iraqi trade dollars.

"Iraq is using money and oil as a weapon against the international community," said James B. Cunningham, former acting U.S. ambassador to the United Nations.

"My government is accustomed by now to Iraq's cynicism toward its own people, and to its bluster and threatening policies. We find it harder to understand, however, why others would join in playing that game when the status quo is clearly not satisfactory."

The question remains if that clout will derail any U.S. notions of forcing the return of U.N. weapons inspectors to Iraq by military force, and holding Saddam Hussein accountable for his support of international terrorism.

Saddam Had the Bomb, Says Top Nuke Physicist

Inside Cover
Sunday, December 30, 2001
As far back as 1990, scientists working for Iraqi madman Saddam Hussein managed to perfect a single nuclear bomb, according to the physicist who ran Iraq's version of the Manhattan Project at the time.

But the device was too heavy to mount on the Iraqi missiles and not enough nuclear material could be obtained for additional bombs, Dr. Khidhir Hamza, who ran Saddam's nuclear weapons program from 1987 through the early 1990s, tells *U.S. News & World Report* this week.

The former top Iraqi physicist — Hamza defected to the U.S. in 1994 — also reveals that a few years earlier Hussein twice tested radiological weapons, known as "dirty bombs," but was disappointed in the results.

By November of 1990, Dr. Hamza's Atomic Energy Department had nearly completed a nuclear device. But it was the size of a refrigerator — far too big to fit into a missile warhead, he explains.

Iraq had been able to extract enough of the key nuclear ingredient enriched uranium, 18 kilograms, from its Osiraq nuclear reactor, the facility bombed into oblivion by the Isaelis in 1981, he tells the magazine.

But two things stopped Hamza and his colleagues from deploying what would have been Saddam's first nuke:

They knew that any such move would set off alarms at the International Atomic Energy Agency, which monitored Iraq's use of uranium.

And once their success had become public, the agency would prevent Iraq from developing any more enriched uranium. Therefore, says Hamza, Iraq would be able to build only one oversize bomb.

Informed of this, Saddam agreed to shift Iraq's WMD focus to chemical and biological weaponry.

Prior to perfecting a genuine nuke, Hamza and his crew were ordered to explore the potential of non-nuclear radiological weaponry — the same sort of "dirty bombs" experts fear Osama bin Laden may have obtained.

Two weapons using irradiated zirconium oxide were tested at a site west of Baghdad in 1987 and 1988 with an eye towards using them in Iraq's then-ongoing war against Iran.

"But the results were poor," Hamza tells *U.S. News.* "The radioactive material did not spread far enough, and the degree of radiation from the device was too weak to cause immediate casualties."

Iraq's radiological warfare program was subsequently terminated, he says, explaining, "We wanted a nuclear yield."

Thatcher: Get Saddam

Inside Cover
Tuesday, February 12, 2002
Margaret Thatcher offers good "Advice to a Superpower" in today's *New York Times,* but the Democrats, America's European "allies" and a certain Iraqi madman won't be happy.

Among the former British prime minister's thoughts:

• The next phase of the war against terrorism "should be to strike at other centers of Islamic terror that have taken root in Africa, Southeast Asia and elsewhere.

   "This will require first-rate intelligence, shrewd diplomacy and a continued extensive military commitment. Our enemies have had years to entrench themselves, and they will not be dislodged without fierce and bloody resistance.

• "The third phase is to deal with those hostile states that support terrorism and seek to acquire or trade in weapons of mass destruction." She notes that Iran and Syria are "enemies of Western values and interests," also singles out Libya, genocidal Sudan and "mad as ever" North Korea.

• Her choice for "most notorious rogue" is Iraqi dictator Saddam Hussein. "His aim is, in fact, quite clear: to develop weapons of mass destruction so as to challenge us with impunity.

   "How and when, not whether, to remove him are the only important questions," Thatcher writes. "America's allies, above all Britain, should extend strong support to President Bush in the decisions he makes on Iraq."

'Saddam's Bombmaker': Iraq Working on 'Hiroshima Size' Nuke

Inside Cover
Monday, February 18, 2002
Iraqi madman Saddam Hussein will likely have a "Hiroshima size" nuclear bomb within the next 24 months, the physicist who headed up Iraq's nuclear weapons research program said Monday.

Citing U.S. intelligence estimates, Dr. Khidhir Hamza told nationally syndicated radio talker Sean Hannity, "I don't think he has [nuclear capability] right now but it may not take long for him to have it — a year or two probably.

"U.S. intelligence estimates at least a year. Germany estimates by 2005, three nuclear weapons," the top Iraqi nuke scientist said.

Dr. Hamza, who defected to the U.S. in 1994, warned about Hussein's nuclear weapons program in his autobiography, *Saddam's Bombmaker*, three years ago. More recently he has been working closely with U.S. intelligence agencies.

He declined to describe the precise nature of his cooperation with those agencies, telling Hannity, "I cannot talk about that. You know that."

Hamza did reveal that the 1991 Gulf War interrupted Iraq's A-bomb program in its final stage, just as he and the rest of Saddam's nuke team were in the process of acquiring materials for the bomb's nuclear core.

HAMZA: We [scientists] dragged our feet. We really had enough material to make the bomb then. We delivered it now back to the French but we claimed that we could not extract enough uranium to put in a nuclear core....

HANNITY: So you're saying you did have enough — you could have built nuclear weapons but you dragged your feet?

HAMZA: We could have, yes. Actually, everybody [dragged their feet], including the chemists who were in the process of extracting the uranium from the French bureau. Nobody wanted to give Saddam a bomb because we knew he would use it recklessly and finish Iraq with it.

End of excerpt

German intelligence now believes Hussein once again has all the bomb-making materials he needs except for the enriched uranium necessary for the nuclear core.

"According to the Germans he, more or less, has 30 to 35 percent of the technology needed to enrich uranium for bomb grade," said Hamza, adding, "so he will have enough uranium, and he already has a stockpile of uranium to use."

The top Iraqi nuclear scientist said that, based on what he witnessed, Hussein is working on "Hiroshima size" weapons of "12 to 20 kilotons."

But he cautioned: "There was some enhancement to the bomb that could raise it to 40 kilotons. So you are looking at [a] realistic nuclear weapons stockpile equivalent to that of, say, at least India and Pakistan — and if it continues, probably larger."

Iraq–al Qaeda Bombshell: Mag Documents New Links

Inside Cover
Sunday, March 17, 2002

A report set to hit newsstands Monday documenting ties between Iraq's Mukhabarat intelligence service and Osama bin Laden's al Qaeda terrorist organization is being called a "blockbuster" by former CIA Director James Woolsey.

The New Yorker magazine report details cooperation between al Qaeda agents in Northern Iraq and intelligence operatives working for Saddam Hussein, Woolsey told CNN's *Late Edition,* including:
- details of the 10-year-long working relationship between al Qaeda and Mukhabarat agents in attacks on the Kurdish minority;
- evidence that the Mukhabarat smuggled weapons into Afghanistan to help al Qaeda forces;
- accounts of al Qaeda refugees being brought into Iraq.

The New Yorker report also quotes Kurdish sources as saying the CIA had no interest in the Mukhabarat–al Qaeda links, prompting this reaction from ex-Director Woolsey:

"The CIA has over recent years not been real enthusiastic about the Iraqi resistance and I think that's a shame. If they got beat on this story by *The New Yorker* and [its reporter] Jeff Goldberg, three cheers for the fourth estate."

"I think [*The New Yorker*] piece is a blockbuster," added Woolsey.

Iraqi Terrorists Detail Ties to Bin Laden

Dave Eberhart, NewsMax
Monday, March 18, 2002

A terrorist group operating in northern Iraq told *The New Yorker* magazine's Jeffrey Goldberg that their organization "has received funds directly from al Qaeda."

In interviews conducted in a prison in Kurdish-controlled territory, captured members of Ansar al-Islam also alleged:
- The intelligence service of Saddam Hussein has joint control, with al Qaeda operatives, over Ansar al-Islam.
- Saddam Hussein hosted a senior leader of al Qaeda in Baghdad in 1992.
- A number of al Qaeda members fleeing Afghanistan have been secretly brought into territory controlled by Ansar al-Islam.
- Iraqi intelligence agents smuggled conventional weapons, and possibly even chemical and biological weapons, into Afghanistan.

If these charges are true," Goldberg writes in the current issue of the magazine, "it would mean that the relationship between Saddam's regime and al Qaeda is far closer than previously thought."

The prisoners Goldberg spoke to last month are kept in a jail that is run by the intelligence service of the Patriotic Union of Kurdistan, whose director told Goldberg that American intelligence officials had not visited the site. "The FBI and the CIA haven't come out yet," the director said.

According to Kurdish officials, Goldberg reports, "Ansar al-Islam grew out of an idea spread by Ayman al-Zawahiri, the former chief of the

Egyptian Islamic Jihad and now Osama bin Laden's deputy in al Qaeda."

One official explained, "Zawahiri's philosophy is that you should fight the infidel even in the smallest village, that you should try to form Islamic armies everywhere. The Kurdish fundamentalists were influenced by Zawahiri."

The group has between 500 and 600 members, according to Kurdish officials, including Arab Afghans and at least 30 Iraqi Kurds who were trained in Afghanistan.

Last September, the officials said, representatives of Osama bin Laden gave Ansar al-Islam $300,000. These officials added that the real leader of Ansar al-Islam is an Iraqi known as Abu Wa'el, who has spent a great deal of time in bin Laden's training camps but is also, they said, an officer of the Mukhabarat, Saddam's principal intelligence service.

"A man named Abu Agab is in charge of the northern bureau of the Mukhabarat," one official told Goldberg. "And he is Abu Wa'el's control officer."

Smuggling al Qaeda Members

Kurdish intelligence officials said that there is no proof that Ansar al-Islam has ever been involved in international terrorism or that Saddam Hussein's agents were involved in the attacks on the World Trade Center or the Pentagon. But they claimed that several men associated with al Qaeda have been smuggled over the Iranian border into an Ansar al-Islam stronghold near the city of Halabja.

Two of these men, who go by the names Abu Yasir and Abu Muzaham, are high-ranking al Qaeda members, they say. An Iraqi intelligence officer, Qassem Hussein Muhammad, one of the prisoners with whom Goldberg spoke, said that his own involvement in Islamic radicalism began in 1992 in Baghdad, when he met Zawahiri after being assigned to help guard him.

After reports surfaced that Abu Wa'el had been captured by American agents, Qassem says, he was sent by the Mukhabarat to Kurdistan to find out what was going on. "That's when I was captured," he said. Asked if he was sure that Abu Wa'el was on Saddam's side, Qassem said, "He's an employee of the Mukhabarat. He's the actual decision-maker in the group — Ansar al-Islam — but he's an employee of the Mukhabarat."

In the prison, Goldberg also spoke to a young Iraqi Arab named Haqi Ismail, whom Kurdish officials described as a middle- to high-ranking member of al Qaeda, who was captured as he tried to get into Kurdistan three weeks after the start of the American attack on Afghanistan.

Jawad, a 29-year-old Iranian Arab who is a smuggler and bandit from the city of Ahvaz, and whom Kurdish intelligence officials said was most recently employed by bin Laden, told Goldberg that he began to smuggle for bin Laden in the late 1990s.

Liquid Might Be Bioweapon

In 2000, Jawad's al Qaeda contact told him to smuggle several dozen refrigerator motors into Afghanistan for the Mukhabarat; a canister filled with liquid was attached to each motor. Jawad told Goldberg that he had no idea what liquid was inside the motors, but he assumed that it was some type of chemical or biological weapon.

"There's been a relationship between the Mukhabarat and the people of al Qaeda since 1992," Jawad said.

In his *New Yorker* article, "The Great Terror," Goldberg also provides a comprehensive account of Saddam's massive conventional, chemical and possibly biological attacks on the Kurds in the late 1980s, during which as many as 200,000 Kurds in northern Iraq were killed, out of a population of about 4 million.

Christine Gosden, an English geneticist who has been studying the attacks on the Kurds since 1998, says, "The Iraqi government was using chemistry to reduce the population of Kurds. The Holocaust is still having its effect. The Jews are fewer in number now than they were in 1939. That's not natural. Now, if you take out 200,000 men and boys from Kurdistan, you've affected the population structure. There are a lot of widows who are not having children."

Gosden believes it is quite possible that the countries of the West will soon experience serious chemical and biological weapons attacks. "Please understand," she said, "the Kurds were for practice."

Gosden told Goldberg that she cannot understand why the West has not been more eager to investigate the chemical attacks in Kurdistan. "It seems a matter of enlightened self-interest that the West would want to study the long-term effects of chemical weapons on civilians, on the DNA," she says, pointing out that "for Saddam's scientists, the Kurds were a test population. They were the human guinea pigs. It was a way of identifying the most effective chemical agents for use on civilian populations, and the most effective means of delivery."

Khidhir Hamza, an Iraqi defector who was formerly a high official in Saddam's nuclear program, told Goldberg that he had direct knowledge of the army's plans for Halabja. "The doctors were given sheets with grids on them, and they had to answer questions such as 'How far are the dead from the canisters?'"

Fouad Baban, a pulmonary and cardiac specialist in Kurdistan who led Goldberg on his tour of Halabja, and other experts "now believe that Halabja and other places in Kurdistan were struck by a combination of mustard gas and nerve agents, including sarin (the agent used in the Tokyo subway attack) and VX, a potent nerve agent."

Baban told Goldberg that the Iraqis could conceivably have used aflatoxin as well; aflatoxin is a biological agent that causes long-term liver damage. Baban said, "Here is a civilian population exposed to chemical and possibly biological weapons, and people are developing many varieties of cancers and congenital abnormalities."

In 1995, the Iraqis admitted that they had weaponized aflatoxin, Charles Duelfer, then the deputy executive chairman of the United Nations Special Commission weapons-inspection team in Iraq, told Goldberg. "This was the first time Iraq actually agreed to discuss the presidential origins of these programs," Duelfer said.

Although "it is unclear what biological and chemical weapons Saddam possesses today," Goldberg writes, August Hanning, the chief of the BND, the German intelligence agency, provided information on another type of weapon. "It is our estimate," he said, "that Iraq will have an atomic bomb in three years."

CIA 'Licensed to Kill' Saddam

NewsMax Wires
Monday, June 17, 2002

President George W. Bush early this year signed an intelligence order directing the CIA to undertake a comprehensive, covert program to prepare the way to topple Saddam Hussein, including authority to capture the Iraqi president or kill him, if necessary, *The Washington Post* reported Sunday.

The Bush intelligence order suggests that the administration has begun to put money and resources into a policy that has publicly consisted mostly of tough rhetoric.

The presidential order, an expansion of a previous presidential finding designed to oust Saddam, directs the CIA to use all available tools, including increased support to Iraqi opposition groups and expanded intelligence collection efforts, and possible use of advance teams in Iraq.

The order authorizes any CIA in-country team to defend itself with the use of lethal force if necessary, the newspaper said.

Tens of millions of dollars have been allocated to the covert program, according to the story by *Post* reporter Bob Woodward.

Slim Chance to Succeed

CIA Director George Tenet has told Bush that the CIA effort alone, without the deployment of troops and the use of economic and diplomatic pressure, probably has only about a 10 percent to 20 percent chance of succeeding, sources told the *Post*.

The CIA's covert program, one source said, should be viewed largely as preparatory to a military strike, devoted to the identification of targets and building relationships with alternative future leaders within the country. The CIA declined to comment, the newspaper said.

Sources said the CIA initiative is part of a broader Bush administration plan to remove Saddam that includes economic pressure, diplomacy and what officials believe will eventually include military action on a large scale.

COPYRIGHT 2002 BY UNITED PRESS INTERNATIONAL. ALL RIGHTS RESERVED.

Order to Kill Saddam: A Time Bomb

Christopher Ruddy
Monday, July 1, 2002

A ticking time bomb? The president's signed order to topple Saddam Hussein, or to kill him in "self-defense," has now been widely publicized. This is like sending a dinner invitation to Charles Manson with the expectation that he plans to use the butcher knife to cut the roast beef only.

By gangster rules, Saddam now has the right to hit Bush or the top leadership of the U.S. government. We should not be surprised.

Saddam has now had too much time to prepare. If we believe that Iraq poses such a threat, then Richard Perle, chairman of the Defense Policy Review Board, is right: We should have struck them early and hard. By waiting to get our ducks in a row here and in Afghanistan, we have given Saddam all the time he needs to launch a major counteroffensive here on American soil.

Why hasn't al Qaeda struck again? Al Qaeda terrorists could easily have struck again on American soil. Yet they haven't. This suggests to me that they are not calling the shots but that one or more nations are behind them masterminding the plan. In my mind, the September 11 attacks involved one or more nations. (I wouldn't be surprised if some of the hijackers took pilot training abroad before they arrived here to take the training again.)

The anthrax attacks were also the work of al Qaeda or its allies. I still don't buy the FBI line of domestic terrorism. The powers behind al Qaeda and its friends are picking their method and time carefully.

Window of opportunity. I have discussed this before, soon after 9/11. The adversaries of the U.S. know that time is not on their side. After eight years of Clinton, they were gifted with a vulnerable America. Now Bush is rebuilding. The ability of adversaries to strike with success at every level will diminish with each passing year. For example, with millions of anthrax and smallpox vaccinations on the way, the terrorists and their friends may be thinking they have to "use or lose" these weapons.

Al Qaeda is a most convenient "cutout." A cutout is another term for a front group. The president has rightfully named a host of nations abetting terror, including Iraq, Iran and North Korea. There are several others. All are backed by either Russia or China, both countries that would like to see America brought down a peg or two.

U.S.-Iraq War Plans: Debating the Dangers

Dave Eberhart, NewsMax.com
Monday, July 8, 2002

Recipe for "pre-emptive strike" debate stew: Take one portion of the reported leaked "war plans" of the U.S. plotting to take out Iraq's Saddam Hussein, which surprisingly reveal only a moderate concern about the dictator's levels of chemical and biological weapons, and simmer gently with the concession by even the most steadfast doomsayers amongst Iraq watchers that the country's nuclear capability is at present nil.

For extra spicy debate stew, add a volatile measure of enigma: Attacking Saddam would vaporize a decade-long policy of containment that has deterred him from using weapons of mass destruction, replacing the uneasy status quo with provocation that experts say virtually guarantees their use.

John Hillen, a veteran of the 1991 Persian Gulf war and an adviser to the 2000 Bush campaign, opined, "Any buildup would be seen by Saddam as a spear pointed at his heart, and he would be smart to act pre-emptively with chemical weapons against the first units showing up."

Reportedly, Pentagon officials do not believe that Hussein's development of weapons of mass destruction has advanced seriously since the Gulf War — which is not to suggest that Saddam has stopped pursuing a program of weapons of mass destruction (WMD) since U.N. inspectors left in December 1998.

What exactly do the experts say Saddam has in his present arsenal to possibly make the marshaling of U.S. troops in the area dangerous and the march into Baghdad fraught with biochemical hazards?

If you listen to controversial former U.N. weapons inspector Scott Ritter, not much. In fact, Ritter maintains, Saddam's WMD inventory was pretty much flattened in 1991, and despite administration rhetoric to the contrary, there is no hard proof that he has successfully rearmed.

As Ritter recently told CNN: "[T]hey tend to traipse out former [U.N. inspector] boss Richard Butler, who has said that the biological program is a black hole. Maybe it is, maybe it isn't. But the fact is they have not made a substantive case that Iraq continues to possess or is in pursuit of developing a biological weapons program."

Others are not so sanguine.

Saddam's Inventory

Saddam's inventory of WMD is thought to include sarin and VX gas, which attack the central nervous system, often lethally — as well as anthrax and botulism, said Charles A. Duelfer, the former deputy chairman of the United Nations commission that monitored Iraq's chemical and biological weapons programs until 2000.

Duelfer estimates that Iraq has between one dozen and three dozen advanced Scud missiles that can travel up to 375 miles, as well as drones, artillery shells and bombs capable of dispersing chemical and biological agents. "Whatever he's got now, it's less than what he had in 1991," Duelfer said. "But in 1991 we weren't going to Baghdad. It's different now."

And Duelfer is not alone. Based on U.N. reports, Iraq Watch estimates that Baghdad has an ample supply of aerial bombs, munitions and missile warheads that could deliver chemical weapons such as VX nerve gas.

According to Iraq Watch, a website devoted to monitoring Iraq's progress in building weapons of mass destruction, Saddam has 157 bombs and 25 missile warheads suitable for germ agents: anthrax, aflatoxin and botulinum.

"We know that they built such things before the Gulf war, and we know not all of them have been found," said Gary Milhollin, director of the Wisconsin Project on Nuclear Arms Control, which includes Iraq Watch.

Additionally, Iraq Watch believes the country may still have as many as 50 Scud missiles standing by as potential delivery vehicles.

Training for the Worst

Signals of official "moderate" concerns aside, the Army's biochemical warfare school at Fort Leonard Wood in Missouri continues to crank out about 5,000 trained soldiers a year.

A recent report put the total number of trained troops ready to mount out full tilt into whatever clouds of poison Saddam throws their way at 17,587. This number is enough to flesh out a specialized brigade, as well as attach chemical warfare specialists to most combat units.

Also belying the moderate concern label: Some key details of invasion scenarios, including the location of an initial assault and the best time of year to begin, are contingent upon some perceived measure of biochemical threat. Certainly, say the experts, any U.S. invasion would not come in the hot weather, as it makes the wearing of the cumbersome protective suits at best problematic.

Scenarios include a cornered and frantic Saddam firing missiles tipped with chemical or biological warheads — not only at U.S. assembly areas but also at Israel and other allies.

Countering this scenario: more accurate U.S. airpower and more extensive intelligence than in 1991. Reportedly, intelligence officials have already pinpointed the most likely chemical and biological weapons sites in Iraq.

Ready to engage such targets in a pre-emptory, pre-emptory attack: scads of "smart" bombs. One in 10 bombs dropped in the Gulf War were smart. Six in 10 were smart during the initial softening up of Afghanistan last fall. It has been suggested that in Gulf War II, that number will increase.

During the Gulf War, it took hours to get intelligence on the movement of Scud missile launchers. Defense officials say bombers can now strike such targets within 30 minutes.

Farrakhan: We Pray for Iraq to Defeat U.S.

Inside Cover
Tuesday, July 9, 2002

Nation of Islam leader Louis Farrakhan says American Muslims are praying for an Iraqi victory in a war with the United States, according to Iraq's state-run media.

Farrakhan held meetings over the weekend in Baghdad with Iraqi officials on a "solidarity" trip billed as an effort to avoid a U.S. military campaign against dictator Saddam Hussein, United Press International and *The Washington Times* reported.

Farrakhan held talks with Islamic Affairs Minister Abdul Munem Saleh on "ways to confront the American threats against Iraq," Iraqi News Agency reported.

Saleh was quoted as urging a worldwide effort by Muslims to "expose the American and Zionist crimes toward the people of Iraq and Palestine."

The agency quoted the Black Muslim leader as saying "the Muslim American people are praying to the almighty God to grant victory to Iraq."

A State Department official said he was aware of the news but was not prepared to comment.

'Not a Muslim Outfit'

One of America's leading Muslim organizations today denounced Farrakhan's comments as "outrageous."

"Of course, he does not represent our views or the views of American Muslims," Faiz Rehman, a spokesman for American Muslim Council, told CNSNews.com.

"The mainstream American Muslim community does not consider the Nation of Islam as part of the Muslim community. They claim they have the name of Islam attached to them, but they are not Muslims. Nation of Islam is not a Muslim outfit," Rehman said.

Saddam's War Plan Includes Bioweapons to Make U.S. a 'Living Hell'

Arnaud de Borchgrave
NewsMax.com Wires
Thursday, July 11, 2002

WASHINGTON — If President Bush doesn't have a war plan on his desk to unhorse Saddam Hussein — maybe he doesn't allow *The New York Times* to touch his desk — the Iraqi dictator most assuredly has one on his desk.

It will include everything in Iraq's arsenal, according to what Hussein told his inner circle of advisers and two sons during a five-hour meeting last month that was leaked to a Saudi newspaper. "Everything" in this instance means weapons of mass destruction. Iraq is known to possess chemical and biological weapons of mass destruction.

Hussein made clear to his acolytes he would wait for the United States to throw the first punch — and then hit back with everything he's got, both on the battlefield and "all other fronts." This presumably means the activation of "sleeper" cells in the United States.

The beneficiary of the Iraqi leak was Saudi newspaper *Al Watan Al Arabi*, which quoted sources close to the ruling family in Baghdad. Present at Hussein's war council were two new officials "who were recently assigned by [Hussein's son] Qusay to organize intelligence cells abroad."

'Sabotage of U.S. Targets'

It's a safe bet that "intelligence cells" in this instance is Iraqi jargon for "sabotage of U.S. targets of convenience."

Referring to the green light Bush gave the CIA to "assassinate or arrest me," Hussein, according to the leaker, said the U.S. president "has left Iraq no room to be tolerant. … His war on us is now declared, and he is publicly leaking information today that he gave orders to use all means and weapons to violate Iraq's sovereignty and international law by assassinating me in Iraq."

Hussein then told the participants he wanted to hear their views and analysis "calmly without getting emotional." That is asking the impossible of people whose culture is hyperbole. So one after another, they emoted from the same sheet, working up to a crescendo to take the war to America.

'Take the Fight to Their Own Homes in America'

The first to speak was Ali Hasan al-Majid, a presidential cousin who is widely known as Chemical Ali and is accused of being responsible for the massacres in the south following the 1991 uprising at the end of the Gulf War. "Mr. President, the Iraqi people have tolerated the intolerable from these Americans. … [H]as the time not come to take the fight to their own homes in America?

"They wanted this to be a war on all fronts, so let it be a war on all fronts and using all weapons and means."

Samples from the others:

- "The Americans must know that the heroes of Iraq can become human bombs in the thousands, willing to blow up America in particular."

'We Can Make America's People Sleepless'

- "With a simple sign from you, we can make America's people sleepless and frightened to go out in the streets. … I swear upon your head, sir, that if I do not turn their night into day and their day into a living hell, I will ask you to chop off my head before the brothers present."
- "I am confident that our entire nation will be set aflame [by the

Americans], and they must know that the entire region will turn into rubble, with Israel at the forefront."

- "If [Osama] bin Laden truly did carry out the September attacks as they claim, then as God is my witness, we will prove to them that what happened in September is a picnic compared to the wrath of Saddam Hussein."

After five hours of "fiery elocution," all agreed "on the need for a strong response to the now public hostile U.S. plan and the importance for Iraq not to wait or hesitate." All except Hussein, that is.

He said the United States was using "all its dominion and tyranny not just to humiliate Iraq, but ... every Arab in the land of Arabs and every Muslim in the land of Islam ... just as [Bush] rejected [Palestinian Authority President] Yasser Arafat, he will reject Saddam Hussein, and tomorrow [Syrian President] Bashar al-Assad, and after that another Arab leader, until U.S. dominion reaches the rights, wealth and destiny of the Arab. ...

"Bush, his gang and his intelligence bodies should know that as soon as they start this battle or we get wind of its beginning, Iraq will turn from reaction to action. ... At that moment everything will be handed over to Qusay Saddam Hussein to directly oversee the retaliation plans ... using all the weapons and fronts available."

Hussein's son Uday, according to the leaked minutes in the Saudi paper, still insisted Iraq should launch pre-emptive attacks against the United States.

The dictator reminded him that "so far the U.S. has done nothing except take a decision on paper. A number of officials know from experience that implementation will not be easy. [The Americans] have taken many decisions over the past 12 years, and we have foiled them all.

"What's important today is to wait for the U.S. to throw the first punch, and then we will not just react, but will act and take actions."

Bigger Than the Gulf War

At the very least, concluded an anonymous top security official in a large Arab nation — widely rumored to be Saudi Prince Turki, the retired chief of Saudi intelligence who held the job for 25 years — what will happen between Bush 43 and Hussein will be larger and more dangerous than what happened between Hussein and Bush 41.

Hopefully the U.S. Senate will get to debate war powers for the commander in chief for Gulf War II before the battle of leaks transmogrifies into an alliance between Hussein and bin Laden — weapons of mass destruction terrorism in the United States.

Arnaud de Borchgrave, editor-in-chief of UPI, is on NewsMax's board of directors.

COPYRIGHT 2002 BY UNITED PRESS INTERNATIONAL. ALL RIGHTS RESERVED.

Experts Warn Senators of Iraq's 'Incredibly Dangerous' Threat

NewsMax.com Wires
Thursday, August 1, 2002

WASHINGTON — Experts warned senators weighing options for a strike against Iraq Wednesday that it would be foolhardy to underestimate the danger of Saddam Hussein, who already has chemical and biological weapons capabilities and could be close to constructing a nuclear bomb.

"I do not regard his as a massive force. But I think that it is incredibly dangerous to be dismissive of Iraq's capabilities," Anthony Cordesman of the Center for Strategic and International Studies told the Senate Foreign Relations Committee.

'Body Bags'

"It is easy to send people home unharmed. It is far harder to send them home in body bags because we do not have enough force to engage Saddam Hussein properly. That would be a disaster," Cordesman said.

The grim remarks came during the first of two days of hearings to consider the appropriate U.S. policy against Iraqi dictator Saddam Hussein and determine if he poses an immediate threat to American interests.

President Bush has labeled Iraq part of the "axis of evil" that includes Iran and North Korea. These countries, the White House says, could supply weapons of mass destruction to terrorists.

Bush has called for the eventual ouster of Hussein and demanded that Iraq permit U.N. arms inspectors back into the country.

Amid numerous news reports quoting unidentified "sources" claiming there are plans to invade Iraq, congressional leaders said Wednesday that it was vital to bring the discussion of war into public view.

'Informed Consent'

"The decision to go to war can never be taken lightly. I believe that a foreign policy, especially one that involves the use of force, cannot be sustained in America without the informed consent of the American people," said Senator Joseph Biden, D-Del., chairman of the committee.

Senate Minority Leader Trent Lott, R-Miss., however, scoffed that it would be foolish for the U.S. to give Hussein the advantage of airing details of any plans to attack him, Fox News Channel reported Wednesday night.

The senators spent more than three hours questioning a panel of three experts on Iraqi military capability. The primary concern, they said, was to determine if the threat posed by Hussein was sufficient to justify a pre-emp-tive strike against Iraq, which would be the first such attack in recent American history.

All Agree: Better Now Than Later

The experts differed on the exact composition of the Iraqi nuclear, chemical and biological arsenal, and none said they believed Hussein had developed a nuclear bomb. But all agreed that it would be better to act now than wait until he got stronger.

Ambassador Richard Butler, the former chief of U.N. weapons inspections in Iraq, stressed the shortcomings of the U.S. policy of containment. He said that, because of a lack of enforcement, weapons of mass destruction continue to exist in Iraq and more weapons technology continues to flow in, largely through Syria.

"It is essential to recognize that the claim made by Saddam's representatives, that Iraq has no weapons of mass destruction, is false. Everyone concerned, from Iraq's neighbors, to the U.N. Security Council and secretary-general of the U.N., is being lied to," he said.

Details of Bioweapons

Butler said that despite years of attempted international weapons inspection, Iraq still has an array of biological weapons and missiles tipped with anthrax. It also retains some chemical weapon technology from before the Gulf War. A lack of fissionable material, said Butler, is the only thing that keeps Iraq from developing a bomb.

"We do not know and never have known fully the quantity and quality of Iraq's weapons of mass destruction. Its policies of concealment ensured this. We do know that it has had such weapons, has used them, and remains at work on them," he said.

Khidhir Hamza, a former chief scientist in Iraq's nuclear program, stressed that "regime change" would be the only real way to reduce the threat from Iraq. Before his 1994 defection, Hamza cited a German intelligence report stating that Iraq had more than one ton of slightly enriched uranium — enough to generate enough bomb-grade uranium for three nuclear weapons by 2005.

But Cordesman, the most cautious of the speakers, stressed that intelligence reports available to the public are notoriously false. And with the Iraqi dictator's skill at concealing weapons, it will likely never be possible to know exactly what Hussein has and if and when he is willing to use it.

'Our First Pre-emptive War'

"We have to be prepared for the fact that if we do this, it will in many ways be our first pre-emptive war. We will not have a clear smoking gun. There will not be a central cause," he said.

Cordesman stressed throughout his remarks that quick, surgical strikes against the Iraqi leader would be extremely dangerous. Cornered, Hussein would be most likely to use whatever weapons of mass destruction he has accumulated.

He said that he believed the U.S. needed a major military expeditionary force of the type it used to drive Iraq out of Kuwait in 1991.

At that time, the U.S. led a coalition of nations including France, England, Egypt, Qatar and Saudi Arabia, which fielded 500,000 troops. This time around, Cordesman warned, some of that support would not be available.

Some 'Allies'

"I think we will have the support of the British government. Most of our NATO allies will at best be reluctant and will seek, if anything, to delay [the strike] through use of the U.N.," he said.

Cordesman also stressed the importance of regional allies if the attack is to proceed successfully. He singled out the need for Turkish air bases and the use of Saudi Arabian airspace, as well as cooperation from Qatar, Bahrain, Kuwait and Oman.

Support for Terrorists

The senators asked if Hussein might provide weapons of mass destruction to terrorists, who would use them against the U.S. mainland. The experts said that though Hussein supported terrorists, there was little, if any, evidence, that such weapons transfers had taken place.

As the senators sought to determine if the level of threat could justify an immediate U.S. invasion, Senator Russ Feingold, D-Wis., asked the panel members if they felt that the American mainland was immediately at risk.

The panelists agreed that Hussein still lacked the capability to strike America. But Cordesman warned, "There's this to keep in mind: Things are going to get worse, not better."

COPYRIGHT 2002 BY UNITED PRESS INTERNATIONAL. ALL RIGHTS RESERVED.

Admiral Moorer's Advice on Iraq: Embargo First

Christopher Ruddy
Friday, August 2, 2002

Yesterday I chatted by phone with Admiral Moorer, the former chairman of the Joint Chiefs of Staff.

Last week, Admiral Moorer had joined me for a luncheon speech by former CIA Director James Woolsey at the Institute of World Politics.

Woolsey told the group the U.S. should invade Iraq with 100,000 to 200,000 troops as part of World War IV, which he said began on September 11, 2001.

Admiral Moorer told me he didn't like the talk of world war.

Few can appreciate war like the admiral, who landed on his first aircraft carrier in 1935.

He was at Pearl Harbor on December 7, 1941, and later saw his own plane crash in the Pacific. He was rescued by a supply ship that was later destroyed by the Japanese.

Miraculously, he was saved in a small lifeboat and went on to see more action in that war, as well as combat in the Korean War and, of course, the Vietnam War.

During Vietnam he served as chairman of the Joint Chiefs, and it was his advice to begin the Christmas bombings of 1972 that brought the war to a quick end.

Speaking as a military man — he can speak and think no other way — Admiral Moorer says we need to proceed carefully with Iraq.

While he sees the danger of Saddam Hussein, he thinks an invasion could be very costly in American lives. He wonders why other options haven't already been implemented that could help reduce Hussein's power and make an invasion easier.

"The way I would deal with Iraq," the Admiral said, "is cut them off now and make them starve."

He continued: "I would cut off all of their oil, cut all shipping, all air traffic in and out of the country. I would interrupt their telecommunications.

"What would Hussein be able to do?" the admiral asked. "His army has no mobility."

The admiral's thinking is wise. Squeeze Iraq first. If they don't accept unfettered U.N. inspections, the strict embargo will weaken Saddam. He may be overthrown from within. Certainly, he will be weaker when and if the U.S. decides to invade.

Admiral Moorer's advice should have been heeded months ago.

Instead, Saddam has been allowed to steadily sell oil for billions. He also has had plenty of time to prepare his army and perhaps his terrorist agents here in the U.S. Arguably, a strict air and sea embargo may have tightened the noose around Saddam and limited his ability to harm us.

But Americans need to remember that as we prepare to go to war with Iraq, we continue to buy oil from them and fund the regime we so despise.

Back in 1998, when Bill Clinton was facing impeachment, he made a big fuss about Saddam's weapons programs.

Saddam refused to give inspectors complete access. Instead of forcing the issue, Clinton did what he always did: He caved.

Saddam thumbed his nose at us, and what did we do? The U.S. agreed as the U.N. lifted its sanctions and implemented its "Oil for Food" program. While the program was intended to help the Iraqi people, it has also freed up resources for Saddam to spend on his military and terrorist activities.

In addition to the Oil for Food program, Clinton also turned a blind eye to massive Iraqi oil smuggling in violation of U.N. sanctions. Illegal oil shipments reportedly net Hussein an additional $2 billion in war money a year.

If the U.S. government had been thinking in military terms, Admiral Moorer's advice would have been heeded long ago.

Instead, political thinking is at work in Washington.

Fearing a complete embargo would cut off all Iraqi oil and cause a dramatic rise in oil prices, the politicians in Washington fear such a move could seriously harm the already teetering U.S. economy.

Clearly, Washington wants both cheap oil and an ousted Saddam. But we may not be able to have it both ways, and the present policy may make ousting Saddam more dangerous and difficult.

Saddam Warns Attackers

NewsMax Wires
Thursday, August 8, 2002
BAGHDAD, Iraq — Iraqi President Saddam Hussein warned potential attackers of "disgraceful failure" in a speech to the nation Thursday.

Although he did not mention any names, Saddam said any aggression against Iraq was doomed to failure.

"One of the lessons of recent and distant history is that all empires and bearers of the coffin of evil, whenever they mobilized their evil against the Arab nation, or against the Muslim world, they were themselves buried in their own coffin," he said. "This is the inevitable outcome awaiting all those who try to aggress against Arabs and Muslims."

Saddam's speech, made on the anniversary of the end of the 1980–88 Iran-Iraq war, comes amid reported U.S. plans to attack Iraq and topple its leader.

"The forces of evil will carry their coffins on their backs, to die in disgraceful failure, taking their schemes back with them," Hussein said.

Washington wants Baghdad to allow U.N. weapons inspectors back into the country. Iraqi diplomats recently met with U.N. Secretary-General Kofi Annan and have asked a U.S. congressional team to come to the country to look for weapons of mass destruction. Washington has rejected those moves.

Saddam said the U.N. Security Council "should reply to the questions raised by Iraq and should honor its obligations under its own resolutions."

In March, Iraqi diplomats gave Annan 19 questions on Iraqi complaints, which have been circulated to Security Council members, who have not replied. The Security Council resolutions on Iraq call for a lifting of sanctions — imposed following Baghdad's invasion of Kuwait — once weapons of mass destruction are eliminated and other requirements are fulfilled. Iraq says it has fulfilled the conditions.

COPYRIGHT 2002 BY UNITED PRESS INTERNATIONAL. ALL RIGHTS RESERVED.

About the Editors

Christopher Ruddy is editor of NewsMax.com. In 1999, *Newsweek* named him one of America's top 20 new media personalities. He has worked as an investigative reporter for the *New York Post* and the Pittsburgh *Tribune-Review*.

Carl Limbacher Jr. edits the Inside Cover section of *NewsMax.com*. A former columnist for the *Washington Weekly*, Limbacher has appeared on numerous national television and radio shows.

Bitter Legacy

Edited by Christopher Ruddy and Carl Limbacher Jr.

NewsMax.com editors tell you the story you didn't get on the evening news ...

In *Bitter Legacy* NewsMax.com reveals the *Untold Story of the Clinton-Gore Years*. You will learn how the corruption of the Clinton-Gore administration robbed America of its political integrity and national security — and how the Clinton-Gore administration engaged in a massive abuse of power.

Deceit, Lies, Scandal, Criminal Acts ...

Bill Clinton and Al Gore have survived the most scandal-ridden administration in the history of the nation — all with the help of the media. Phrases and words such as strange deaths, bribes, missing documents, threatened employees, perjury, Chinagate, funneled campaign cash and impeachment all came to symbolize a massive abuse of power at the highest levels of government.

Skeletons you didn't know about...

Bitter Legacy also details the unbelievable story of a state trooper who guarded Bill and Hillary Clinton and was an eyewitness to corruption in the highest places. Ruddy and Limbacher also offer a case-by-case study of people in the Clinton inner circle who were murdered or met other untimely deaths. *Bitter Legacy* is more than just a book, it is a shocking account of the political corruption of the past decade that caused the weakening of America's military and national security.

Softcover, 424 pages
List Price: $24.95
NewsMax Price $19.95
A-21-138

Order today by calling **1-800-485-4350** or
Mail to: **NewsMax.com**
P.O. Box 20989
West Palm Beach, FL 33416
Please make check payable to: NewsMax.com.
Include product number, shipping address, and $4.95 for shipping and handling with all orders.

Unrestricted Warfare:
China's Master Plan to Destroy America

By Cols. Qiao Liang and Wang Xiangsui
Introduction by Al Santoli

Amazingly *three years* before the Sept. 11 bombing of the World Trade Center a Chinese military manual titled *Unrestricted Warfare* touted such an attack — suggesting it would be difficult for the U.S. military to cope with such an act.

Surprisingly, Osama bin Laden is mentioned frequently in this book.

Now NewsMax.com is making the CIA translation of this shocking book available to all Americans.

Our media and government were quick to declare the acts of Sept. 11, 2001 as simply terrorism by a nationless group known as al-Qaeda.

In reading China's military manual *Unrestricted Warfare*, you will learn that the events of Sept. 11 were not a random act perpetrated by independent agents.

The doctrine of total war outlined in *Unrestricted Warfare* clearly demonstrates that the People's Republic of China is preparing to confront the United States and our allies by conducting "asymmetrical" or multidimensional attacks on almost every aspect of our social, economic and political life.

The media and Congress are keeping a lid on this book because of the implications of U.S.-China economic and trade relations.

Here's what others say about *Unrestricted Warfare*:

"You need to read *Unrestricted Warfare* because it reveals China's game plan in its coming war with America ... China thinks it can destroy America by using these tactics."

— Adm. Thomas Moorer
Former Chairman, Joint Chiefs of Staff

Softcover, 206 Pages
List Price: $24.95
NewsMax Price: $19.95
A-21-238

Order today by calling **1-800-485-4350** or
Mail to: **NewsMax.com**
P.O. Box 20989
West Palm Beach, FL 33416

Please make check payable to: NewsMax.com.
Include product number, shipping address, and $4.95 for shipping and handling with all orders.